THE EXPERT LIBRARY
STAFFING, SUSTAINING, AND ADVANCING THE ACADEMIC LIBRARY IN THE 21ST CENTURY

edited by

Scott Walter and Karen Williams

Association of College and Research Libraries
A division of the American Library Association
Chicago, Illinois 2010

The paper used in this publication meets the minimum requirements of American National Standard for Information Sciences–Permanence of Paper for Printed Library Materials, ANSI Z39.48-1992. ∞

Library of Congress Cataloging-in-Publication Data

The expert library : staffing, sustaining, and advancing the academic library in the 21st century / Scott Walter and Karen Williams, editors.
   p. cm.
  Includes bibliographical references and index.
  ISBN 978-0-8389-8551-9 (pbk. : alk. paper) 1. Academic libraries--Personnel management. 2. Academic librarians--Selection and appointment. 3. Academic libraries--Employees. 4. Academic libraries--Effect of technological innovations on. 5. Academic libraries--Forecasting. 6. Academic libraries--United States--Case studies. I. Walter, Scott, 1967- II. Williams, Karen, 1957-
  Z675.U5E95 2010
  023--dc22
                        2010033332

Printed in the United States of America.

14 13 12 11 10   5 4 3 2 1

TABLE OF CONTENTS

THE HYBRIDIZATION OF LIBRARY PERSONNEL RESOURCES
NEW RESPONSIBILITIES DEMAND STAFF DIVERSITY

James G. Neal
Columbia University

Academic libraries have entered a period of gross mutability, a state of constant change, productive and powerful chaos, hybrid strategies, and essential creativity in advancing their individual and collective visions.

Academic libraries are about users: faculty and students who demand an expanding array of dynamic and responsive services, and learners and researchers across the network who routinely reach beyond their institutional boundaries. Academic libraries are about a shifting array of professional, technical and support personnel who bring critical expertise and experience to both the sustained responsibilities and the new roles that higher education libraries are advancing. This volume, for the first time, brings together fresh thinking and insights about what will be required to advance library relevance and success through people.

Each chapter teases out a new perspective on the changes which are redefining the library in the academy. Academic libraries will remain focused on the core functions of: identifying (selection), getting (acquisition), organizing (synthesis), finding (navigation), distributing (dissemination), serving (interpretation), teaching (understanding), using (application), and archiving (preservation) information in support of teaching and learning, and in support of research and scholarship.

The boundaries of the library are expanding in areas such as publishing, teaching and learning, research and development, entrepreneurial initiatives and new business development, and information policy advocacy. And the extension and professionalization of the administrative functions in the academic library are demanding backgrounds and capabilities that respond to the complexities of space management, fundraising, human resources, information technology, financial management, and digital services, for example. This will demand, in some cases, a new suite of credentials and skills that enable credibility and effectiveness, whether we speak of ferals or hybrids, or a new organizational ecosystem based on mutualism.

The developments and projections described in each chapter, directly or by implication, call out a new and more rigorous set of expectations for staff at all levels of the academic library. We must seek individuals who have a clear sense of mission and a well-developed self-vision, with the requisite base of knowledge, an understanding of strategic positioning, and a commitment to continuous improvement.

A critical element is rethinking the ways the academic library workforce is attracted and developed. The library needs new skills, but also a new attitude. It is essential that the role of professional education be rethought, and that the recruitment and employment of staff be reengineered to embrace a wide range of academic and professional credentials and a more fluid definition of job responsibilities. This will have a wide impact on the values, outlooks, styles and expectations of the library organization. And it will influence academic community understanding, recognition, respect and support for the work of the library.

We need to redefine our expectations for the professional working in the library, with a particular focus in the following areas: a commitment to rigor, a commitment to research and development, a commitment to evaluation and assessment, communication and marketing skills, political engagement, project development and management skills, entrepreneurial spirit, resource development skills, leadership and inspirational qualities, an embracing of ambiguity, a sense of adventure, and deep subject or technical expertise. An academic library cannot thrive as a learning and scholarly organization without a staff that is dominated by these essential qualities and characteristics.

Similarly, we need a rethinking of organizational structure and purpose. We can think of an organization as individuals and groups carrying out roles and working together to achieve shared objectives within a formal social and political structure and with established policies and processes. Organization is the tool through which goals and priorities are established, decisions are made, resources are allocated, power is wielded, and plans are accomplished. An organization considers carefully how administrative responsibility and authority are distributed and shared, how operations and procedures are integrated and flexible, how policies and norms are designed and enforced, and how fluidity and vitality contribute to productivity and success. Academic libraries are increasingly embracing organizational models which support new thinking and action. They are moving away from conventional administrative hierarchies and academic bureaucracies to a combination of centralized planning and resource allocation systems, loosely coupled academic structures, and maverick units and entrepreneurial enterprises. The key characteristics which support a new culture are: decentralization, distribution, adhocracy, complexity, informality, innovation, and collaboration. Can academic libraries adapt?

The 21st century academic library is driven by innovation, a focus on redefining the physical, expertise and intellectual infrastructure, and on understanding the geography, psychology, economics, and process of progress. This book expands our understanding of these complex elements.

INTRODUCTION

Scott Walter
University of Illinois at Urbana-Champaign

Karen Williams
University of Minnesota

Though we sometimes forget to celebrate this fact, the library's most valuable collection is its people. As we look back on a decade of extraordinary change in academic libraries—change driven by information technology, by new approaches to teaching and learning, by new models for scholarly communication, and by new user expectations for the ways they will be able to discover, share, and make use of information—there is nothing so important to the future of the library and its continued place at the heart of the academic enterprise than its people and the expertise that they bring to the design, development, and delivery of library services. But, what will those services be, and who are the library professionals who will provide them?

The impetus for the current collection can be found in James Neal's oft-cited essay on the future of library staffing, "Raised by Wolves: Integrating the New Generation of Feral Professionals into the Academic Library" (2006).[1] Making what has since become a familiar argument, Neal concluded that the academic library should be home not only to librarians who are re-thinking the design and delivery of traditional services in light of broader changes in the academic and information environments, but also to professionals in fields such as fundraising, human resource management, educational technology, and scholarly publishing, who can help the library to meet the service challenges inherent in those changes. While there have been many studies of the changing nature of academic library work and of how those changes are reflected in position descriptions and professional responsibilities, Neal moved the discussion of change beyond studies of specific job types (e.g., reference librarians, catalogers, subject specialists) toward a more fundamental questioning of the variety of professional services that an academic library must provide if it is to remain relevant to campus concerns in the twenty-first century.[2] "Feral professionals," Neal argued (using an evocative term for our colleagues who have come to find their home in the library without taking the traditional path through an accredited Library and Information Science education program), provide critical support to the academic library as it moved more systematically into discussions of its ongoing role in areas of critical campus concern, including undergraduate research, e-learning, data curation, intellectual property management, scholarly publishing, and e-science.

In the years since the publication of Neal's essay, we have seen continued study both of the evolution of traditional academic library positions and of the emergence of new positions that represent the expansion of librarian expertise into areas of campus concern to which the library can contribute support, e.g., first-year experience, instructional design, and support for multicultural user communities.[3] At the same time, we have seen broader discussions of how to ensure the ongoing contribution of library professionals to campus initiatives such as data services, university publishing programs, and e-science.[4] As Lori Goetsch, President of the Association of College & Research Libraries (ACRL), wrote in 2008, the "evolution of library positions will play a key role in... [our] effort to remain relevant [to our users]," and the critical nature of our thoughtful study of library staffing for the future can be seen in the recent attention to this topic by the Association of Research Libraries (ARL), which has made the study of "new roles for new times" a key component of its inquiry into the transformation of research libraries in the twenty-first century.[5]

The broad question of how we will build capacity in our libraries to undertake these new roles is the subject of the essays that open this collection. David W. Lewis reviews trends in academic librarianship (some of which have been shaken even since the initiation of this project by the impact of the global economic downturn on campus hiring plans) and notes that a library's "human capabilities" will be a crucial component in its ability to successfully meet the challenges represented by changes in teaching, learning, and scholarly practice. Articulating themes that echo throughout this collection, Lewis argues that we will need to be creative in our approach to library staffing, and that we will need to find ways both to recruit new professionals into our libraries who can contribute to emergent initiatives and to support the continuing professional education and development of colleagues who find the nature of their work fundamentally changed. John Lehner suggests that our ability to engage in these creative approaches to professional recruitment may be hampered by traditional approaches to personnel selection, and argues for the adoption of personnel selection approaches informed by the broader field of organizational development that will allow us to recruit more effectively both for the core competencies required of our professional staff and for the behavioral characteristics associated with success in our quickly-changing professional environment, including flexibility, adaptability, and a commitment to continuous learning. Finally, R. David Lankes challenges us to consider how best to support innovation in our organizations by promoting an ideal of "participatory librarianship"—a model both for individual professionals and for organizations committed to fostering collaboration across campus in support of the goal shared by libraries, information technology units, student affairs programs, and academic departments to "build knowledge in our community."[6]

Identifying "core competencies," both for our libraries and for individual library professionals, is a theme introduced by Lehner, but explored in greater depth in the next set of essays in this collection. Heather Gendron introduces the basic tools required for any discussion of establishing core competencies in your library, as well as examples of how professional associations have addressed the issue of core competencies for academic librarianship. Craig Gibson and Jamie Wright Coniglio explore the question of how the core competencies for subject specialists and other liaison librarians have evolved over the past decade, as well as how they will continue to change as the demands placed on liaison librarians to serve as key agents for the promotion of strategic initiatives in information literacy instruction, scholarly communications, data services, and e-scholarship continue to grow. Finally, Stephanie H. Crowe and Janice M. Jaguszewski bring the ideas found in the previous chapters together in a case study of the reorganization of the Academic Programs Division of the University of Minnesota Libraries in which a redefinition of liaison librarian roles around core competencies aligned with strategic initiatives was one driver for successful change.

While Gibson and Coniglio and Crowe and Jaguszewski explore the evolution of the subject specialist position (a position that has likewise been recognized by ARL as "[essential] to fulfilling the library's mission in a digital age"),[7] the next set of essays address the question initially raised by Neal: who are the "new professionals" whose skills must complement those of traditional library professionals in order to meet the demands of the contemporary campus? Marta L. Brunner opens this discussion by providing an overview of the Council on Library and Information Resources (CLIR) Postdoctoral Fellowship in Academic Libraries—a program designed to bring recent recipients of the doctoral degree into libraries "to forge, renovate, and strengthen connections between academic... [libraries] and their users."[8] Mike Furlough explores the professional partnerships required for the successful development of a publishing program in the library, and demonstrates how the commitment to re-envisioning the library's role in the scholarly communication process requires both the integration of new professionals into the library, as well as the re-thinking of traditional positions to promote the relationships between author, publisher, and reader at the heart of the scholarly communications enterprise. Similar issues are explored in Jake Carlson and Jeremy Garritano's study of Purdue University's approach to building professional capacity within the library for the emergent commitments to data curation and support for e-science. Kevin Clair considers how the emergence of the metadata librarian position represents not only an evolution of traditional responsibilities for cataloging and content management, but also how it challenges traditional divisions within the library organization between public services, technical services, collections, and information technology. Finally, Eric Bartheld provides a view from the "other side" of our increasingly diverse professional community from his position as a communications and marketing professional operating as a leader for library public affairs. Together, these essays highlight how rich and diverse are the commitments that our libraries have undertaken for professional service on our campuses, as well as the challenges faced both by traditional library professionals and "new" library professionals working together to meet those commitments.

The collection concludes with studies of how to support our colleagues as they navigate these new roles and responsibilities. Beth S. Woodard and Lisa Janicke Hinchliffe provide a case study of professional development for librarians with teaching responsibilities at the University of Illinois at Urbana-Champaign—a case study focused on supporting the librarian as teacher, but with clear lessons that may be applied to areas of more recent concern, including scholarly communications outreach and education, data services, and support for e-science. Finally, Elaine Z. Jennerich and M. Sue Baughman return to organizational development, a field introduced to the collection by Lehner in his study of professional recruitment, but relevant much more broadly to the professional development of the library professional and to the successful conduct of the change management process in academic libraries.[9]

As we complete this initial foray into what we expect to be our own continued study of the future of academic library staffing, we are reminded of a scene in the most recent version of "Star Trek" (a franchise that, like the academic library, revisits its own future on a regular basis). In this scene, Montgomery Scott explains the complexities of interstellar transport, or, as he says, "[You're] talking about beaming aboard the Enterprise, while she's traveling faster than light, without a proper receiving pad…. The notion of transwarp beaming is like trying to hit a bullet with a smaller bullet whilst wearing a blindfold, riding a horse."[10] We have often thought of ourselves on that horse as we tried to hit the target we set for ourselves when we began this project, i.e., to take Neal's idea of the "feral professional" and to identify the full range of new and re-defined professional expertise required for the 21st-century library.

There are many areas of expertise, and many emergent library positions, not represented in this collection, e.g., user experience librarians, assessment librarians, emerging technology librarians, and student services librarians, and many changes to traditional service programs and responsibilities still to be explored. We hope that this collection, and the call found throughout its essays to focus on re-thinking our organizations, diversifying our professional complement in order to meet a broader array of core service programs, and committing to foster both the development of the library as a learning organization and the development of our human resources through continuous professional education, will serve as a starting place for further discussion and will help to promote the wide-ranging thinking about professional expertise in the library that we saw earlier this decade in Neal's work. We expect this discussion to benefit not only from the contribution made by this collection, but by complementary efforts currently being pursued by the Association of Research Libraries, the Council on Library and Information Resources and by researchers such as those currently at work at the University of North Carolina at Chapel Hill and other LIS education programs.[11]

We know that this discussion will continue in professional associations like ACRL, but we also know that the proof will be in the work conducted at individual libraries and on individual campuses, and in the state and regional consortia to which many of us belong. Will we be able to think creatively about the people we hire, perhaps fostering the collaboration across library and academic departments in the ways suggested by the CLIR program? Will we be able to collaborate across institutions on support for specialized library positions, e.g., in the Area Studies, in the same way that we have discussed collaborating on shared collections? Can we better articulate the spectrum of lifelong professional education required for contemporary library work that moves across LIS education programs to local continuing professional education programs to continuing professional education programs coordinated or provided by professional and scholarly associations (and, thus, leave behind, once and for all, the tired debate over the "crisis in LIS education")? No single collection could address this range of questions, but we know the discussion must continue because, as we confront the known challenges of changes in the information, technology, and academic environments, as well as the emergent challenges of the current economic crisis, the need for creative thinking and strategic planning for the future of library human resources has never been greater.

We appreciate the opportunity that ACRL has provided for us to engage the question of the expert library, and the contributions that our colleagues have made to this important collection of case studies and exploration of fundamental questions. We would also like to acknowledge the work done in the early stages of this project by our colleague, Vicki Coleman (Arizona State University), who helped us to define that target before we decided to jump on the horse and try on the blindfold. We look forward to continuing these discussions in the future.

Notes

1. James G. Neal, "Raised by Wolves: Integrating the New Generation of Feral Professionals into the Academic Library," *Library Journal* 131, no. 3 (2006), http://www.libraryjournal.com/article/CA6304405.html.

2. For broad studies of changes in traditional library positions, see, for example, Penny M. Beile and Megan M. Adams, "Other Duties as Assigned: Emerging Trends in the Academic Library Job Market," *College & Research Libraries* 61, no. 4 (2000), http://crl.acrl.org/content/61/4/336.full.pdf+html; Janice Simmons-Welburn, *Changing Roles of Library Professionals* [ARL SPEC Kit No. 256] (Washington, DC: Association of Research Libraries, 2000); and Beverly P. Lynch and Kimberly Robles Smith, "The Changing Nature of Work in Academic Libraries," *College & Research Libraries* 62, no. 5 (2001), http://crl.acrl.org/content/62/5/407.full.pdf+html. For more specific studies, see, for example: Christen Cardina and Donald Wicks, "The Changing Roles of Academic Reference Librarians Over a Ten-Year Period," *Reference & User Services Quarterly* 44, no. 2 (2004): 133-142; Lois Buttlar and Rajinder Garcha, "Catalogers in Academic Libraries: Their Evolving and Expanding Role," *College & Research Libraries* 59, no. 4 (1998), http://crl.acrl.org/content/59/4/311.full.pdf+html; and Stephen Pinfield, "The Changing Role of Subject Librarians in Academic Libraries," *Journal of Librarianship and Information Science* 33, no. 1 (2001): 32-38.

3. For studies of the evolution of traditional positions, see, for example: Sally Glasser, "The Changing Face of Cataloging Positions in Academic Libraries: What Skill Set is Needed, and How Can Students Prepare?," *The Serials Librarian* 51, no. 3/4 (2007): 39-49; Jung-ran Park, Caimei Lu, and Linda Marion, "Cataloging Professionals in the Digital Environment: A Content Analysis of Job Descriptions," *Journal of the Association of the American Society for Information Science and Technology* 60, no. 4 (2009): 844-857; and Karen Williams, A Framework for Articulating New Library Roles," *Research Library Issues*, no. 265 (2009), http://www.arl.org/bm~doc/rli-265-williams.pdf. For studies of the evolution of new positions, see, for example: Colleen Boff, Cheryl Albrecht, and Alison Armstrong, "Librarians with a First-Year Focus: Exploring an Emerging Position," in *The Role of the Library in the First College Year*, ed. Larry L. Hardesty (Columbia, South Carolina: National Resource Center for the First-Year Experience and Students in Transition, 2007), 99-107; Lori Mestre, *Librarians Serving Diverse Populations: Challenges and Opportunities* (Chicago: Association of College & Research Libraries, 2010); and John D. Shank, "The Blended Librarian: A Job-Announcement Analysis of the Newly-Emerging Position of Instructional Design Librarian," *College & Research Libraries* 67, no. 6 (2006), http://crl.acrl.org/content/67/6/514.full.pdf+html.

4. Tracy Gabridge, "The Last Mile: Liaison Roles in Curating Science and Engineering Research Data," *Research Library Issues*, no. 265 (2009), http://www.arl.org/bm~doc/rli-265-gabridge.pdf; Elspeth Hyams, Luis Martinez-Uribe, and Stuart Macdonald, "Data Librarianship: A Gap in the Market," *Library & Information Update* (2008), http://hdl.handle.net/1842/2499; Joint Task Force on Library Support for E-Science, "Agenda for Developing E-Science in Research Libraries" (Washington, DC: Association of Research Libraries, 2007), http://www.arl.org/bm~doc/ARL_EScience_final.pdf ; Richard E. Luce, "A New Value Equation Challenge: The Emergence of E-Research and Roles for Research

Libraries," in *No Brief Candle: Reconceiving Research Libraries for the 21st Century* (Washington, DC: Council on Library and Information Resources, 2008), http://www.clir.org/pubs/reports/pub142/luce.html; Laura Brown, Rebecca Griffiths, and Matthew Rascoff, "University Publishing in a Digital Age" (2007), http://www.ithaka.org/ithaka-s-r/strategy/Ithaka%20University%20Publishing%20Report.pdf.

5.   Lori A. Goetsch, "Reinventing Our Work: New and Emerging Roles for Academic Librarians," *Journal of Library Administration* 48, no. 2 (2008): 167; Association of Research Libraries, "New Roles for New Times: An ARL Report Series in Development" (2010), http://www.arl.org/rtl/plan/nrnt/index.shtml.

6.   For more on participatory librarianship, see: Information Institute of Syracuse, "The Participatory Librarianship Starter Kit" (n.d.), http://ptbed.org/. For one model of a library service initiative shaped by the "team approach" Lankes advocates, see: University of Illinois at Urbana-Champaign Library, "Scholarly Commons" (2010), http://www.library.illinois.edu/sc/.

7.   Karla Hahn, "Introduction: Positioning Liaison Librarians for the 21st Century," *Research Library Issues*, no. 265 (2009), http://www.arl.org/bm~doc/rli-265-hahn.pdf.

8.   Council on Library and Information Resources, "CLIR Awards and Fellowships: Postdoctoral Fellowship in Academic Libraries" (2010), http://www.clir.org/fellowships/postdoc/postdoc.html.

9.   On the application of organizational development principles in academic libraries, see, for example: Denise Stephens and Keith Russell, "Organizational Development, Leadership, Change, and the Future of Libraries," *Library Trends* 53, no. 1 (2004), http://hdl.handle.net/2142/1727.

10. Internet Movie Database, "Star Trek (2009)—Memorable Quotes" (2010), http://www.imdb.com/title/tt0796366/quotes

11. Association of Research Libraries, "New Roles for New Times"; Council on Library and Information Resources, "CLIR Awards and Fellowships"; University of North Carolina at Chapel Hill School of Library and Information Science and University of North Carolina at Chapel Hill Institute on Aging, "Workforce Issues in Library and Information Science" (2005), http://www.wilis.unc.edu/index.html; Jose-Marie Griffiths, et al., "The Future of Librarians in the Workforce" (2009), http://libraryworkforce.org/tiki-index.php; and Joanne Gard Marshall, Paul Solomon, and Susan Rathbun-Grubb, "Introduction: Workforce Issues in Library and Information Science," *Library Trends* 58, no. 2 (2009): 121-125.

CHAPTER 1

ACADEMIC LIBRARY STAFFING A DECADE FROM NOW

David W. Lewis
Indiana University Purdue University at Indianapolis

Introduction

Everyone knows that the world libraries inhabit is changing and that the revolution wrought by the Internet and related technologies will have a profound impact on academic libraries and on most other institutions that have information at their core. As academic libraries look to adjust their missions and the ways that they do business, they need to develop their core resource—their staff. The human capabilities a library possesses will either empower or constrain it, particularly in the next decade when an ability to change will be a prerequisite for academic library success.

Assembling a strong staff has always been a central concern, but the stakes are higher today and the challenges greater. Academic libraries will need to adjust their services and their approach to collections, and to do so they will need a staff with a different mix of skills and a willingness to explore new approaches and to break out of established ways of doing things. Libraries will have to build these new capacities at a time when resources will be constrained and when qualified staff will be difficult to find and hard to attract. The established patterns of professional status may also limit flexibility, and MLS programs may not bring us individuals with everything we are looking for.

In this chapter, I will try to provide a summary of the challenges facing academic libraries as they attempt to assemble the staffs they will need in the coming decade. I will begin by identifying the trends I see developing, which will define the kind of staff libraries will require. I will then look at what we can expect of the academic library workforce

1

in 2015. Many of the trends are already clear: the change in the mix of staff between librarians, other professionals, and clerical staff; the increasing need for technology skills for all staff; and the increased need for nonlibrarian professionals—both technologists and those with other expertise, such as human resources and development. Like many service professions, librarianship faces demographic challenges as the Baby Boom generation approaches and enters retirement, but in librarianship these trends are exacerbated by the increasing age of MLS graduates. Finally, I will also consider the organizational development and financial implications of these changes and how academic libraries can manage the transition from the staff they have now to the staff they will need to have a decade hence.

Trends—What the Future Holds

Looking out a decade at the work of academic libraries, what do we see? I would suggest that there are several trends, which are now evident, that will continue to play out and will shape the things that academic libraries do.[1]

The first of these trends is that information tools will continue to grow in power and ease of use, and they will continue to migrate from commercial products purchased and provided by libraries in an access-controlled environment to network-level services that are freely available to anyone connected to the Internet. Google, Google Scholar, Wikipedia, and similarly structured tools will come to be the norm.[2] They will be powerful, easy to use, and free. A decade from now, academic libraries will still be purchasing materials, but this will be a less significant part of their work than it is today.

The second trend is related. Because many tools will be simpler to use and free, information-finding and evaluation skills will move from a profession practiced by librarians to a mass amateur activity. As Clay Shirky points out, this will parallel the mass amateurization of literacy that took place after the invention of the printing press.[3] Information skills will be taught and learned from the earliest grades and across the curriculum. This will mean that most students will be able to find the information they need in most cases. Reference work will need to be focused on the truly difficult questions and may move from assistance in finding information to assistance in using it.

The third trend is that the growth of open scholarship will continue. We can expect commercial publishers to resist and fight this trend, and traditional publishing will not totally disappear, but the economic advantages of open scholarship are compelling, and it will be an increasingly important means of distributing knowledge. This will mean that many of the things libraries would previously have collected will be freely available on the Web. Mass digitization projects, especially the Google Book project, and the efforts of many libraries and other cultural heritage organizations to digitize their collections will add to the corpus of freely available, high-quality scholarly content.

The fourth trend builds on the third. Libraries and librarians will spend more time and effort in supporting users in creating knowledge rather than in consuming knowledge. They will assist researchers and students in archiving and making accessible the results of scholarship. This will include developing and supporting repositories of various sorts and assisting in a variety of open-access publishing initiatives. Some of these efforts may be straightforward, but others, such as those involving e-science, digital humanities, and new forms of publishing, will be complex and require skill sets not possessed by many academic librarians.

So in 2015, what will the landscape look like? Libraries will still be engaged in the traditional roles of building and organizing collections and assisting students and faculty in the use of these collections. However, this will represent a declining portion of the library's activities. The majority of the collections will be digital. The selection of materials will be less time-consuming, as many materials will be bought as large collections rather than on an item-by-item basis. The acquisition and cataloging of these collections will also be easier and cheaper because there will be fewer discrete purchases, and in many cases, cataloging records will be provided as part of the deal. The reference desk, if it exists at all, will be staffed mostly by nonlibrarians. Many questions, perhaps a majority, will not be posed in person; rather, they will be asked from a distance, using chat, texting, or whatever comes next. Instructional activities will be focused on incorporating information skills into the curriculum and on creating learning objects and developing assignments that can be integrated into course management systems.

The library building will be less a warehouse for print materials and more a center for a variety of informal and formal learning activities. It will contain a wide variety of study spaces for individuals and groups. In addition to traditional library services, it will house a variety of activities and centers, many of which will not be part of the library organization, that support student learning and faculty research.

Users, especially students, will be more information literate and will use network-level tools to find scholarly resources, the majority of which will be freely available and not provided as part of purchased library collections. Faculty will have come to expect that the library will provide a place to archive the results of their research, and librarians will be more closely engaged in research activities. This will require a deeper level of technological and subject knowledge than is often possessed by today's generalist librarians. Special collections in both tangible and digital forms will be more important and will be a larger part of what academic libraries do. Because of the technical and human capacities developed by many academic libraries, they will partner with other cultural heritage organizations in their communities to develop and manage digital archival collections.

What will all of this mean for library staffing?

The Academic Library Workforce in 2015

A Decade is not that long a time, and while academic libraries and the information ecology they are a part of will change significantly, staffing in academic libraries will be much slower to adjust. We can look at established trends to indicate where we are heading. Although the pace may quicken some, the changes to come are already well established.

The most important of the trends are these:

- The mix of academic library staffing will change, with the number of nonprofessional and student staff declining and the number of professional staff holding steady or increasing slightly.
- The mix of professional staff will change, with more professionals with special skills, most often some form of technical expertise. Many of these staff will not hold MLS degrees. The number of generalist librarians will decline.
- The workforce, especially the librarian portion of it, will continue to age. In 2015, as many as 50% to 60% of the librarians in many academic libraries will be over 55 years of age. While

there will be some retirements before then, the bulk of the Baby Boom generation will not yet be retired. The real wave of retirements will not come until about 2020.

These trends will be discussed in detail below.

Composition of the Workforce: The NCES Data

The statistics compiled by the National Center for Educational Statistics (NCES) show some trends in academic library staffing.[4] Between 1992 and 2004, the number of employees in academic libraries in the United States declined by 1.8%. The number of nonprofessional staff declined by 13.7%, and the number of student assistants declined by 9.0%. The number of librarians and other professionals increased by 22.5% during the period. NCES did not track librarians and other professionals separately until 1998. In the period between 1998 and 2004, the number of librarians increased by 4.5%, and the number of other professionals increased by 21.4%. While this is a significant increase in other professionals, it is from a low base. A better way to view the data may be that from 1998 to 2004, other professionals as a percentage of total professionals went from 17.4% to 19.7%. So while the number of other professionals increased at a significantly higher rate than librarians, both groups increased, and the overall balance did not change a great deal. In 2004, 27.6% of the staff in academic libraries were librarians, 6.7% were other professionals, 39.1% were nonprofessional

TABLE 1.1						
NCES Data on Academic Library Staffing, 1992–2004						
	1992	**1994**	**1996**	**1998**	**2000**	**2004**
Librarians & Other Professionals	26,341	26,726	27,268	30,040	31,016	32,280
Other Paid Staff	40,421	40,381	40,022	38,026	37,899	36,767
Student Assistants	29,000	28,411	27,998	28,373	26,521	25,038
Total	95,762	95,518	95,288	96,439	95,436	94,085
Librarians	27.5%	28.0%	28.6%	31.1%	32.5%	34.3%
Other Paid Staff	42.2%	42.3%	42.0%	39.4%	39.7%	39.1%
Student Assistants	30.3%	29.7%	29.4%	29.4%	27.8%	26.6%
Total	100.0%	100.0%	100.0%	100.0%	100.0%	100.0%

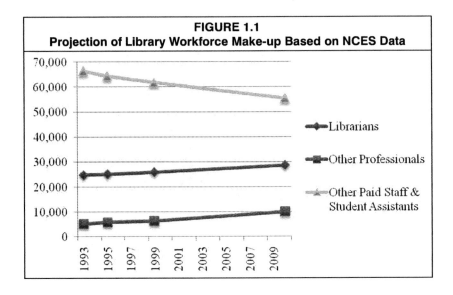

FIGURE 1.1
Projection of Library Workforce Make-up Based on NCES Data

staff, and 26.6% were student assistants. If the 1998 to 2004 trends are extended to 2015 as straight-line extrapolations, 30.4% of academic library staff will be librarians, 10.7% will be other professionals, 35.7% will be nonprofessionals, and 23.2% will be student assistants. The NCES data are shown in table 1.1, and the projections through 2015 are shown in figure 1.1.

The straight-line extrapolation in figure 1.1 is probably conservative and likely underestimates the decline in the number of nonprofessional staff and student assistants, as we are likely to see an accelerating decline in the acquisition and use of paper collections. I also suspect that more other professionals will be hired as more specialized expertise is required. Stanley J. Wilder has documented the rise of "functional specialists" in ARL libraries.[5] From 1985 to 2000, the number of positions in this category increased 169% to become the second largest category of new hires in ARL libraries. The majority of these positions involved information technology.

I would predict that the mix of staffing in 2015 is more likely to be 30% librarians, 20% other professionals, and 50% nonprofessionals and student assistants.

The breakdown between other staff and student assistants is difficult to predict. If the existing trends continue, 30% of library staff would be other staff and 20% student assistants, but it could easily be the other way around if libraries opt to maintain levels of student assistants, either to provide student work opportunities for their campuses or to save money.

The number of librarians is likely to continue to increase gradually; however, most of the new members of academic library staffs will be other professionals. This group could go from representing 20% of the professional workforce to being close to 40%.

Current Trends in the Academic Librarian Job Market

Analyzing the academic library job market has been the focus of a number of studies. They are useful in establishing trends and pointing out the directions the field is heading.

In 2000, Penny M. Beile and Megan M. Adams reviewed 900 academic library job announcements published in four journals in 1996.[6] They noted a significant decrease in technical services positions generally and in cataloging positions in particular. They also noted that there were more specialist positions, a growing preference for computer skills, and what they described as the "most dramatic trend"—an increase in the acceptance of degrees other than the MLS for professional positions. Karen Croneis and Pat Henderson reviewed the position announcements that appeared in *College & Research Libraries News* between 1990 and 2000 that included the word *electronic* or *digital*.[7] Not surprisingly, they found a dramatic increase in the number of such announcements. Many of the positions were traditional activities in, as the authors put it, "technologically sophisticated surroundings." At the same time, they noted an increase in the number of digital project and project management positions. These positions appear to be for responsibilities that few libraries undertook in the past.

Claudene Sproles and David Ratledge analyzed entry-level position announcements for a 20-year period beginning in 1982 and noted an overall decline in the number of position announcements.[8] They also found a decline in the number of technical services positions. The number of systems positions increased but remained a small portion of the total positions, though the demand for computer experience increased in all types of positions. Joan Starr's similar study comparing job announcements in 1983 and 2003 had similar findings, as did a study by Beverly P. Lynch and Kimberley Robles Smith that reviewed announcements in *College & Research Libraries News* between 1973 and 1998.[9] Jane Kinkus attempted to document an increase in the requirement for project management skills by reviewing job announcements in 1993, 2003, and 2004.[10] Her data are not conclusive but seem to indicate an increased demand for this set of skills. John Shank's 2006 study of instructional design librarian job announcements yielded a very small number of announcements, but the existence of "blended librarian," with both traditional library credentials and instructional design skills, as an emerging library specialty was given some support.[11]

This research confirms the NCES data and documents several trends that we can expect to continue. First, there is an increased demand for technological expertise, whether in the form of computer skills for traditional positions or in the form of new roles such as management of digital projects or instructional design. Second, we see a decline in some areas of traditional library practice, particularly cataloging. Finally, we see an increase in specialist, often technology, positions, some of which have degree requirements other than the MLS.

Demographics

Academic librarians are old and have become increasingly older in comparison to similar professions such as teaching, social work, or nursing. To quote Wilder's frank assessment, "librarians are unusually old."[12]

In 1995, Wilder projected that in 2010 in ARL libraries, nearly 25% of academic librarians would be 50 to 54 years old, nearly 25% more would be 55 to 59 years old, and about 9% more would be over 60 years of age. Only approximately 15% of academic librarians in ARL libraries in 2010 would be under 40 years old. By 2020, according to Wilder's 1995 projections, not quite 45% of ARL librarians will be over 50, and about 23% will be under 40.[13] In 2020, the last of the Baby Boom generation will still be a decade from retirement.

Wilder's 2003 study confirms his earlier findings and provides a more nuanced analysis of the demographics of academic libraries. Beyond the aging of the Baby Boom generation, several factors are at work. The first is the decline in the number of young women choosing traditionally female-dominated professions, especially librarianship, because of increased opportunities in other professions, such as law and medicine. Secondly, there has been a marked increase in the age of those receiving MLS degrees. Between 1983 and 2001, the percentage of those receiving MLS degrees who were 40 years old or older rose from 16.4% to 35.0%.[14] In 2001, over a third of the newly minted MLS graduates were of the Baby Boom generation.

Wilder's 2003 study also provides some assessment of management and leadership positions in ARL libraries. As with the general population of ARL librarians, he notes an aging in managerial positions. Between 1986 and 2000, the percentage of ARL managers under 45 years of age declined from 54.5% to 21.7%.[15] A similar trend can be seen with ARL directors. In 1986, 47.2% of ARL directors were under 50 years old. By 2000, this number had fallen to 25.0%.[16] One implication of the increase in the age of managers and directors is that the current generation of young librarians will have less opportunity to advance into management positions until much later in their careers than the generation that preceded them. Wilder's data do not address this issue particularly, but it seems likely that advancement opportunities are increasingly unavailable until individuals are at a stage of their lives when they are less mobile. Thus libraries may find that they have mid-career librarians who have had few advancement opportunities and are now geographically constrained by family and community ties.

As noted above, in 2015 the trends that Wilder documents will still be playing out and academic libraries will still have a large cadre of aging Baby Boomers occupying most of the managerial and leadership positions. But the end will be in sight. The Baby Boomers will begin retiring in 2015, though the majority will not be leaving the workforce until a few years later. As Wilder points out, "The management issue resulting from the aging of librarianship is thus not retirements; it is how to obtain new entrants in sufficient numbers, quality, and expertise to replace retirees and to keep the cycle turning."[17] Wilder concludes on an optimistic note: "Libraries have discovered needs for new kinds of expertise. We may be fortunate that at the very moment that information undergoes its biggest revolution since Gutenberg, librarianship appears positioned to take on substantial numbers of new people with new skills to help it adapt."[18] I am not so sure. There is a decade to go before there will be significant openings; this is a long time, and recruitment of the required level of talent will be challenging. This will create a pipeline problem that will be discussed below.

Generational Changes

The Baby Boom generation of librarians came of age in the time before catalogs were computer-based. They were the generation that brought automation and the library instruction movement to academic libraries. But many of the changes that were wrought by Baby Boomers in their youth are now being overwhelmed by the newer network-level technologies. In 1980, Brian Nielsen predicted the demise of online searching as a responsibility of professional librarians.[19] While it seems hard to imagine today, Nielsen's thesis created quite a stir. This early loss of the need for professional expertise was followed by many more losses both large and small, so that much of the knowledge and many of the skills that 25 years ago comprised the core professional competencies of an academic librarian are now unimportant or irrelevant. This is not to say that librarians of this generation have not adapted, for in many cases they have. In many cases, these librarians have a deep knowledge of their campuses and strong relationships with faculty. When the Baby Boom generation of librarians retires, it will be a loss.

Lynne C. Lancaster provides a good summary of the generational differences and the issues they raise for libraries.[20] She cautions that libraries need to watch out for Boomer burnout as the Boomers deal with multiple pressures from job and family or as they get restless and bored. Lancaster describes Gen Xers in this way: "Highly independent, entrepreneurial, and comfortable with change, this group entered the work world with a healthy degree of skepticism. Not deluded by the idea that employers would keep them around for a lifetime, Xers took charge of their careers early on and have been willing to leave a job if their needs weren't being met."[21] Boomers often misunderstand Gen Xers, who they see as not appropriately dedicated to their jobs. Arthur P. Young, Peter Hernon, and Ronald Powell found that there was a difference in the views of leadership attributes between Gen X librarians and library directors and that the differences were in line with other observations of Gen Xers.[22] As Pixey Anne Mosley puts it in her article on mentoring Gen X managers, "To many Generation Xers, because of their lack of tolerance for bureaucracy and hierarchies, being a library director is not a presumed goal."[23]

Susanne Markgren and her colleagues surveyed librarians who had switched jobs in the past five years, most of whom where Gen Xers, and found most of the moves were to new institutions, and many were lateral moves.[24] Lack of opportunity, financial constraints, and lack of challenging work were cited as reasons for leaving. A lack of support and encouragement for professional development and continuing education was also cited as a concern. Reviewing their findings, Markgren and her colleagues state:

> New librarians certainly feel that a generational gap exists between them and their senior colleagues. Many are worried that their more seasoned peers view them as disloyal professionals who are only using their current positions as stepping stones and will resent them for their mobility. In fact, many attribute the dissatisfaction with their positions and the profession to the inability of older generations to understand and accept them as peers.[25]

The generational difference, especially between Boomers and Gen Xers, will exacerbate the demographic challenges academic libraries face in the recruitment and retention of talented librarians.

Organizational Challenges

It is clear that the coming decades will require staff, particularly librarians, who are not wed to traditional roles and who are flexible and willing to learn new skills and to remake their jobs.

There will also be an influx of new professional staff, most of whom will work with technology and many of whom will not have MLS degrees. This will be particularly true in light of what will likely be problems in the recruitment of librarians. The skills these non-MLS professionals bring will be required for organizational success in academic libraries, but they will often be outside the traditional power structures that have been dominated by librarians.

There will be a decline in the number of nonprofessional and student staff. This decline will be gradual and in most libraries should be manageable through attrition. There may be some tension in libraries that try to maintain their current levels of student staffing at the expense of nonprofessional staff.

There are several trends that are likely to lead to organizational challenges in the near future of many academic libraries. The two most pressing challenges will be these:

- recruiting librarians
- resolving the tensions that can be expected from the increase in non-MLS professionals in libraries

To meet these challenges, we must develop organizations and embrace organizational cultures that foster a new balance of power among professional communities or that eliminate the distinction between traditional library professionals and "new" library professionals.

Recruiting Librarians: The Pipeline Problem

There are a variety of issues confronting academic libraries as they attempt to recruit the new librarians they need. There are questions about the pool of MLS students, about what is taught in MLS programs, about salaries, and about the geographic mobility of beginning librarians. All of this leads to fewer applicants for academic library positions, as well as disappointment about the quality of the preparation these applicants have received for our changing profession. Stephen T. Bajjaly's study of recruitment in libraries indicates that a typical applicant pool contains 15 individuals, and 43% of those conducting the search rated the quality of the applicant pool as "less than they expected."[26] In addition, there is what Malcolm Gladwell calls the "mismatch problem," whereby inappropriate criteria are used to limit applicant pools, which makes hiring librarians even less likely to be successful.

Who Gets an MLS Degree?

In 2003, *Library Journal* ran a series of three articles assessing the recruitment and retention of MLS students. The survey of students in MLS programs showed that 70% had worked in libraries and that this experience was a primary reason for their choosing to pursue the degree. Deans and directors of graduate programs estimated that 50% to 80% of their students were recruited from full-time jobs in libraries.[27] As noted above, students in MLS programs are getting older. Given the role of library work experience in the decision to pursue the degree, this should come as no surprise.

In concluding the article reporting on the *Library Journal* survey results, John Berry summarized the situation as he saw it:

> While the body of people recruited from libraries is gener-
> ally diverse and guarantees new librarians with great faith in
> the profession, it tends to make for an older constituency of
> students, deeply rooted in libraries as they exist. The library of
> the future may have difficulty being born in that culture. . . .
> If the field needs new blood, if it needs younger librarians who
> have more of their careers ahead of them, if it needs thinking
> that is brand new, out of the box, to create the library of the
> future, it needs a younger generation of recruits to go with the
> strong librarians brought in from libraries today. To find that
> new generation, LIS schools will have to seek candidates from
> somewhere beyond libraries. The best place will be among the
> general undergraduate population.[28]

What Library Schools Teach

The MLS degree is most often a one-year program that faces the challenging task of squeezing in instruction in a wide variety of competencies. Critics of the results are everywhere. Youngok Choi and Edie
Rasmussen end their article on the educational requirements of future
digital librarians by saying, "Based on this survey, it appears that LIS
education needs to pay attention to additional education in interpersonal and communication skills and integration of practical skills and
experience with digital collection management and digital technologies
into curricula."[29] Mark Winston and Gretchen Ebeler Hazlin document
a lack of marketing training in MLS programs.[30] Ingrid Hsieh-Yee
expresses concerns about the quality of cataloging instruction.[31] Patricia
Promís makes a case for Emotional Intelligence (EI) as a critical competency for librarians. While stressing that many parties are responsible for assuring that librarians develop this competency, she focuses
attention on library schools: "For obvious reasons, library schools have
traditionally focused on developing cognitive and hard skills. Today,
they are looking for ways to expand and enhance the curriculum by
incorporating soft competencies into programs."[32] As John Berry says in
a 2004 *Library Journal* editorial entitled "Don't Dis the LIS 'Crisis'":

At every school I've visited in the past three years, students complain about the lack of courses and choices in traditional library areas. The other very common grievance comes from recent graduates about the courses they were mandated to take, either because they were the only ones available or because they were required technology courses. Many found their studies of little use on their first jobs.[33]

There are many complaints, but in the end, the state of library education may not really matter. Stephen T. Bajjaly documents that employers don't seem to care what courses were taken in MLS programs or where the degree was earned.[34] In his study, only 1% of employers ranked courses taken during the MLS program as critical, and 44% ranked this factor as not that important. Only 6% ranked MLS program attended as critical, and 47% ranked it as not that important.

Salaries and Other Constraints
The most recent *Library Journal* survey of salaries and placements reports a median starting salary of $40,000 and mean starting salary of $39,000 for 2006 MLS graduates finding work in academic librarians.[35] ARL reported a $40,000 median starting salary for beginning librarians in its 2006–07 salary survey.[36] Figures collected by the National Association of Colleges and Employers show that the salaries of beginning academic librarians trail salaries commanded by undergraduates with degrees in science, engineering, or business, often by more than 25%. Beginning academic library salaries are about 15% above those received by undergraduate liberal arts graduates, however.[37]

Many new MLS graduates are not geographically mobile. The *Library Journal* followed up its 2007 placements and salaries survey with a survey that indicated that only 16% of 2006 MLS graduates moved outside their home region and that, "As a group, graduates said that finding the ideal location, one where they were willing to move their families and where salaries were acceptable, was tricky."[38]

We can expect that the best MLS graduates, who have the personal and technical characteristics libraries desire and who are geographically mobile, will be in high demand, and this may drive up salaries for these beginning librarians. This upward push on salaries will either ripple up to previously hired librarians, or it will create salary compression.

The Mismatch Problem

In his talk at the 2008 New Yorker Conference "Stories from the Near Future," Malcolm Gladwell discussed the challenge of hiring in the modern world and what he calls the "mismatch problem."[39] Citing the sports combine as a clear example, Gladwell argues that the predictors most of us use in hiring do not match the skills that will be required to do the job. For those not familiar with professional sports, a "combine" is an event held before the annual draft that brings together the most promising athletes and puts them through a series of physical, intellectual, and psychological tests aimed at providing teams with the information required to make the most successful draft picks. As Gladwell notes, it turns out that there is almost no correlation between success in a sports combine and success as a professional player. As is often the case in regard to the criteria set up for teachers under the No Child Let Behind law, he argues, the criteria used by professional sports teams to evaluate the future success of top recruits may appear reasonable, but their application routinely limits the pool of applicants at precisely the point when it should be expanded. Gladwell argues that the sports combine and similar procedures that we put in place to aid in hiring are an attempt to create certainty when that certainty is illusory. As the workplace has become more complex, as it has in every profession, the only real way to tell whether or not someone can do the job is to let the person do it and evaluate his or her success. The world has changed, Gladwell concludes, but the way we staff our organizations has not.

Not surprisingly, Gladwell does not mention librarians in this talk, but it seems obvious to me that libraries also face a mismatch problem when hiring. We use the MLS degree as a filter when it is far from clear that what is taught or the criteria for getting into MLS programs are at all related to what we need in professionals in academic libraries.

The MLS degree is certainly not an indicator of the soft skills, such as flexibility, initiative, and ability to work in teams and with diverse populations, that academic libraries need in professional employees. It is also the case that many libraries do not structure new hires in a way that allows for relatively quick assessment and decision on continuing employment. Rather, many faculty librarian positions have what amounts to a five- to seven-year probationary period, and many nonfaculty positions follow similar patterns. In addition, as Promí notes, libraries often do not advertise for what they really want. As she says, "The present study demonstrates that a significant percentage of job advertisements are not designed to attract emotionally intelligent individuals, but rather those with specific hard skills. On the one hand, the profession is clamoring for these missing soft skills. On the other hand, employers are not soliciting them at the point when positions are advertised."[40]

It is not clear how academic libraries can solve their mismatch problem, but the most likely approach would be to expand the talent pool by looking for professionals without the MLS.

Librarians and Non-MLS Professionals

I believe it is likely that this area will be among the most problematic facing academic library leaders over the next decade. It requires addressing the fundamental issues of who is a librarian and what are the appropriate roles for other library professionals. It requires new organizational solutions in the light of deeply entrenched traditional practice. Success in this endeavor is critical if libraries are to develop new and innovative resources and services, but such success will be very challenging to achieve.

The Balance of Librarians and Other Professional Staff

It is likely that the number of librarians in academic libraries will grow slightly over the next decade, but there will be a significant influx of other professionals. The new balance of professional staffing between librarians and other professional staff will have the potential to create tensions between the two groups. As Wilder points out, these new functional specialists are "simply different from their colleagues elsewhere in the library. They have fewer MLS degrees, there are more males, and they have fewer years of professional experience but earn higher pay."[41]

To the extent that class distinctions and salaries, benefits, and expectations of research and service based on them persist, especially between librarians and other professional staff, it could easily lead to conflicts that will make the work of the organization difficult. Librarians have, in the past, always run academic libraries. The change in the balance of staff will change this at least to some degree and could require a reworking of the way academic libraries are managed. The change is likely to have an impact on the identity of librarians.

Who Does Library Work?
Another way to view this issue is to ask this question: Who does library work?

One can distinguish between what librarians with MLS degrees do and "library work." It is the work that is important, not who does it. But it is, of course, not that simple. Academic librarians and our professional associations have long held that being a librarian means having an MLS degree, and while not always expressed, the clear implication is that it is librarians who do library work. ACRL is crystal clear on this. The association's "Statement on the Terminal Professional Degree for Academic Librarians" says simply, "The master's degree in library science from a library school program accredited by the American Library Association is the appropriate terminal professional degree for academic librarians."[42] Typical of the general sentiment of academic librarians is the title of John Berry's article on a Council on Library and Information Resources program to move PhD holders into research library librarian positions through a fellowship rather than an MLS degree program. Berry's title is "But Don't Call 'em Librarians."[43]

In *War Made New,* Max Boot discusses the challenges military organizations face in confronting change. He says, "Successful adaptation to major technological shifts requires overcoming that dread [of innovation] and changing the kinds of people who are rewarded within a military structure."[44] Boot recounts how 19th-century navies did not treat "line" and "engineering" officers comparably until more than 50 years after the introduction of steam power. Logistics officers in 19th- and early 20th-century armies faced similar inequities. Boot wonders how the Air Force will treat the controllers who fly drones from trailers thousands of miles from the combat zone. Will this time be counted as "flying" hours? He continues: "This is part of a broader challenge confronting all Information Age militaries: how to make room for those who fight with a computer mouse, not an M-16."[45] I would suggest that academic libraries face a similar challenge. We will need to begin rewarding different kinds of staff, many without MLS degrees. In many cases, staff with positions that have received the highest status in the past, primarily librarians, will not appreciate the change.

The MLS and Faculty Status

Academic libraries have a long history of class distinction within their workforces. Librarians, often with some form of faculty status, and clerical staff have long had clearly differentiated roles, benefits, and responsibilities. The addition of technical staff and other professionals, such as personnel and development officers, in recent decades has added a third class to the library mix. It is likely that the skill sets required for library work will increasingly not be found in generalist MLS librarians, but that subject expertise and knowledge of technical areas like geographic information systems, instructional design, or assessment will be better provided by individuals with master's or PhD training in these areas. These individuals will be doing library work, but in many cases they will be classed as professionals with technologists, rather than with librarians.

James Neal has recently suggested that influx of other professionals is already in full force and that it is a good thing.[46] He argues that librarianship has long struggled with how it can define itself as a profession. He goes on, "This ambiguity about the professional characteristics of librarianship suggests that educational preparation for the field does not have an impact on socialization into the field comparable to other professions."[47] Neal argues that staff trained in other disciplines—"raised by wolves" as he puts it—might provide a creative infusion of needed talent. He concludes: "They [non-MLS professionals] may fit effectively or be creatively disruptive in the transformed libraries we are seeking to create. Either way, they are needed for their important contributions to academic library innovation and mutability. They will grow in their influence and relevance to the future academic library."[48]

Among the findings of Thea Lindquist and Todd Gilman's study of academic librarians with subject doctorates was that a sizeable minority of academic librarians with subject doctorates did not have MLS degrees and that younger academic librarians with subject doctorates

were significantly less likely to have also an MLS than their older colleagues.[49] Lindquist and Gilman conclude:

> The fact that so many respondents lack the MLS but are,
> nonetheless, employed as professional librarians indicates that
> a significant number of academic/research library employers
> do not insist upon an MLS if the potential employee has a
> subject doctorate. It also effectively reinforces a widely held (if
> minority) view that, in certain situations, a subject doctorate
> offers many of the essentials that an MLS provides while also
> assuring that the candidate has deep subject knowledge in a
> particular field, advanced knowledge of the research process, or
> both.[50]

These findings demonstrate that, despite the strong sentiment
among librarians and their professional organization for the MLS as the
required terminal degree, academic libraries will forgo this requirement
when subject expertise is required and can be acquired through the
recruitment of individuals who hold the subject doctorates but do not
hold the MLS degree.

It is likely that a small minority of PhD holders without MLS
degrees in subject specialist positions will be acceptable, but this is not
what Neal is talking about. A large number of non-MLS professionals
doing library work with masters' degrees in geographic information
systems, instructional design, informatics, or new media will be something else. This will clearly challenge long-established ways of thinking
about what an academic librarian is and should be, and maybe more
important, who should do library work. We can expect considerable
resistance to the changing of established norms.

There have been many debates and some research on the impact of
faculty or academic status on the work of academic librarians. It is generally concluded that faculty status provides librarians with better job
security and better pay and that librarians with faculty status are more
engaged with campus governance.[51] Despite this, some research seems
to argue that faculty status does not correlate with the quality of the
institution.[52] Rachel Applegate, in a review of the research on faculty
status, found no evidence for the claims made by its proponents.[53] That

classic naysayer, Blaise Cronin, blasted faculty status for librarians in his 2001 *Library Journal* article, "The Mother of All Myths," which he concluded by saying:

> If anything, the obsession with faculty status merely detracts from customer service and weakens the profession's public image. Librarians, along with information systems specialists and sundry other members of the campus community, are professional employees whose role is to support, not define or negotiate, the academic mission of the university. Fifty years of conceit is probably enough.[54]

The response of the library academic library community was quick, and Cronin was soundly taken to task.[55]

What is important for our discussion is not the merits of faculty status for librarians, but rather, since it is firmly entrenched in many institutions, its implications for organizational change in academic libraries. It is my view that to the extent that faculty status increases the class distinctions between librarians and other professionals who do library work, it is likely to create tensions and to limit the flexibility in the use of staff. On the other hand, especially on larger campuses, faculty status often enhances the relationships between librarians and faculty, and this could be a compensating advantage. As Charles B. Lowry put it 15 years ago: "If closer affinity with classroom teaching and with research are logical outcomes of the new paradigm, then the case for faculty status during the next twenty years will be a persuasive one."[56]

Faculty status, while it has, in my view, many advantages, may exacerbate library's ability to blend staff with and without MLS degrees; it could be a significant impediment to the construction of productive working relationships and organizational structures.

Merged Organizations as a Model

One way to look at the likely future of academic libraries is to look at the experience of those colleges and universities that have chosen to merge their libraries and computer centers. John K. Stemmer reviewed such organizations, sometimes called a "merged information services organization" or MISO, in liberal arts colleges and provides an effective summary of the justifications for this organizational change. He documents a slow but steady growth of this organizational structure and cites four reasons for pursuing it:

- improved service to faculty and students through better technology and information support and through the effective implementation of new technology
- increased efficiencies and greater organizational flexibility with budget and staff
- improved visibility and enhanced reputation for the campus
- the evolution of a new "information profession" that will encourage and support campus technical leadership and increased staff cooperation[57]

Stemmer found, "The MISO model is an effective organizational structure with which to deliver information resources and services on a liberal arts campus. Both academic deans and CIOs had favorable impressions and perceived the MISO organization as effective."[58] However, he identified a number concerns: a champion for the merger is required, the merging of the cultures of computing and library organizations takes time and requires a significant staff development program, and at times there is a loss of focus among constituent elements of the MISO.

Peggy Seiden and Michael D. Kathman reviewed the history of merged organizations and found that the mergers were generally driven from the top down and that, in general, while there were some examples of merged help/reference desks: "Even those that have 'merged' basically have two separate units that report to the same individual."[59]

Mary K. Bolin examines the organizational structures of land grant universities and finds that very few have adopted a merged model. She concludes by observing, "The library has synergy with everyone, and, in a different way, so does the computer center. While organizationally imposed synergy may have worked for some institutions, it may be that the library and computer center can find 'synergy,' 'convergence,' and so on, by remaining organizationally distinct, preserving the strengths of each."[60] Edward D. Garten and Delmus E. Williams concur when, after reviewing the cultural difference of libraries and computing organizations, they say, "Those who manage academic libraries and those who manage computer centers cohabit a common information universe. But cohabitation is just that—cohabitation—not marriage."[61] Deborah Ludwig and Jeffrey Bullington studied the merged organization at the University of Kansas and conclude that they see promise in the organization's current "adolescence." They suggest that for the structure to achieve its promise, librarians must learn to work alongside technologists and not feel that it "lessens their status on the faculty playing field" and has not "eroded traditional library roles and the benefits those roles provide library users."[62]

What we should take from the experience of merged libraries and computing organizations is not that doing it or not doing it is right or wrong, but rather that it cannot be accomplished without considerable difficulties, and that a truly harmonized and integrated organization is the rare exception. It may be the same as the number of non-MLS professionals increases inside academic libraries. The same cultural differences will be present and, because the change is happening inside the library, the threat to library values may seem more dangerous—more like a cancer than an external assault.

Financial Implications

There are several ways in which the trends I have identified might impact that financial situation of academic libraries.

First, the decline in the number of clerical and student staff will provide some opportunities for salary savings, though it is unlikely that these savings will be enough to offset fully the requirements for new professional staff.

Second, salaries for professional staff will increase, probably at rates greater than the cost of living. While it may not feel like it for most librarians, at least as measured by the ARL Salary Survey, academic librarians in the United States have had salary increases that are greater than the increase in the Consumer Price Index over the past 20 years.[63] In recent years, this growth may not have been distributed equally, as Martha Kyrillidou and Mark Young point out in their introduction to the most recent *ARL Annual Salary Survey*: "Libraries need staff with high-level technical skills to operate the more sophisticated and complex information environments that are in place. As people are hired with higher beginning salaries, the inability to adjust the overall salary structure to achieve some equity for the experienced staff members is another factor that contributes to slow salary growth for higher salaries."[64] It is likely that the need for more specialized positions, whether librarians or non-MLS professionals fill them, will continue to drive this trend. It is also likely to be the case that the most desirable new MLS graduates will command higher salaries. The salary compression that is likely to result will exacerbate the generational and librarian/specialist tensions we have already noted.

I have suggested that libraries over the next decade will need to move a significant portion of the resources devoted to collections from purchasing published material to curating content that either is produced at or is important to the campus.[65] To the extent that this can be done, it will provide funding for the new positions that will be devoted to this task. While I believe this is the appropriate course for libraries, it will be a difficult one, as the press of cost increase for scientific journals will continue and, while it is reasonable to have faith in the long-term success of open access, the transition to it will be difficult, and carving funds for staffing from funds currently devoted to the purchase of science journals will be a difficult political challenge.

Conclusion: Getting from Here to There

It is quite clear that staffing academic libraries for the transitions they face will be challenging. As organizations, academic libraries will need the ability to be flexible with their staffing, but our traditional structures and long-term commitment to individuals will make this difficult. The aging of academic librarians will at some point lead to a large number of retirements and will result in openings, but this will not come soon enough in many cases. The aging of MLS graduates and their increasing recruitment from traditional library settings will make the MLS a less effective filter for the hiring of library professionals, but it is likely that moving away from this standard, though it might, as Neal has argued, make good sense, will be difficult and will likely create tension between older librarians and younger non-MLS professionals. The distinct class structure that is imposed on libraries where librarians have faculty status will likely limit needed flexibility.

We will need to reduce the number of clerical and student staff, and though this may well be an accomplished through attrition, it will understandably create anxiety within this group.

There will be a particular challenge in recruiting professionals into leadership roles. In part this will be because Gen Xers are less inclined than Boomers to make the sacrifices necessary, but probably of more importance is the fact that there will be fewer leadership opportunities for the next generation until they are much older than was the case for the current generation of library leaders.

I believe there are several things that can be done to help academic libraries get from where they are now to where they need to go:

- It is critical that the library's leadership be frank and realistic and make the realities clear to current staff. Everyone understands that our world is changing quickly, but if we sugarcoat how these changes will impact our staffs, this can only lead to surprises for them later. This is not what we want.

- Money will need to be found to pay both librarians and non-MLS professionals competitive salaries.

- We need to be generous with support for staff development. When a staff member from any part of the organization is interested in acquiring new skills that could benefit the library, encouragement and support should be provided.

- It will be important for the current generation of librarians, especially those in leadership positions, to recognize that individuals coming into libraries today may not see their lives and their careers in the same way the Boomer generation did 20 or 30 years ago. Accommodations need to be made for different work/life balances and to provide meaningful work early in careers.

- Every library should have a clearly articulated strategy for managing its recruitment, retention, and leadership development. At a minimum, every director should know the demographics of his or her staff and when retirements can be expected. Retirements will be critical opportunities, and they should be used strategically.

- It is inevitable that academic libraries will be looking for new staff with a wide range of skills. Libraries need to be clear about how they will fill these positions. Several questions are particularly important. First, when do they need librarians, and when are non-MLS professionals a better alternative?

Second, what is the salary strategy? Will they pay the salary needed to attract the required talent even when this leads to salary compression or inequity? There are many possible answers to these questions. What is important is not answering them on the fly.

- It seems to me that it will be very difficult to avoid a growing tensions between librarians and non-MLS professionals. There are any number of strategies for minimizing these, including teams and other types of collaborative projects that expose different staff to the skills and abilities of the other group. The opposite approach would be to create separate parts of the organization—a "skunk works"—and live with the animosity that will follow.

The next decade will be challenging for academic libraries from a variety of perspectives. Finding, retaining, and developing the staffs we need will be one of the central challenges. If we recognize this and confront it, I think those libraries that are doing exciting things, where good work is recognized and rewarded and where the culture is not cutthroat or overly political, can be successful.

Notes

1. These predictions are an extension of the work presented in David W. Lewis, "A Strategy for Academic Libraries in the First Quarter of the 21st Century," *College & Research Libraries* 68, no. 5 (Sept. 2007): 418–434. A nice summary of the overarching issues facing academic libraries can be found in "Part I: A Continuing Discussion on Research Libraries in the 21st Century," in *No Brief Candle: Reconceiving Research Libraries for the 21st Century*, CLIR Publication No. 142 (Washington, DC: Council on Library and Information Resources, August 2008), 1–12; available at www.clir.org/pubs/reports/pub142/contents.html (accessed Sept. 3, 2008). Similar conclusions can be found in Ross Housewright and Roger Schonfeld, *Ithaka's 2006 Studies of Key Stakeholders in the Digital Transformation in Higher Education*, Aug. 18, 2008, available at www.ithaka. org/research/Ithakas%202006%20Studies%20of%20Key%20Stakeholders%20 in%20the%20Digital%20Transformation%20in%20Higher%20Education.pdf (accessed Sept. 3, 2008).

2. Mark J. Ludwig and Margaret R. Wells's preliminary study of the superior effectiveness of Google Books over a library catalog is indicative of the changes that are coming; see Mark J. Ludwig and Margaret R. Wells, "Google Books vs. BISON: Is the BISON Catalog Going the Way of Its Namesake?" *Library Journal* 133, no. 11 (June 15, 2008), www.libraryjournal.com/article/CA6566451.html (accessed July 5, 2008). The recent announcement by Encyclopædia Britannica that it will be accepting "participation and collaboration from experts and read-

ers" is a similar sign. See "Britannica's New Site: More Participation and Collaboration from Experts and Readers," Encyclopædia Britannica Webshare blog, June 3, 2008, http://britannicanet.com/?p=86 (accessed July 5, 2008).

3.   Clay Shirky, *Here Comes Everybody: The Power of Organizing without Organizations* (New York: Penguin Press, 2008), 77–78.

4.   National Center for Educational Statistics academic library statistics are collected every two years. They can be found at "Publications & Products: Library Statistics Program," http://nces.ed.gov/pubsearch/getpubcats.asp?sid=041# (accessed July 5, 2008).

5.   Stanley J. Wilder, *Demographic Change in Academic Librarianship* (Washington, DC: Association of Research Libraries, 2003), 20–23.

6.   Penny M. Beile and Megan M. Adams, "Other Duties as Assigned: Emerging Trends in the Academic Library Job Market," *College & Research Libraries,* 61, no. 4 (July 2000): 336–347.

7.   Karen S. Croneis and Pat Henderson, "Electronic and Digital Librarian Positions: A Content Analysis of Announcements from 1990 through 2000," *Journal of Academic Librarianship* 28, no. 4 (July 2002): 232–237.

8.   Claudene Sproles and David Ratledge, "An Analysis of Entry-Level Librarian Ads Published in *American Libraries,* 1982–2002," *E-JASL: Electronic Journal of Academic and Special Librarianship* 5, no. 2–3 (Fall 2004), http://southernlibrarianship.icaap.org/content/v05n02/sproles_c01.htm (accessed July 5, 2008).

9.   Joan Starr, "A Measure of Change: Comparing Library Job Advertisements of 1983 and 2003," *LIBRES: Library and Information Science Research Electronic Journal* 14, no. 2 (Sept. 2004), http://libres.curtin.edu.au/libres14n2/index.htm (accessed July 5, 2008); Beverly P. Lynch and Kimberly Robles Smith, "The Changing Nature of Work in Academic Libraries," *College & Research Libraries,* 62, no. 5 (Sept. 2001): 407–420.

10.   Jane Kinkus, "Project Management Skills: A Literature Review and Content Analysis of Library Position Announcements," *College & Research Libraries* 68, no. 4 (July 2007): 352–363.

11.   John D. Shank, "The Blended Librarian: A Job Announcement Analysis of the Newly Emerging Position of Instructional Design Librarian," *College & Research Libraries* 67, no. 6 (Nov. 2006): 515–524.

12.   Wilder, *Demographic Change in Academic Librarianship,* 3.

13.   Stanley J. Wilder, *The Age Demographics of Academic Librarians: A Profession Apart: A Report Based on Data from the ARL Annual Salary Survey,* (Washington, DC: Association of Research Libraries, 1995), 41.

14.   Wilder, *Demographic Change in Academic Librarianship,* 17–18.

15.   Ibid., 42.

16.   Ibid., 46.

17.   Ibid., 27.

18.   Ibid., 57.

19.   Brian Nielsen, "Online Bibliographic Searching and the Deprofessionalization of Librarianship." *Online Review* 4, no. 3 (Sept. 1980): 215–224.

20.   Lynne C. Lancaster, "The Click and Clash of Generations," *Library Journal* 128, no. 17 (Oct. 15, 2003): 36–39.

21.   Ibid., 37.

22.   Arthur P. Young, Peter Hernon, and Ronald R. Powell, "Attributes of Academic Library Leadership: An Exploratory Study of Some Gen-Xers," *Journal of Aca-*

demic Librarianship 32, no. 5 (Sept. 2006): 489–502.

23. Pixey Anne Mosley, "Mentoring Gen X Managers: Tomorrow's Library Leadership is Already Here," *Library Administration & Management* 19, no. 4 (Fall 2005): 191.

24. Susanne Markgren, Thad Dickinson, Anne Leonard, and Kim Vassiliadis, "The Five-Year Itch: Are Libraries Losing Their Most Valuable Resources?" *Library Administration & Management* 21, no. 2 (Spring 2007): 70–76.

25. Ibid., 75.

26. Stephen T. Bajjaly, "Contemporary Recruitment in Traditional Libraries," *Journal of Education for Library and Information Science* 46, no. 1 (Winter 2005): 55.

27. John N. Berry III, "LIS Recruiting Does It Make the Grade?" *Library Journal* 128, no. 8 (May 1, 2003): 39.

28. Ibid., 41.

29. Youngok Choi and Edie Rasmussen, "What Is Needed to Educate Future Digital Librarians," *D-Lib Magazine* 12, no. 9 (Sept. 2006), www.dlib.org/dlib/september06/choi/09choi.html (accessed July 5, 2008).

30. Mark Winston and Gretchen Ebeler Hazlin, "Leadership Competencies in Library and Information Science: Marketing as a Component of LIS Curricula," *Journal of Education for Library and Information Science* 44, no. 2 (Spring 2003): 177–187.

31. Ingrid Hsieh-Yee, "Cataloging and Metadata Education in North American LIS Programs," *Library Resources & Technical Services* 48, no. 1 (Jan. 2004): 59–68.

32. Patricia Promí, "Are Employers Asking for the Right Competencies? A Case for Emotional Intelligence," *Library Administration & Management* 22, no. 1 (Winter 2008): 26.

33. John N. Berry III, "Don't Dis the LIS 'Crisis'," *Library Journal* 129, no. 16 (Oct. 1, 2004): 10.

34. Bajjaly, "Contemporary Recruitment in Traditional Libraries," see chart on page 56.

35. Stephanie Maatta, "What's an MLS Worth?" *Library Journal* 132, no. 17 (Oct. 15, 2007): 36.

36. Martha Kryllidou and Mark Young, comps. and eds., *ARL Annual Salary Survey 2006–07* (Washington, DC: Association of Research Libraries, 2007), 14.

37. The National Association of Colleges and Employers data are available only to members, but the summary information is widely reported. See for example, "More Jobs, Higher Pay for New College Graduates in 2008," CourseAdvisor, http://resources.courseadvisor.com/education-trends/starting-salary (accessed July 5, 2008).

38. Maatta, "What's an MLS Worth?" 38.

39. Malcolm Gladwell, "Reinventing Invention" (talk, 2008 New Yorker Conference, "Stories from the Near Future," May 8, 2008); video available at www.newyorker.com/online/video/conference/2008/gladwell (accessed July 5, 2008).

40. Promí, "Are Employers Asking for the Right Competencies?" 30.

41. Wilder, *Demographic Change in Academic Librarianship,* xv.

42. Association of College & Research Libraries, "Statement on the Terminal Professional Degree for Academic Librarians," approved by the Board of Directors of the Association of College and Research Libraries, on Jan. 23, 1975; reaffirmed June 2001 and June, 2007; available at www.ala.org/ala/mgrps/divs/acrl/standards/statementterminal.cfm (accessed July 5, 2008).

43. John N. Berry III, "But Don't Call 'em Librarians," *Library Journal* 128, no. 18 (Nov. 1, 2003): 34–36.

44. Max Boot, *War Made New: Technology, Warfare, and the Course of History, 1500 to Today,* (New York: Gotham Books, 2006), 465.

45. Ibid.

46. James G. Neal, "Raised by Wolves," *Library Journal* 131, no. 3 (Feb. 15, 2006): 42–44.

47. Ibid., 42.

48. Ibid., 44.

49. Thea Lindquist and Todd Gilman, "Academic/Research Librarians with Subject Doctorates: Data and Trends 1965–2006," *portal: Libraries and the Academy* 8, no. 1 (Jan. 2008): 31–52, http://muse.jhu.edu/journals/portal_libraries_and_the_academy/toc/pla8.1.html (accessed July 5, 2008).

50. Ibid., 43.

51. See for example Danielle Bordrero Hoggan, "Faculty Status for Librarians in Higher Education," *portal: Libraries and the Academy* 3, no. 3 (July 2003): 431–445, http://muse.jhu.edu/journals/portal_libraries_and_the_academy/toc/pla3.3.html (accessed July 5, 2008); Jeanie M. Welch and Frada L. Mozenter, "Loosening the Ties That Bind: Academic Librarians and Tenure," *College & Research Libraries* 67, no. 2 (March 2006): 164–176.

52. Dorita F. Bolger and Erin T. Smith, "Faculty Status and Rank at Liberal Arts Colleges: An Investigation into the Correlation among Faculty Status, Professional Rights and Responsibilities, and Overall Institutional Quality," *College & Research Libraries* 67, no. 3 (May 2006): 217–229; Bruce R. Kingma and Gillian M. McCombs, "The Opportunity Costs of Faculty Status for Academic Librarians," *College & Research Libraries* 56, no. 3 (May 1995): 258–264, especially their analysis of ARL rankings, pages 261–262.

53. Rachel Applegate, "Deconstructing Faculty Status: Research and Assumptions," *Journal of Academic Librarianship* 19, no. 3 (July 1993): 158–164.

54. Blaise Cronin, "The Mother of All Myths," *Library Journal* 126, no. 4 (Feb. 15, 2001): 144.

55. See letters to the editor in *Library Journal* by Stephen Karetzky, April 1, 2001; Jane D. Schweinsberg, April 15, 2001; Lisa Dunn, May 1, 2001; and Robert Eno, June 1, 2001.

56. Charles B. Lowry, "The Status of Faculty Status for Academic Libraries: A Twenty-Year Perspective," *College & Research Libraries* 54, no. 2 (March 1993): 172.

57. John K. Stemmer, "The Perception of Effectiveness of Merged Information Services Organizations," *Reference Services Review* 35, no. 3 (2007): 344–359.

58. Ibid., 357.

59. Peggy Seiden and Michael D. Kathman, "A History of the Rhetoric and Reality of Library and Computing Relationships," in *Books, Bytes, and Bridges: Libraries and Computer Centers in Academic Institutions,* edited by Larry Hardesty (Chicago: American Library Association, 2000), 10.

60. Mary K. Bolin, "The Library and the Computer Center: Organizational Patterns at Land Grant Universities," *Journal of Academic Librarianship* 31, no. 1 (Jan. 2005): 10.

61. Edward D. Garten and Delmus E. Williams, "Clashing Cultures: Cohabitation of Libraries and Computing Centers in Information Abundance," in *Books, Bytes,*

and Bridges: Libraries and Computer Centers in Academic Institutions, edited by Larry Hardesty (Chicago: American Library Association, 2000), 69.

62. Deborah Ludwig and Jeffrey Bullington, "Libraries and IT: Are We There Yet?" *Reference Services Review* 35, no. 3 (2007): 374.
63. Kryllidou and Young, *ARL Annual Salary Survey 2006–07,* see "Table 3: Salary Trends in U.S. ARL University Libraries," 20.
64. Ibid., 15.
65. Lewis, "A Strategy for Academic Libraries," 425–428.

CHAPTER 2

NEW CHALLENGES IN ACADEMIC LIBRARY PERSONNEL SELECTION

John Lehner
University of Houston

Libraries face accelerating and potentially transformational change as the end of the first decade of the new millennium approaches. A variety of forces are shaping our institutions and jobs, but evolving information technologies are having an especially profound impact on our work in libraries.

As we face the technological, as well as economic and social, forces that are reshaping our work, we must understand how these changes affect our organizational processes. Personnel selection is a key process for our organizations. As transformational change challenges our organizations, effective personnel selection becomes more important than ever. Who we choose to bring into our organizations, and who we choose to exclude, are critical decisions. We should be concerned that our established processes for selecting personnel are ill suited, however, to dynamic environments. In fact, many of our institutionalized approaches for selection assume a static work environment and do not contemplate high rates of change in the nature of work to be performed or much flexibility in job roles.

A fundamental premise of this chapter is that our usual personnel selection processes, and much of our understanding of selection, have evolved around jobs with strictly defined roles and very stable, unchanging content. We are now faced with a significant challenge in identifying and implementing selection processes that are appropriate for positions with frequently changing job content and less-defined boundaries within organizations that must be dynamic. Our selection concerns are also compounded by the need to articulate a new set of organizational expectations to candidates and to attract suitable candidates oriented to meeting these expectations.

The dynamic library work environment is shaped by a number of forces, but especially by the pervasive application of complex information technologies. Increasingly, interdependencies across traditional organizational boundaries are required. These trends, which drive ongoing change in job content, require us to develop a new focus on candidate characteristics beyond a specific skill set derived from a specific and delimited set of tasks. New approaches are required that emphasize broad attributes such as adaptability, predisposition to continuous learning, creativity, and innovative problem-solving skills that support working in an environment of continuous change. In addition, we must select for interpersonal and communication skills to support working in highly interdependent cross-functional team environments that are increasingly culturally diverse.

The need to select employees based on more than immediate and readily defined job responsibilities is made more pressing by the traditions and cultural expectations of job security in academia. The Association of College and Research Libraries, in its standards for faculty status for academic librarians, specifically calls for librarians to be "covered by a stated tenure policy."[1] Faculty tenure models are overtly adopted for librarians in many institutions and are an influential model even in institutions that don't grant full tenured status to librarians. Somewhat modified versions of tenure that offer job security and the assurance of due process protections, such as continuing appointment status, are common. Such forms of job security, seen as inherently linked to academic freedom, are deeply ingrained traditions. Such forms of job security will also, of course, be valuable in recruiting and retaining the type of deeply engaged and committed workers needed to fulfill the requirement of our increasingly complex and demanding positions. If we are to sustain our practice of ensuring job security to librarians, we must identify, recruit, and select individuals who will be able to continually adapt to changing job duties and new assignments. Long-term employment commitments by our institutions require that employees be adaptable and willing to engage in a process of continuous learning.

There is a small body of literature on library and librarian personnel selection. Some of the literature focuses on the faculty model of

selection using a peer or collegial search committee, and the procedural aspects of conducting a search have been elucidated.[2] The general
standards for this approach to librarian hiring are well established and
endorsed by our professional association.[3] The literature also includes
some analysis of the need for improvements in the methods and procedures, such as Gregory K. Rashke's 2003 article urging a more streamlined and less risk-averse approach to library recruiting and selection.[4]

There is some emerging discussion in the library literature on
selection that we need to hire for "traits and potential as well as skills
and experience."[5] The proposition that libraries should select and hire
individuals for wider skill sets or broader attributes has probably been
most advanced by Giesecke and McNeil's work on core competencies.[6]
Giesecke and McNeil's approach is cast in the context of organizational
development and transformation of the academic library into a learning
organization.

The established models for selection procedures that have been
studied for reliability and validity presume stable job roles and static
job content. These established models deeply shape our thinking about
selection and present a formidable obstacle to change. The underlying presumption of stability may be profoundly wrong for academic
libraries. The challenge we face is twofold. First, we must develop a new
understanding that we are often selecting personnel for tasks and work
that we can't yet imagine or foresee, much less clearly enumerate. Secondly, we must move forward in attempting to identify and implement
new approaches for selection that are not constructed around narrowly
defined job content that is presumed to be static.

The Changing Nature of Our Work

The changing nature of work is not a phenomenon limited to the
library field. The issue of the fast-changing jobs and job content, and
its impact on selection, has been identified as an important concern for
business and industry. Academic researchers in personnel selection have
recognized the changing nature of work and its implications for selection processes. Schmitt and Chan identify five major changes that will
affect how personnel selection is done in organizations. They enumerate speed of technological change, use of teams to accomplish work,
changes in communications technology, globalization of large corpora-

tions, and increased service orientation of organizations.[7] Globalization is perhaps the only one of these trends that has not profoundly affected academic libraries as much as private-sector corporations, although it has had an impact.

There is a lot of anecdotal evidence of the changing nature and mutability of library jobs and broad awareness of this as a professional concern. A set of "provocative statements" developed to stimulate discussion at a national library forum in 2006 included several statements that specifically addressed changes in our work. The provocative statements included "traditional library organizational structures will no longer be functional. Reference and catalog librarians as we know them today will no longer exist [and] there will be no more librarians as we know them. Staff may have MBAs or be computer/data scientists. All library staff will need the technical skills equivalent to today's systems and web services personnel."[8] Although these assertions were developed to be provocative and stimulate discussion, they make it clear that the changing nature of our work is a preeminent concern for many of us.

There is also empirical evidence of the dynamic and changing nature of our work. A survey of ARL libraries' position descriptions conducted in 2000 found that "ARL institutions presently desire many different types of new positions that are designed work with technology, networked environments, information systems, and digital libraries. In addition, many other positions have been redesigned to integrate technological competencies as part of the overall requirements and desired characteristics of their positions."[9]

Lynch and Smith, in their comprehensive review of library job advertisements, also found important changes in job requirements over a 25-year period. They conclude, "The field has incorporated computing technologies into all jobs."[10]

The enormous impact of technological change and new communications technology are the change forces to which we are most attuned in academic libraries. From institutional repositories and digitized collections to social networking software and user-generated content to federated search engines, we are constantly working with the challenges of new information and communication technologies. The increasing integration of information technologies into library services and the accelerating rate of change of these technologies have dramatically reshaped work in libraries. The much-discussed "blended librarian" is one characterization of how the nature of our work is changing because of the pervasiveness of information technology. According to one definition, the blended librarian is "an academic librarian who combines the traditional skill set of librarianship with the information technologist's hardware/software skills, and the instructional or educational designer's ability to apply technology appropriately in the teaching-learning process."[11]

The use of teams in the workplace is a major trend that has been embraced by academic libraries over the last 20 years and is having a profound impact on the nature of our work. The early adoption of work teams by the University of Arizona Libraries proved influential.[12] What was once a unique organizational structure has become increasingly commonplace in academic libraries. As long ago as 1998, one survey found that "teams are at least being experimented with in most ARL libraries."[13] The previously mentioned survey and analysis of position descriptions in ARL libraries noted that many "ask for the possession of team skills—the ability to work in 'team-based' or 'team-oriented,' 'client-centered' environments."[14]

Teams in academic libraries have grown out of the total quality management movement and from the recognition that many of our service functions in the contemporary library environment are too complicated to be addressed by individuals, but must draw from expertise held by multiple individuals. In team-working, employees "are increasingly interdependent, and work is coming to be seen more and more as the completion of projects."[15] Employees' ability to function effectively in a team-based structure requires skills and attributes that are not just related to the technical task at hand. It appears that there are additional skills or attributes individuals must possess to be effective members of teams.

Libraries also share in the broader trend of adopting a stronger customer service focus. As we compete for resources within our institutions, we have had to become much more concerned about assessing and demonstrating the value of the services we provide. The assessment movement of recent years and the emphasis on user-centered services reflects a growing customer service orientation of libraries. Lynch and Smith, in the previously mentioned study of job advertising, noted certain new behavioral requirements appearing in advertisements. They suggest that there is a new model of the library as an "active agency providing information services [and] requirements for 'flexibility,' 'creativity', and 'leadership' also suggest that jobs were changing and that libraries were paying closer attention to interactions between librarians and library users."[16]

The trend of greater customer service orientation is certainly evidenced by the LibQUAL+ survey, administered under the auspices of ARL. It is a user satisfaction survey, and ARL reports that 282 libraries participated in the 2007 iteration of the survey.[17] Many of the major research libraries in North America now routinely participate in this survey.

It appears that the forces that are driving change in the nature of our work will continue for the foreseeable future. As David W. Lewis recently observed, "Library staff will need to recognize that they are unlikely to be doing, ten or even five years hence, the same things they are doing now."[18] Employees will have to do new things in new ways at an accelerating pace. It seems clear that academic libraries must select employees who are prepared to learn at the individual level and prepared to support development and deployment of knowledge at the collective, organizational level. The demands of a changing environment will require it.

The Longstanding Model

Approaches to personnel selection have been shaped by empirical research in industrial/organizational psychology and the legal environment. The conventional methods tell us a job analysis should be conducted and that the job analysis results in the development of a job description that identifies, based on the job tasks, the knowledge, skills and, abilities required to be successful in the position. The knowledge, skills, and abilities required for the position indicate the selection methods and content of interview questions. This classic model, of course, is structured around a strictly defined, stable set of job tasks. This approach has the support of empirical research and seems, intuitively, to be valid and appropriate. We should be mindful, however, that it is a model that ignores "characteristics of the person that are irrelevant to immediate job requirements."[19]

In many and probably most academic library organizations, this highly structured approach is not strictly followed. It is the model, however, that deeply influences our thinking and the way we conceptualize selection processes. This model is also the dominant paradigm that pervades university human resources departments and university affirmative action offices. We must question the usefulness of this approach as we acknowledge the continuous change in job content and the changing nature of the work in many library positions. Some academics in the field of industrial/organizational psychology have raised the issue succinctly: "Post-bureaucratic forms of work organization have shifted the ground under the feet of personnel psychologists, resulting in the dominant paradigm becoming increasingly maladaptive."[20] These commentators characterize the dominant paradigm in the field of personnel and selection psychology to include, as fundamental assumptions, that "work is done by individuals, work consists of tasks, groups of tasks form jobs, [and] jobs do not change very much."[21] These assumptions seem to have less and less legitimacy in many work environments, including academic libraries.

Equal employment opportunity and the legal environment have also been key elements in shaping what have become the standard and conventional selection approaches. Selection procedures must have a valid and reliable linkage to job content. The influential "Uniform Guidelines on Employee Selection Procedures,"[22] initially promulgated in 1978, have had a profound impact on selection practices. These guidelines address the validation of selection methods when selection methods have a disparate impact. *Disparate impact* refers to a disproportionate disqualification of women or minority applicants for positions. The conventional structured approach to selection processes has been driven, in part, by the need to use selection tools with empirically demonstrable validity and "job-relatedness." The approaches to validation necessarily employ a clearly defined and enumerated set of tasks and functions for a job. The demands of equal employment opportunity law have supported and entrenched this highly structured approach to selection processes that focus on clearly defined jobs with carefully delineated sets of unchanging tasks composing the job content.

Constraints on New Approaches

Another important aspect of the challenge we face is the institutional and organizational constraints imposed on selection processes. Psychometric testing, or any type of paper-and-pencil test, is unlikely to be accepted in academic libraries, especially for librarian positions. Though sometimes used by corporate employers, sophisticated psychometric approaches are apt to be viewed with suspicion, if not outright hostility, in the academic library environment. The literature on personnel selection procedures notes the issue of face validity. *Face validity* refers to the concept that a selection tool simply, on its face, appears to measure what it should—an attribute relevant to job performance. It is critical to the perception of candidates and members of the organization that the selection methods being employed are on their face valid and appropriate. Highly technical selection processes suffer from poor face validity and will be largely eschewed in organizations shaped by the traditions of academia.

It is also important to consider applicant acceptance of selection methods in an increasingly competitive employment market. Many of our organizations find that the pools of applicants for many positions, particularly those requiring specialized technical skills, are quite limited. Under such circumstances, we are reluctant to impose selection processes that applicants may find distasteful. There are research findings that a positive correlation exists between face validity and applicants' perception of procedural justice.[23] That is, a selection process that enjoys face validity is more likely to be seen by applicants as fair and just. Given the research evidence that selection methods do affect applicant perceptions about the desirability of an employer, we must be sensitive to such applicant concerns. Indeed, research on applicant reaction to selection methods shows us that interviews are perceived as fairer than cognitive ability tests, which are perceived as fairer than personality inventories.[24] Applicants faced with what they perceive to be inappropriate or invasive selection methods will be less likely to accept offers of employment. Equally worrisome is the negative effect that may occur when unhappy applicants persuade other potential applicants not to apply.

The influence of faculty selection models on librarian selection has shaped a selection process largely based on oral interviews with a search committee at the center of the selection process. The faculty selection model is based on evaluation and selection by peers, who are subject-matter experts. The subject-matter experts are presumed to be the best judges of other subject-matter experts' work and the best judges of who should be allowed admittance to organizational membership. The importance of peer participation in selection is also linked to the tradition of peer evaluation in faculty promotional processes. The deeply ingrained traditions of peer evaluation in academic organizations dictate that selection tools be readily understandable and enjoy face validity with both candidates and their professional peers in the organization who will participate in personnel selection. Selection tools requiring administration by trained psychologists or other highly technically sophisticated methods are likely to be seen as unacceptable by both candidates and by librarian peers in the organization. There are powerful tools available for selecting candidates for behavioral and psychological attributes, but these tools enjoy little acceptance in the academic environment.

The Selection Challenge

How can we select for positions with continuously changing job content and fluid job roles? It seems counterintuitive to assert that we can select appropriate candidates for a position if we can't clearly articulate the knowledge, skills, and abilities that are needed, based on the responsibilities and functions of the position. Indeed, it may be impractical for us not to consider the current job content of most our positions when we engage in the recruitment and selection process. It does seem increasingly clear, however, that selecting employees based on a static, specific set of current job tasks will not serve our organizations well in our environment of fast-paced change. Perhaps the most appropriate approach is to acknowledge that we are selecting for the ability to undertake the current responsibilities of a position, but to place even greater emphasis on the ability to adapt to new, often unforeseen, job duties in a fluid and increasingly unstructured organization. Another perspective might even be to consider selecting individuals for the interest and potential to learn the current set of job tasks because learning new, changing job tasks will be one of the central responsibilities of many of our positions.

Moving towards more effective personnel selection requires several modifications to the current, widely used approach seen in academic libraries. First, we must overtly accept and acknowledge that we are selecting personnel with a conceptually different set of selection criteria than we have used in the past. We cannot continue to focus on the existing configuration of a job and its tasks as the key drivers of selection criteria, but must broaden the criteria. From the technical perspective of personnel psychology:

> First, *flexibility* and adaptability, in technical and social competencies, attitudes to work, and task- and not-task related behaviour will be called for. As work roles will themselves be transient, assessment criteria for selection will widen from being the evaluation of specific technical competencies, to the assessment of flexibility as a psychological-behavioral construct.[25]

The next step is that we must be more mindful of the processes of attracting and recruiting potential candidates. We need to communicate to potential candidates that we seek employees who will thrive in dynamic environments with all of the demands and challenges that entails. Finally, we need to focus on changes to selection methods. We are selecting for different candidate attributes and therefore must consider different selection techniques to assess those attributes. One method of potential value that should be considered is behaviorally oriented interviewing.

New Criteria for Selection

Selection of personnel to work in positions with fast-changing job content and fluid job roles requires identification and development of different selection criteria than those used in the traditional model. Selection criteria need to be focused on a broader set of attributes, and the evolution of a more broadly based approach has appeared in disparate forms across the management and personnel psychology literature. It has been presented as the person/organization fit, organizational competencies, or core competencies. This general trend has also recently been characterized as a shift from "task-based selection" to "person-centered assessment."[26]

The notion of selecting employees using more than just the limited job specifications has some longstanding precedent in the human resources and management literature. A 1991 article titled "Hiring for the Organization, Not the Job"[27] lays out an approach that moves away from the overwhelming focus on the person/job fit and considers the importance of the person/organization fit. The authors look to organizational analysis and assessment of fit to the organization in addressing broader attributes employees will need to succeed in the organization. They assert that organizational analysis "is important because job analysis data may quickly become outdated as rapidly changing products and technologies reshape employees' jobs"[28] Although the authors examine the selection processes of three private sector firms that are quite unlike academic libraries, the approaches of these firms reflect a response to forces that are similar to the forces reshaping academic library work.

A discussion of organizational issues and adaptations in environments of fast-paced change must include the concept of the learning organization. An important part of the rising recognition of the need for broader, less job-specific criteria for selection and assessment of employees is rooted in the growth of the idea of the learning organization. As Peter Senge posed it from the organizational perspective, "The organizations that will truly excel in the future will be the organizations that discover how to tap people's commitment and capacity to learn at all levels in an organization."[29]

The term *learning organization* arose, in part, around the identification of attributes that permit organizations to succeed in highly dynamic, competitive environments. The literature on learning organizations has helped us articulate and understand the capabilities required of academic libraries to succeed in the fast-changing and increasingly competitive information environment. A learning organization "is an organization skilled at creating, acquiring, and transferring knowledge and at modifying its behavior to reflect new knowledge and insights" and one that "translates new knowledge into new ways of behaving."[30] The learning organization supports individual, team, and organization-wide learning and is capable of deploying new knowledge in pursuit of its business purpose. In a fast-changing environment, the ability to learn and the predisposition to engage in continuous learning are critical employee attributes. As organizations increasingly identify themselves as learning organizations, new expectations for employees emerge. New entrants to such organizations "can expect to face a cultural emphasis on learning, strategies to enhance development beyond conventional training and an expectation that they will take responsibility for their own learning."[31]

It seems obvious that organizations that aspire to be learning organizations would very consciously recruit and select employees in ways that would support and advance this aspiration. Interestingly, there appears to be little research, or even discussion, in the management and organizational development literature about personnel selection in the learning organization. One research effort, attempting to establish the relationship between organizational learning and human resources practices, included selective hiring as one of the practices that positively influenced organizational learning. It concludes that "organizations that have identified learning as their primary objective can begin to address it by matching new employees to their requirements and attracting those people with creative ideas and a desire to share learning."[32]

Another approach to broader, less job-specific criteria for selection is the previously mentioned core competencies put forth in the library literature by Giesecke and McNeil. Their work focuses on transformation of library organizations into learning organizations. They provide one of the few discussions of employee selection as it relates to the learning organization. Giesecke and McNeil describe core competencies as "the knowledge and skills that make the organization a success and help the organization change to meet a changing environment."[33] This is an important way to address the context of jobs and the larger organizational environment in establishing criteria for personnel selection.

The approach of using organization-wide competencies as criteria in selection helps us to move the selection process away from the excessively job-specific model. Indeed, "when organization-wide competency modeling is used, technical and functional distinctions, between job roles and positions are not included in the overall competency model."[34] The competencies approach has a history that is intertwined in the literature of learning organizations. The concept of organizational competencies has been characterized as being inherently based in identifying characteristics that give an organization competitive advantage, or in some discussions of the concept, "speed of adaptation in the market-place."[35] The competencies approach has a lineage that is connected to organizational learning and the idea that organizations can consciously respond to environmental change.

The core competencies presented by Giesecke and McNeil were developed as set of library-wide competencies that are a part of all positions in the library. The core competencies include a number of skill sets that are crucial in environments of fast-changing job content and collaborative, cross-functional job responsibilities. Among the core competencies enumerated are analytical skills/problem solving/decision making, communication skills, creativity/innovation, and interpersonal/group skills. Giesecke and McNeil note that flexibility/adaptability is a key competency and "one of the most important core competencies in today's changing library environment."[36] The authors also include a valuable appendix of sample interview questions for these core competencies, including questions to address the critical attribute of flexibility and adaptability.

Attracting and Recruiting

Attracting and recruiting potential candidates for positions is critical for success in the hiring process and ultimately for organizational success. Conveying to potential applicants the information about jobs and attracting appropriate applicants is increasingly challenging for library organizations given the nature of many positions. The types of positions that have been described here, with expectations of employee flexibility, innovative problem skills, continuous learning, and teamwork skills, are high-involvement jobs that require deeply engaged employees. The burden is on our organizations to convey the positive aspects and attractiveness of such positions. Attracting the best candidates for such positions will require communicating information about the job, but also much more about the organization itself. If we are to apply organizational competencies, or increasingly focus on the person/organization fit in selection, we should first seek to shape our applicant pools by conveying more information about the organization and its culture, climate, mission, and goals.

The actual selection process, of course, must be preceded by development of the applicant pool. Important tools for developing the pool are our position announcements and job advertisements. Advertisements and job announcements must be more carefully constructed to articulate organizational needs and expectations. If we seek employees who are adaptable, creative, and predisposed to continuous learning and who possess interpersonal skills for teamwork, our position announcements need to express this. For some candidates, the promise of working in a dynamic environment requiring these attributes may be a strong attractor. Position announcements should explicitly address organizational expectations of continuous learning, creative problem solving, and adaptability. We must also convey that we fully support professional development and learning, innovative thinking, and risk taking. To do so evokes some level of self-selection by applicants. Those who seek a dynamic work environment will be attracted, and those who desire greater stability in day-to-day work and have little enthusiasm for ongoing learning can select themselves out. We should not hesitate to be explicit and detailed about the nature of the organization and its jobs in our position announcements. There are research findings that "recruitment materials have a more positive impact if they contain more specific information."[37]

Although there is relatively little research on readers' reactions to employment advertising, there are some emerging ideas that can inform us in developing job advertisements. Anat Rafaeli proposes that employment ads are an important part of providing people with information on alternative employment relationships. In addition, the differences in the text of job ads represent a variable "labeled 'the implicit motivational agreement between employees and organizations,' which is proposed to be conveyed by the text of the ads."[38] In summarizing his exploratory study examining readers' reactions to the content of ads, he suggests:

> higher-order needs, more personalized discourse, and more detail about the advertising organization are proposed to represent an employment relationship that is more enriched and involving. In contrast, the emphasis of lower-order (existence) needs, the use of impersonal discourse, and the failure to provide insight into the organization is proposed to reflect an employment relationship that is constrained, calculated, and formal.[39]

Clearly, what we need to be conveying to potential applicants through our job announcements and advertising is the more enriched and involving relationship. I believe the type of employees we will increasingly require will be those who will find the more enriched and engaged relationship more attractive than other alternatives. The professionals we most seek are those who have many alternative employment choices.

Peter Drucker put forth the intriguing notion that knowledge workers will need "to be managed as if they were *volunteers*. They are paid, to be sure. But knowledge workers have mobility."[40] In academic and research libraries, we will increasingly have to acknowledge that employees will also have to be attracted and recruited as if they were volunteers. We will need to convey that we offer the opportunity to undertake work that is engaging and fulfilling. The importance of the mission of our libraries, as well as that of the larger institutions we are part of, must also be conveyed to potential employees. If we must recruit employees as if they were volunteers, these will be key elements of the message we must convey.

Behavioral Interviewing

Behavioral interviewing is an approach that offers considerable promise in helping assess broader employee attributes beyond the specific, technical requirements of a position. In some forms, it's called behavioral description pattern interviewing or behavioral description interviewing. It is an approach that is readily adaptable to the widely accepted selection practices of academic libraries, while helping move past some of the limitations of our usual practices.

In our current selection processes we must overcome the tendency to emphasize highly position-specific questions: Are you familiar with searching in a particular database? Have you edited and uploaded records in a specific integrated library system? Search committees often seem most comfortable with candidates who have previously held a job just like the one the committee is seeking to fill. The focus is all too frequently on very concrete, job-specific skills. This focus on current, strictly defined job specifications leaves little time or attention for consideration of other, perhaps more important qualifications. Instead, we need to move to questions that focus on broader candidate attributes we know will be required as position duties change, job roles evolve and organizational structures become more flexible.

There are certain attributes that will be crucial to success in positions with constantly changing job content and evolving job roles. A predisposition for continuous learning, personal flexibility and adaptability, interpersonal and communication skills will all be very important employee characteristics. These are attributes that are more behavioral in nature and not job-specific skill sets. Of course, assessing these behaviors is more challenging than assessing a very concrete set of job skills. Behavioral interviewing offers a reasonable way to examine and assess such attributes.

Behavioral interviewing is a structured interview process employing the use of questions about past candidate behaviors. Questions are posed in the interview process that elicit descriptions of the candidates' previous performance and behavior. An example might be to ask candidates if they've ever had to assume a significant new job responsibility and how they responded and went about preparing themselves for the new responsibility. Another example, from Gisecke and McNeil, is "Tell me about the most challenging relationship you had with a coworker. Why was it challenging? What did you do to try to make it work?"[41] Another example would be asking the candidate "to relate how he or she dealt with difficult people at school as a way of getting at how well the applicant will handle difficult people in the future on the job."[42] Behavioral interviewing is grounded in the idea that past behavior is a strong indicator of future behavior. In constructing such an interview, at least several different questions, requiring descriptions of responses to several past situations, are used to assess each attribute or competency to be measured. This is to ensure that patterns of behavior are identified, not a candidate's unique or anomalous responses.

Discussions of behavioral interviewing in the industrial/organizational psychology literature frequently focus on it as one of several methods to structure interviews. Generally, the validity of behavioral interviewing has been found to compare very favorably to other interview methods.[43] It is important to note that the findings of validity are based on the technique being used in the context of structured interviews, in which basic structuring methods are in place. This includes practices such as asking all candidates the same questions and interviewing and evaluating interview results by panels, not individuals.

Behavioral interviewing is a technique that lends itself to looking at much broader traits of candidates than just specific technical skills. If properly constructed, behavioral interview questions can provide rich data for assessing candidates. As one writer puts it, "by understanding past behaviors as they relate to specific incidents, we find out more about a person's motivations, values, work styles, and instincts than we—or even the candidate—could ever imagine."[44]

A related, but somewhat different approach is situational interviewing. Situational interviewing questions pose a hypothetical fact situation and then ask candidates to describe how they would respond to the situation. Situational interviewing assumes "that the future performance of applicants can best be predicted by finding out their goals and intentions for dealing with the dilemmas they might encounter in specific job situations."[45] Like behavioral interviewing, it offers a tool for examining broader behavioral attributes that may be critical for job success. There is evidence that this approach, too, enjoys reasonable validity as a method of structuring interviews.[46] Some researchers have concluded that research comparing situational and behavioral questions presents mixed results and suggest that "The best advice is to use a mix of questions rather than limiting the interview to any one type."[47] Other research proposes that although differing approaches all have benefits and shortcomings, behavioral interviewing may well serve many organizations.[48]

Behavioral interviewing can readily be incorporated into existing search committee processes. It enjoys fine face validity. It appears that behavioral interviewing is perceived by applicants as fair.[49] It can be readily explained to both candidates and search committee members. It provides a tool to assess what have been described as the harder to measure "'softer' competencies."[50] It allows consideration of these potentially key attributes without resorting to highly technical assessment techniques. Search committees can learn to develop behaviorally oriented questions and continue to take a major role in the selection process. Incorporation of behavioral interviewing into our existing selection structures permits us to move forward with an improved process while retaining the strengths of the existing process.

Applying the Tools

Clearly, our organizations will grow more proficient in addressing issues of change as we continue to experience the accelerating rate of technological change that so deeply shapes our work. I have attempted here to enumerate some of the issues we face in academic library recruitment and selection in our high-change environment. There are approaches available now that library organizations can use to more actively tailor some of these key human resource management activities to better address the high-change environment.

The University of Houston Libraries recently added a statement to all of its librarian position announcements expressing the expectation of continuous learning. Our announcements now state that the libraries support the ongoing professional development of librarians and our goal is to recruit librarians committed to continuous learning. Our position announcements also speak to our strategic directions and that we seek individuals interested in advancing this plan. We routinely include a statement that the University of Houston reflects the multicultural community of the metropolitan area and is one of the most diverse research universities in the country. I believe that this type of information is the beginning of what will be an ongoing effort to more effectively convey meaningful organizational information to candidates. Like many academic libraries, we must thoughtfully develop more compelling and engaging information to attract prospective employees.

Libraries that have substantially restructured into the team model need to convey not just that fact, but some of the organizational expectations that accompany such a model. Libraries that aspire to be learning organizations need to be articulate in expressing the expectations and employment environment that such an aspiration entails. Position announcements for these libraries need to address the candidate attributes and high level of engagement that are sought in prospective employees. It may be important to convey certain statistical and basic descriptive data to candidates, but enumerating better information about the organizational culture, climate, and expectations will be critical for successful attraction and recruitment. Our goal must be to focus less on excessively detailed statements of qualifications and provide more information about the working environment and the context of positions.

Libraries can readily adopt behavioral interviewing methods. As I've previously suggested, search committees can easily understand and incorporate behavioral interviewing approaches into their existing processes.

Search committees often struggle in their efforts to identify the best candidate for a position, and committee members are very open to new ideas that support improving their decision-making process. It has been my experience that search committee members quickly embrace behavioral interviewing as a method that gives them better information about candidates and therefore greater confidence in their recommendations.

The application of broader, less job-specific selection criteria into existing selection processes may be somewhat more challenging for some organizations. Many academic libraries may need to engage in a process of organizational conversations to develop understanding and support for the use of core, or organization-wide, competencies. Once consensus is achieved about the value of such broader selection criteria, there are fine examples of these competencies in the library literature that can be readily borrowed and applied.[51] For some organizations, it may be valuable to undertake the more demanding exercise of collectively developing statements of their own organization-wide competencies. Such an effort, in addition to supporting recruitment and selection work, has its own value as an organizational development effort.

Looking to the Future

It will be important for us to be attentive to new developments in the academic research on personnel recruitment and selection, as well as new practices that develop in organizations. The emerging concerns of academic researchers in the field of industrial/organizational psychology regarding the relevance of long-established approaches are significant. Hopefully, this signals what will be a burgeoning interest in identifying and examining new approaches to selection that consider this activity in the context of high-change organizations. The challenges we face are not unique to the academic library environment, but are shared with many other types of organizations and industries. These are areas in which we need to continue to be open to both ideas from the academic library environment and new approaches that develop in business and industry. Personnel recruitment and selection are critical organizational processes that will require us to be engaged in continuous learning and adaptation. Like many of the services we offer to users, these internal processes will also require thoughtful management and high levels of responsiveness to change.

Notes

1. ACRL Committee on the Status of Academic Librarians, "Standards for Faculty Status for College and University Librarians: Approved at ALA Annual Conference, June 2007," *College & Research Libraries News* 68, no. 8 (Sept. 2007): 530.
2. William Fietzer, "World Enough, and Time: Using Search and Screen Committees to Select Personnel in Academic Libraries," *Journal of Academic Librarianship* 19, no. 3 (July 1993): 149–153.
3. American Library Association Committee on the Status of Academic Librarians, "A Guideline for the Screening and Appointment of Academic Librarians Using a Search Committee: The Final Version," *College & Research Libraries News* 65, no. 4 (April 2004): 220-221.
4. Gregory K. Raschke, "Hiring and Recruitment Practices in Academic Libraries: Problems and Solutions," *portal: Libraries and the Academy* 3, no. 1 (Jan. 2003): 53–67.
5. Ibid., 60.
6. Joan Giesecke and Beth McNeil, "Core Competencies and the Learning Organization," *Library Administration & Management* 13, no. 3 (Summer 1999): 158-166.
7. Neal Schmitt and David Chan, *Personnel Selection: A Theoretical Approach*, Foundations of Organizational Science (Thousand Oaks, CA: Sage, 1998), 263.
8. Taiga Forum Steering Committee, "Taiga Forum Provocative Statements," March 10, 2006, www.taigaforum.org/documents/ProvocativeStatements.pdf.
9. Janice Simmons-Welburn, *Changing Roles of Library Professionals: SPEC Kit 256* (Washington, DC: Office of Leadership and Management Services, Association of Research Libraries, 2000), 1.
10. Beverly P. Lynch and Kimberley Robles Smith, "The Changing Nature of Work in Academic Libraries," *College & Research Libraries* 62, no. 5 (Sept. 2001): 417.
11. Steven J. Bell and John Shank, "The Blended Librarian: A Blueprint for Redefining the Teaching and Learning Role of Academic Librarians," *College & Research Libraries News* 65, no. 7 (July 2004): 374.
12. Laura J. Bender, "Team Organization—Learning Organization: The University of Arizona Four Years into It," *Information Outlook* 1, no. 9 (Sept. 1997): 19-22.
13. George J. Soete, *Use of Teams in ARL Libraries: SPEC Flyer 232* (Washington, DC: Association of Research Libraries, Office of Leadership and Management Services, 1998).
14. Simmons-Welburn, *Changing Roles of Library Professionals*, 11.
15. Neil Anderson and Peter Herriot, "Selecting for Change: How will Personnel and Selection Psychology Survive," in *International Handbook of Selection and Assessment, eds.* Neil Anderson and Peter Herriot (New York: Wiley, 1997), 9.
16. Lynch and Smith, "Changing Nature of Work in Academic Libraries," 418.
17. Association of Research Libraries, "LibQUAL+® Survey Participants," www.

libqual.org/Information/Participants/index.cfm (accessed June 1, 2008).

18. David W. Lewis, "A Strategy for Academic Libraries in the First Quarter of the 21st Century," *College & Research Libraries* 68, no. 5 (Sept. 2007): 430.

19. David E. Bowen, Gerald E. Ledford, Jr., and Barry R. Nathan, "Hiring for the Organization, Not the Job," *Academy of Management Executive* 5, no. 4 (1991): 35.

20. Anderson and Herriot, "Selecting for Change," 2.

21. Ibid., 11.

22. United States Department of Labor, "Uniform Guidelines on Employee Selection Procedures," www.uniformguidelines.com/uniformguidelines.html (accessed June 1, 2008).

23. John P. Hausknecht, David V. Day, and Scott C. Thomas, "Applicant Reactions to Selection Procedures: An Updated Model and Meta-Analysis," *Personnel Psychology* 57, no. 3 (Sept. 2004): 652.

24. Ibid., 639–640.

25. Anderson and Herriot, "Selecting for Change," 24.

26. Christopher Rees and Derek Eldridge, "Changing Jobs, Changing People: Developing Employee Selection Processes in Radical Change Settings," *EBS Review* 22, no. 1 (2007): 61.

27. Bowen, Ledford, and Nathan, "Hiring for the Organization, Not the Job."

28. Ibid., 38.

29. Peter M. Senge, *The Fifth Discipline: the Art and Practice of the Learning Organization,* rev. and upd. (New York: Doubleday, 2006), 4.

30. Joan Giesecke and Beth McNeil, "Transitioning to the Learning Organization," *Library Trends* 53, no. 1 (Summer 2004): 55.

31. Rees and Eldridge, "Changing Jobs, Changing People," 67.

32. Susana Pérez López, José Manuel Montes Peón, and Camilo José Vazquez Ordás, "Human Resource Management as a Determining Factor in Organizational Learning," *Management Learning* 37, no. 2 (June 2006): 215–239.

33. Giesecke and McNeil, "Core Competencies and the Learning Organization," 158.

34. Robert A. Schmieder and Mark C. Frame, "Competency Modeling," in *Encyclopedia of Industrial and Organizational Psychology,* ed. Steven G. Rogelberg (Thousand Oaks, CA: Sage, 2007), 86.

35. Dexter Dunphy, Dennis Turner, and Michael Crawford, "Organizational Learning as the Creation of Corporate Competencies," *Journal of Management Development* 16, no. 4 (1997): 238.

36. Giesecke and McNeil, "Core Competencies and the Learning Organization," 161.

37. Ann Marie Ryan and Nancy T. Tippins, "Attracting and Selecting: What Psychological Research Tells Us," *Human Resource Management* 43, no. 4 (Winter 2004): 311.

38. Anat Rafaeli, "Employee-Organizational Relationships in Employment Ads," in *Work Motivation in the Context of a Globalizing Economy,* ed. Miriam Erez, Uwe Kleinbeck, and Henk Thierry (Mahwah, NJ: Erlbaum, 2001), 248.

39. Ibid., 257.

40. Peter F. Drucker, *Management Challenges for the 21st Century,* 1st ed. (New York: HarperBusiness, 1999), 20.

41. Giesecke and McNeil, "Core Competencies and the Learning Organization,"

165.

42. Robert L. Dipboye, Kevin Wooten, and Stefanie K. Halverson, "Behavioral and Situational Interviews," in *Comprehensive Handbook of Psychological Assessment,* ed. Michel Hersen (New York: Wiley, 2004), 301.

43. Jean M. Barclay, "Improving Selection Interviews with Structure: Organisations' Use of 'Behavioural' Interviews," *Personnel Review* 30, no. 1 (2001): 84.

44. David S. Cohen, *The Talent Edge: A Behavioral Approach to Hiring, Developing and Keeping Top Performers* (New York: Wiley, 2001), 6.

45. Robert L. Dipboye, "Situational Interview," in *Blackwell Encyclopedic Dictionary of Human Resource Management,* ed. Lawrence H. Peters, Charles R. Greer, and Stuart A. Youngblood (Malden, MA: Blackwell, 1998), 314.

46. Elaine D. Pulakos and Neal Schmitt, "Experience-Based and Situational Interview Questions: Studies of Validity," *Personnel Psychology* 48, no. 2 (June 1995): 289–308.

47. Dipboye, Wooten, and Halverson, "Behavioral and Situational Interviews," 301.

48. Barclay, "Improving Selection Interviews with Structure," 10–11.

49. Arla L. Day and Sarah A. Carroll, "Situational and Patterned Behavior Interviews: A Comparison of Their Validity, Correlates and Perceived Fairness,*" Human Performance* 16, no. 1 (2003): 41.

50. Pérez López, Montes Peón, and Vazquez Ordás, "Human Resource Management as a Determining Factor in Organizational Learning," 219.

51. See ASERL Education Committee, "Shaping the Future: ASERL's Competencies for Research Librarians," Nov. 10, 2000, www.aserl.org/statements/competencies/competencies.htm (accessed June 1, 2008); Karen L. Holloway, "Developing Core and Master-Level Competencies for Librarians," *Library Administration & Management* 17, no. 2 (Spring 2003): 94-98

CHAPTER 3

INNOVATORS WANTED
NO EXPERIENCE NECESSARY?

R. David Lankes
Syracuse University

Introduction

There is no doubt that technology evolves rapidly. Keeping on top of new technologies and being able to evaluate their utility to the mission of the library are essential skills for librarians today. It is understandable that many libraries look to new hires to bring new technology skills into the organization. However, such a strategy can be problematic when a library begins to depend on new hires as its dominant innovation mechanism. All too often, these new staff are seen as change agents who will propel the library into new environments and services or, worse, relieve the rest of the library staff from having to gain new technology skills. In either case, placing the burden for innovation on the least experienced and lowest status employee is not a method towards success. These new employees often grow restless and frustrated. They are also often prepared in terms of technology innovation, but have little instruction in the role of change agent or how to bring the whole organization into new services. These realities are often even worse when recruiting nonlibrary technical expertise. This chapter will examine these problems and seek to outline the skills needed for today's innovators.

Uncharted Seas

Ancient mariners always kept the shore in view as they sailed.[1] All the navigation charts were based on visual landmarks on land. To lose sight of the coast was almost certain death because without a compass or any concept of longitude and latitude, they would quickly become disoriented and lost at sea.

Eventually, civilization developed means of determining latitude—that is, the distance either north or south of the equator. Using the position of stars and tools like a sextant, sailors could determine their rough distance from port. However, because star constellations differed in the northern and southern hemispheres, European sailors couldn't explore past the middle of Africa.

It wasn't until centuries later, with the development of fine metal work and accurate clocks, that the concept of longitude became meaningful and the whole of the oceans became available for navigation. Today, we still use some of the basic concepts of stars and time for navigation. The stars have been replaced by GPS satellites, and the time is measured in the difference of signals from these satellites.

Why the history lesson on sailing? It is an interesting analogy for today's world of library science. Without core concepts to propel the field forward, we are restricted to using obvious landmarks close to the shore to navigate our future. It also highlights the need for deep conceptual structures. There are no physical lines banding the Earth. There is no single starting point for the lines of longitude. These are human constructs created to help a group achieve new goals. In a very real way, the depth of these concepts limits the world of possibilities available. As Susser said, "to practice without theory is to sail an uncharted sea; theory without practice is not to set sail at all."[2]

It is for this reason that a chapter on innovation and staffing in the academic library starts with a much larger question: what is the conceptual foundation upon which we build our world of possibilities? Until we have that, we are constantly looking to close-to-shore landmarks to guide us. Instead of rock formations and lighthouses, we most often use technology developments like Google's latest feature or the Web 2.0 site of the day. Because we are running in shallow waters, we must constantly rely on the skills of new hires to navigate the new coast line.

Our "close to the shore" focus leads to additional problems when we look to librarian preparation. As a profession, we have instituted a system that by and large believes that a two-year master's program at the beginning of one's career is sufficient preparation to be a cataloger, reference librarian, webmaster, director, or any other professional position in a library. This in turn has created long-standing pressure between library schools and libraries. This tension has been simplistically cast as "*L* word" versus "*I* word," or as a crisis, or some lack of unified core curriculum. However, the real problem, felt on both sides, is that there is too much to include in any one degree—particularly when the essentials keep changing as we all chase the next near-shore landmark.

The remainder of this chapter will explore these ideas in greater depth. First a conceptual framework, participatory librarianship, will be explored in terms of needed skills. Special attention will be paid to a team approach that looks beyond a model of librarians doing it all themselves. Then the implications of that changing library environment and participatory librarianship for library science education will be explored.

Staffing for the Right Business

Any question of staffing must begin with agreeing upon the core objectives of the organization hiring. Even though there will no doubt be a myriad of functions and specialties needed in an organization, there is still some core that binds them together. For example, the McDonald's corporation is famous for instilling a sense of mission in all of its employees. If you go to the corporate headquarters and ask the receptionist what he or she does, the response will be "I make hamburgers." If you ask the CEO, he will respond likewise. Answering the phone, manning the stove, or cleaning the floors are all functions necessitated by a core mission.

So, what is the core mission of an academic library? Buying books? Licensing databases? Cataloging? Of course not; the core mission of an academic library is to build knowledge in its community. That knowledge may be represented in an undergraduate paper, or a Nobel laureate researching the foundations of existence. This of course is a very abstract mission, and clearly could be accomplished in a near-infinite number of ways. However, already it provides an interesting insight into how the library compares to other information-driven organizations.

Take those "near-shore" landmarks that libraries have been using to help navigate the future. Is Google in the same business as libraries? No. While a lot of the tools and even language that Google uses seem in line with those used by libraries, Google is in the advertising business. What Google does, it does to draw users' eyes to paid placements.

Is Amazon in the same business as libraries? Certainly Amazon and libraries share a common tool set of bibliographic data and document delivery. However, Amazon is about selling things—books, CDs, lawn chairs. Does this mean there is nothing to learn from Amazon and Google? Certainly not. Libraries simply cannot wait for them to figure out the future of libraries or library staffing.

But what separates the library from other agents in the knowledge business? Even within the academy, computing services and faculty are seeking to build knowledge—as are food service and parking, if we take the earlier McDonald's example to heart. It is the method by which these agents build knowledge that defines at once the role of the library and the skills the staff needs to have. It is also the method that will help define natural points of cooperation to build a team of professionals to help chart the future beyond the shoreline.

A large focus of current librarianship, and indeed librarianship over the past century, has been around bibliographic tools. That is, libraries build knowledge by providing efficient and effective access to documents. Unfortunately, over time these tools and methods have at times crowded out the true mission: knowledge. So the answer for too many librarians to the McDonald's question above—what do you do?—is "organize and disseminate documents (books, video, and such)." It is not that librarians don't understand the larger picture of building knowledge; they have just allowed their methods to limit the mission.

In 2006, the American Library Association and scholars at Syracuse University set out to understand the value of social networking technologies to libraries. In the course of the project, it became increasingly obvious that focusing on functions and tools was missing a larger and more important conversation related to the future of libraries. This ongoing effort saw learning and conversation at the core of librarianship.[3] This approach to understanding and service through conversation is called participatory librarianship. It is this frame of reference that this chapter uses to chart a course for libraries in terms of hiring and skills. The rest of this chapter will first lay out the basics of participatory librarianship, then talk about its implications for staffing, and finally discuss innovation and the preparation of innovators in librarianship.

Participatory Librarianship as a Method of the Library

The foundation of participatory librarianship is conversation theory. Developed by Gordon Pask, conversation theory sets out how people learn, or, in his terminology, how they go about "knowing."[4] At the heart of conversation theory is the tenet that knowledge is created through conversation. Pask presents a far-reaching theoretical framework in which agents engage in a conversation, using different levels of language, to reach agreements that are stored as relationships in a memory. The "agents" can be people or organizations (or states or countries), or they can be parts of a single individual. While talking to oneself may seem an odd act, instructional specialists call it critical thinking, or metacognition.[5] If you are asking yourself what I mean by "metacognition," you are in fact engaged in it. Who are you asking and expecting a response from?

Why this abstract foray into conversation theory? Because if libraries are in the knowledge business, and if knowledge is created through conversation, then libraries are in the conversation business. Specifically, libraries are in the facilitation of conversation business. This facilitation forms the basic method academic librarians use to accomplish the ultimate goal of knowledge creation that is shared across the academy. It also differentiates the role of the librarian from that of instructional and support staff.

Conversations are occurring all over the academy. They are happening in classes where faculty and students are engaged in conversations of differing levels of formality. They are happening in administration in terms of academic policy and initiatives. They are happening between researchers and their wider disciplines in the form of scholarly publishing.

This is not an entirely new concept for libraries. As early as 1968, Taylor, while talking about the importance of question negotiation in libraries, wrote:

> This paper is not concerned with the usual library automation. ...routine automation is merely an extension of the control and warehousing functions of libraries. The work here is an early effort to understand better the communications functions of libraries ...because that is what libraries are all about.[6]

In 1986, Joan Bechtel presented conversation as an organizing metaphor for academic libraries:

> As a more powerful alternative to the images of librarianship already available or proposed, I suggest that we begin to think of libraries as centers for conversation and of ourselves as mediators of and participants in the conversations of the world.[7]

Bechtel's focus on information instruction is illustrative of how the library is really a place of conversation.

Researchers engage in some knowledge discovery process. They formulate questions, muster methodology, gather data, and arrive at conclusions. However, they rarely, if ever, do this in isolation. Aside from conversations with colleagues, they are engaged in a much larger conversation within their chosen area. The methods they choose are derived from previously published articles. The questions they ask are often the result of previous studies. Even the publishing outlets they choose are often a result of an ongoing conversation about what constitutes a "quality" journal. The conversation is made explicit at the end of the paper with citations, etching out the lines of conversation that may span decades.

Those citations are also evidence of one means by which libraries facilitate these academic conversations; namely, access. Libraries have seen their role in the conversations of the academy in terms of access for some time. Simply put, access is enriching conversations with information such as articles, books, websites, databases, and the like. This means of facilitation has dominated library practice, education, and hiring for well over a century. To hire for access skills is to hire staff that can find and catalog materials. Yet access is only one means of facilitating conversations—facilitating knowledge.

Participatory librarianship defines four broad methods of facilitation. Each method requires its own set of skills. Aside from *access,* there is providing requisite *knowledge* to understand a conversation, a safe *environment* to engage in a conversation, and *motivation* to engage in conversation. The following sections detail these means of facilitation and their implications for core skills the academic library workforce needs.

Access

Access is simply getting a person to a conversation or some artifact of a conversation. Books, videos, journal articles, and so on aren't conversations, but they come from conversations—therefore, they are artifacts. This is an important distinction because while libraries have been focused on access to artifacts, digital networks allow libraries and their users to get closer and closer to the actual point of knowledge creation, the conversation itself. Now libraries can not only provide an article, but can get a user in touch directly with the article's author.

This new reality of access is easily seen in the sciences, where open-access publishing and online conversations have supplanted published journal articles as the primary means of sharing knowledge. In many science disciplines, published articles have become archives of new knowledge and ex post facto forums of official review. If one truly wants access to the physics conversation, for example, the best "resource" to point people to is online, real-time, and ongoing. This trend seems to be expanding into other disciplines, and while open-access publishing models have been adopted to various degrees, they have put real pressure on faculty to post preprint versions of their papers online and on associations and traditional journal publishers to provide increasingly low-barrier access to articles.

Much of library education, and indeed library science as a whole, is focused on access. Cataloging, metadata, even information retrieval and search engines are examples of access. Libraries have created an array of tools, such as subject classification, that seek to make access to information and materials efficient and effective. To be precise, however, much of library science has been focused on providing access to artifacts. Access to actual conversations and knowledge has been a much more recent development and still is not well integrated into common library practice.

Knowledge

If access to artifacts or conversations were sufficient for knowledge, then anyone with Internet access would be brilliant. In fact, some have argued that access can in fact provide on-demand, or commoditized knowledge. Today there is a discussion of the end of memory and the end of theory because of the massive quantity of easy-to-access information.

David Weinberger, the author of *Everything Is Miscellaneous,*[8] talks about meetings where the topic of the 1996 Telecommunications Act was being discussed.[9] One colleague not familiar with the act went online and read a Wikipedia article on the topic, increased her knowledge in real time, and therefore could better participate in the conversation. This is true, but it misses the fact that the increase in knowledge did not come from simply accessing the page. For example, she had to know how to read. She had to know English. She had to know that Wikipedia exists. She probably had to have a basic concept of telecommunications. The point is, she was adding to her existing knowledge, the result of a huge number of previous conversations.

Libraries have understood this need to go beyond access for some time; hence, instructional librarians. Going beyond earlier concepts of bibliographic instruction, instructional librarians have now engaged library users to increase their basic information-seeking skills. Academic libraries are offering students tutoring services, creating spaces to collocate library and instructional assistance services as well. This concept of instruction is also evident in how reference librarians are prepared. Reference staff are taught to go beyond simply providing answers and to provide instruction—not only providing information, but teaching users how to search on their own.

However, libraries are only now confronting the reality of instruction, and that is the need for better integration into the complete instructional environment of their users and the reality that true instruction requires evaluation. For example, if a professor simply stood before a room and talked on a topic for 30 minutes, does that necessarily mean that anyone learned? It is impossible to tell without evaluating the impact of the talk on the audience members. Whether it is a test, accomplishment of a task, or even some ethnographic study on changed behaviors, without evaluation, it is impossible to determine if learning truly occurred. It is this logic that underlies an increasing shift from outputs to outcome-based evaluation by accrediting agencies.

The need for libraries to move beyond access grounds the need for instructional skills in the academic library workforce. However, since learning is at the heart of participatory librarianship, it also points to the need for instructional and evaluation skills throughout the library workforce regardless of title or function. Reference staff, technical staff, administration are all part of the instructional process and need to have a true sense of how to teach and how to evaluate the effectiveness of that teaching. While certainly some librarians will develop a deeper understanding and set of instruction skills, basic knowledge of learning is important to all librarians.

Environment

Access to a conversation and sufficient foundational knowledge to engage in a conversation are still insufficient for true conversation and true knowledge generation. A safe environment is also needed. Safety here refers to a sense of both physical safety, often emphasized in public library settings, and intellectual safety. Academic libraries have long considered questions of intellectual safety. With concepts of intellectual freedom and privacy, one could argue that safety is a core value of any library.

It would be simple to say that librarians need to have policy skills and a deep understanding of privacy and intellectual property and leave it at that. However, the question of environment is more complicated than that. Let us take two examples in the area of privacy and intellectual freedom.

Participatory librarianship tells us that memory, the ability to recall concepts and artifacts and their relationships, is vitally important. In essence, new learning is scaffolded on previous learning. If the library is about facilitating knowledge, it must be about supporting a learner's (student's, scholar's, staff member's) memory. Yet, can the learner find out from the library the books he or she checked out previously? Can the learner annotate journal articles in our online tools? Can the learner see all the articles flagged in a previous search? To be sure, there are some libraries, and fortunately an increasing number, that can say yes to some of those questions. However, many library policies and library software prevent such memory features because of a fear of retaining user data. In essence, the policy of many library environments works against the intended work of libraries and facilitating knowledge.

There is an additional unintended consequence to building the library environment on a simplistic view of learner privacy. Rather than teaching users how to make effective privacy choices (understanding the consequences of giving out personal information) in the safe library environment, libraries tend to enforce a monolithic view of retaining no personal data, making any real conversation of privacy in the library meaningless. Rather than libraries choosing a single approach to privacy, it would be better for librarians to be equipped to have a privacy conversation with their user communities and determine appropriate privacy policies based on the needs and understanding of that community.

Another more nuanced approach to policy can be seen in content filtering. While the example is one of a public library, it is intended to demonstrate how strict adherence to global concerns on intellectual freedom can actually get in the way of good service. A local public library did not filter its computers. Patrons could visit any site they wished. The local police learned that registered sex offenders were visiting this public library, as was their right. The police, as was their right, started visiting the library on a regular basis and standing behind patrons using the public access computers, watching for banned Internet usage by these sex offenders. The net effect was that they were watching all users, in an obvious way, creating a chilling effect within the library. In order to get the police not to display such an obvious and chilling presence, the library installed content filters (which could be turned off by librarians). The effect was a greater sense of intellectual safety for the patrons because they didn't have authorities watching over their shoulders. The public library example is hardly an endorsement of filtering. Rather, it demonstrates that true environmental facilitation requires a complex understanding of policy and principles.

Many additional examples could be given of good services, particularly participatory services, that were shut down by lawyers and managers out of fear of breaching policy. If a librarian does not have a good grasp of policy and legal issues (or, as will be talked about, a strong relationship with a policy/legal expert), service may suffer out of an "assume the answer is no" mentality.

Motivation

So the user is at the conversation, knows what is going on, and feels safe to participate—mission accomplished, right? Well, it may seem obvious, but if the user does not want to engage in the conversation, or the user is not motivated to do so, the conversation will not occur. Libraries often underplay the importance of motivation in conversations. Users often seek out the library and its resources of their own accord (intrinsic motivation) or are compelled to do so, as in assignments (extrinsic motivation).

Efforts to market the library are a partial response to the question of motivation. Marketing campaigns seek to raise awareness of the library, and if they are properly targeted, they can motivate a user to use the library. However, all too often these approaches seek to bring people to the library rather than to bring the library to the user.

Take for example the question of faculty tenure in the academy. A colleague preparing his tenure package called the library looking for help doing a citation analysis. Since publication and citation analysis form the bulk of tenure consideration at his university, he wanted to know how many times he had been cited and by whom. The library staff told him they would be glad to spend an hour to show him or his GA how to use Web of Science. Take a look at that response and ask yourself what it is really saying. It is saying that the most important professional task in a professor's career warranted about an hour of time, and even worse, that the entire considerable bibliographic skill set of a professional librarian could be imparted to a GA in an hour.

What if, knowing that faculty are highly motivated in terms of citation analysis and tenure, librarians proactively reached out to faculty coming up for tenure to interview them and work with them to do a citation analysis. Recognizing the intrinsic motivation of the faculty member (the need for tenure) and the crucial extrinsic motivation from the faculty member's department, there is no better opportunity to demonstrate the value of the library. What's more, if the tenure decision is positive, the library has become a trusted resource that the faculty member can start recommending to students and colleagues. If the tenure decision is negative, the faculty member won't be around long enough to badmouth the library service.

The point is that a librarian must understand motivation to build services that aren't simply useful to learners, but that recognize and reward the learners' reasons for using the service. Marketing is one approach in a broad way, but each conversation has its own motivation dynamic.

Participatory Skills

So how do these methods of facilitation (access, knowledge, environment, motivation) translate into a specific skill set for library staff? The following skills were identified in the preceding section:

- *access skills:* most of what is traditionally taught in LIS programs, including information organization and information searching
- *knowledge skills:* a background in instruction and evaluation
- *environment skills:* deep knowledge of policy issues and the ability to create a sense of physical and intellectual safety
- *motivational skills:* the ability to recognize and reward users in their knowledge activities.

The underlying tenets of participatory librarianship also indicate needed skills in conversations, including these:

- identifying conversations within a target community of users (whether they are occurring within the library or not)
- identifying the conversants within those conversations (who are the authoritative voices, for example)
- recognizing the nuances of language being used in those conversations,
- understanding the method by which agreements are reached (are they dictated, or do they come about in true consensus, for example)
- remembering these agreements and how they relate to each other over time

Most of these skills could be summed up as better communication skills. This is not coincidental, since the root of librarianship is conversation and conversation is all about communication. Library managers have been calling for these skills, if not by name, for some time. Phrased as customer service skills or simply as librarians that smile, there is an implicit understanding that libraries need skills in engaging users, not artifacts.

There are a few additional skills that, while not derived from the conceptual framework of participation, are necessitated by the current environment of libraries. They can be seen as special cases of the above list. For example, to truly participate in the ongoing conversation of how libraries are administered and their roles in the academy, political skills are needed. Also, in today's digital world, technical skills are needed (how to build access and motivational conversation spaces online).

This list, from communications skills to technical knowledge, can seem overwhelming. How can one librarian, given on average two years of master's-level education, truly master all of these skills? More importantly, how can these librarians constantly innovate in these areas to assure they are providing the optimal facilitation to conversations when the underlying channels of communication (the Web, the phone, mobile, and so on) and tools of conversation enrichment (primarily in terms of artifacts) are in constant flux? The answer is twofold: teams and reformed LIS education.

No Librarian Is an Island

Learning theory, policy, legal issues, technology, and information organization: these are just some of the skills mentioned so far in this chapter. To advocate that one person (with one type of degree) could be a master of all of these skills is ludicrous. While a librarian should be aware of these areas (and master some), the ultimate answer to bringing an expanded, participatory skill base to the library is a team approach. Librarians must work with lawyers, technologists, educators, and content experts to choreograph the necessary facilitation within the academic community. By working in functional teams, a librarian can bring necessary resources to a community beyond simple artifacts and materials.

Often when the idea of an interdisciplinary team approach within an academic library is proposed, several obstacles are quickly identified. Almost all of these are based on the assumption that the whole team is organizationally and physically located within the library. Certainly there have been issues with nonlibrarians (like technologists) feeling like second-class citizens or lacking a peer group. Libraries often complain about a lack of resources to attract highly qualified specialists or point out how salary discrepancies caused by a competitive marketplace can alienate librarians. These are real concerns.

There is nothing, however, that says that all team members must be under the aegis of the library. Certainly, crossing administrative lines is possible in academia, even beyond university committees. In fact, there is an advantage to pulling teams from across these boundaries.

There is, however, one essential factor in effective teams—clear respect and identification of the value of team members. Effective teams require a team member to feel valued and to value other team members. All too often in the library profession, facilitation is seen as a primarily passive and often invisible task. The goal seems to be to interject as little of the voice of the librarian as possible to avoid bias. As stated by Lankes and colleagues:

> As knowledge is developed through conversation, and libraries facilitate this process, libraries have a powerful impact on the knowledge generated. Can librarians interfere with and shape conversations? Absolutely. Should we? We can't help it. Our collections, our reference work, our mere presence will influence conversations. The question is, in what ways? By dedicating a library mission to directly align with the needs of a finite community, we are accepting the biases, norms and priorities of the community. While a library may seek to expand or change the community, it does so from within.
>
> When Internet filtering became a requirement for federal Internet funding, public and school libraries could not simply quit, or ignore the fact, because they are agents of their communities. School libraries had to accept filtering with federal funding because their parent organizations, the schools, accepted filtering. We see, from this example, that libraries may shift from facilitating conversations to becoming active conversants, but they are always doing both. Thus, the question is not whether the library shapes conversations, but which ones, and how actively?
>
> These questions are hardly new to the underlying principles of librarianship. And nothing in the participatory model seeks to change those underlying principles. The participatory model does, however, highlight the fact that those principles shape conversations and have an impact on the community.[10]

This realization that facilitation is a proactive shaping activity also provides a foundation for a team approach to service and technological innovation. Teamwork requires a strong sense of identity.

Without a strong sense of purpose, method, and underlying conceptual frame, librarians can have great difficulty working in teams. It is, in essence, a form of professional insecurity that often sees other skill sets and conversants as competition. This realization once again points out the dangers of using technological landmarks outside of the library profession as pointers to some preferred future. It leads to a sort of schizophrenia whereby the profession is at once looking externally for innovation, and on finding it, seeing the innovators as competition and a threat.

This situation was apparent in much of the discussion of the library in relation to Google, Yahoo, and Amazon over the past decade. It was not unusual to go to conferences where Google was described as a great threat to libraries in an era of "good enough" information ("Google will put us out of business because people would rather have it quick than right") and in the next session a discussion of using a simple single search box to search library websites, catalogs, and databases ("All library search has to look like Google because that is what they expect"). Before Google "forced" libraries to adopt simple search boxes, Yahoo forced us to fit all of our services and resources into 13 categories on a homepage. The truth is that if libraries continue to try to be a better Google or a better Yahoo or a better Amazon, the best they can ever achieve is coming in second. Adopting innovation without a matching mission is a follower's game.

Now consider Amazon, Google, Yahoo, and any technological company through a lens of conversation and facilitation. Take that single search box that has become the norm. Why does it seem to work so well for Google when repeated studies show that in fact richer structured metadata provides better precision and recall? The answer is obvious—those same studies show that structured systems document representations are more effective for experts—in other words, for those already well versed in the conversations they are searching. So doctors can be very effective searchers in PubMed because they know the name of disease and common terms for symptoms and interventions. Likewise, librarians are more effective searchers in library catalogs.

The revolution Google brought to search was building its search engine on the output of conversations. That may sound odd: after all, Google is searching webpages. That is true, but the text on the webpage is only one factor used in determining which pages are presented to users and in what order. The ranking algorithm, known as page rank, uses the number of times a webpage is linked to and by who in determining the relevance of that page to a user's query. Those links, like the citations in a scholarly journal, act as the evidence of a conversation. Google makes the assumption that the pages most pointed to are seen as the most important artifacts in a conversation, and therefore most likely to be relevant to a query. Clearly, this system has issues. It tends to prioritize shopping sites, it tends to point to technical information, and it stresses the popular over the precise. However, as a gross tool, it has proven amazingly successful.

The current logic, seeing the Google search box as a user interface element, seems to say if it works on the open Web, it should work on library websites as well. The problem, of course, is that by and large, academic websites, and certainly bibliographic collections, don't represent explicit conversations. For example, library catalogs are populated with items with the only thing resembling a conversation being a tie to some classification system (classification systems being the artifact around a conversation among librarians on the topic of "how do we organize the world"). A Google-like algorithm simply won't have enough data to work with unless libraries incorporate more conversational linkage between items—for example, using circulation data so that items most circulated get ranked higher, or incorporating citation data from the items themselves (like Web of Science) or from reference transactions (these items were most cited by our reference staff).

The Google example is presented as one instance where innovation needs to come from core concepts. It also demonstrates the need to match librarians who may understand the concepts of conversation with other experts who may understand the content of a conversation (like faculty) or technological tools (like computing services). The work of librarians is not diminished in such a team because they have a clear foundation for their contributions. Further, a librarian's core skill in facilitation is essential to making such a team work. Increasingly, librarians are finding themselves embedded in teams well outside the confines of physical libraries. This makes sense—the librarians are going to the conversations rather than waiting for the conversants to come to the library.

Facilitating Innovation

Ultimately, fostering innovation in the staff of an academic library comes down to facilitating a conversation about innovation among the staff. The same framework that defines the needed skills for academic librarians also defines the necessary factors for innovation. Staff members need access to resources with which to innovate. They need knowledge to innovate. They need a safe environment in which to innovate. They need to be motivated both intrinsically and extrinsically.

Access for Innovation

Lewis Hyde of Harvard's Berkman Center discusses how genius and creativity are often talked of as individual attributes, but in fact are the product of a complex interaction between a person and his or her environment.[11] Einstein's theory of relativity, for example, had its origins in synchronizing clocks along train routes by means of telegraphs. Without the invention of those technologies, would Einstein still have arrived at his famous physics work? Many of Shakespeare's plays were based on earlier folktales. Could Steve Jobs have introduced the iPhone without a digital telecommunication grid?

Innovators need a rich and diverse environment from which to draw. Access to diverse technologies and diverse examples is helpful, but the key is access to diverse conversations. The unique perspectives and the diverse knowledge of communities are the fertile ground of innovation.

Knowledge for Innovation

Simply throwing library staff in the midst of diverse thought and acknowledged innovation is insufficient. There are two pieces of knowledge librarians must have to capitalize on the fertile ground: topical knowledge and, most importantly, knowledge of what the end result of innovation needs to be.

Innovation exists only in relation to some goal. Something cannot simply be better; it must be better than something else. So simply implementing some new technology or creating some new piece of software is not in and of itself innovative. It becomes innovative only if it advances some mission. Did the new thing (process, tool, approach, concept) advance a user's knowledge? Did it more efficiently or effectively facilitate a conversation?

This is not to say that experimentation without a direct goal is worthless. It does build knowledge. Play is an essential part of innovation, just not an end in itself. Experimentation outside of theory or a goal is really an access activity. It is building a set of ideas and skills available for directed innovation. Play and experimentation are part of making fertile ground, not planting seeds. It is for this reason that even though much of librarianship has been following a near-shore strategy of innovation, libraries are well positioned for true innovation from core principles. Work with wikis, blogging, Twittering, Google, Amazon, social networking, Facebook, MySpace, and Flickr, while possible innovations, are certainly a set of rich concepts and tools that can lead to innovation.

Environment for Innovation

Just as users must feel safe in our libraries, so too innovators—not safe as in protected and unchallenged, but safe to try and fail. If the library environment is seen as unsupportive of new ideas or punitive, innovators will find other environments in which they can innovate. While sometimes this is in personal endeavors, it is increasingly in librarianship outside of organizational confines. This is particularly true in technology.

Time was when staff members who wanted to try a new technology were restricted to the infrastructure of the institution. Early experimentation with the Web, for example, happened on academy computers. With the current trend towards applications being hosted by third parties, this is no longer the case. If a staff member wants to blog and is prevented from doing so by institutional policies, that person can simply blog on Blogger or LiveJournal or WordPress. A staff member who wants to set up a social network no longer has to download source code; that person can set one up in a few clicks on Ning. Rather than restrictive policies suppressing activity, they now drive innovation, and often institutional identity, to third parties.

Of course, if one person sees a policy as limiting innovation, another may well see it as preventing some negative consequence. By having a large number of staff blogs, the institutional voice might be diluted. By hosting some social network activity, the college might be opened up to some legal action. In the real world, the ideal of innovation must always be tempered with respect for the larger institutional good. The problem does not occur from the policies; it is a result of insufficient shared knowledge on the institutional goals. If a policy is seen as limiting innovation, it must be explained. If it can't be explained, it must be eliminated.

Also, positive policies that stimulate innovation can be put in place—for example, requiring continuing education of staff. A policy that requires liaison staff to spend time physically located with their communities not only provides greater access to new ideas, but can locate library service at the point of need.

Motivating Innovation

Just as with users, providing staff members with a fertile environment of ideas, preparing them with knowledge of the conversation and their core mission, and building a safe environment for risk are insufficient for innovation. Motivation is a key element. For innovation, intrinsic motivation is much more important than extrinsic.

The old saying about leading a horse to water but not being able to make it drink is not quite true. If you hold a horse's head underwater long enough, it will take in water. Of course, it will also drown. This would be an extreme example of how extrinsic motivation is insufficient for innovation. At best, extrinsic motivation can reward an internally motivated individual. There is increasing talk in the management literature on the importance of ritual, for example.

It is the intrinsic motivation of the individual that will drive innovation. However, there is no one universal motivation that will drive people. A librarian may innovate out of a need for recognition, or simple curiosity, or competition, or a sense of duty to either the organization or the function. Frustration, while a dangerous tool, is also a motivator. People will innovate to relieve stress or minimize frustration. The key as an organization is to find out what motivates an individual and create conditions that match that motivation.

Starting the Innovation Conversation

While the ultimate responsibility for innovation lies with the individual and the organization for which he or she is innovating, LIS education also has a responsibility to prepare future innovators. It must provide a foundational set of skills and conversations that a librarian can bring into the workplace.

To date, foundational skills have focused on facilitation of conversations through access—that is, classification, searching, and practice focused on artifacts. Technology skills have always been a significant part of the curriculum, from electric pens, to early online databases, to the current focus on Internet-enabled services. However, much of this curriculum is still centered on using applications and is currently in flux.

What has been lacking in many LIS cores is an understanding of the importance of communication skills, an obligation to innovate, and sufficient real-world settings to experiment within. These holes are obvious when viewing documents like the draft of "ALA's Core Competencies of Librarianship."[12] Here the focus is overwhelmingly on access skills, and every item is modified with "recorded knowledge." Even in the areas of reference, where there is some mention of communication skills, the apparent purpose is solely to get someone to a document:

> The methods used to interact successfully with individuals and
> groups to provide consultation, mediation, and guidance in
> their use of recorded knowledge and information.

The only mention of innovation in the entire document is in recognizing technical innovation:

> The principles and techniques necessary to identify and analyze
> emerging technologies and innovations in order to recognize
> and implement relevant technological improvements.

If librarianship and library education adopt such an approach (or worse, if the document represents current practice), the field will have competent functionaries, but will lack the engine of new thought needed by any important and growing field.

The lack of stressing innovation in LIS education is troubling considering a disturbing practice the author has perceived in the field—that of hiring for innovation. In too many libraries, new LIS hires are being brought on board to innovate the institution. Often referred to as "the young librarian," the newly minted MLS is often looked to for leadership and advice in technology. This situation is based on an assumption that recent graduates have a better sense of technology and what is new. This assumption does not take into account that increasingly, cutting-edge practice and developments are not centered in the academy, but come from the field of practice and other information industries. Also, these new graduates are expected to innovate against a mission they do not fully understand, that of their new workplace. In essence, too many libraries place the most vital of their functions—innovation—in the hands of the least experienced person, with the least institutional knowledge, and the fewest political skills.

It should be noted that the author is not suggesting that a new perspective is not valuable, or that new hires should not be an important part of an institution's innovation process. Instead, the author stresses that innovation is the job of every librarian, not just new ones. Further, if innovation is handed to the newest employees with the added responsibility of institutionalizing these innovations, they will fail.

LIS education can improve the odds of success of innovators by matching a fertile sandbox for exploration with political and change agents' skills. MLS students must be taught not simply how to dream up new ideas, but how to work within an organization to implement these changes. One of the keys to teaching these skills is providing as many real settings as possible. Internships are a nearly universal part of LIS education, and yet this only provides a semester of access to real-world settings, and internships are often directed towards existing practice. What are needed are real clients for project work throughout the curriculum. Such learning allows for inventive exploration with real clients.

The stress on real projects and real settings should not be taken as advocating a sort of apprenticeship approach to education. Instead, the focus must be on bringing innovation to the real-world settings and showing the students the reality of implementation. One must avoid the "Florentine" dilemma. The Accademia di Belle Arti di Firenze was the center of Renaissance art. It instructed masters such as Michelangelo in sculpture and painting. Within the Accademia is a sculpture room. It is a long room with high ceilings. The walls are filled floor to ceiling with plaster busts. The busts on the bottom are those of the masters. The sculptures above are those of students—in essence, final projects. The dilemma is that it is nearly impossible to tell the students' final work from that of the masters. The point was to replicate the skills and styles of the teacher, not to surpass them or deviate from them. This approach to imparting a style where there was a single definition of perfection, and one that did not change from class to class, master to master, led to an eventual stagnation in the Italian art world.

Library science must avoid the Florentine dilemma. It must teach innovation and experimentation over simple skills replication. The culture of LIS education must begin modeling such innovation by adopting more co-teaching in classes, where the instructor and students are learning a topic together. LIS programs must provide ample opportunities to professors to update their own skills and translate those into classroom experiences. Ultimately, LIS programs need to see their own schools as ongoing participatory networks with a vigorous ongoing conversation into the future of libraries.

In order to truly accomplish these changes, the very nature of LIS master's preparation must be re-examined. Just as no one librarian can master all the participatory skills at great depth, one can argue that teaching all the needed skills to librarians in a single master's degree is impossible. The idea that a single one- to two-year degree at the outset of a professional's career is sufficient preparation to be webmaster, reference librarian, cataloger, instructional librarian, or library director is optimistic at best. Skills instruction is often a bachelor's degree–level education in today's universities. Masters' degrees make a great deal of sense for innovators and managers, while for large academic libraries, doctoral level education makes sense.

Library and information schools do an excellent job with the time they have. However, the lock into a single degree has led to a distinct tension between the profession and the academy. Libraries want a better prepared workforce, and so does the academy. Libraries want a new employee to have more experience, and so does the academy. Without expanding the LIS education cycle to include more time and more preparation in both formal education programs and coherent professional training, integration of innovation, technology, and communication skills into the curriculum will remain a zero-sum game. There is simply too much the field would like to impart to preprofessionals. This problem is only made worse without a coherent conceptual framework for the profession.

Conclusion

Seafaring allowed a small nation like Portugal to thrive in a globalized economy. The navies of nations from Spain, to the United Kingdom, to the United States of America brought great wealth and power. All of this might and power relies in a real way on ideas. The globe became open to flesh and wood through the ocean, and the ocean became open through the concepts of longitude and latitude. Today, libraries are all too often limited by a lack of navigational concepts. All too often, innovation is measured against nonlibrary metrics of success. All too often, innovators become frustrated by scant charts of the future.

It is essential for the academic library to embrace change and innovation. However, it must do so from core values and a shared vision of what "better" means. By creating an environment welcoming risk and change, by providing ongoing learning opportunities throughout the library, by providing access to a fertile field of ideas, and by recognizing and rewarding what is important to the innovator, the academic library has a bright future.

Notes

1. Dava Sobel, *Longitude: The True Story of a Lone Genius Who Solved the Greatest Scientific Problem of His Time* (New York: Walker, 1995).
2. Mervyn Susser, *Community Psychiatry: Epidemiologic and Social Themes* (New York: Random House, 1968), quoted in Pauline Hardiker and Mary Baker "Towards Social Theory for Social Work" in *Handbook of Theory for Practice Teachers in Social Work*, ed. Joyce Lishman (London: Jessica Kingsley, 1991), 87.
3. R. David Lankes, Joanne Silverstein, and Scott Nicholson, "Participatory Networks: The Library as Conversation," *Information Technology and Libraries* 26, no. 4 (Dec. 2007): 17–33.
4. Gordon Pask, *Conversation Theory: Applications in Education and Epistemology* (New York: Elsevier, 1976).
5. Linda H. Bertland, "An Overview of Research in Metacognition: Implications for Information Skills Instruction," *School Library Media Quarterly* 15 (Winter 1986): 96–99.
6. Robert S. Taylor, "Question Negotiation and Information Seeking in Libraries," *College & Research Libraries* 29, no. 3 (May 1968): 178.
7. Joan M. Bechtel, "Conversation, A New Paradigm for Librarianship?" *College & Research Libraries* 47, no. 3 (May 1986): 219.
8. David Weinberger, *Everything Is Miscellaneous: The Power of the New Digital Disorder* (New York: Holt Paperbacks, 2008).

9. David Weinberger, "The Commoditization of Knowledge," KMWorld, Feb. 5, 2008, www.kmworld.com/Articles/Column/David-Weinberger/The-commoditi-zation-of-knowledge-40810.aspx

10. R. David Lankes, Joanne Silverstein, and Scott Nicholson, "Participatory Networks: The Library as Conversation," *Information Technology and Libraries* 26, no. 4 (Dec. 2007): 31.

11. Lewis Hyde, *The Gift: Creativity and the Artist in the Modern World,* 25th anniversary ed., (New York: Vintage, 2007).

12. American Library Association, "ALA's Core Competencies of Librarianship," May 2008, http://wikis.ala.org/professionaltips/images/e/e7/ALA_Core_Competences_June_6_2008.pdf

PUT THE PIECES TOGETHER AND YOU GET THE PERFECT ACADEMIC LIBRARIAN... OR DO YOU?

WHAT COMPETENCY STANDARDS TELL US ABOUT ACADEMIC LIBRARIANSHIP IN THE 21ST CENTURY

Heather Gendron
University of North Carolina

Introduction

Many factors contribute to a rapidly evolving workplace in today's academic libraries, and many library staff may feel they are ill prepared to meet changing expectations. A recent *Environmental Scan* by the Association of College and Research Libraries (ACRL) identifies numerous challenges academic libraries face, including the effects of social computing on research, the necessity to incorporate intellectual property management into library service models, an overall view of libraries as "businesses serving customers," and an increased need to protect library patrons' privacy and a support of intellectual freedom.[1] Another factor is an increase in the privatization and digitization of information products. In a continuously changing environment, how can academic librarians best prepare and develop their staff to respond rapidly and appropriately to these changes? Just as important, how can librarians prepare their staff to be *agents* of change and innovation in higher education?

Through a competency modeling process, librarians and their staff can better prepare themselves to perform successful transformations of information products, library services, and traditional leadership roles. The development of a core competency framework is a way to identify the baseline and expert skills, knowledge, and abilities that are specific to a particular field and is applied in a different ways:

- Competency guidelines written by library organizations communicate to the world *what librarians do expertly.* They act as a vehicle to move forward the profession of librarianship as a whole. Such guidelines can also help individual librarians identify and plan what personal competencies they need to *achieve personal career goals* that may or may not be directly tied to their current job.
- Individual libraries that utilize a core competency framework to devise *strategic planning goals* (that may also trickle down to personal competence via performance planning) can home in on and develop what gives their library an edge over competing units at their home institutions.
- Competency standards created within libraries and for library staff provide frameworks for *personal and job-specific competence* so that librarians can zero in on, and ultimately achieve, the goals related to their specific jobs.

Academic libraries today that wish to be at the heart of their universities tomorrow would be wise to consider core competence. In order to not only sustain, but to also successfully reshape academic libraries, it is essential to define what the core competencies of individual librarians are. This includes "next-generation competencies."[2] Equally important, although perhaps more challenging, is the need to define what competencies the profession of academic librarianship as a whole can offer. Competency planning done effectively will help ensure that academic libraries continue to be the ultimate and most relevant resource for students, faculty, and researchers and will help promote libraries as leaders in the delivery of information for scholarly research. In order to do this, librarians need to first understand the concepts behind core competence and choose good methods for creating competency statements.

What We Say We Do—Defining Baseline Competence

Confusion about what exactly are "core competencies" stems from the phrase being used in the literature of library science to mean different things, depending on the goals of the authors or their respective institu-

tions. Most library organizations provide a clear definition of *competence* in their competency statements, but individual authors commonly
use this term without clearly defining what it means. It is important for
the authors of any competency document to define clearly what they
mean by the term *competence* because competency standards are created
for different reasons and are utilized in wide range of scenarios.

The majority of libraries and library organizations with competency
standards define competencies, in one way or another, as the *skills,
knowledge, abilities, and behaviors* individuals need in order to perform
specific jobs. This definition follows closely the original concept of
competence as defined by psychologist and author David McClelland.
His 1972 article for *American Psychologist* entitled "Testing for Competence Rather Than for Intelligence" sharply criticizes the validity of the
Scholastic Aptitude Test (SAT) and similar tests used in order to determine intelligence (and therefore, a person's ability to excel in college or
to be successful in a particular career).[3] McClelland argues that these
tests measure best how well test-takers can complete, for instance, word
analogies, but that they do a terrible job of testing a person's ability to
perform successfully in social situations or in a particular line of work.
The alternative McClelland proposes is the development of competency
measures through "criterion sampling." This involves identifying what
criteria are essential to perform a job well. For example "If you want
to test who will be a good policeman, go find out what a policeman
does, follow him around, make a list of his activities, and sample from
that list in screening applicants."[4] However, the trick is not to simply
make a laundry list of job skills but to identify instead "competencies
that are more generally useful in clusters of life outcomes, including
not only occupational outcomes but social ones as well, such as leadership, interpersonal skills, etc."[5] The four general areas of competence
McClelland identifies are communication skills; patience, or response
delay; moderate goal setting; and ego development.[6] He also makes a
distinction between testing for selection and testing for improvement
over time. The competency guidelines for each should be different.
McClelland's approach to competencies is what "performance planning" is based upon. Performance planning is a process with which
most librarians and library staff are familiar, as it is typically tied to the
annual evaluation process. In fact, McClelland's critique of testing and

of performance analysis prompted what has culminated in a nearly 40-year interest in the development of competency guidelines for the field of library science.[7]

Current discussions about the future of academic libraries identify several evolving areas of competence that include, but are not limited to, the digitizing of collections, social computing, e-scholarship, e-learning, assessment of library services and products, the "student as customer" model, privacy and intellectual freedom, collaborative and interactive learning models, a shift away from collection building and an increasing emphasis on library service and outreach, interdisciplinary studies, and intellectual property issues.[8] Very few competency statements list the skills and knowledge needed in order to innovate or cope effectively with these changes. Instead, competency statements are typically written with the goal of identifying baseline competence necessary for a particular type of job.

For instance, in ALA's "Need to Know" series, broad competencies for librarians are outlined.[9] "What Librarians Need to Know" is extremely baseline. In this document, there is little difference between what librarians and managers need to know and what library directors need to know. It is assumed that each set of competencies will build on the next; however, it is questionable that the only difference in competence between a library manager and a library director is number of years of experience (according to ALA, library managers and library directors require the exact same skill set, but library directors need "typically ten years of experience as a librarian with five years of managerial or administrative experience").[10] Additionally, while many of the competencies listed in the ALA "Need to Know" series are applicable to any type of library, they are written with a slant towards public librarianship (e.g., "In a rural setting, the director may be the only regularly scheduled employee. In a large urban setting, the 'city librarian' or director may oversee a staff of hundreds and fifty branches. In the small library the director may handle everything from locking the doors to paying the bills.")[11] While these statements serve to communicate what skills are needed by most public librarians, it is necessary for ACRL and other organizations that serve academic libraries to continue to explore and define what are the competencies unique to academic librarianship.

Academic Librarianship Competency, a Closer Look

Numerous library organizations have, in recent years, developed competency standards for various areas of librarianship, but only two library organizations have identified core competencies specifically for academic librarianship.[12] In 1999, the Association of College and Research Libraries (ACRL) produced a statement on the professional education of academic librarians. This document is not strictly a core competency document, but it is one of the few documents written for academic librarianship that come close. It was written primarily to guide library and information science curricula for academic librarianship.[13] In the same year, the Association of Southeastern Research Libraries (ASERL) created, for the same reason, a more defined set of competency standards for research librarians.[14] In 2007, ACRL once again created a competency document, but this time with a focus on competencies for instruction librarians specifically. Of the three, this most recent document lists the greatest number of competency areas that are specifically geared towards academic librarianship and is a model of competency guidelines intended to guide the professional development of librarians. However, the two documents that most resemble a comprehensive statement of competence in academic librarianship (ACRL's statement on professional education and ASERL's competency document) identify only a handful of competencies that are unique to academic librarianship. For the most part, these competencies are shared by librarians working in any type of institution.[15]

ASERL's competency guidelines for academic librarianship include 14 areas of competence that are necessary for many public service positions (not only in libraries), 11 competencies that are needed in most library positions (not only in academic libraries), and 9 competencies that are more specific to academic librarianship. Portions of the ASERL document point to areas of competence that may require new skill sets (e.g., fund-raising and information policy, copyright laws, licensing, intellectual property); however, these competencies are communicated in passive terms such as "understanding the implications of" or "participates in," rather than in terms that put the librarian and libraries in a leadership role. In ACRL's statement on professional education, only 3 of the 11 areas of competence listed are specific to academic librarianship. As in the case of the ASERL document, these are stated in support of the status quo in academic librarianship and outline very broad and baseline competence. In contrast, ACRL's statement on proficiencies for instruction librarians and coordinators is the most thorough of the three in that it identifies areas of competence specific to academic librarianship. As the authors note, many of the competencies can be applied to instruction positions in any type of library; however, the wording of the document places it squarely in the academic library environment. In addition, several of the competencies point to opportunities for innovation (e.g., an instruction coordinator "encourages librarians to experiment and take risks, to try new approaches and technologies, and to share experiences and materials").[16]

A further comparison of these few competency standards in the field of academic librarianship shows little to no attention given to identifying the "next-generation competencies" that will be required in order to move academic libraries forward in a competitive and sustainable way, let alone competencies that are currently required of academic librarians. In an environment in which required skills are quickly changing, old roles are being redefined, and new positions are being created with regularity in all academic libraries, the profession would benefit from a deeper analysis of what it is that librarians and libraries do expertly.

Identifying a Methodology

Individual authors writing on the issue of core competence in academic librarianship, tend not to mention any kind of methodology used in developing standards for competence.[17] Of the three competency documents written for academic librarianship by library organizations, two utilized literature review (the ASERL document and ACRL's piece on instruction librarianship), and one makes no mention of methodology (the ACRL statement on professional education). Utilizing research methodology to develop standards not only adds a layer of professionalism and authority to the work, but can also help authors of competency standards ground their work in objectivity. This is especially important when working to identify emerging skill sets. Typically, the menu of methodologies available to authors writing competency standards includes literature review, job description analysis, DACUM exercise, survey, and member checking. (Brief descriptions of these methods are included below.) Several of these methods involve seeking input from workers, which allows for greater equity in the ownership of the competency writing process.

In order to write competency standards that address a specific type of job (e.g., library instruction coordinator or distance education librarian), it is essential to conduct analyses of these jobs in order to gain an objective understanding of what skills, knowledge, and behaviors are required on the job. This can be achieved through several methods, chiefly job description content analysis, a DACUM exercise, or in some cases through survey or focus groups.

Job Description Analysis

A job description analysis involves the review of library job descriptions or job ads in order to identify common and emerging skills and job duties. To identify what competencies are needed by academic librarians for development and fund-raising, Mark Winston and Lisa Dunkley performed an analysis of 432 university-level development and fundraising job announcements during a six-month period in 2000 in order to define the competencies in this area.[18] Beverly P. Lynch and Kimberley Robles Smith conducted an analysis of job advertisements that appeared in *College & Research Libraries News* over a period of 25 years (in the month of March during the years 1973–1998) in order to track changes in the work of academic librarians and more specifically how library jobs incorporated computer technology over time.[19]

While the job description analysis process works well to identify general job skills required of a specific job, job descriptions are typically not comprehensive views of what workers actually do on the job day to day. Job ads or announcements are even less specific. Additionally, it is important to make a distinction between a *job duty* (e.g., manages a staff of three full-time librarians) and a *competency* (e.g., "well-developed interpersonal skills that promote collegiality and mutually respectful relationships with others"[20]). A job duty is what someone does on the job. A job competence is the skill, knowledge, or behavior that is evidenced by job performance. The job description analysis should be coupled with at least one other method in order to round out the description of a particular job. Competency standards that simply list what librarians do on the job are helpful in creating job descriptions, but these are not actual competencies. Authors who write competency standards can take data from a job description analysis, identify broad job responsibilities, and then use another method (e.g., survey, member checking, focus groups, or DACUM) to examine more deeply what are the actual skills, knowledge, and behavioral traits needed to perform these job duties.

DACUM Exercise

The DACUM exercise was used by the Alliance of Libraries, Archives and Records Management (ALARM) in partnership with the Cultural Human Resources Council in Canada to create the *Information Resources Management Specialists' Competency Tool Kit.*[21] DACUM is short for "developing a curriculum" and was created in Canada in the 1960s. The DACUM is an occupational analysis process that determines what are the duties, tasks, knowledge, skills, and traits typically required to perform a specific job.[22] This type of process is typically initiated at a state level by human resources staff. DACUM utilizes a "small group method" that includes a team of six to ten "veteran workers" (staff members with two or more years of experience and who do quality work), a neutral facilitator, a recorder, and an observer. Together, this group identifies the duties, tasks, skills, and individual knowledge necessary to do a specific job well. The steps of this process are outlined on the DACUM Archives and Resource Website.[23] As the DACUM website points out, other techniques of job analysis, such as observation or shadowing, can be utilized. The benefits of DACUM are that it is a cost-effective, relatively quick process that involves workers in a participatory way "that honors their expertise."

Member Checking and Survey

Another method that promotes participation and ownership of the competency process is member checking. For this reason, member checking is a necessary component of competency standards development. It simply involves checking in with members of the community who are the subjects of the research being conducted and who will ultimately be affected by the outcomes of the research project. Member checking can involve conducting a survey of, for instance, the members of a library organization in order to get their feedback on proposed

competency standards. This method was utilized by the Art Libraries Society of North America (ARLIS/NA), in addition to a literature
review and a job announcement analysis.[25] Member checking creates
an opportunity for people to participate actively in the development of
competency standards and in the process reduces bias.

Literature Review

Literature reviews are commonly found in the work of library competency authors; however, this should not be the only method used to
write competency standards. Much of the literature that is reviewed in
the creation of competency standards tends to contain mostly anecdotal information. That is not to say such information is not timely
or insightful. It simply calls into question how objective authors of
competency standards can be when they refer to secondary information. Conducting a literature review is a good way to find out what
work has already been done in competency standards development and
can help in understanding broader concerns in the field that affect the
work people do, but a literature review should not be the sole source of
information in the development of competency standards.

The Next Generation of Academic Library Competence

McClelland's type of competency framework is an effective tool for
measuring individual staff performance and can help identify ways a
person can build upon a baseline of skills and knowledge through professional development. This method typically supports the status quo
in libraries and provides some latitude for the inclusion of professional
development skills that are tied to innovation.[26] However, applied
independently of strategic planning and other larger goals, this method
can be too narrowly focused to address the fairly radical changes being faced in the field of academic librarianship. For instance, ACRL
published an essay called "Changing Roles of Academic and Research
Libraries" that recommends librarians let go of the idea of libraries as
"the domain of the book" and instead embrace the idea of libraries as
"pathways to high-quality information in a variety of media and information sources."[27] It suggests that libraries move beyond a model that
supports the control and ownership of collections to "one that seeks to
provide service and guidance in more useful ways, helping users find

and use information that may be available through a range of providers, including libraries themselves, in electronic format" and that libraries need to become better at "assert(ing) their evolving roles in more active ways" in order to be more competitive.[28] What do competency guidelines for this type of change look like?

In his article, "The Innovator's Dilemma: Disruptive Change and Academic Libraries," David Lewis suggests ways in which librarians can better cope with the evolution of their academic libraries.[29] Essentially, his suggestions read as a list of broad competencies that support change to the culture of a workplace. Lewis proposes that "porous organizational boundaries" be set in order to allow for the flow of ideas, in addition to "collaboration among all staff that creates the ability and willingness to share knowledge and expertise freely."[30] In contrast to McClelland's suggested baseline competence "patience, or response-delay," Lewis calls on librarians to be *im*patient, "which leads to a desire to explore, innovate, and change."[31] While McClelland is referring to a type of personal competence that is critical for a healthy work environment and involves having patience in coping with change, difficult situations, and challenging coworkers, Lewis's version calls for impatience in order to create a climate in which innovation can take place. Lewis also suggests that libraries embrace "the ability and willingness to measure results and make consequences visible" and for library staff to "trust that colleagues will exercise competence and good professional judgment even, or especially, when they are doing things differently than you would."[32] These are competencies that could not only be linked to strategic planning, but could also be included in library staff performance plans as behavioral competencies that support an increasingly innovative climate in the workplace.

In addition to strategic planning and performance planning, there is a type of competency framework that could be utilized by academic libraries to identify next-generation competencies. The framework was proposed by C. K. Prahalad and Gary Hamel in their *Harvard Business Review* article entitled "The Core Competence of the Corporation."[33] This article is frequently mentioned in the library literature, but tends to be misunderstood and inappropriately applied, likely because it is written with a corporate workplace in mind. It appears that this article spurred a surge of writing on competence in librarianship during the

1990s.[34] In the case presented by Prahalad and Hamel, *core competence* refers to the competencies of an entire corporation and how the knowledge and skills of each staff person can be harnessed in order to achieve the most competence in a particular industry. Core competence is not considered something that diminishes over time like physical assets; rather, competence is something that grows and develops over time.[35] The authors define core competence as the "collective learning in the organization, especially how to coordinate diverse production skills and integrate multiple streams of technologies" within a corporation.[36] According to Prahalad and Hamel, core competence "provides potential access to a wide variety of markets . . . makes a significant contribution to the perceived customer benefits of the end product," and "should be difficult for competitors to imitate."[37] At first glance, it appears that academic librarians may not be interested in their libraries having "access to a wide variety of markets," until they consider how to situate their libraries to become expert in, for instance, institutional repositories (which could be considered a "market"), forcing the need for new competence in areas outside traditional library roles.

Prahalad and Hamel also point to a need to build "people-embodied skills" in organizations that "sustain product leadership," rather than outsourcing these skills.[38] Librarians, when considering outsourcing, should ask whether or not their library would be better off streamlining by handing over areas of competence to outsourcing, or if in doing so key library organizational competence is diminished. Other attributes of a corporation's competence as identified by Prahalad and Hamel include "communication, involvement, and a deep commitment to working across organization boundaries."[39] Librarians who are able to achieve these goals in their libraries can be better prepared to respond quickly and effectively to the changing needs of the people they serve.

Librarians do not typically speak of "competitors" or "end products," but within academic institutions there is always competition for resources between libraries and other departments or units on campus, and it is easy to identify what are considered library "end products." Academic librarians are more often in a position to identify "partners" or "collaborators," as minimal staffing and tight budgets common in the field generally do not allow for much room to "compete." Nonetheless, competitors could include any organization whose activities overlap with or mimic the services provided by academic libraries (e.g., ask-us type services provided by private companies). A competitor could also be a peer library that ranks slightly higher in ARL rankings or a library that is achieving better results in a particular area of competence (such as partnering with faculty and publishers in e-scholarship ventures or creating and managing institutional repositories). End products could be defined as anything from a library catalog to instructional services.

The framework proposed by Prahalad and Hamel as applied to the field of academic librarianship as a whole could help to identify and communicate better what academic libraries and their staff excel at, what core competencies they can build upon, and critically, what are the areas of the "marketplace" in which academic librarianship serves "customers" best. This kind of exercise can help library organizations (such as ACRL and ARL) identify where academic libraries could become stronger, gain core competence, and outpace their "competition." The point is not necessarily to gain enough competence in an organization or within the profession to simply copycat the competition, although that could be a goal. To be truly competitive, libraries can identify emerging areas of competence that they are already superior in and develop these competencies in order to create new models of service and information delivery. Libraries can identify strengths in particular areas that their competition has yet to discover and that ultimately provide exemplary service to library patrons.

One example where a core competency framework could be integrated is in the work of library organizations to identify trends and emerging concerns in the academic library field. It is common for groups such as ACRL and ARL to produce reports that provide guideposts for where they see academic librarianship is headed. The aforementioned "Changing Roles" piece by ACRL and its *Environmental Scan* of 2007 are two examples. While this type of reporting typically offers useful information about trends, there is little in the way of *how* to deal with these changes. A competency framework forces the question "What distinguishes academic librarianship from other disciplines?"—essentially, "What is core to the field of academic librarianship?" In the development of forecast-type reports, organizations could include accompanying material that identified the competencies needed in order to effectively engage in the creation of next-generation competence. Concrete discussion could take place around what skills, knowledge, and behaviors are needed in order to make changes that are responsive to user needs—changes that are needed not only to keep up with change, but also to innovate.

For instance, a review of ACRL's *Environmental Scan* reveals numerous key areas for potential competency development needed in academic libraries, including "assessment." Assessment competencies can be broken down into three areas: profession-level competence (delivered at the level of a library organization such as ALA, ACRL, and ARL); library-level competence (delivered at the level of the individual academic library); and staff-level competence (delivered at the level of the individual staff person).

One example of professional-level competence related to *assessment* in academic libraries is:

- Academic libraries are leaders in the development and application of assessment methodology, as evidenced by the ability to identify where assessment is needed, the execution of effective and methodologically sound assessment programs, and the accurate analysis of assessment data—with the end result being sustained support of or additional support gained for library services and collections.

Library-level competence could be:

- The university library is a campus leader in the development and application of assessment methodology that promotes a better understanding of information-seeking behavior and the acquisition and use of information in academic settings.

At the staff level, a competency could read:

- Librarians possess baseline knowledge of and expertise in the assessment methodologies that shape and support academic library services and collections (e.g., survey, focus groups, statistical analysis). Their ability to conduct assessments is evidenced by the existence of assessment projects and programs that directly address the needs of academic library users.

Providing clear guidelines such as these could also help library science faculty more easily and successfully integrate the necessary skills and knowledge into library science coursework, ensuring that courses are current and forward-looking.

Looking Ahead

The changes that shape the field of academic librarianship can be exciting for librarians but are also anxiety-making as they tend to tap precious and hard-won resources and because they stretch and redefine what skills are needed. A competency framework can be utilized in variety of settings to reach different goals in order to help mitigate the stress of change in library organizations. Typically, competency frameworks are developed by library organizations to identify competence for individual staff professional development. However, little exploration has been done to look at how competence developed at the profession level or library level could benefit the profession of academic librarianship. Through a more holistic approach to competency development and an identification of competence at each level of the profession libraries will be better positioned to react successfully to the evolving needs of their patrons.

Notes

1. ACRL Research Committee, *Environmental Scan, 2007* (Chicago: Association of College and Research Libraries, Jan. 2008), www.ala.org/ala/mgrps/divs/acrl/publications/whitepapers/Environmental_Scan_2007%20FINAL.pdf.
2. The phrase *next-generation competencies* is borrowed from C. K. Prahalad and Gary Hamel, "The Core Competence of the Corporation," *Harvard Business Review* 68, no. 3 (1990): 90; Business Source Premier, EBSCOhost (accessed June 24, 2008).
3. David McClelland, "Testing for Competence Rather Than for Intelligence," *American Psychologist* 28, no. 1 (Jan. 1973): 1–14.
4. Ibid., 7.
5. Ibid., 9.
6. Ibid.
7. A search of the database *Library and Information Science Abstracts* (LISA) for the term *competencies* that excludes the term *literacy* results in a total of 745 citations (covering the years 1960 through the middle of 2008). Before 1970, there is no mention of the term in the literature cited in LISA. The first mention of *competencies* in relation to librarian performance (after 1969) was an article entitled "The Education of Community College Librarians" published in 1975 in the *Journal of Education for Librarianship*. By 1980, 16 articles mentioned competencies, and each year since new material has been added.
8. See Jerry D Campbell, "Changing a Cultural Icon: The Academic Library as a Virtual Destination," *Educause Review* 41, no. 1 (Jan./Feb. 2006): 16–30; David W Lewis, "The Innovator's Dilemma: Disruptive Change and Academic Librar-

ies," *Library Administration and Management* 18, no. 2 (Spring 2004): 68–74; and ACRL Research Committee, *Environmental Scan, 2007.*

9. American Library Association, "What Librarians Need to Know," www.ala.org/ala/educationcareers/careers/librarycareerssite/whatyouneedlibrarian.cfm (accessed February 14, 2008).

10. American Library Association, "What Library Managers Need to Know," www.ala.org/ala/educationcareers/careers/librarycareerssite/whatyouneedlibrarymgr.cfm (accessed February 14, 2008) and "What Library Directors Need to Know," www.ala.org/ala/educationcareers/careers/librarycareerssite/whatyouneeddirector.cfm (accessed February 14, 2008)

11. ALA, "What Library Directors Need to Know."

12. See Heather Ball, "Competency Issues in the Library Profession: An Annotated Bibliography," in *Core Competencies and Core Curricula for the Art Library and Visual Resources Professions.* Occasional Paper of ARLIS/NA 15 (2006): 19–34. Library organizations that have written competency statements include American Library Association (ALA), Association of College and Research Libraries (ACRL), Special Libraries Association (SLA), Art Libraries Society of North America (ARLIS/NA), Music Library Association (MLA), Association of Southeastern Research Libraries (ASERL), California Library Association (CLA), American Association of Law Libraries (AALL), Alliance of Libraries, Archives and Records Management (ALARM).

13. Association of College and Research Libraries, "Statement for Congress on Professional Education: Issues in Higher Education and Library and Information Studies Education" (March 1999), www.ala.org/ala/hrdrbucket/1stcongressonpro/1stcongressassociation.htm (accessed June 23, 2008).

14. ASERL Education Committee, "Shaping the Future: ASERL's Competencies for Research Librarians" (Atlanta, GA: Association of Southeastern Research Libraries, Nov. 10, 2000), www.aserl.org/statements/competencies/competencies.htm.

15. The original ACRL statement is not a formal competencies document and was in large part written by a single author, rather than by a committee. However, it is one of only three competency-type documents published by a parent library organization representing academic librarianship and as such is given attention here. In the ACRL document, 11 broad areas of concern for professional education in librarianship are outlined and present a foundation for competence in academic librarianship. Of the 11 areas, just 5 directly address concerns specific to academic librarianship (although it could be argued that at least 2 of these 5 could also apply to most fields of librarianship): "Broad and in depth knowledge of the higher education environment; preparation for scholarly work; educational role of libraries and librarians; knowledge of legal and policy issues, including areas such as intellectual property and intellectual freedom; and the accreditation of graduate LIS programs that focus on school librarianship (i.e., there is a need to focus more attention on the accreditation of LIS programs that support information literacy and school librarianship, thereby supporting information literacy across the educational spectrum)." The ASERL document outlines 5 broad areas, only 2 of which specifically address issues of academic librarianship—the competencies outlined under the headings "The research librarian understands the library within the context of higher education (its purpose and goals) and the needs of students, faculty, and researchers" and "The research librarian knows the structure, organization, creation, management, dissemination, use, and preserva-

tion of information resources, new and existing, in all formats." The competencies under each heading number fewer than 10 and range from very general ("is able to help users learn") to very specific ("participates in fund-raising efforts on behalf of the university").

16. Association of College and Research Libraries, "Standards for Proficiencies for Instruction Librarians and Coordinators" (Chicago: ACRL, June 24, 2007), www.ala.org/ala/mgrps/divs/acrl/standards/profstandards.cfm.

17. Mary Cassner and Kate E. Adams, "Assessing the Professional Development Needs of Distance Librarians in Academic Libraries," *Journal of Library Administration* 45, no. 1&2 (2006): 81–99; Wanda Dole, Jitka M. Hurych, and Anne Liebst, "Assessment: A Core Competency for Library Leaders," *Library Administration and Management* 19, no. 3 (Summer 2005): 125–132; Mary Anne Kennan, Patricia Willard, Concepión S. Wilson, and Fletcher Cole, "Australian and U.S. Academic Library Jobs: A Comparison," *Australian Academic & Research Libraries* 28, no. 2 (June 1997): 111–128; Beverly P. Lynch, Catherine Murray-Rust, Susan E. Parker, Deborah Turner, Diane Parr Walker, Frances C. Wilkinson, and Julia Zimmerman, "Attitudes of Presidents and Provosts on the University Library," *College & Research Libraries* 68, no. 3 (May 2007): 213–227; Beth McNeil, *Core Competencies: SPEC Kit 270* Washington, DC: Office of Leadership and Management Services, Association of Research Libraries, 2002);Thomas Shaughnessy, "Approaches to Developing Competencies in Research Libraries," *Library Trends* 41 (Fall 1992): 282–298; and Mark D. Winston and Lisa Dunkley, "Leadership Competencies for Academic Librarians: The Importance of Development and Fund-Raising Analysis of Job Announcements, January–June 2000," *College & Research Libraries* 63, no. 2 (March 2002): 171–182.

18. Winston and Dunkley, "Leadership Competencies for Academic Librarians."

19. Beverly P. Lynch and Kimberley Robles Smith, "The Changing Nature of Work in Academic Libraries," *College & Research Libraries* 62, no. 5 (Sept. 2001): 407–420.

20. Heather Ball with Sara Harrington and members of the ARLIS/NA Professional Development and Core Competencies Subcommittees, "ARLIS/NA Core Competencies for Art Information Professionals," in *Core Competencies and Core Curricula for the Art Library and Visual Resources Professions.* Occasional Paper of ARLIS/NA 15 (2006): 13.

21. Alliance of Libraries, Archives and Records Management (ALARM) in partnership with the Cultural Human Resources Council with the support of Human Resources Development Canada, *Information Resources Management Specialists' Competency Tool Kit,* (Ottawa: CHRC, 2002); full document available to CHRC members at www.culturalhrc.ca/for_members/Competencies/IRMS/CHRC_IRMS_Competency_Tool_Kit-en.pdf; preview available to nonmembers at www.culturalhrc.ca/minisites/Heritage/e/PDFs/CHRC_IRMS_Competency_Tool_Kit_SAMPLE-en.pdf.

22. DACUM Archive and Resource Website, www.dacum.org (accessed June 23, 2008).

23. Ibid.

24. McNeil, *Core Competencies,* XX.

25. Ball et al., "ARLIS/NA Core Competencies for Art Information Professionals," 7–18.

26. Many fine examples of academic library competency planning at the individual

library level are presented in ARL's *Core Competencies: SPEC Kit 270.*

27. American Library Association, Roundtable on Technology and Change in Academic Libraries, convened by the Association of College and Research Libraries (ACRL) on November 2–3, 2006, in Chicago, "Changing Roles of Academic and Research Libraries," www.ala.org/ala/mgrps/divs/acrl/issues/value/changingroles.cfm.
28. Ibid.
29. Lewis, "The Innovator's Dilemma."
30. Ibid., 73–74.
31. Ibid., 74.
32. Ibid., 74.
33. Prahalad and Hamel, "Core Competence of the Corporation."
34. Two hundred seventy citations for this article are listed in the database LISA for the period 1990–1999.
35. Prahalad and Hamel, "Core Competence of the Corporation," 82.
36. Ibid., 82.
37. Ibid, 83–84.
38. Ibid, 84.
39. Ibid, 82.

CHAPTER 5

THE NEW LIAISON LIBRARIAN
COMPETENCIES FOR THE 21ST CENTURY ACADEMIC LIBRARY

Craig Gibson and Jamie Wright Coniglio
George Mason University Libraries

Librarians who believe that their job is to care for and manage their places and their collections will need to accept that their role in society, and their importance to their communities, will continue to shrink. But for those who see that their role is deeper than that, the great age of librarianship is just beginning. Our places and our collections will never become unimportant—we are, after all, physical beings. But in order to become the fabulously successful librarians that we have the capability to be, we will need, in significant ways, to leave our libraries behind.[1]

Liaison Librarianship in the Current Higher Education Context

One of the most familiar themes concerning the future of academic librarianship is the unrelenting change facing the profession and, indeed, the viability of academic libraries themselves.[2] This theme has most recently focused on the impact of technology upon all of higher education, with attendant changes in relationships among faculty, students, and other stakeholders in the academy. However, technology as driver of change raises many additional questions and creates uncertainties about emergent forms of scholarship, student and faculty research behaviors, and the blurring of lines of responsibility and authority in the academy in the face of technological advances. As a result, many in the academy are uncertain about their traditional roles.

Within academic and research libraries, one cohort of professionals whose traditional roles are now questioned is the subject specialist
or liaison librarian group. This group has been variously called subject
librarians, subject specialists, or most traditionally bibliographers; the
term *liaison* itself has emerged as a designation for those librarians
with assignments to academic programs and departments, centering
on certain combinations of discipline-based knowledge or affiliation,
with a limited set of functional responsibilities (collection development,
reference or research assistance, and instruction). The combinations of
responsibilities in liaison positions have varied from institution to institution, depending on breadth and depth of academic programs, number of liaison positions available, individual educational backgrounds
and expertise, and in some cases, individual preferences, talents, and interests. The "standard" portfolio for liaison librarians, however, includes
the major elements of collection development/management, reference,
research advisory, specialized instruction, and communication or "liais-
ing" with assigned departments.

The contemporary environment in higher education and academic libraries places great pressure on liaison librarians. The current
milieu for colleges and universities involves much greater accountability, a focus on research productivity, learning outcomes, "return on
investment," and new metrics beyond the traditional inputs associated
with the activities in which liaison have been engaged in the past:
building collections, answering research questions, and teaching individual instruction sessions. Thus, academic libraries are challenged
by the need to demonstrate "added value" and to integrate expertise
into the research and teaching processes of their institutions. Indeed,
this pressure transcends academic institutions in the United States.
Rodwell and Fairbairn of Australia, for example, have identified the
intensifying pressures on the traditional roles of the liaison librarian
and the mounting pressures for liaison librarians to take on responsibilities related to learning and program outcomes, special campus
projects, and grants.[3]

Redefined roles for subject specialist librarians are, at this point,
most closely linked with the changing patterns of scholarly communication, changing research practices focused on collaboration, and the
impact of digital and distributed technologies. As Lougee notes in the

CLIR position paper *Diffuse Library,* the academic library itself is now positioned to redefine its role:

> With the incorporation of distributed technologies and more open models, the library has the potential to become more involved at all stages, and in all contexts, of knowledge creation, dissemination, and use. Rather than being defined by its collections or the services that support them, the library can become a diffuse agent within the scholarly community.[4]

Repositioning the academic library within scholarly workflows, research practices, and application of new knowledge in the curriculum and with the institution's varied constituencies is the path to engagement for the library. The entire library organization will need to change to chart the path into this integrative role, but subject specialist or liaison librarians will be the key change agents in shaping this new role for academic libraries. Because they are the "public face" of the library organization and possess strong lines of communication with faculty and students, liaison librarians are ideally positioned to understand shifting patterns of scholarship and learning and, in turn, to reinterpret the library's mission in mutually intelligible ways for external constituents (faculty, students, academic administrators) and for library colleagues (digital programs/systems, technical services, access services, collections management). In effect, liaison librarians can expand their repertoire of knowledge and skills to be the key mediators in promoting the new "diffuse," permeable library throughout the institution.

To accomplish this transformation, liaison librarians will need to expand their competencies, learn new skills, and become more integrative players on the academic scene. Their traditional roles will need to be delegated, transformed, or managed by their organizations so that newer roles focused on membership on research teams, communities of practice focused on curriculum change, and projects focused on knowledge management, virtual laboratories, digital publishing, information management tools, and other opportunities receive their time, attention, and expertise. To transform the liaison librarian role, however, the legacy issues associated with that role must be understood, and the valuable elements within that role must be strengthened, expanded, and linked with a new knowledge-and-behavior repertoire.

Liaisons and Legacy

While one can trace librarians and librarianship back to antiquity, the role of the liaison librarian is relatively recent in academic libraries. As such, "it is useful to examine the classic or traditional model of the modern era. In the variations of this model, the work of the faculty and the work of the librarian have been basically distinct or discrete, but have increasingly merged or coalesced in areas of instructional delivery, assessment of student learning, and other scholarly activities. Recent emphasis on information literacy and the ongoing reexamination of the role and responsibilities of academic librarians in teaching and learning in the academy are intensifying the faculty-librarian coalescence."[5] How did the academic library liaison model originate? It is rooted in the classic response—a library reflects its environment.

Subject librarian positions were created in response to change and "designed to take advantage of 'the best features of a branch library system' and improve communications between the library and academic departments."[6] With the post–World War II GI Bill providing an impetus, universities and colleges grew with new faculty hired to teach increasing numbers of students. Library budgets and local research collections boomed as research and teaching grew significantly nationwide.[7] To foster improved communications as new collections were built, libraries created the "subject specialist," "subject bibliographer" or "subject librarian," who sustained and maintained local collections and increased his or her own subject expertise, formally and informally.

Subject librarians focused on comprehensive collection depth, based on specific faculty, departments, or colleges, as well as the available budget. Organizationally, these librarians reported through a collection development division or department—ostensibly a link between public and technical services divisions or departments. Bright boundaries between academic disciplines created a clear environment in which the subject librarian was the gatekeeper to local resources, as interlibrary loan and regional cooperatives began to emerge as viable services. Interactions were, primarily, on the librarian's turf of office or service desk in a general reference room, a "graduate" reference room, or a specific branch subject library. Dempsey succinctly speaks of "four facets of the library: place, collections, expertise and service. In a pre-network age these are vertically integrated around the collections. Place exists to hold the collections. Expertise is devoted to organizing and interpreting the collection for local needs. And services tend to be around acquisition and delivery of the collections."[8]

While automating library tasks, providing "online searching" (mediated or "end-user"), SDI services, and so on, librarians worked with wonder as they adapted, adopted, and adjusted to these tools. Simultaneously, machine-driven separations between academic technical staff (computer technicians) and library staff (content experts with technical needs) appeared on campuses. Computer centers and labs, usually distinct, separate spaces from the library, were created and placed under the jurisdiction of campus information systems technology or computing divisions or departments. Library technology became a distinct professional specialty: subject librarians with technical skills, of varying levels, were assigned to develop and deploy library automation systems and packages. Formally or not, all librarians in any given library were exposed to, aware of, and retooled for the "new world" of librarianship.

During the 1980s through the mid-1990s, higher education moved toward targeted, market-driven curricula as higher education programs proliferated and institutional competition increased. Multidisciplinary and interdisciplinary scholarship, teaching, and research appeared on campuses. In addition, multidisciplinary and interdisciplinary campus-wide research centers and institutes sprouted; they also needed librarian support. Although approval plans and online library systems started to streamline tasks, subject librarians' collection development duties continued as an artful craft as those budgets stagnated or declined. Library budgets were viewed through the "automation" prism as well as the "books and materials" lens to keep up with new and ever-evolving technologies. More and more, subject librarians found themselves delighting in and coping with the rampant changes in publishing, resource formats, resource transparency, and improved delivery systems.

During this time, many academic libraries reviewed and recast traditional subject bibliographers into "liaison" librarians, who typically encouraged and facilitated communication between the library and academic departments. Formalized liaison programs, emphasizing proactive services to foster communication and visibility, were created and assessed.[9] "Guidelines for Liaison Work in Managing Collections and Services," issued by the Reference and User Services Adult Services Association of the American Library Association (ALA-RUSA), defined such work as "the relationship, formal and informal, that librarians develop with the library's clientele for the specific purpose of seeking input regarding the selection of materials."[10] Over the years, traditional hierarchical library organizations were "flattened" and library administrators tried a variety of organizational approaches such as matrixes, work groups, teams, programmatic groups, and other organizational structures to identify and combine staff skills and experience to better serve users.[11] Traditional liaison services and programs are now perceived as a passive, reactive role; times and technologies require a shift into active, affective, and effective models of engaged and enhanced subject librarianship.

"Nontraditional" Models

Shumaker's excellent study of "embedded librarians" describes three forms of embedded librarianship: physical, organizational, and virtual. *Physical embedding* refers to moving the librarian's office into the office area of the customer group. *Organizational embedding* refers to the management and funding of the librarian "who may be supervised and funded either by the customer group or by a central library service." *Virtual embedding* "refers to the delivery of library services in a virtual workspace exclusively for the use of the customer group."[12] Examples of physical embedding are "college" and "field" librarians.

College librarians originated at Virginia Tech in 1995, in response to university restructuring requirements. "Overcoming the disadvantages of central library, the... librarians allocated to... colleges perform outreach from offices among their constituents. This has allowed closer ties to faculty, resulting in more library instruction, more reference requests, and more placement of librarians on college committees and grants."[13] The University of Michigan's Field Librarian Program finds "[i]n the natural course of bumping into faculty in the hall, informal relationships ultimately develop into new collegial patterns. Instead of being... collection-bound, the field librarians are regarded as resources and active partners in the department.... as a result, the field librarian was viewed as a colleague rather than as an external liaison… providing a broad array of services, collections, and instruction… [they are] collaborators in the advancement of scholarship, teaching, and research." Field librarians "are much more aggressive about providing a diverse set of options for users—physical, virtual, and a blending of the two. The FLP has transformed the role of the subject specialist and has encouraged us to move more deliberately toward perpetuating this model across the organization."[14]

The hybrid library is "an environment with physical and virtual services supporting professional activities of the users at their workplace from the discovery of information to the manipulation and analysis of the delivered resources."[15] Librarian roles in this environment "include learning facilitator, who trains and educates the user community, academic liaison, who focuses on building relationships with departmental faculty, and metadata specialist. Responsibilities include management of electronic information, including resource evaluation and provision of access through gateways and digital libraries, and team building, where resource-based learning teams are comprised of faculty, computing professionals, course designers, and web experts.… diversity of skills and technological proficiency are required to thrive in such a hybrid environment."[16]

Bell and Shank promulgate the "blended librarian"—an academic librarian who combines the traditional skill set of librarianship with the information technologist's hardware and software skills and the instructional or educational designer's ability to apply technology appropriately in the teaching and learning process. Blended librarians, they claim, take leadership positions as campus innovators and change agents; commit to developing campus-wide information literacy initiatives; design instructional and educational programs and classes to assist patrons in gaining the necessary skills (trade) and knowledge (profession) for lifelong success; collaborate and engage in dialogue with instructional technologists and designers to facilitate the instructional mission of academic libraries; implement adaptive, creative, proactive, and innovative change in library instruction through instructional technology and design; and transform relationships with faculty to assist them in integrating technology and library resources into (hybrid or blended) courses; and develop a new capacity for collaboration to improve student learning and outcome assessment in the areas of information access, retrieval, and integration.[17]

Common traits of these schemes are user focus, place, visibility, immediacy, and impact. Not unlike solo librarians in special library settings, the subject liaison lives "cheek by jowl" (physically or virtually) with the clientele served. This proactive proximity demonstrates Shumaker's charge: "the librarian has to be familiar with the work and understand the domain and the goals. Doing this, the librarian becomes an invaluable member of the team. So let's not fall into the trap of providing 'the information they desire.' Let's show them what they need, and deliver it."[18]

Library organizations and librarians continue to seek the balance between access and ownership, paper and electronic, virtual and physical, hardware and software, visibility and viability, resources and relevance as budgets teeter and users are all becoming distance learners, remotely accessing resources and staff in lieu of in-library transactions and face-to-face interactions. At the end of the first decade of the 21st century, liaisons find themselves in the midst of the perspicacious prediction by Lancaster and Smith of either becoming "redundant" or "exploiter[s] of a vast electronic 'library without walls'"[19] where "ambiguity and uncertainty replace routine and rote responses to information seeking."[20]

Skills and Knowledge Areas of Traditional Subject Specialists

The traditional subject specialist role has been (and continues to be) a tripartite one: that of bibliographer or collection developer, of reference desk consultant, and of instructor in course-related sessions. With variations of emphasis across institutions, these three roles have become the defining features of liaison librarianship. The competencies needed for these roles have usually been internally (library) determined rather than externally influenced by the larger academy. These roles have evolved into "orthodoxies" with unvarying assumptions about what liaison librarians should value, work toward, and spend time upon. The bibliographer role, for example, depends on strengthening the local collection for a defined constituency (in a defined academic discipline) and being a "full steward" (in Lougee's phrase) on behalf of the library of specific parts of that local collection. The reference desk consultant role grows out of that "full stewardship" role: the interpretive function to assist users in understanding the local collection is placed with the liaison librarian who develops and manages specific parts of the collection and understands its relationship to the overall local collection and the bibliographic apparatus used by the library to provide access to the collection and to resources beyond the collection. The instructor role, like the reference desk consultant role, is often a reactive one: the subject specialist is invited to present to classes of students at the request of faculty on specific resources so that students can complete course-related assignments.

Each of these roles in the tripartite structure has its own orthodoxies that limit the redefinition of the liaison role to advance larger aspirations of the library. For example, how does the subject specialist as "full steward" of parts of the local collection develop that expertise into the diffuse digital, networked environment? Is "full stewardship" even possible in the digital environment with which most faculty and students are now familiar? The orthodoxy of the reference desk consultant role, which depends upon a place-bound view of information resources and services, breaks down with the reality that faculty in most disciplines do not employ the library-as-place and that most students have 24/7 expectations for research assistance. Finally, the bibliographic instructor role has its own orthodoxy: that course-related instruction provides sufficient help to enable students to meet the requirements for an assignment, which can therefore be leveraged by linkages with other "one-shot" presentations. This orthodoxy quickly breaks down in the face of little learning transfer or programmatic development, based on infrequent interactions with students in such classes (and the overall lack of information literacy training, systematically, across the curriculum). Thus the tripartite liaison roles, with their orthodoxies, limit the impact of liaison librarians—whether they have nascent expertise in these areas that can be expanded in a more integrative fashion to become part of the scholarly enterprise cannot be discovered through the inadequacies of the traditional liaison roles.

The skills needed for the traditional liaison or bibliographer role are well known and have been reported on widely in the literature.[21] Even those surveys and studies that report a growing emphasis on outreach and interaction with faculty are still rooted in the fundamentals of collection development and acquiring scholarly content—the golden age of collection development and building the local collection echoes clearly in this legacy role.[22]

Liaison librarians' intellectual roots are clearly located in the bibliographer role, with ancillary roles of reference service, associated instructional roles, and faculty outreach in various forms. The primacy of the bounded local collection has historically also "bounded" the traditional bibliographer within a passive, place-dependent role; this traditional role continues to be reinforced by faculty responses to such surveys as LibQUAL (with cross-institutional findings showing the priority, for faculty, of some elements of the "information control" dimension of that survey), and to locally designed surveys eliciting faculty priorities regarding their libraries.[23]

Several knowledge and skill clusters are apparent in any review of the traditional liaison librarian role:

- *Disciplinary knowledge:* familiarity with the academic disciplines through formal education or through training on the job; understanding of the chief theories, theorists, research methods, scholars, schools of thought, subdisciplines, controversies, and lines of scholarly discourse over time within a discipline
- *Knowledge of information structure and scholarly communication patterns within the discipline:* familiarity with publishing practices, publication channels, formats, and less familiar types of "grey literature"
- *Familiarity with bibliographic and knowledge organization:* understanding of the bibliographic apparatus and intellectual "mapping" of information resources within a local library and understanding of the resources available from major national research libraries such as the Library of Congress and such international networks as OCLC
- *Understanding of the assigned academic departments' curriculum:* familiarity with the content of academic courses and the teaching methods employed by faculty in them and with the accreditation requirements of discipline-specific accrediting agencies

- *Understanding of the research interests, priorities, and publications of faculty* within assigned academic departments
- *Research consultancy expertise:* ability to interact with faculty and students on a range of research projects and informational needs
- *Instructional ability:* most typically, the ability to give a "guest lecture" or presentation to groups of students, at the request of faculty, on specific resources of the library and on any other aspects of the library's collections or services deemed appropriate for a specific assignment or course[24]
- To these clusters of knowledge and skills might be added reading knowledge of appropriate foreign languages, depending on the discipline, knowledge of the collecting emphases of the local library; and some familiarity with the culture of the college or university. These familiar knowledge and skill clusters have, in recent years, been augmented by needed skills in the following areas:
- *Scholarly communication changes:* knowledge of changes in publishing in the digital environment; understanding of vendors and ability to interact with vendors
- *Emerging technologies* and their application in teaching, learning, and research
- *Understanding of demographic changes in both students and faculty,* with attendant implications for changes in information and research habits of those groups
- *Marketing, communication, and public relations*

However, these newer knowledge and skill clusters cannot be grafted onto the traditional liaison roles without a more fundamental consideration of the academic libraries' strategic position within the academy. Too, there are significant workload and priority issues in many academic libraries for liaison librarians as they are asked to take on new responsibilities that transcend their traditional responsibilities. Finally, the values and attitudes of liaison librarians themselves must change. The contemporary environment for academic libraries is a challenging one, given the many options available to students and faculty for research and information. As Anne Kenney has noted in Cornell University Libraries' Strategic Plan for Public Services, "Ensuring

Relevancy: Key Challenges in Public Services, 2006–2010," academic libraries are *not* any of the following:

- center of the information solar system
- starting point for information inquiry
- only trusted kid on the block
- easy to use
- 24/7
- essential to all academic experiences
- as user-centric as we'd like

For Kenney, there are seven key challenges facing academic libraries:

- "Deliver the goods"
- "Focus on points of contact"
- "Invest in knowledge management"
- "Leverage the library as place"
- "Foster strategic partnerships"
- "Prioritize human-intensive work"
- "Utilize measures of success"[25]

These key challenges obviously involve all library staff in every academic library and require changing deeply rooted cultural habits and assumptions, but these challenges can be addressed fundamentally only through enculturation of the subject specialist or liaison librarian cohort within those libraries.

Same Old Song, with a Different Meaning?

In a network age… library space is being reinvented to serve learning and social behaviors. Library collections are diversifying, including not only purchase and licensing of published materials but also the outputs of institutional research and learning, selectively harvested web pages, and other materials. Library expertise is being applied to all aspects the creation, transmission and use of knowledge to support user productivity. And there is a major new focus on developing network services that reach out into the research and learning behaviors of library users.[26]

Are traditional library values clashing with new research methods and needs?

The values and attitudes across liaison librarian generations are increasingly complex, as newer librarians enter the workplace without the perspectives, tacit knowledge, and rich history of more experienced subject specialists. Concomitantly, some experienced subject specialists may be so firmly grounded in the traditional "orthodoxies" of the tripartite role of bibliographer, reference desk consultant, and one-shot lecturer, it is intimidating to imagine new and more integrated ways of contributing their expertise within the larger scholarly enterprise and information flows of academia. As evidenced by various blog commentaries and exchanges, "new" librarians may see the library organization (and hence their colleagues) as hidebound, technophobic, slow to regroup, recharge, and revive—and break ground. Older librarians may perceive the "newbies" as ill-educated in the profession: they don't understand how anyone can be a librarian without the traditional courses of basic reference, cataloging, and collection development. Thus, there can be an internal disconnect within departments as librarian managers try to motivate staff to "take the hill"—and one half of the group thinks the other half of the group doesn't even know what the hill is.

Basic professional values are still core to the work; quality services, sources, and stewardship remain hallmarks. Perhaps resistance to change and clinging to the tried and true are centered more on the librarian's need for organization, stability, and control? It is no secret that academic librarians have been affected by change since the dawn of time (stone vs. papyrus? handwritten vs. typed? open vs. closed? access vs. ownership?); the change is that "The Change" is constant. The literature of academic librarianship is rife with reports, studies, slide shows, blogs, and more on "the change" and what is required, needed, demanded in the modern era. "Traditional" library values, expressed and embodied by liaison librarians, are not lost, ignored, or in transition. The expectations for the librarian, articulated by the library or the institution in which those values are practiced (hopefully) are. Coupled with sense of urgency driven by the academy and burgeoning technologies, change-resistance is not necessarily due to lack of understanding or a lack of faith in the "vision, mission, and goals" of a library. It may be in play due to the librarians' sense that everything old is new again, just faster, glitzier. For example, it may daunting to move from the "one-shot" to the integrated—particularly since most academic librarians are not equipped or trained as instructional designers.

Adding value is as important for today's liaison as adding volumes. But to the change-resistant, the implicit or explicit expectation to add value may also be perceived as a professional slight: aren't *they* valued? Hasn't *their work* been valued? A librarian is told (assigned, expected) to "engage in more 'user-centered' initiatives," when from his or her perspective, he or she has been user-centered throughout his or her career. He or she has been an "ambassador" for the library and its programs and services all along. The change-resistant may also be change-reluctant based on the academy's general tendency to "hurry up and wait." Nimbleness is not necessarily an academic virtue or characteristic. And, to some, it can be disheartening to read such statements as, "Now we have an opportunity to move up the value chain, becoming more valuable by delivering highly customized and targeted services."[27] Haven't they been doing that all along?

Depending on the local institution and the librarian's academic status and credentials, he or she taught subject-based research methods courses (for credit, through a subject department), served on departmental or university committees, and so on. Other common ways the subject librarian developed and fostered the collection was through the faculty lounge or club, faculty researchers in their library offices or study carrels, students referred by faculty to the librarian expert. Standards set and rankings produced by professional associations, regional accrediting bodies, and even state agencies provided many a college or university library mission and goal statement to reach the "gold standard" reflecting institutional intellectual capacity and campus pride through its library's collection subject strengths and volume counts. Incorporated, as needed, into nascent and burgeoning undergraduate "bibliographic instruction" schemes to expose students to myriad materials as types and forms of resource access increased and student populations boomed, subject librarians found themselves, ready or not, expected to teach as well as collect and evaluate resources.

Control, bibliographic and otherwise, shifted into the hands of users, literally and figuratively. Subject silos are breached through interdisciplinary research and teaching. Most academic library users are now distance users (whether they are formally enrolled in a distance ed course or not). On many campuses, physical divisions between computing centers and libraries no longer exist; computing technicians and librarians work side by side in the information commons. Citation management is as important as collection management. Scholars communicate through blogs and open-access journals as well as published "controlled" literature. Librarians are expected to possess technical skills and experience, as well as subject degrees; collection development responsibility now includes Web-based collections, digital collections, keeping up with "Library 2.0" and "Web 4.0" periodical embargoes, and a host of other things too numerous to list as the liaison strives to serve his or her target populations, both seen and unseen.

So, what's new? Haven't liaisons be doing these professional duties and activities (using different subject headings and keywords) for years? The "new" is a combination of an unsettling sense of urgency, heightened professional expectations, and an intense pressure to get directly involved in learning and research. Urgency is driven by a host of changes in the academy (research dollars, straitened library budgets, shifting means and modes of learning, increasing demand for full-text online materials, keeping up with trends, shifting accreditation standards, etc.), new and revolutionary technologies, and the "loss" of the old days, when stability and predictability reigned on campus and in the library. Urgency is also driven by upper management's expectations for deeper, broader, targeted, and focused professional relationships. Based on this, it becomes imperative that upper management set the stage for these deeper professional relationships for liaisons. Liaison librarians don't work in a vacuum: the value placed on the changing expectations is related to the support, vision, and advocacy of library administration. Library administrators are liaisons as well and need to plow the field at their administrative levels so the liaison can plant the seeds and the library, faculty, and students reap the harvest.

Competencies for Liaison Librarians of the Future

The skills needed for future liaison librarians are more wide-ranging than ever. Libraries are facing challenges of relevance (or potential marginalization) in the ambiguous environment of rapidly changing user habits and preferences, the uncertain system of scholarly communication, and the ubiquitous impact of digital content instantly available to all. A recent CLIR report, *No Brief Candle: Reconceiving Research Libraries for the 21st Century,* based on a symposium of academic library administrators, leaders, and teaching faculty, identifies a number of key challenges for academic and research libraries: a risk-averse culture, the need to cocreate new library services with students and faculty, engaging with faculty in digital scholarship and a range of data problems specific to disciplines, identifying libraries' 'competitive advantage' vis-à-vis other information providers, forging new collaborations across institutions, fostering experimentation and reallocating resources to sustain it, and rethinking the library workforce. [28] These intertwined challenges call for far-reaching changes in the cultures, organizational structures, belief systems, self-conceptions, and work practices of many academic librarians—away from individual expertise to collaborative capacities and away from the valorized, perfected "product" of the local collection-and-service model to participation in evolving and emerging research and knowledge-discovery processes at both institutional and transinstitutional levels.

Given their front-line contact with faculty and students, liaison librarians are already facing these challenges of relevance and regard— they are the "public face" of the academic library and are therefore most often looked to by faculty as the key representatives of the library's mission and goals. Liaison librarians are therefore in a key position to articulate, and also to create, a new future for their organizations: one based on taking risks, integrating their collaborative expertise into interdisciplinary and transdisciplinary research projects, and understanding the transformations in scholarly communication, collaborative research, and teaching and learning practices so that their libraries add value at carefully calibrated points as research projects develop and as curricular changes occur across their universities. Kenney has identified the need to "Focus on points of contact" as a key challenge, with outreach as "the key public service."[29] More and more, libraries are asking liaison librarians to focus on adding value through outreach. However, the outreach role cannot be seen as "add-on" to the more traditional roles. Outreach must be woven in as an integral part of the work all liaison librarians do.

Building up the new liaison skill set will require transforming the tripartite structure of bibliographer, reference desk consultant, and occasional course-related instructor; the orthodoxies associated with these three roles must give way to a reconceptualized, more integrated liaison librarian professionalism, one that connects deeply with the scholarship and research, teaching, and outreach missions of colleges and universities.

Competencies for future liaison librarians will need to be organized into the following *transformed* clusters of professional expertise:

- *Enhanced client services:* This will take the traditional, reactive "reference desk" service role into another dimension of knowing the user and collaborating with the user. What is gleaned anecdotally from interactions through reference desk and research consultation interactions will be systematized into ongoing knowledge advisory services for all users through a more detailed and finely grained understanding of user perspectives, needs, habits, and preferences. The client services skill set includes the ability to conduct research studies and to be familiar with appropriate research methodologies in order to understand the clientele more systematically; such studies should be ongoing, conducted *as preparation for* integrating the liaison's expertise within the workflow and research practices of the client base, as discussed by Lorcan Dempsey. In effect, liaison librarians of the future will need to participate in the "upstream" spectrum of research, in its earlier stages. The set of skills needed will include

  - data collection and analysis, standard research methods, and quantitative measures, as well as anthropological research methods

  - creating research tools and integrated research environments for the clientele (information management tools, widgets, research portals, current awareness services placed within client's workflow)

  - working with faculty on research teams: understanding research behaviors and faculty perspectives on all stages of their work; knowing the life cycle of research processes and products in order to contribute at strategic points on these research teams

  - contributing to new digital scholarship initiatives, projects, and process (e-scholarship); connecting with digital humanities centers and other enterprises that create new tools, services, products, and perspectives for scholars

- *Knowledge management:* This large and somewhat ambiguous role moves the liaison librarian beyond local collection development tied to expanding the traditional collections, regardless of formats. Liaison librarians at most institutions will continue to develop collections, of course, but "content development"[30] and knowledge management—creating new layers of usability and positioning the library more integrally within the scholarly communication system—will become much more prominent. As ever more content migrates to digital form; as formats proliferate, blur, blend; as various "open-access" initiatives grow and complicate the scholarly communication landscape; as scholarship and research become more ubiquitous through global connections; and as faculty priorities and time pressures create an even greater need for enterprise-level knowledge management systems at their institutions, liaison librarians are faced with a major challenge in keeping up with the shifting information and research environment.

  Traditional collection development practices, focused on traditional formats and the local bounded collection, are insufficient. Branin has written of the Ohio State University Libraries' experience with knowledge management in creating an enterprise-level infrastructure, with associated policies and practices, for helping a large research university manage its knowledge assets.[31] Many other academic libraries have implemented institutional repositories, digital repositories, data curation projects, e-science and e-scholarship initiatives that all involve the library's taking responsibility for a life-cycle approach to knowledge or research assets. Liaison librarians of the future will need to understand the full range of possibilities associated with such knowledge management initiatives. Liaison librarians will need the following skills to contribute effectively to knowledge management:

  - understanding of, and the ability to articulate, their library's potential contribution to knowledge management, whether in intake of research products into a repository or the policies associated with stewarding, curating, and preserving those research products

- understanding of the scholarly communication process as it manifests itself in the disciplines with which they work and identification of the particular points in that process at which their libraries can optimally position support or expertise

- the ability to monitor emerging research practices of faculty in the academic departments served and to engage in conversations about potential contributions to those research practices

- the ability to monitor the constantly shifting communication patterns and conduits for dissemination of research findings among researchers and scholars (including those based only on Web 2.0 technologies) and to direct attention to these for primarily clientele

- sufficient technical knowledge to collaborate with digital repository library staff or data curation specialists

- knowledge of copyright, intellectual property, and other policy issues affecting the management of institutional (locally produced) scholarly content

- *Teaching and learning expertise:* Liaison librarians have in the past offered episodic "BI" sessions at the request of disciplinary faculty, often limited to explaining the resources needed to complete a particular assignment. This model continues to serve a useful, though limited, purpose—that of helping students tap into a specific set of resources immediately useful to them in a particular course. The "content" of these one-shot sessions is often disconnected, however, from effective teaching and learning practices, becoming, in effect, an inventory of immediately useful databases, resources, and services. The liaison librarian of the future will need to work much more collaboratively with faculty, instructional designers, assessment specialists, and technologists to create, deploy, and assess effective learning environments specific to a discipline. In order to contribute to teaching and learning teams, liaison librarians of the future will need the following skills:

- knowledge of student research and information behaviors (how to develop this knowledge more systematically)
- knowledge of discipline-specific pedagogies
- instructional design and assessment skills
- knowledge of, and experience with, "open" technologies and "open" knowledge environments that promote transformation of pedagogy
- knowledge of emerging teaching and learning practices and curricular models within the academy and how to connect information literacy competencies of students with them

- *Outreach, advocacy, and communication:* This set of abilities has often been honored in theory, but not observed rigorously among liaison librarians. In the future, liaison librarians will require competence in this area that includes both traditional relationship-building skills with faculty and students and also expands into a "nonpositional leadership" role in the library. The liaison librarians' so-called "soft skills" will be crucial in the future: the ability to exercise emotional intelligence in dealing with colleagues from other areas within the library, and understanding their perspectives, while advocating for the library to the academic departments or programs or other constituencies served, will require astute and wise management of self and the ability to think holistically about the mission of the library and its strategic purpose—rather than just serving as ambassador to the assigned departments. Competencies needed include:
  - knowledge of communication style of self and communication styles and patterns of constituents
  - collaborative skills rather than "service mentality" skills in working with faculty
  - ability to communicate at a high level and present oneself positively as representative of the library
  - ability to market oneself strategically to the assigned departments

In addition, a fuller range of advocacy, communication skills, and other "soft skills" for liaison librarians is discussed by Rodwell and Fairbairn. These include the following:

- risk taking
- flexibility and comfort with ambiguity
- networking skills, being able to build coalitions and cultivation of clients and supporters
- relationship or "account management" skills
- negotiation, persuasion, and influencing skills
- reflection on practice and ability to learn and play
- project management skills[32]

Taken together, this set of competencies is crucial in sustaining academic libraries' visibility and relevance and should become part of all liaison librarians' training and education. Most library school curricula, of course, do not focus on these competencies—they are assumed to be an integral part of the individual's personality or attributes that can be developed "on the job" through other forms of staff development. However, this set of "soft skills" is ripe for much more concerted action by professional development programs in the academic library community, to build on the technical skills and deep subject knowledge increasingly called for in the liaison librarian cohort. Building relationships, sustaining them, and instigating new conversations, communities of practice, and collaborations with specific groups of faculty, researchers, and students is essential for other competencies needed for client services, knowledge management, and teaching and learning practices to flourish.

A special point must be made about the thread unifying these enhanced competencies for liaison librarians: they all depend on strong relationship building, a finely attuned sense of timing, positioning of expertise, professional presentation of self, and a collaborative mindset—one that transcends traditional library categories and explanations in order to expand capacities of faculty and students who seek solutions to problems not framed in "library terms." Social skills and a collaborative attitude, rather than some of the traditional library perfectionism and rule-bound strictures, will be the future liaison librarian's entrée into wider and deeper participation in academic programs.

Core Questions for Library Administrators, Supervisors, and Coordinators of Liaison Librarians

The discussion in this chapter of the issues, context, history, and challenges of liaison librarianship raises some central questions for any library administrator to ponder in developing or enhancing a liaison program, in redesigning liaison roles and positions, in reorganizing work of liaisons, and in promoting liaison librarians' expertise throughout the institution. These questions center on values as well as competencies, on the overall mission and strategic directions of the library as well as on functional expertise. The history of liaison librarianship shows a gradual and uneven shift from a place-bound collections-oriented focus, originally rooted in the bibliographer role, to active communication and visibility with traditional academic programs and departments. However, the digital revolution, the networked environment, interdisciplinary research, perpetually connected students, greater focus on learning across the lifespan, and uncertain and permeable professional boundaries mean that libraries and their administrators must grapple with the following "role definition" issues for liaison librarians now, and in the foreseeable future:

- *Subject/discipline-focused role versus project-focused role:* Most liaison librarians or subject specialists are assigned to work, over time, with specific academic departments, schools, or colleges: biology, history, cultural studies, environmental engineering, public policy. The great advantage of this approach is that it allows for specialization and potential matching of previous training, education, and experience of the librarian with the research and scholarship of the faculty and students in the assigned unit. However, many colleges and universities are creating initiatives and projects that span the entire institution: green/sustainability research or initiatives, undergraduate research projects, and various interdisciplinary research clusters. These projects and initiatives may last for one or two years or longer; their hallmark is project- and collaborative-based work across the institution. What can liaison librarian expertise contribute to such initiatives? Thinking outside the traditional academic department "silo" is a challenge for librarians as well as for many faculty, and the ability to match project management skills in one or more liaison librarians for these initiatives will call upon creativity and imagination on the part of library administrators and other supervisors.

- *Audience or clientele:* Library administrators and coordinators of liaison librarians need to reflect on which constituencies and units in the university have no formal connection with the library because they fall in the interstices of the library's own response to the organization of the institution. For example, in addition to subject- or discipline-focused liaisons, librarians could assume liaison responsibilities for student life, university life, disability services, the office of institutional assessment, the center for teaching excellence, the office of global education, and other units. Liaison roles in these cases may not focus on many traditional elements such as collections or reference service, but will instead consist of "intelligence gathering" about the life of the institution in emerging areas.

- *Overlaps between internal library organization and external university strategic directions:* Many traditional liaison librarians have worked and developed their expertise individually, rather than collaboratively, because of their specific departmental, discipline-based assignments. With the advent of interdisciplinary research within and across institutions, the need for liaison librarians to work together in teams is much greater—to be aware of emerging research areas that fall between disciplinary boundaries and to act collaboratively to position the libraries' collective expertise on interdisciplinary research projects at the institutional level. Library administrators face the challenge of fostering a collaborative, team-based, action-oriented culture among liaisons—collective action that transcends occasional coordination among liaisons that is often the norm.

- *Internal knowledge management within academic libraries:* Related to the challenge of interdisciplinarity, research teams in the sciences (and other disciplinary clusters) among faculty, and potentially parallel teams of liaison librarians, are emerging. This is particularly true at larger research institutions with multiple libraries, geographically dispersed, but is true in any library organization of any size. How can the expertise and tacit knowledge of expert liaison librarians be best employed in mentoring or training younger liaison librarians? Conversely, how can the newer skill sets of more technologically oriented librarians, trained in a different era, be used to expand the expertise of an older generation? While it is possible to over-simplify these intergenerational dichotomies, the main point is that tacit knowledge among liaison librarians, of whatever generation or background, is not usually captured and made useable for others in a way that advances the organization. Library administrators will need to consider this "knowledge management" problem in order to sustain momentum in a constantly changing environment for libraries and for the academy. Strong mentoring relationships, rather than explicit training, are probably best suited to address the challenge of tacit knowledge and expertise among liaison librarians—hearing stories of successes and failures, observing colleagues in action, and absorbing the process, over time, of relationship building with faculty and students.

- *The meaning of "outreach" or "engagement":* The final crucial decision element for reconfiguring the work of liaison librarians is to reflect on what these words mean in practice. Most academic library administrators believe in the outreach role of their liaison librarians—that is, they want their liaisons to be the library's advocacy network for promoting the collections, services, and expertise of the library and making the library's services highly visible on campus. However, the interest among university administrators in forging closer bonds with constituencies in their communities, cities, localities, states, and regions means that liaison librarians have, potentially, an expansive "community engagement" role that transcends outreach to academic departments. Liaison librarians can become familiar with the information challenges and research needs of other cultural institutions such as museums, historical societies, and other community organizations in order to form partnerships that integrate the resources of the university into the life of the community, and vice versa. Similarly, the loyalties of alumni in the community (and beyond) are now much an issue for university administrators (for fund-raising, obviously, but also for building institutional capacity and prestige over time); this potential link with alumni as ongoing clientele is another important facet of "community engagement" that offers the academic library, through the communication of the liaison librarian (and development/advancement officers), an expansive, intergenerational cohort of supporters.

Recommendations for the Future Education and Training of Liaison Librarians

For academic libraries to flourish, they must become more expert, agile, and well positioned. These attributes will not develop spontaneously, but only through astute recruitment of, or development of, talented, innovative, risk-taking staff with a "research-and-development" mind-set who are attuned to the large changes sweeping higher education rather than just to their particular functional roles. The new liaison librarian must become an integral partner with faculty in the research, teaching, and learning agendas through complementary expertise. To develop these partnerships, liaison librarians will need disciplinary knowledge and a grasp of information structure as in the past, but will need to recast that knowledge and expertise in more immediately visible, available, and useful ways.

Recent environmental scans in the academic library profession show the increasing need for expertise in a digital environment, with uncertain disciplinary boundaries (a challenge to traditional subject specialists), technology-mediated services, and ambiguous and overlapping areas of responsibility. A comparison of the 2007 ACRL Top Ten Assumptions[33] with the 2002 ACRL Top Issues[34] illustrates recent professional concerns and the accelerating emphasis on expertise; information technology; customer-centric, business-oriented approaches; and accountability.

By aligning 2007's top ten assumptions with 2002's top issues, it is interesting to note that "the role of the library in academic enterprise" does not appear in the 2007 list. This does not imply inaction or invisibility; it illustrates that the role of the library in the academic enterprise is the overarching topic, with recruitment, education, and retention of librarians and their evolving skill sets as the "top" elements. People first. As T. Scott says in a recent blog posting, "Frankly, my dears, I don't give a damn if the 'library' is successful. But I will make sure that this organization of talented, dedicated *people* is."[35]

TABLE 5.1
2002 ACRL Top Issues and 2007 ACRL Top Ten Assumptions

2002 ACRL Top Issues		2007 ACRL Top Ten Assumptions	
Rank	*Element*	*Rank*	*Element*
1.	Recruitment, education, and retention of librarians	1.	Increased emphasis on digitizing collections, preserving digital archives, and improving methods of data storage and retrieval.
2.	Role of library in academic enterprise	2.	The skill set for librarians will continue to evolve in response to the needs and expectations of the changing populations (students and faculty) that they serve.
3.	Impact of information technology on library services	3.	Students and faculty will increasingly demand faster and greater access to services.
4.	Creation, control, and preservation of digital resources	4.	Debates about intellectual property will become increasingly common in higher education.
5.	Chaos in scholarly communication	5.	The demand for technology-related services will grow and require additional funding.
6.	Support of new users	6.	Higher education will increasingly view the institution as a business.
7.	Higher education funding	7.	Students will increasingly view themselves as customers and consumers, expecting high-quality facilities and services
		8.	Distance learning will be an increasingly more common option in higher education, and will coexist but not threaten the traditional bricks-and-mortar model.
		9.	Free public access to information stemming from publicly funded research will continue to grow.
		10.	Privacy will continue to be an important issue in librarianship.

	TABLE 5.2	
	2007 ACRL Top Ten Assumptions aligned with 2002 ACRL Top Issues	
2002: ACRL Top Issues		**2007 ACRL Top Ten Assumptions**
Rank	*Element*	*Element*
1.	Recruitment, education, and retention of librarians	• The skill set for librarians will continue to evolve in response to the needs and expectations of the changing populations (students and faculty) that they serve.
2.	Role of library in academic enterprise	
3.	Impact of information technology on library services	• Students and faculty will increasingly demand faster and greater access to services. • Distance learning will be an increasingly more common option in higher education, and will coexist but not threaten the traditional bricks-and-mortar model. • Privacy will continue to be an important issue in librarianship.
4.	Creation, control, and preservation of digital resources	• Increased emphasis on digitizing collections, preserving digital archives, and improving methods of data storage and retrieval.
5.	Chaos in scholarly communication	• Debates about intellectual property will become increasingly common in higher education. • Free public access to information stemming from publicly funded research will continue to grow.
6.	Support of new users	• Students will increasingly view themselves as customers and consumers, expecting high-quality facilities and services.
7.	Higher education funding	• Higher education will increasingly view the institution as a business. • The demand for technology-related services will grow and require additional funding.

Given the emerging consensus with academic librarianship about the very large challenges of recruiting new professionals and reorienting those already in the profession toward a more integrative role in the academic enterprise, a wide-ranging agenda for educating "the new liaison librarian" needs to become a priority. Liaison librarians of the future will be best educated, trained, and re-acculturated in the following ways:

1. Separate courses in library school curricula on the role of the "new generation" liaison librarian or subject specialist, integrating perspectives on higher education, changes in users, technological impacts, collaborations with faculty, and line leadership skills. Such courses must transcend the traditional knowledge imparted through courses in reference, collection development, instruction, and management.

2. Courses, practicums, or other vehicles for training in project management, presentation skills, instructional design skills, persuasion, and advocacy skills.

3. Focused, work-related training, where appropriate, in instructional/information technology skills that will enable greater productivity and collaborative capacities with faculty and students.

4. In-house continuing education programs featuring outreach and "positioning" strategies for liaison librarians and a range of in-house seminars on digital initiatives, copyright and intellectual property, knowledge management, disciplinary research, and interdisciplinary research clusters.

5. Summer or annual institutes, already well known in other areas of specialization such as information literacy, scholarly communication, or leadership. Such institutes afford another opportunity to re-educate liaison librarians in the competencies identified in this chapter, while also leveraging the existing expertise of many liaison librarians with their colleagues at their home institutions.

6. A repository of best practices, training materials, and curriculum materials for re-educating liaison librarians in the new competencies, developed by consortia and/or library associations such as the Association of College and Research Libraries. Such materials can be adapted for local staff development

needs. Multi- and interinstitutional continuing education for liaison librarians will become more important as libraries grapple with the very large issues of the data deluge, the globally connected research community, and the ambiguities of roles among librarians, information technologists, and faculty engaged in new forms of scholarship.

7. Acculturation into "research teams" at local institutions through new reward structures co-created by deans of libraries and their counterparts among academic deans that will add an experiential dimension for liaison librarians in learning new roles. Individual liaison librarians who find such opportunities to participate in such research teams should of course be supported strongly, but a library-wide cultural shift will be sustained only through intentional, programmatic leadership from library administration collaborating with other leaders across campus in order to afford librarians this deeper participatory role.

8. Related to item 5 above, a particular focus on e-science, cyberinfrastructure, and digital humanities. This focus will need to become part of the professional re-education of traditional liaison librarians. The Association of Research Libraries formed a Joint Task Force on Library Support for E-Science, which issued a report in 2007; one of its chief recommendations concerns libraries' human capacities to support e-science, with a call for "a library workforce with relevant new skills and knowledge about emergent forms of documentation and research dissemination" in support team science and associated endeavors.[36] In the humanities, interinstitutional initiatives underway, such as Project Bamboo, offer opportunities for liaison librarians to contribute their particular perspective on digital scholarship in its "upstream" manifestation and to engage in collective action across institutions to advance new forms of humanities research and scholarship.[37]

9. Redesigning a number of liaison positions in each library to focus on new roles rather than on competencies (however transformed) connected to the more traditional library functions of collec-

tion development, reference service, or instruction. Such positions should focus on outreach to new constituencies (new users, student services), or on research-and-development projects and initiatives identified as ongoing (digital products and services, the overall user perception or experience of the library). Each library's liaison librarian cohort will benefit from this internal "re-acculturation" that expands the boundaries of professional discussion and places innovation in the service of new or nontraditional library users (or those who don't use library services at all).

10. An active support network of liaison librarian mentors available virtually and at conferences. What is well known in the library profession (as in others) is that the rich tacit knowledge of expert practitioners is rarely articulated or made explicitly useful to beginners. Professional library associations and library consortia could develop and promote such mentoring networks to showcase best practices for engagement with faculty and to create sustainable interinstitutional collaborations among liaison librarians facing similar challenges at home.

11. Strong institutional support for liaison librarian participation in disciplinary   conferences outside librarianship. Collaborative research between librarians and faculty partners should be presented at such conferences.

Conclusion

The time is ripe for academic and research libraries to redefine the roles of liaison librarians, whatever they may be called at local institutions. The very future of libraries depends on the visibility, leadership, political acumen, subject expertise, grounded experience, and social skills of these professionals. They are a crucial cohort of librarians in forging a vital future at the crossroads where communities of researchers, digital technologies, proliferating forms of scholarship, and the possibilities for institution-wide collaboration all meet. The new competencies for liaison librarians will, among much else, assist their own libraries in developing a keen sense of possible futures, created through greater sensitivity to the myriad facets of the academic enterprise. The recent Ithaka Report, "Studies of Key Stakeholders in the Digital Transformation of Higher Education," notes:

Libraries… could be well served to engage in local intelligence-gathering to better understand how their faculty, students, and administrators use and perceive the library and its services. Information gleaned in this process may suggest otherwise unconsidered changes which could greatly improve user satisfaction, identify initiatives which are liable to be particularly controversial, and more… [b]y understanding the needs and research habits of scholars in different disciplines, libraries can identify products and services which would be appreciated by and of use to these scholars. Such efforts to be involved in the research process offer benefits to scholars, by providing them with services to improve their efficiency and effectiveness, as well as to libraries, recapturing the attention of scholars and contributing to a general awareness of and respect of the library's contributions.[38]

The intelligence gathering possible through liaison librarians makes them the "eyes and ears" of their organizations in creating organizational intelligence and new strategic directions. Such intelligence gathering arises through assertiveness, positioning and political skills, knowing the clientele, creativity, and an innovative, risk-taking spirit. Liaison librarians of the future will help envision and create new futures for libraries and all of their collaborators.

Notes

1. T. Scott, "What Do You Call 'Success'?" T. Scott blog, Jan. 5, 2007, http://tscott.typepad.com/tsp/2007/01/what_do_you_cal.html (accessed Dec. 11, 2008).
2. Jerry Campbell, "Changing a Cultural Icon: The Academic Library as a Virtual Destination," *Educause Review* 41, no. 1 (Jan./Feb. 2006): 16–31. Lyman Ross and Pongracz Sennyey, "The Library is Dead, Long Live the Library! The Practice of Academic Librarianship and the Digital Revolution," *Journal of Academic Librarianship* 34, no. 2 (March 2008) 145–152.
3. John Rodwell and Linden Fairbairn, "Dangerous Liaisons? Defining the Faculty Liaison Librarian Service Model, Its Effectiveness and Sustainability," in "Change Management in Academic Libraries—2," special issue, *Library Management* 29, no. 1/2 (2008): 116–124, available at http://ses.library.usyd.edu.au/handle/2123/1898.
4. Wendy Pradt Lougee, *Diffuse Libraries: Emergent Roles for the Research Library in the Digital Age* (Washington, DC: Council on Library and Information Resources, 2002), 4.
5. Donald G. Frank and Elizabeth Howell, "New Realities, New Relationships:

New Relationships in Academe: Opportunities for Vitality and Relevance," *College & Research Libraries News* 61, no. 1 (Jan. 2003), www.ala.org/ala/mgrps/divs/acrl/publications/crlnews/2003/jan/newrelationships.cfm (accessed Sept. 17, 2008).

6. Georgina Hardy and Sheila Corrall, "Revisiting the Subject Librarian: A Study of English, Law and Chemistry," *Journal of Librarianship and Information Science* 39, no. 2 (June 2007): 80.

7. Lauren Matacio, "Library Liaison Programs in the 21st Century" (paper presented at the 22nd annual conference of the Association of Seventh-Day Adventist Librarians. Libertador San Martin, Entre Rios, Argentina, June 30, 2002), www.asdal.org/minutes/matacioliaison.html.

8. Lorcan Dempsey, "Library Services." Lorcan Dempsey's weblog, Oct. 4, 2007, http://orweblog.oclc.org/archives/001444.html (accessed Sept. 17, 2008).

9. See, for example, Tom Glynn and Connie Wu, "New Roles and Opportunities for Academic Library Liaisons: A Survey and Recommendations," *Reference Services Review* 31, no. 2 (2003): 122–128; John N. Ochola, and Phillip J. Jones, "Assessment of the Liaison Program at Baylor University," *Collection Management* 26, no. 4 (2002): 29-41; Cynthia C. Ryans, Raghini S. Suresh, and Wei-Ping Shang, "Assessing an Academic Library Liaison Programme," *Library Review* 44, no. 1 (1995): 14–23; Frada Mozenter, Bridgette T. Sanders, and Jeanie M. Welch, "Restructuring a Liaison Program in an Academic Library," *College & Research Libraries* 61, no. 5 (Sept. 2000): 432–440; Carla A. Hendrix "Developing a Liaison Program in a New Organizational Structure: A Work in Progress," *Reference Librarian* 32, no. 67 & 68 (2001): 203–224; Raghini Suresh, Cynthia C. Ryans, and Wei-Ping Zhang. "The Library-Faculty Connection: Starting a Liaison Programme in an Academic Setting," *Library Review* 44, no. 1 (1995): 7–13; M. R. Tennant et al., "Customizing for Clients: Developing a Library Liaison Program from Need to Plan," *Bulletin of the Medical Library Association* 89, no. 1 (Jan. 2001): 8–20; Zheng Le (Lan) Yang, "University Faculty Perception of a Library Liaison Program: A Case Study," *Journal of Academic Librarianship* 26, no. 2 (March 2000): 124–128.

10. Liaison with Users Committee, Collection Development and Evaluation Section, Reference and User Services Association, "Guidelines for liaison work in managing collections and services," American Library Association, 1992, rev. June 2001, www.ala.org/ala/mgrps/divs/rusa/resources/guidelines/guidelinesliaison.cfm (accessed Sept. 16, 2008).

11. Dan Hazen, "Twilight of the Gods? Bibliographers in the Electronic Age," *Library Trends* 48, no. 4 (Spring 2000): 821–841.

12. David Shumaker and Laura Ann Tyler, "Embedded Library Services: An Initial Inquiry into Practices for Their Development, Management and Delivery" (paper presented at the Special Libraries Association Annual Conference, Denver, CO. June 6, 2007), 21.

13. Jane E. Schillie, Virginia E. Young, Susan A. Ariew, Ellen M. Krupar, and Margaret C. Merrill, "Outreach through the College Librarian Program at Virginia Tech," *Reference Librarian* 34, no. 71 (2001): 71.

14. Brenda L. Johnson and Laurie A. Alexander, "An Innovative Role Puts Academic Librarians Right in the Departments They Serve," *Library Journal* 132, no. 2 (Feb. 1, 2007), www.libraryjournal.com/article/CA6407750.html (accessed Sept. 15, 2008).

15. Lisa Allen, "Hybrid Librarians in the 21st Century Library: A Collaborative Service-Staffing Model," in *ACRL 13th National Conference Proceedings,* ed. Hugh A. Thompson (Chicago: ACRL, 2007): 292.
16. Ibid., 293.
17. Steven J. Bell and John Shank, "The Blended Librarian: A Blueprint for Redefining the Teaching and Learning Role of Academic Librarians," *College & Research Libraries News* 65, no. 7 (July 2004): 372–375.
18. David Shumaker, "Embedded Librarians Seize the Initiative," The Embedded Librarian, Feb. 16, 2008, http://embeddedlibrarian.wordpress.com/2008/02/16/embedded-librarians-seize-the-initiative. (accessed Sept. 17, 2008).
19. F. W. Lancaster and L. C. Smith, "Science, Scholarship and the Communication of Knowledge," *Library Trends* 27 (Winter 1979): 370.
20. Mary Lynn Rice-Lively and J. Drew Racine, "The Role of Academic Librarians in the Era of Information Technology," *Journal of Academic Librarianship* 23, no. 1 (Jan. 1997): 37.
21. Hazen, "Twilight of the Gods?"; Edward Shreeves, "Selectors, Subject Knowledge, and Digital Collections," *Journal of Library Administration* 39, no. 4 (2003, appearing in spring 2004), also appearing simultaneously in *Improved Access to Information: Portals, Content Selection and Digital Information,* edited by Sul Lee (Binghamton, NY: Haworth Press, 2003); Glynn and Wu, "New Roles and Opportunities."
22. Hazen, "Twilight of the Gods?".
23. Zheng Le (Lan) Yang, "University Faculty Perception of a Library Liaison Program: A Case Study," *Journal of Academic Librarianship* 26, no. 2 (March 2000): 124–128.
24. Hazen, "Twilight of the Gods?"
25. Anne Kenney, "Ensuring Relevancy: Key Challenges in Public Services, 2006–2010" (presentation to Cornell University Libraries' Academic Assembly, Feb. 2, 2006), www.library.cornell.edu/insidecul/200602/PublicServices.html.
26. Dempsey, "Library Services."
27. David Shumaker, "Dangerous Liaisons?" An Article Worth Reading," The Embedded Librarian, March 5, 2008, http://embeddedlibrarian.wordpress.com/2008/03/05/dangerous-liaisons-an-article-worth-reading (accessed Sept. 17, 2008).
28. *No Brief Candle: Reconceiving Research Libraries for the 21st Century,* CLIR Publication No. 142 (Washington, DC: Council on Library and Information Resources, August 2008) www.clir.org/pubs/reports/pub142/contents.html (accessed Dec. 1, 2008).
29. Kenney, "Ensuring Relevancy."
30. Shreeves, "Selectors."
31. Joseph J. Branin, "Knowledge Management in Academic Libraries: Building the Knowledge Bank at the Ohio State University," *Journal of Library Administration* 39, no. 4 (2004): 41–56.
32. Rodwell and Fairbairn, "Dangerous Liaisons."
33. James L. Mullins, Frank R. Allen, and Jon R. Hufford, "Top Ten Assumptions for the Future of Academic Libraries and Librarians: A Report from the ACRL Research Committee," *College & Research Libraries News* 68, no. 4 (April 2007): 240–246.
34. W. Lee Hisle, "Top Issues Facing Academic Libraries: A Report of the Focus

on the Future Task Force," *College & Research Libraries News* 63, no. 10 (Nov. 2002): 714-15,30.

35. Scott. "What Do You Call 'Success'?"

36. Joint Task Force on Library Support for E-Science, "Agenda for Developing E-Science in Research Libraries," Association of Research Libraries, Nov. 2007, available at: www.arl.org/bm-doc/ARL_EScience_final.pdf (accessed Dec. 1, 2008).

37. Project Bamboo website, http://projectbamboo.uchicago.edu (accessed Dec. 1, 2008).

38. Ross Housewright and Roger Schonfield, "Ithaka's 2006 Studies of Key Stakeholders in the Digital Transformation of Higher Education," August 18, 2008, http://www.ithaka.org/ithaka-s-r/research/Ithakas%202006%20Studies%20 of%20Key%20Stakeholders%20in%20the%20Digital%20Transformation%20 in%20Higher%20Education.pdf (accessed Dec. 3, 2008).

CHAPTER 6

PREPARING OUR LIBRARIANS FOR THE FUTURE

IDENTIFYING AND ASSESSING CORE COMPETENCIES AT THE UNIVERSITY OF MINNESOTA LIBRARIES

Stephanie H. Crowe and Janice M. Jaguszewski
University of Minnesota

Library leaders have been discussing the changing nature of our profession for some time now,[1] but it is only recently that the widespread adoption of numerous technological advances and the "emergence of open/collaborative models"[2] have presented academic librarians with a wide range of new opportunities. With fewer in-person reference transactions and more automated approval plans for collection development, less emphasis is now placed on traditional librarian roles. Instead, there is an increasing need for "blended" or versatile librarians who collaborate with faculty to actively contribute to an institution's research and instructional mission. For example, new models of scientific research, often referred to as "e-science," offer opportunities for creating virtual communities by discipline, shaping new modes of scientific communication, and preserving and serving up large data sets.[3] In addition, the movement away from "one-shot" instructional sessions and toward a more holistic approach of integrating information literacy into the curriculum requires increased collaboration with faculty in developing assignments and creating online tutorials and digital learning objects. In general, academic librarians now need to possess a higher level of technical expertise as well as an understanding of a whole host of emerging issues, from new models of scholarly publication, to data curation, to learning theory and instructional design. It has become clear that what librarians do and the skills they possess must change in order for us to remain relevant to our faculty and students. We must align our roles and responsibilities with the goals and mission of our institutions. As Andrew Dillon notes, "The future of academic libraries will be determined by the extent to which they amplify the mission of their host institutions... Libraries must enable and accelerate learning and discovery."[4]

In 2004, the University of Minnesota began a strategic positioning process that culminated in a final report in 2007.[5] This three-year planning process resulted in the university's goal to become one of the top three public research universities in the world, emphasizing collaborative, interdisciplinary research; new modes of scholarship; student learning communities; a new undergraduate writing curriculum; and a greater role in civic engagement. The libraries participated in several aspects of this planning process and read and evaluated task force reports as they were written to consider how we could support the university's new mission and vision.

At the same time, the University of Minnesota Libraries began the process of transforming the role of our subject and reference librarians to reflect this changing environment. We conducted a number of focus groups, interviews, and surveys to better understand the needs of our undergraduate and graduate students and to further define ways in which the libraries could support research in the humanities and social sciences[6] and the sciences.[7] These assessments were useful in two ways: we learned a great deal about user needs and were able to identify new ways to meet these needs, and the assessments themselves served to model new roles for our librarians. The assessment process emphasized the need for us to move from a traditionally passive role in which the user typically initiates contact through reference questions and collection requests, to an increasingly active role in which we continuously seek to identify new needs and then collaborate to develop customized solutions. The process helped us not only to learn that researchers needed help in areas such as keeping current in their fields and managing the primary research materials that they collect, but also that the libraries had a responsibility to assist the liaison librarians and the entire library staff through a period of considerable change. To do this, the libraries focused on defining responsibilities, clarifying expectations, and supporting liaison librarians throughout this transition from a more passive supportive role to an active partnering role.

In this chapter, we share the libraries' process, the documents that were developed, and the results of a staff assessment that we conducted to identify any gaps between the skills that librarians need in the near future and the skills that they currently possess. The libraries' goals were to develop a framework for liaison positions that aligns with the mission and vision of our university and with trends in higher education overall, and to assist our librarians through a period of tremendous change in the profession.

Restructuring

Prior to 2003, the University of Minnesota Libraries was a team-based organization in which collection development and management (CDM) and reference and consultative services (RCS) were separate teams. Some librarians were strictly "bibliographers" who reported through CDM, some were strictly "reference librarians" who reported through RCS, and some had blended roles and were arbitrarily assigned to one team or the other. In addition, we had a user education coordinator, but librarians who offered instruction did not report to this coordinator and instead reported through either CDM or RCS, a reporting structure that diluted her authority and effectiveness.

In 2003, the University of Minnesota Libraries formed a new division entitled Academic Programs (AP), which was an explicit merger of collections, reference, and instructional responsibilities. The name "Academic Programs" was chosen to emphasize the libraries' role in developing partnerships with academic departments on campus and stressed the importance of working with students and faculty to develop new tools and services. For some staff in broad subject areas in which reference librarians and bibliographers had traditionally been separate positions, the merger took time and required a clearer articulation of the new, blended roles. For all staff, the idea that librarians not only supported departments but also developed partnerships with them was a new and not necessarily comfortable concept. Many librarians were not certain about what it meant to be a partner. They were hesitant to initiate conversations that did not revolve around collection needs or reference questions and unsure of methods to identify new needs in their user communities and ways to address them. Ultimately, the libraries wanted to help the liaison librarians thrive in an environment of ambiguity, of constantly changing user needs.

An Associate University Librarian (AUL) for Academic Programs was hired in fall 2004, and in the fall of 2005, the AP division began a planning process to clarify these roles and better define the expectations of liaison librarians in the division, moving the emphasis away from reference desks and collection activities toward an active liaison model that required initiative, comfort with ambiguity, and an ability to form collaborative relationships with our user communities. In addition, the process sought to restructure the division to address an imbalance in the size of departments within the division and to regulate system-wide activities such as e-mail and chat reference services, information literacy, learning spaces, and the development of online tools.

As a result, one new department was formed, and the humanities and social sciences were divided, resulting in six departments: Coordinated Educational Services, Arts and Humanities, Social Sciences and Professional Programs, Archives and Special Collections, Physical Sciences and Engineering, and Agricultural, Biological and Environmental Sciences. Directors were appointed to lead each department.

Redefining Professional Expectations and Position Descriptions

A set of general professional expectations that are considered essential for successful job performance was developed. These expectations included anticipating and responding to the changing needs of users, leading from within, being flexible and adaptable, and thriving in a collaborative environment. A complete list of these professional expectations is provided in Appendix A.

In addition, a new framework for librarians' position descriptions was drafted. The overarching role for almost all AP librarians was defined as liaison to academic departments. The framework includes examples of what constitutes good interaction with faculty and students and goes on to address traditional roles, such as collections and reference work, as well as newer roles such as participation in issues of scholarly communication and the development of new online learning and digital tools. The emphasis for liaisons is currently on assigned departments, but the libraries are now considering explicitly including research centers and institutes and addressing the need for liaisons to work across disciplines to better support interdisciplinary research. The entire position description framework, as well as an introduction for staff about how it is a living document that will change over time, is included in Appendix B.

Both the professional expectations and the position description framework served to facilitate a better understanding of responsibilities and to ensure more consistency across the division. However, it should be noted that while both documents focused on what the libraries needed and expected of our librarians, the AP directors acknowledged that not everyone yet had the knowledge, skills, and abilities (KSAs) to carry out their new responsibilities. These KSAs, or job competencies, included both task-based requirements for carrying out individual responsibilities, such as the ability to conduct a needs assessment, and softer skills, such as responding to changing needs and aligning individual goals with larger institutional goals.

Developing a KSA Assessment

It therefore became important for the AP division directors to accomplish two goals: to create an atmosphere in which librarians were fully informed of the responsibilities of their newly structured positions, and to support librarians' professional development in areas in which they were less skilled or comfortable. To meet these goals, the AUL for the AP division brought in an ARL Academy Fellow, who worked with an AP department director, to spearhead the creation and administration of a self-assessment of the current knowledge, skills, and abilities of all AP librarians.[8]

It was our intention to use this assessment to analyze the gaps in desired competencies among AP division librarians and provide a focus for a professional development program and future hiring goals. Just as useful, we hoped that current AP librarians, simply by taking the assessment, would become more fully aware of the KSAs that the administration believed to be vital for the future success of the division.

We began this project by using the libraries' newly created position description framework to delineate the desired categories for the

KSAs. We added several additional broader areas of importance, and then used a detailed, multistep process—scans of the existing literature, discussions with staff who possess expertise in each category, interviews with current practitioners, and suggestions from a group of AP directors—to create a draft list of KSAs for the assessment.

KSA categories and sample statements follow. For the entire assessment, please see Appendix C.

- Teaching and Learning
  - Understand and apply principles of learning theory.
- Reference and Research Services
  - Collaborate/partner with the user in the information-seeking process.
- Collections Management
  - Look for collaborative ways to accomplish collections goals.
- Liaison/Relationship Building/Communications
  - Participate in the development of new tools and services in response to user needs.
- Archives and Special Collections
  - Understand the nature and purpose of primary research and the significance of original artifacts.
- Technology
  - Demonstrate the value of technological tools to users and colleagues.
- Scholarly Communication
  - Advocate for sustainable models of scholarly communication.
- Leadership
  - Understand and apply program management skills.
- Professional
  - Know the basics of using statistics and understand their misuse.

We decided to structure the assessment using a method that we felt would best analyze gaps in competencies: for each section of KSAs, we created a matrix of multiple-choice statements, each of which required the respondents to rate their perceived current level of competency. The options were as follows:

- Basic or less
- Basic or less, but need to know more
- Intermediate
- Intermediate, but need to know more
- Advanced
- N/A

Respondents were also given the opportunity, at the end of each category, to add in a comment field any KSAs that they felt had not been covered or emphasized sufficiently.

In creating this assessment, we did not intend to produce a statistically valid tool. Rather, we believed that the best method would be to create the means for addressing both where librarians believed their current skill levels to be and where they felt they did or did not need to know more. This method allowed us to identify the division's actual gaps, and it helped us to identify the KSAs that respondents believed were important (or unimportant) to their positions and to the division.

The assessment, which we created and administered online using a service called SurveyMonkey (www.surveymonkey.com), was piloted with a group of five volunteer pretesters (all AP division librarians from various departments). The pretesters' critiques and suggestions were considered in the final version of the assessment.

The final assessment was administered to all AP librarians and archivists, a group of 53 individuals. We received a response rate of 65% At the beginning of the assessment, respondents were asked to identify their department, and department directors received the results for their department as well as for the AP division as a whole. However, aside from department identification, the assessment results were anonymous.

Each department director discussed the results with the librarians in his or her department, providing insight, responding to concerns, and seeking feedback on the results. The feedback received from each department was brought back to a meeting of all AP directors. The data that we received from the assessment responses, along with the verbal feedback that we received from division librarians, proved to be quite useful. First, AP directors were able to work with individual librarians to set professional development goals for the coming year. Second, the directors worked with the AUL to build a staff development program that focused on specific identified needs. And third, the program directors and AUL considered which skills could not easily be developed within and across staff (for example, instructional design and computer programming) and should be built into new positions as they became available.

In general, respondents appeared to be honest in their self-assessments. If anything, respondents tended to be overly self-critical when evaluating their knowledge, skills, and abilities. In at least one department's follow-up discussion, several librarians indicated that they checked "advanced" very rarely because they believed that they always had more to learn in almost every area.

From the aggregate data that we received in the results, we were able to identify some overarching needs. Throughout the assessment, it was clear that many librarians felt they needed to improve their knowledge of and skill in various technologies, or at least to improve their ability to maintain an awareness of new technologies in all aspects of their jobs. For instance, many librarians responded "Basic or less, but need to know more" for "Understand and effectively incorporate instructional technologies (e.g., online tutorials) into instruction." Assessment was another broad topic in which respondents repeatedly indicated a need for further education, with, for example, many responding "Basic or less, but need to know more" for both performing a user needs assessment and analyzing its data. Finally, scholarly communication and teaching and learning (i.e., information literacy) were two categories in which we identified some professional education needs based on the results of the assessment. However, it should be noted that the needs identified in the information literacy category may have lessened somewhat after the assessment was administered due to a series of information literacy workshops offered soon after individuals took the assessment.

Results also indicated some other specific educational needs. In the area of leadership, respondents felt that they needed improvement in both project and program management and, more generally, in leading from within (rather than simply leading when assigned a traditional leadership role). The data also identified a gap in the understanding of the relevance of archives and special collections to other areas of librarianship. Finally, librarians responded that they needed to know more about identifying grant opportunities, grant writing, using statistics and understanding their misuse, creating effective professional presentations, writing for publication, and presenting information or data in an understandable format.

The assessment also allowed us to identify areas in which our librarians already viewed themselves as competent. One of these areas was collections management, although many librarians indicated that they needed training in understanding and evaluating license agreements and in generating collections reports to guide selection. In addition, AP librarians were fairly confident in the reference and research category, particularly when responding to questions about specific knowledge and skills. Many felt less confident in broader or less traditional areas, such as "understanding the broad universe of information in order to create content and tools that anticipate and respond to questions without mediation" and "contributing to the development and refinement of existing tools." Likewise, many felt that they needed some training in keeping current with new information resources, a result that may point to the rapidly increasing numbers of available resources and formats.

Other KSAs for which a significant portion of respondents rated themselves as advanced included the following:

- "Respond to changing needs by taking on short-term responsibilities that move the Libraries forward"
- "As a group member, contribute actively and constructively to help the group achieve its goals"
- "Identify and take advantage of opportunities for professional growth and development"
- "Develop collaborative relationships within the library profession"
- "Work comfortably in a multicultural environment"
- "Communicate effectively with diverse groups, including those whose first language is not English"

As the first step in addressing the division's apparent gaps in knowledge, skills, and abilities, a list of professional education goals was added to the AP division's overall goals for the 2008–2009 fiscal year. These goals were explicitly based on the perceived gaps from the KSA assessment results and included development of the following offerings:

leadership and leading from within; development, donor relationships, and grant-seeking; integration of archives and special collections into research, teaching, and learning; and training in collections management selection tools. It also included the goals of continuing professional education offerings for staff in information literacy and scholarly communication. AP directors then worked with individuals to incorporate these professional development opportunities into their personal goals.

In summary, our process may be reflected as shown in figure 6.1.

FIGURE 6.1
Summary of KSA Process

Restructured Division → Developed Professional Expectations →

Redefined Position Descriptions → Conducted KSA Assessment →

Included Training Needs in Division Goals → Considered Skills Needed for Future Hires

---

Summary

Ultimately, this KSA project will be part of a continuum of efforts to position University of Minnesota Libraries' staff for the future of academic librarianship, as it supports and aligns with the mission and vision of the university overall. The libraries will keep these needs in mind as we hire new liaisons and rethink open positions, particularly relevant since a retirement incentive will result in a large number of new openings in the coming year. Positions will be reconsidered in light of new emphases at the university, including new directions in e-science, scholarly communication, and information literacy. The required qualifications for these positions will reflect the new knowledge, skills, and abilities needed to support these responsibilities, and we will continue to address the needs of current staff as we develop our professional education offerings.

Conducting a division-wide self-assessment at this time in our profession has presented us with both challenges and opportunities. We believe that we captured a snapshot of the current needs of the AP division, and we further think that the KSAs we listed identify many of the current and developing areas of importance within academic librarianship. However, the changing nature of librarianship and higher education today means that some of our identified KSAs could become much less significant in the near future, while at the same time new competencies will become important. For instance, as we began administering the assessment, an ARL task force published a report on e-science, detailing the ways in which research libraries should become important players in the increasing role of e-science in the scholarly community.[9] Although we referenced topics related to this field in the assessment (data curation, for instance, as it relates to our University Digital Conservancy), we did not mention e-science by name or refer to other aspects of this developing field. This experience supports an assumption about our future that was discussed recently in the ACRL *Environmental Scan 2007:* "the skill set for librarians will continue to evolve in response to the needs and expectations of the changing populations (students and faculty) that they serve."[10]

The administration of this KSA assessment was a positive experience that has enabled us to be more proactive and strategic in shaping the future of our profession. It initiated a conversation among staff about the changes taking place within academic librarianship, and it has helped position the libraries for the future. It was one tool in a continuum that the University of Minnesota Libraries have used to assist our staff through a challenging period of transition, and we believe other libraries could apply this process as well: define expectations, align liaison positions with the goals and needs of the larger institution, discuss strategies for working in an environment of ambiguity, clarify what work should be given up in order to assume new roles, acknowledge the sense of loss that many staff will experience as they shift away from areas in which they were expert (e.g., reference work), and provide a strong professional development program based on identified needs to support and empower liaisons as their roles continue to evolve. Constant communication is critical, and an assessment can be one effective way to position your library to thrive in an ever-changing and exciting environment.

Notes

1. Sheila D. Creth, "A Changing Profession: Central Roles for Academic Librarians," *Advances in Librarianship* 19 (1996): 85–98; Beverly P. Lynch and Kimberley Robles Smith, "The Changing Nature of Work in Academic Libraries," *Col-*

lege & Research Libraries 62, no. 5 (Sept. 2001): 407–420; Mary Anne Kennan et al., "Changing Workplace Demands: What Job Ads Tell Us," *Aslib Proceedings* 58, no. 3 (2006): 179–196.

2.   Wendy Lougee, "Diffuse Libraries," (presentation, Association of Research Libraries 142nd Membership Meeting, Lexington, KY, May 15, 2003), www.arl. org/resources/pubs/mmproceedings/142mm-lougee.shtml (accessed March 27, 2008).

3.   Association of Research Libraries Joint Task Force on Library Support for E-Science, "Agenda for Developing E-Science in Research Libraries (Nov. 2007), www.arl.org/bm-doc/ARL_Escience_Final.pdf (accessed March 27, 2008); Margaret Henty, "Developing the Capability and Skills to Support eResearch," *Ariadne* 55 (April 2008), www.ariadne.ac.uk/issue55/henty (accessed June 3, 2008).

4.   Andrew Dillon, "Accelerating Learning and Discovery: Refining the Role of Academic Librarians," (presentation, meeting of the Council on Library and Information Resources: Core Functions of the Research Library in the 21st Century, Feb. 21, 2008), http://www.clir.org/pubs/reports/pub142/dillon.html (accessed June 10, 2008).

5.   Robert H. Bruininks, "Transforming the U for the 21st Century: Strategic Positioning Report to the University of Minnesota Board of Regents" (2007), http://www1.umn.edu/systemwide/strategic_positioning/pdf/SPReport_FINAL.pdf (accessed August 21, 2008).

6.   University of Minnesota Libraries, "A Multi-Dimensional Framework for Academic Support. Final Report" (June 2006), http://purl.umn.edu/5540 (accessed August 21, 2008; page now discontinued).

7.   University of Minnesota Libraries, "Understanding Research Behaviors, Information Resources, and Service Needs of Scientists and Graduate Students: A Study by the University of Minnesota Libraries" (June 2007), http://conservancy. umn.edu/handle/5546 (accessed August 21, 2008; page now discontinued).

8.   See "ARL Academy: Careers in Academic & Research Libraries," www.arl.org/ leadership/academy/index.shtml for further information about the ARL Academy program.

9.   ARL Joint Task Force on Library Support for E-Science, www.arl.org/bm-doc/ ARL_Escience_Final.pdf (accessed March 27, 2008).

10. ACRL Research Committee, *Environmental Scan, 2007* (Chicago: Association of College and Research Libraries, Jan. 2008), www.ala.org/ala/mgrps/divs/acrl/ publications/whitepapers/Environmental_Scan_2007%20FINAL.pdf (accessed June 10, 2008).

APPENDIX A

UNIVERSITY OF MINNESOTA LIBRARIES ACADEMIC PROGRAMS DIVISION PROFESSIONAL EXPECTATIONS

General Professional Expectations

The performance expectations listed below are considered essential for successful job performance. They will be considered in setting an individual's goals and in reviewing the quality of the staff member's performance.

Knowledge of Role / Expertise

- Demonstrates a clear understanding of one's role and responsibilities as a member of the University of Minnesota and the University Libraries.
- Keeps current with the literature, issues and trends pertinent to the position, including the University's curriculum and research foci and trends.
- Cultivates a thorough understanding of the University Libraries' system and approaches all work with a philosophy of serving and educating users of the system.
- Strives to provide outstanding customer service, meeting and exceeding customer wants and needs.
- Fulfills responsibilities in a professional manner.
- Anticipates and responds to changing needs of users.
- Knows and follows ethical standards of the profession.
- Develops a breadth of knowledge of technological possibilities and applications.
- Applies good judgment, analytical skills and subject knowledge to job performance.

Leadership / Initiative

- Contributes to setting directions and developing and carrying out goals for the department, division, and the Libraries, displaying leadership and vision.

- Provides leadership (supervisory and other) that guides individual and unit/departmental performance, inspires a shared purpose, and contributes to the forward movement of the organization.
- Leads by example, conveying to the external world positive support for University Libraries, division, departmental and unit goals and priorities.
- Takes the initiative in recognizing, analyzing and constructively solving problems and overcoming barriers.
- Makes recommendations for program and service improvement.
- Develops leadership skills and innovative ideas to contribute to the advancement of the profession by participation in professional organizations, initiatives, and scholarship.
- Seeks to be a full partner in the educational and research process, anticipating and adopting technology advances and changing behaviors in research, teaching, learning and information seeking.
- Involves staff and others, as appropriate, in analyzing tasks and investigating alternative ways of doing things.
- Demonstrates innovation, creativity, and informed risk-taking.

Flexibility / Adaptability
- Demonstrates flexibility, openness, and receptivity to new ideas and approaches and encourages others to embrace this attitude.
- Anticipates and adapts to new challenges, changing priorities, situations, and demands.
- Handles multiple tasks and priorities well.
- Recognizes and embraces ambiguity in our environment.
- Anticipates how to be a vital partner in the changing research and learning enterprise.

Collaboration
- Demonstrates ability to work well in groups within individual units and beyond.
- Seeks ways to build team efforts to solve problems and achieve common goals.

- Offers constructive input as appropriate.
- Participates in multiple groups as necessary.
- Works effectively and cooperatively with others.
- Shares knowledge and information in support of goals.
- Demonstrates sensitivity and respect for others.
- Offers assistance, support, and feedback to others.
- Works independently and collaboratively.
- Works with scholars and experts in other disciplines to contribute a library and information perspective to those areas.

Interpersonal Relations

- Exhibits a positive attitude.
- Is approachable/accessible to others and responds in a cooperative, diplomatic, and courteous manner.
- Treats differences of opinion in a serious, non-judgmental fashion.
- Demonstrates fair and equal treatment towards everyone.
- Exercises sound, ethical, and accountable judgment.
- Respects the demands made on colleagues and those in formal leadership positions.
- Maintains appropriate confidentiality and respect for individual privacy.
- Guides and influences the future of libraries and librarians by developing mentoring relationships with colleagues, especially new staff, and by imparting a firm foundation in the values and ethical standards of the profession.
- Strives to help people be successful.

Communication

- Identifies internal and external users and stakeholders and communicates with them effectively and in a timely manner.
- Effectively promotes our services and resources to users.
- Is mindful that messages are sent and received both verbally and non-verbally, whether intentional or not.
- Demonstrates effective "listening" skills (regardless of medium) and provides opportunities for input.
- Promotes an environment where communication is encour-

aged, open, and flows in all directions in the organization.
- Evaluates communication effectiveness, checking for and removing barriers, both personally and within the unit/department.
- Provides timely feedback to individuals and their supervisors on substantial contributions or significant negative impacts to a project, committee, or unit for which one is responsible.

Resource Management
- Demonstrates a broad knowledge of our organization and recognizes the responsibility to be informed.
- Demonstrates effective, efficient, and responsible use of resources to best support goals and objectives.
- Practices good time management and respects others' time.
- Prioritizes work appropriately.
- Demonstrates a strong commitment to improvement of operations and services (for example, by improving performance and productivity, reducing redundancy and bottlenecks, automating labor intensive efforts and instituting collaborative arrangements where appropriate).
- Looks beyond the daily work of the library to the larger picture, forming a vision and appropriate work plan for the future.

Integrity
- Honors commitments.
- Holds self accountable and behaves in a consistently ethical and responsible manner.
- Acts with consistency, honesty, fairness and professionalism.

APPENDIX B

UNIVERSITY OF MINNESOTA LIBRARIES ACADEMIC PROGRAMS DIVISION POSITION DESCRIPTION FRAMEWORK

Introduction to the Framework

There a several reasons for making position descriptions more uniform. The first is so that expectations of the job are clear to everyone, and people doing similar work have similar position descriptions. Clear and current position descriptions, along with division and department goals, will help individuals write annual personal goals. With a framework in place directors and individuals will easily be able to create and update position descriptions.

Our profession faces significant change and this is reflected in the changing and expanding roles of librarians. The framework is intended to help articulate both ongoing and new roles and responsibilities. This is why examples are included in a number of areas. The examples are illustrative, but not exclusive. This is a living document, suggestions are always welcome.

The framework includes most work performed by librarians, but not every individual will do everything in the framework. Position descriptions will be designed in consultation with individuals; department directors have responsibility for the final document.

Campus Engagement

- Actively engage with faculty, students, and staff in assigned areas, developing strong working relationships.
- Promote current services and collections.
- Be knowledgeable about and be able speak to a range of library issues, including scholarly communication, the emerging digital conservancy, the development of new online tools, and the integration of information literacy skills into the curriculum.
- Assess user needs to develop and maintain relevant, high-quality services and collections.
- Analyze trends in departmental teaching and research pro-

grams, stay abreast of scholarship in the disciplines themselves, and use this knowledge to respond to departmental needs.

- Seek opportunities to collaborate and establish partnerships with departments, including the creation of digital content and services. Examples include:
  - Collaborating with data producers and repository contributors to develop cost-effective and efficient strategies for managing data and information.
  - Seeking opportunities to partner with researchers in projects or grants that require intense information and data management.
- Examples of good interaction include:
  - Engaging in individual conversations, especially as we increase the amount of time we spend outside the Libraries, in departments, research centers, and areas in which students gather
  - Seeking participation in departmental, college and campus committees
  - Attending and presenting at departmental meetings, seminars, and colloquia
  - Forming and working with library advisory committees.
  - Content / Collections (Acquisition, Stewardship, Promotion)
- Build and manage library collections in the subject areas of XXX by:
  - Systematically selecting material in all formats (print, manuscripts, digital, data sets, fixed and streaming multimedia), to serve the current and future research, teaching, and learning needs of University of Minnesota clientele.
  - Building on collections of distinction that may also serve regional, national and international users.
  - Managing collection funds efficiently, effectively and in a timely manner.
  - Strategically assessing and making decisions regarding the acquisition, retention and preservation of collections.
  - Working proactively with technical and access services staff on appropriate arrangement, description, catalog-

ing and provision of access to traditional collections and electronic resources.

- Discovering and recruiting institutional scholarly output, research data and other content for inclusion in the University Libraries' digital initiatives.
- Developing and maintaining relationships with dealers and donors (of both in-kind and monetary gifts).

Teaching and Learning

- Actively engage with faculty and graduate teaching assistants as partners in programmatically integrating information literacy concepts and skills into the curriculum
- Using sound instructional design practice, develop learning materials and instructional sessions in a variety of formats that teach students to:
  - Recognize information needs, create successful search strategies, and evaluate and effectively use information resources in all formats, including archival and other primary materials as well as secondary sources.
  - Understand the research and scholarly communication patterns of their chosen disciplines.
  - Understand the economic, social, and legal issues around the use of and access to information.
- Deliver effective instructional sessions as appropriate. Determine when it is more appropriate to have students use online tools; or to give learning materials to faculty and teaching assistants for their incorporation into class sessions.
- Conduct needs assessment as appropriate and selectively measure instructional outcomes in order to ensure effectiveness of instructional initiatives.
- Maintain an up-to-date knowledge of relevant University and department curriculum initiatives, in order to keep information literacy program consistent with University curriculum.
- Develop and manage physical and/or online learning spaces.

Scholarly Communication

- Educate and inform faculty, graduate students, and campus

administrators about scholarly communication issues. Examples include:

- Helping faculty and graduate students to understand their rights as authors.
- Contributing content to copyright and/or scholarly communication web sites.

- Advocate for sustainable models of scholarly communication.
- Work closely with faculty and students to understand their changing workflows and patterns of scholarly communication; assist in the development and creation of tools and services to facilitate scholarly communication.
- Support and promote the University Digital Conservancy by
  - Helping administrators, faculty, and students understand the role of the UDC in building and preserving digital collections.
  - Working with faculty and departments to promote the UDC as a scholarly communication tool.
  - Assisting in content recruitment; Identifying digital resources that require long-term preservation and merit sustained access.
  - Helping to shape the infrastructure in which digital preservation and access can successfully evolve.

E-Scholarship and Digital Tools

- Identify areas where new online learning and digital tools can place the Libraries into the flow of teaching, learning and research.
- Collaborate in the design, implementation, and maintenance of online tools and services that meet the needs of discipline/interdisciplinary research communities.
- Actively participate in the coordination and integration of online tools in support of teaching, learning and research.
- Develop knowledge of current practice and future directions in e-scholarship and help to identify gaps in existing support.
- Participate in defining library roles in e-scholarship.

"Ask Us" Services

- Actively seek opportunities to provide customized reference and research services, which include:
  - Providing consultations that involve subject or other specialized areas of expertise (e.g., in-depth knowledge of copyright or scholarly communication issues or specific collections).
  - Answering referred questions in all formats (chat, e-mail, phone, desk/in-person) and individual / group consultations.
  - Applying knowledge of how research is conducted in certain disciplines.
  - Extending services such as mobile librarian activities, administrative research service, blog creation in partnership with departments, partnerships with the Office of Business Development, morning report type activities, etc.
- Provide high quality reference and research support on demand by:
  - Providing assistance and one-to-one instruction in finding and evaluating information.
  - Providing assistance in accessing library resources and services.
  - Providing feedback about user success with resources and services.
  - Providing support in using information effectively in all formats.
  - Documenting and analyzing data on reference transactions, both at service points and for customized reference transactions.

Outreach

- Contribute to the University of Minnesota's commitment to serve the citizens of Minnesota. Examples include:
  - Seeking speaking engagements and other opportunities to address community groups to inform them of resources available to them.
  - Seeking opportunities to address local, regional, and state

government agencies, to foster better communication and understanding of each other's programs and services.
- Pursuing partnerships with other organizations (e.g., libraries, library organizations, business community, etc.).
- Developing, maintaining and promoting services and resources that will benefit the broader community.

Fundraising
- Identify and monitor relevant government agencies and private foundations for funding opportunities.
- Identify potential projects / activities for grant funds; prepare and submit grant proposals.
- Identify potential donors and work with the Libraries Development Office to cultivate donors as appropriate.
- Seek input from academic department heads and faculty about needs that might be met with external funding.

Exhibit and Event Planning (Not all librarians will engage in this every year)
- Identify potential topics for exhibits or events that promote services or collections or support campus goals; share with appropriate planning bodies (Exhibits Committee, First Fridays Planning Committee, Events Planning Committee, etc.)
- Prepare exhibit content and mount exhibits.
- Plan and execute events.
- Work closely with Communication Office on publicity for exhibits and events.

Leadership
- Contribute to the goals and strategic initiatives of the Libraries through active participation in collaboratives, working groups and task forces.
- Manage projects and develop programs as assigned in consultation with sponsors, supervisors and other stakeholders.
- Share expertise with colleagues and administrators to further Libraries and University goals and strategic initiatives (leading from where you are within the organization).

- Facilitate successful group processes including meeting management, conflict resolution, and consensus building.

Management and Supervision (where applicable)

- Coordinate overall operational activities of [name of unit or library], facilitating relationships with other groups in the Libraries, evaluating needs and processes, and addressing staffing requirements, physical plant needs, and the implementation of policies and procedures.
- Provide direct supervision of [positions]. In consultation with department director write position descriptions, hire, assign job responsibilities, coach and mentor, conduct performance evaluations, and facilitate staff development and training opportunities.
- Prepare narrative and statistical reports for [name of unit or library] and prepare additional documentation on activities and progress as required. Prepare recommendations and proposals for long range projections in terms of staffing, space and equipment, and collection facility needs.

APPENDIX C

UNIVERSITY OF MINNESOTA LIBRARIES ACADEMIC PROGRAMS DIVISION KNOWLEDGE, SKILLS AND ABILITIES SELF-ASSESSMENT

Ratings:
- Basic or less
- Basic or less, but need to know more
- Intermediate
- Intermediate, but need to know more
- Advanced
- N/A

1. I am a member of:
   - Archives and Special Collections
   - Arts and Humanities
   - Coordinated Educational Services
   - Physical Sciences and Engineering
   - Social Sciences and Professional Programs
   - Agricultural, Biological, and Environmental Sciences

2. Teaching and Learning

Please rate your current knowledge, skills, and abilities in the following areas:
- Understand and apply principles of learning theory
- Understand and accommodate different learning styles
- Understand and incorporate the principles of instructional design into information literacy activities
- Be familiar with the *Information Literacy Standards for Higher Education*
- Understand information literacy needs for assigned or relevant disciplines
- Understand the methods of disciplinary instruction in assigned or relevant areas
- Proactively partner with faculty, curriculum committees, and/or departments to integrate information literacy into their curricula
- Develop and manage physical learning spaces

- Develop and manage online learning spaces
- Work with faculty to design effective assignments
- Find and incorporate previously created instructional resources
- Create engaging and effective instructional materials
- Incorporate active learning techniques into instruction as appropriate
- Deliver dynamic presentations to large groups
- Understand and effectively incorporate educational technologies (e.g., online tutorials) into instruction

3. Reference and Research Services

Please rate your current knowledge, skills, and abilities in the following areas:

- Understand the broad universe of information in order to create content and tools that anticipate and respond to questions without mediation
- Contribute to the development and refinement of existing tools
- Understand and apply knowledge about the process of information seeking to structure information services for users
- Have an understanding of assigned or relevant disciplines and reference tools that support advanced help in these areas
- Understand the flow of information and how that flow may differ by subject
- Keep current with new information resources
- Understand and apply best practices in effective customer service
- Collaborate/partner with the user in the information-seeking process
- Work well with diverse users who possess varying skill levels
- Communicate effectively in synchronous online reference situations (i.e., chat)
- Communicate effectively in asynchronous online reference situations (i.e., e-mail)
- Communicate effectively in face-to-face and telephone reference
- Conduct an effective reference interview that investigates a user's stated and unstated research needs
- Construct effective database searches and instruct users in effective techniques
- Create research and bibliographic tools

4. Collections Management

Please rate your current knowledge, skills, and abilities in the following areas:

- Understand current economic and market issues that affect collection development
- Understand how to represent needs of specific areas within the context of larger collection needs
- Look for collaborative ways to accomplish collections goals, such as pooling money or selecting common resources
- Understand the publication trends and develop familiarity with publishers in assigned or relevant areas
- Evaluate resources in terms of the University of Minnesota Libraries' curricular and research needs; select and manage resources in all formats in assigned or relevant areas
- Strategically assess and make decisions regarding the acquisition, retention, and preservation of collections
- Understand and evaluate a license agreement
- Compile data and information about collections in assigned or relevant areas and update it regularly (e.g. usage data, expenditures, price increases over time, gifts received in ASC)
- Effectively use the acquisitions component of integrated library system
- Track and effectively manage collections budgets
- Understand and effectively use selection and approval tools
- Know what kinds of collections reports can be generated and use these reports to monitor and guide selection
- Develop and maintain foreign language competencies appropriate to the University of Minnesota collections and the needs of its researchers

5. Liaison/Relationship Building/Communications

Please rate your current knowledge, skills, and abilities in the following areas:

- Maintain awareness of current trends in assigned or relevant disciplines
- Maintain awareness of departmental focuses for research and teaching in assigned or relevant areas
- Proactively develop working relationships with faculty in as-

signed or relevant areas, identifying opportunities to collaborate on projects, services, and collection decisions
- Proactively develop working relationships with administrative staff in assigned or relevant areas
- Develop working relationships with students in assigned or relevant areas
- Learn about and support the information needs of research groups
- Participate in the development of new tools and services in response to user needs
- Effectively communicate library and information-related news and issues to appropriate audiences in group or one-on-one interactions
- Promote library services and collections to the university and outside communities
- Perform a user needs assessment
- Analyze the data from a user needs assessment

6. Archives and Special Collections

Please rate your current knowledge, skills, and abilities in the following areas:
- Understand and apply the generally accepted theories, standards, and professional practices relating to materials in archives and special collections
- Understand the nature and value of primary research and the significance of original artifacts
- Understand the purpose of finding aids and other access tools for archives and special collections materials
- Develop and maintain in-depth knowledge of the bibliographic, historical, cultural, and institutional aspects of the University of Minnesota archives and special collections
- Maintain familiarity with and selectively implement the technologies that are key to management and dissemination of archives and special collections materials
- Promote an appreciation and use of archives and special collections materials to a variety of audiences
- Actively engage with faculty and other librarians to integrate use of archives and special collections into the curriculum

- Understand and maintain a balance between preservation of and user access to unique artifacts
- Maintain an in-depth knowledge of the book trade and build relationships with dealers
- Understand and apply appropriate processing techniques
- Understand and apply current descriptive standards

7. Technology

Please rate your current knowledge, skills, and abilities in the following areas:

- Maintain awareness of new technologies and their potential applications in libraries and higher education
- Maintain awareness and understanding of the technologies that are currently employed in libraries and higher education
- Understand technological tools that are broadly used by University of Minnesota communities
- Seek opportunities to train in new or unfamiliar information technologies
- Integrate use of relevant current technologies and tools into everyday practice
- In response to user needs, identify new tools that could be developed
- Critically evaluate effectiveness of technologies and tools
- Demonstrate the value of technological tools to users and colleagues
- Effectively use productivity applications (e.g. word processing, spreadsheets)
- Effectively use social networking tools such as blogging and social bookmarking
- Effectively use instant messaging tools
- Effectively use LibData
- Effectively use wikis
- Have a basic understanding of web site design

8. Scholarly Communication

Please rate your current knowledge, skills, and abilities in the following areas:

- Understand the basic issues in scholarly communication
- Be aware of the scholarly communication differences among

disciplines
- Possess a basic understanding of copyright law
- Possess a basic understanding of a variety of publishing models, including open-access
- Understand issues surrounding authors' rights
- Understand the basic roles of the University Digital Conservancy and when to recommend that faculty submit their publications
- Understand the tenure process as it relates to publishing, including the issue of impact factor
- Communicate scholarly communication issues in a balanced way that can be adjusted to meet the needs of a wide range of audiences
- Advocate for sustainable models of scholarly communication
- Assist in the development and creation of tools and services to facilitate scholarly communication
- Assist scholars in identifying publications that allow them to retain their rights
- Advise scholars on how they may manage the articles, preprints, etc. that they gather
- Advise scholars on how they may manage their data
- Discover and recruit institutional scholarly output, research data, and other content for inclusion in the University Digital Conservancy

9. Leadership

Please rate your current knowledge, skills, and abilities in the following areas:
- Share expertise with colleagues and administrators to further Libraries and University goals
- Consider the risk, benefit, and impact of decisions on the present and future library environment before taking action (maintain a system-wide perspective)
- Collaborate successfully within a larger organization and with external partners as appropriate
- Advocate for the library on campus
- Develop individual goals that are strategic and support Division-wide and Libraries-wide goals

- Respond to changing needs by taking on short-term responsibilities that move the Libraries forward
- Understand and apply project management skills
- Understand and apply program development skills
- As a group member, contribute actively and constructively to help the group achieve its goals
- Facilitate meetings that are focused and productive
- Manage conflict between members of a group
- Structure discussions, situations, and assignments to encourage creativity
- Ask open-ended questions, listen actively, and respond in an open, constructive manner
- Build consensus among the members of a group
- Support group decisions and outcomes through actions and communications
- Mentor newer staff

10. Professional

Please rate your current knowledge, skills, and abilities in the following areas:

- Provide library colleagues with constructive feedback
- Request feedback and use it to make improvements
- Identify and take advantage of opportunities for professional growth and development
- Understand and employ effectively principles and techniques of marketing
- Identify grant opportunities
- Write effective grant proposals
- Participate in departmental, college, and campus committees
- Effectively manage time and set priorities for assigned responsibilities
- Set priorities, create plans, and establish a schedule for professional activities
- Develop collaborative relationships within the library profession
- Know the basics of using statistics and understand their misuse
- Have a basic understanding of research methodology
- Write for publication

- Create effective professional presentations
- Present information or data in an understandable format
- Work comfortably in a multicultural environment
- Communicate effectively with diverse groups, including those whose first language is not English
- Cultivate relationships with donors and potential donors of funds and collections
- Understand the principles of censorship and intellectual freedom
- Engage in self-reflection to assess personal strengths and weaknesses

CHAPTER 7

PhD HOLDERS IN THE ACADEMIC LIBRARY

THE CLIR POSTDOCTORAL FELLOWSHIP PROGRAM

Marta L. Brunner
University of California, Los Angeles

Introduction

Academic libraries are feeling the effects of the rapid transition prompted primarily by advances in digital technology, by shifts in campus budget priorities, and by new modes of scholarship and teaching. In redefining the scope of their responsibilities, academic libraries have found themselves needing to create and fill positions that, until very recently, few envisioned the need to create. Administrators face the question of how staffing and recruitment practices will need to change in order to keep up with and direct the transition rather than be pulled along by it. Librarians and other library staff then wonder how their own positions will evolve and whether vacant positions in their departments will be filled at all.

One recent attempt to grapple with these issues regarding academic library staffing and recruitment has been the Council on Library and Information Resources (CLIR) Postdoctoral Fellowship Program, now entering its fifth year. This program aims to bring newly minted PhD holders in the humanities into academic libraries with the goal of producing "a new kind of scholarly information professional."[1] The CLIR Postdoctoral Fellowship Program grew from a seed planted in late 2002 by Deanna Marcum, then president of CLIR. In January 2003, she convened a group of colleagues with whom she had collaborated in the past, individuals likely to be interested in the issue of cultivating leadership in academic libraries. The purpose of this meeting was to brainstorm ideas for a new CLIR program to tackle this issue of leadership. Although the desire to cultivate new kinds of leaders, along with some concerns about the relevancy of library school curricula, prompted this endeavor, the discussion became more focused on collaboration between the scholarly world and the library world. What resulted from this meeting, then, was a vision for a postdoctoral fellowship program to bring humanities PhDs into academic libraries. In February 2003, an announcement was issued to potential host institutions, making them aware of this upcoming opportunity.[2]

CLIR issued a press release announcing the postdoctoral fellowship program and calling for applicants in December 2003.[3] The first cohort of CLIR Fellows joined their host institutions in late summer and early fall of 2004. Host institutions included Princeton University, North Carolina State University, the University of Illinois at Urbana-Champaign, University of Southern California, Lehigh University, Johns Hopkins University, Yale University, University of Alabama, University of Virginia, and Bryn Mawr College. To date, 21 institutions have participated in the program. Not all of these institutions have continued to host fellows each year; to date, there have been as few as four and as many as ten institutions hosting first-year fellows in a given year.

In this program, host institutions draft job advertisements for their CLIR Fellowship positions. Applicants see individual job postings or hear about the fellowship and visit the CLIR website to view all position descriptions. Then they complete a common application, including an essay demonstrating knowledge of and interest in intersections among scholars, libraries, and scholarly information resources. As part of this application, potential fellows indicate their top three choices of host institutions and offer very brief reasons for their choices. These applications are then vetted by the host institutions, which conduct telephone or in-person interviews with candidates. Depending on the institution, project, and funding situation, successful candidates are offered the position as a one- or two-year contract. The host institution pays the salary, benefits, and professional development costs of their fellows, while CLIR provides travel and professional development support for all CLIR-related activities, including the two-week orientation seminar at Bryn Mawr College held in July or August prior to a new fellowship year, a two-day seminar at UCLA in January during the fellowship year, and other related activities, such as attendance at ACRL when CLIR Fellows have presented on behalf of the program.[4]

Although discussions of the CLIR Postdoctoral Fellowship Program have appeared in library literature, there has yet to be an in-depth examination of the CLIR Postdoctoral Fellowship Program, such that those who are outside the program can make informed judgments and those who have participated can take stock of how well it has accomplished what it set out to do and consider where it ought to go from here.[5] I have undertaken in this article to fill this gap. What is evident from my examination of the program is that CLIR Fellows adapt quickly, innovate effectively, and provide knowledge and expertise suited to fit the new roles the library is likely to play in the future. In fact, having recently finished dissertations, CLIR Fellows know research collections, know the latest trends in scholarship, and, in many cases, come with fresh undergraduate-level teaching experience. As such, a fellow is positioned to view the work of academic libraries from the invaluable perspective of one who is well informed about research and instructional needs in the academy but not predisposed to favor traditional definitions of "librarian" or "library work." A survey of past fellows and host institutions suggests that libraries ought to create jobs that serve new, evolving purposes and goals rather than making new library professionals into the image of past library professionals.

In this essay, I will provide a detailed report of the CLIR program's first four years and its outcomes, and draw conclusions about the role of this program in academic librarianship and in higher education more broadly. The experiences of CLIR Fellows are central to this analysis as they illustrate some of the challenges that programs of this sort will present, such as the need for new human resources categories, workflows, and procedures; new ways of capitalizing on the strengths of existing library professionals and providing retraining where needed; and new strategies for educating, retooling, and involving library users (especially faculty and other advanced scholars).[6]

Overall, this report shows that there is much that has worked well in the CLIR program for all involved. There is also much that could be improved, but in spite of this needed change, the CLIR Postdoctoral Fellowship Program embodies the transition that academic libraries, as a whole, are undergoing. Consequently, the academic library profession would do well to learn from the CLIR program experience and explore opportunities to create similar programs to meet other staffing and recruitment needs within the profession.

Staffing Strategies in Academic Libraries: A Brief Overview

Academic librarians have long been concerned about the role of subject doctorate holders in the profession. Although ACRL officially blessed the Masters in Library Science as the terminal degree for the profession over 30 years ago, that decision has not laid to rest questions about the need for or desirability of library professionals who hold a subject doctorate. Nor did the decision close discussions about whether all library professionals must hold the terminal degree. The fact that these debates about librarian credentialing, skills, and education continue to surface—a 1976 article by Rush G. Miller cites already well-worn discussions—suggests that we ought to collectively identify ways to improve academic libraries and plan for future staffing needs accordingly, rather than continue trying to settle, once and for all, the question of which degrees one must hold in order to contribute to the profession.[7]

Professional staffing needs have been addressed in a variety of innovative ways in recent years.[8] One example is ACRL's New Member Mentoring Program, instituted in 2000, which paired new librarians with more experienced colleagues.[9] Mentors and mentees were not based at the same institutions, thereby exposing participants to a broader variety of experiences and perspectives within the profession. Pairs met in person at ALA Annual and Midwinter meetings and kept in regular touch via e-mail. Networking and professional development were key outcomes for mentees; mentors likewise benefited from fresh perspectives offered by these newly minted library professionals. One challenge was that the burden for fruitful learning outcomes rested with mentees, who had to take initiative with their mentors. For mentors, this fact ensured that the time commitment was not onerous, but for mentees who are not self-starters, this program may have proved less satisfying.[10]

Other programs have addressed concerns with the need for diversity within the library profession. For example, the University of Arizona's Knowledge River Program attempts to achieve the goal of promoting academic librarianship to those who might not otherwise consider that career path by recruiting Hispanic and American Indian individuals into a professional library degree program and mentoring these students into internships in academic libraries. Importantly, the authors of an article on this program caution that a well-designed residency program should not "take newly graduated students, insert them into often hostile environments, and expect them to address all the problems of diversity."[11] This caution highlights a crucial point: if we recruit with an eye toward encouraging diversity in the profession—diversity of racial and ethnic background, diversity of sexual orientation, diversity of education and training, diversity of work experience—we need to understand the needs of these less traditional members and recognize the valuable contributions they can make, contributions that may challenge the profession in uncomfortable ways and improve it in unexpected ways.

One argument for recruiting PhD holders to academic librarianship has been a need for in-depth subject or language expertise; certain programs have been developed to address this specific concern. Because it has become challenging for academic libraries to fill librarian positions requiring such expertise, the University of Colorado at Boulder (CU-Boulder) Libraries teamed up with the campus's Graduate Teacher Program to develop a new recruiting program. According to an article by Sean Patrick Knowlton and Becky Imamoto, the resulting Provost's Fellowship Program introduced graduate students—particularly those at the master's level—to the academic library profession by matching them with volunteer library mentors and having them participate in group sessions and library activities for 150 contact hours in a semester.[12] Training in academic librarianship was built into the mentoring feature of the program. Fellows came out of the program with on-the-job experience as well as knowledge about the faculty tenure system in place at CU-Boulder Libraries. As a recruitment effort, this program appears to have been successful; however, its goals are limited in focus. The program committee turned away applicants who did not express clear interest in academic librarianship as a career possibility and intentionally funneled participants toward library school.[13] Thus, the effects of a program such as this remain within the library profession rather than simultaneously recirculating back into academic departments, as happens with the CLIR Fellowship Program by virtue of the fact that many participants return to the faculty career track after their fellowship.

Considering the strengths and drawbacks of these and similar programs, then, a need clearly exists for the development of a program that will recruit and mentor academic library professionals with deep subject expertise. Data from a survey of PhD holders in academic librarianship by Thea Lindquist and Todd Gilman suggests that there is a correlation between a weak academic job market and the numbers of PhDs entering librarianship.[14] However, survey responses also suggest that these individuals entered the profession for a variety of reasons, not simply because they failed at securing tenure-track teaching positions. For PhD holders who had earned or were in the process of earning their doctorates when they opted for a career in academic librarianship, most appear to have been working in libraries before making the switch. Say the authors of the survey, "this finding suggests that exposing more advanced-degree holders to the profession tends to result in more entering it."[15] This idea is one that prompted programs like the CLIR Postdoctoral Fellowship Program.

The Lindquist and Gilman survey also brings up a key question that is addressed by the CLIR program; that is, which credentials ought to be required for holding an academic library position? After analyzing the results of their survey, the authors conclude that "Those who think that nearly every doctorate holder seeking work in an academic/research library requires an ALA-MLS should think again."[16] As their evidence shows, for a significant number of PhD-holding librarians, the lack of a professional library degree has not hamstrung their careers. Nonetheless, the presence of a PhD does not, in and of itself, mean a librarian will become a leader in the profession and in extending the reach of libraries on campus. Lindquist and Gilman discovered that a large number of their respondents seem to have eschewed supervisory roles in favor of continuing in subject specialist capacities—positions that most directly utilize skills and expertise gained during their doctoral training.[17] It is possible that some of these librarians took less traditional leadership roles within their libraries. Nevertheless, what remain unclear are the reasons why these librarians passed on supervisory roles and whether they would have more readily moved into leadership roles with additional mentoring or professional development opportunities along the lines of the CLIR Fellowship.

The CLIR Fellowship Program: Methods for Collecting Data

After considering the need for innovative staffing strategies in academic libraries, and informed by the strengths and weaknesses of the programs addressed above, I undertook an analysis of the CLIR Postdoctoral Fellowship Program to determine the role it has played thus far in addressing the future of academic libraries. I surveyed CLIR Fellows and interviewed selected participants in the program, including fellows, their direct supervisors, and host library administrators. For the survey, I attempted to contact all past and present fellows. Of the 29 CLIR Fellows to date, I was able to locate contact information for all but one individual. Of the 28 fellows then invited to participate, 22 completed the online survey, resulting in a 76% response rate. I conducted the survey using Zoomerang software, a product to which my institution has a license.[18] The survey consisted of 34 questions covering fellows' experience of the postdoctoral fellowship, career aspirations, motivations for participating, skills and experience, perceptions about the "librarian" role, and demographic information. Although I devised the survey to suit the goals of the present article, I did model some questions on the survey instrument used by Thea Lindquist and Todd Gilman in their recent study of PhDs in academic librarianship, mentioned above.[19]

Given the relatively small number of research subjects and the fact that most questions allowed respondents to select multiple answers and offer prose comments, I opted not to use a statistical analysis program beyond the tabulation and graphing provided by Zoomerang. My goal for this study was not to provide detailed statistical information but to identify broad themes and trends and to elicit information about the experiences and perspectives of CLIR Fellows—to begin to sketch a picture of the fellowship program for others in the profession and provide an opportunity for reflection to those who have participated in the program. The survey and results are archived in the University of California's E-Scholarship Repository.[20]

To this same end, I conducted interviews with a broader cross-section of program participants, including four past fellows and three present fellows, four direct supervisors of CLIR Fellows, and two library administrators from host institutions. I solicited these interviews by asking survey respondents to volunteer, by asking them to suggest direct supervisors and administrators to interview, and by directly inviting particular individuals myself, given my knowledge of their experiences or unique perspectives. I attempted to get representatives from a variety of contexts: CLIR Fellow placements at large universities and small colleges, and placements within main library units (e.g., collections, reference) and elsewhere like special collections or digital humanities units; those individuals who were the only CLIR Fellow at their institution and those who were placed alongside other CLIR Fellows at their host institution; fellows who were pursuing librarianship and fellows who were pursuing tenure-track faculty careers; fellowship assignments with very well-defined structure or projects and fellowship assignments with looser definition; direct supervisors and library administrators from a similar range of settings and experiences. These interviews were conducted in person or over the phone and typically lasted 30–45 minutes. I generally followed an interview protocol of 10 questions but allowed the conversations to develop more organically, depending on what seemed most important to the interviewee. The interview protocol is also archived in the University of California's E-Scholarship Repository.[21]

Experiences and Outcomes
Host Institutions: Motivations for Participating

What prompts libraries to sign on to host CLIR Fellows is not always evident, but it appears that the decision typically has come from the top—from a dean or provost or university librarian who thought that it was a good idea. This is not to suggest that such decisions were capricious or unilateral, but I did not hear of any cases where line librarians or other staff members urged their administration to participate. It makes sense that participation would be prompted by top administrators since these individuals are more likely to have heard of the program from their peers and typically hold the strings of the purse that winds up funding the CLIR Fellow.

Each host institution decides how many fellowship positions to offer and how to craft the position postings for the recruitment process. To date, host institutions have taken different approaches to designing the position announcements, or rather, to imagining the role CLIR Fellows might play in their libraries. Some have identified discrete projects or responsibilities within the library for the CLIR Fellow to complete during his or her tenure, such as participating in a digital project or performing a specific research project for the library. Other institutions describe the position in less bounded terms, hoping that opportunities to utilize particular applicants will present themselves during the application and vetting process. What these latter institutions hope for are self-starters with expertise and skills that complement the collections and services of the library and its campus.

CLIR Fellows: Experiences and Outcomes

Compared with those of host institutions, CLIR Fellows' reasons for applying to the CLIR Postdoctoral Fellowship Program were more straightforward. CLIR Fellows came into the postdoctoral fellowship program for a variety of reasons, but in the survey half of respondents reported interest in a library career as one contributing factor. Slightly less than half of CLIR Fellows entered their fellowships with prior library work experience. Only a third of CLIR Fellows reported pursuing the fellowship, at least in part, because they were unable to find a tenure-track teaching or research faculty job. Specific job advertisements attracted a third of fellows to the program; having run across the fellowship announcements in places like the *Chronicle for Higher Education,* a number of applicants felt that a specific project description "was tailor-made for me." Geographical location was also a factor for fellows who did not want to relocate due to family circumstances. One fellow noted a slightly different appeal in the job advertisement to which she responded: "I saw the announcement for the CLIR Postdoctoral Fellowship and got interested in part because of my work with online resources and in part because it is so difficult to find postdoctoral fellowships in the humanities." Since this individual had already taken a somewhat less conventional route to her PhD, she had already assumed she would not be following the usual faculty career track. For her, as for others as well, academic librarianship was definitely not a substitute for a tenure-track faculty job, but a strategically pursued career track, and this opportunity helped to identify and shape that less standard career track.

Once their fellowships are underway, CLIR Fellows collectively engage in a wide range of activities. Most CLIR Fellows to date have engaged in digital projects and/or special projects, such as exhibit curation, conference planning, or projects for library administration. Some fellows also did collection development, instruction, subject area research, rare books/special collections/archives processing and management, and library-related research. A few did reference. Other activities included writing grants, doing liaison work, making public presentations, and publishing their library-related research.[22]

The survey also revealed that very specific, bounded projects or positions have tended to be more popular with fellows, especially those who are not necessarily planning to pursue an academic library career. The expectations are clear and the outcomes are measurable. Keeping the CLIR Fellow position posting loosely defined in order to allow for a wider range of applicants can also work well but can prove to be unsettling for some fellows. In these positions, fellows must take more initiative, must be willing to live with less structure, and must be prepared to communicate with their supervisors about their own needs and project ideas. Because some fellows in these positions participate in ongoing activities more than bounded projects, it may be challenging to figure out how to identify and measure outcomes. I will speak more to these challenges later in this essay.

TABLE 7.1 What Skills Did You Bring to and Use in the Service of Your CLIR Fellowship? (Check all that apply)		
In-depth subject knowledge/expertise	18	82%
Non-English language skills	7	32%
Advanced research skills	21	95%
Ability to work closely with faculty	21	95%
Digital technology skills (e.g., programming, tagging, web design, web publishing, cyberinfrastructure)	10	45%
Ability to work closely with IT staff	5	23%
Administrative skills	9	41%
Financial skill	0	0%
Intellectual property rights knowledge/expertise	0	0%
Development, grant-writing experience	6	27%
Other	4	18%

In the survey, I asked what skills or experience fellows felt that they brought to their fellowship positions (see table 7.1). Nearly all CLIR Fellows reported having utilized their advanced research skills and ability to work with faculty during their fellowships. Most fellows also drew upon their in-depth subject knowledge and expertise. Almost half of fellows brought digital technology skills or administrative skills to bear in their activities. Less frequently, fellows utilized non-English language skills, their ability to work closely with IT staff, or their experience in the area of grant writing/development. Many commented that teaching experience came into play during their fellowships, as did communication/presentation skills, as well as previous understanding of academic libraries and of the graduate student experience.

TABLE 7.2 What Knowledge and/or Skills Did you Gain in the Course of Your CLIR Fellowship Experience? (Check all that apply)		
Cataloging and metadata	9	41%
Library IT systems	1	5%
Collection management	12	55%
Digital resources creation/management	15	68%
Scholarly communication issues	15	68%
Reference services	9	41%
Library instruction, teaching experience	13	59%
Library administration	11	50%
Library facilities, space issues	8	36%
Development, grant-writing	10	45%
Other	4	18%

Not surprisingly, CLIR Fellows also acquired a wide variety of skills and knowledge in the course of their participation in the program (see table 7.2). Unlike the batch of skills and expertise they reported having brought to the fellowship, which was heavily weighted in two or three areas, the skills and knowledge acquired during the fellowship was spread fairly evenly among eight or nine areas. Between 40% and 70% of fellows reported learning the following: digital resources creation/management, scholarly communication issues, library instruction/teaching experience, collection management, library administration, development/grant-writing, cataloging and metadata, and reference services. Approximately one third of fellows gained knowledge about library facilities and space planning. One reported having learned library IT systems. Other survey comments mentioned learning about academic politics, digital preservation, the library profession, library bureaucracy, and management skills.

CLIR Fellows gained the knowledge and skills listed above mostly through on-the-job training and mentoring. Comments indicated that some of this on-the-job training was more formal—workshops and training/instruction sessions offered to librarians—while some of it was less formal, including "figur[ing] it out" on the fly, doing "research and lots of reading," and "shadowing librarians in almost any department [the fellow] had interest in." For one CLIR Fellow, "conversations with colleagues were most important, and remain [the] most important source of information." Another fellow identified conference attendance as a learning opportunity.

For those fellows who were embedded in library departments—as opposed to digital humanities centers, for example—one of the most valuable aspects of learning on the job was becoming familiar with institutional politics. While politics are endemic to any organization or campus unit, and most fellows come through their doctoral training with plenty of experience with academic department politics, the one- or two-year experience helped fellows learn what to expect and how to negotiate challenging relationships within their library. One fellow gave the example of learning to negotiate effectively with library information technology (IT) staff. She observed that librarian-IT collaboration "is a relationship that often has not worked out well" in libraries but is something that can be learned. With fewer preconceived notions about how things *ought* to work, fellows may actually be in a better position than traditionally trained library staff to navigate these challenging relationships.

Navigating library politics and the fellowship experience overall seems to have been easiest for those fellows who had dedicated mentors, whether that mentor was a direct supervisor or another colleague. Mentoring played a key role in sustaining some fellows and has become somewhat more institutionalized with each passing cohort. Those fellows who had mentors reported that this support was crucial to their success in the program. What this mentoring looked like may have been very different from campus to campus, depending on the types of training and guidance fellows needed. Those who did not receive much, if any, real mentoring reflected after the fact that having a supportive mentor would have helped. One fellow who did have a mentor at her host institution also suggested that there are different levels of mentorship needed: a direct supervisor or "on-the-ground" mentor to consult on daily issues and tasks, an administrative mentor "to oversee our work in a meaningful way," and a CLIR mentor. Currently, Elliott Shore, dean of the CLIR Postdoctoral Fellowship Program, acts as a CLIR mentor to all fellows. For their part, direct supervisors came to realize the need for mentoring of CLIR Fellows and expressed interest in having more direction from CLIR on the needs of its fellows as well as more formal mechanisms in place for mentors to communicate with each other about their experiences on an ongoing basis.

In some ways, mentoring suggests inculcation *into* a community of practice. However, for many participants, the "outsider" status of CLIR Fellows is a valuable resource to be tapped and retained; in other words, the goals of this mentoring should probably not be to make CLIR Fellows "one of us." Here, "outsider's perspective" refers to the perspective of a scholar and a library user; of one not traditionally trained or credentialed; of one who, though respectful of the traditions and track record of the profession, will not take all of its goals, practices, and assumptions without question.

Some fellows come into the program planning to return to the faculty track afterward. For these fellows, their outsider status may get reinforced on the job and in their interactions with other fellows and with CLIR. One fellow, whose project did not involve "traditional" library functions or services, said that she never got past thinking about the library as a user rather than as an insider. Given her own career goals, this way of thinking was not necessarily a problem for her, but she wondered whether CLIR or her host institution would consider her a success in the program. Even one fellow who completed an MLIS after her fellowship noted that this outsider status probably shaped her career plans in a significant way since she now does consulting. Mostly, fellows saw the outsider's perspective as a unique contribution of the program. A fellow explained, "The ability to look at library issues from a multiplicity of perspectives serves the profession well" in terms of being able to spur innovation in productive directions. As a direct supervisor put it, "Libraries need a broader sense of diversity, not just racial and gender diversity, but also a diversity of perspectives," and bringing CLIR Fellows into our libraries is one of many ways to achieve this.

CLIR Fellows: Career Opportunities Postfellowship

The main worry for early critics of the CLIR program concerned the question of what happens when fellows finish the program; however, concerns that the CLIR Postdoctoral Fellowship Program would hasten a flood of PhD holders into the academic library job market should be alleviated by actual outcomes to date (see table 7.3). Of the 22 fellows who responded to my survey, fewer than half reported having been hired into library jobs; three of these individuals have professional library degrees in hand or are in the process of getting them. Four fellows reported being hired into tenure-track faculty positions. Seven respondents said that they had neither library jobs nor tenure-track faculty positions. Most of these individuals appear to be working in areas that may be characterized as "other academic"—adjunct teaching, university IT/instructional technology, consulting in a library setting, and freelancing (this last item may not be in an academic setting).

Former CLIR Fellows working in library jobs, with or without the professional degree, are engaged in a broad range of activities. Half of these individuals perform reference service as part of their duties. Around one third are involved in collection management, instruction, administration, scholarly communication, outreach (e.g., department liaison), and rare books/special collections/archives. Only one individual reported being involved in development. Other areas noted in comments include digital projects, access services, and project management.

Only a little more than one third of CLIR Fellows report that they are actively pursuing a library career. The same number assert that they are not on the academic library track. The rest of the respondents are currently undecided. This overall response illustrates the fact that CLIR Fellows go in different directions and that the fellowship ought not to be viewed solely as a librarian recruitment program. For those respondents who are pursuing an academic library career, the most common factors influencing CLIR Fellows' decisions to do so, by far, were that they wanted to become scholar-librarians—i.e., librarians who pursue independent scholarship—and that they enjoyed library work. For half of respondents, having more job options and increased geographic mobility were contributing factors. Some fellows noted having wanted to stay in academia in a capacity other than as teaching faculty. Only one respondent reported having chosen librarianship due to lack of success on the tenure-track faculty job market.

How has the fellowship experience affected alums' postfellowship job or career plans? For fellows looking to enter the faculty track, the experience was extremely positive. Humanities postdoctoral fellowships are relatively rare but increasingly viewed as a pre-

TABLE 7.3 Are you Pursuing a Career in Academic Librarianship?		
Yes	8	36%
No	8	36%
Undecided	6	27%
Total	22	100%

requisite for securing a tenure-track job, so just having a postdoc from a major university gives candidates an edge in the academic job market. Another fellow who landed a tenure-track faculty position pointed out that improving one's chances on the academic job market is not the only benefit of the CLIR Postdoctoral Fellowship to future faculty members: from his perspective as a soon-to-be junior faculty member, the CLIR Postdoctoral Fellowship Program was a great opportunity because one gets so many things in the fellowship experience that one cannot get in graduate school, including grant-writing experience, contacts with the publishing world, scholarly communication expertise, and so on. "It's good to have time to pause and develop these contacts and perspectives. Senior faculty know this stuff, but not usually junior faculty."

CLIR Fellows and the Professional Degree
Some critics of the CLIR Postdoctoral Fellowship Program will undoubtedly want to reopen the debate about whether participation in the program is enough to turn a PhD holder into an academic librarian. Importantly, most CLIR Fellows do not see this program as an automatic "in" or shortcut to a librarian career. That is, they do not assume that the fellowship *necessarily* equips them to become library professionals. Whether or not a particular fellow is prepared for an academic

library career without the MLIS depends upon the individual, her or his prior library experience, and the shape of her or his experience in the fellowship. It also depends upon a fellow's career goals, including the nature of the work she or he wants to do in libraries or in academia.

Significantly, those fellows who did pursue the library degree during or after their fellowships felt like the CLIR experience equipped them in important ways. One such fellow said that her library school emphasized the idea that things are changing in libraries so one needs to be prepared to adapt to new technology, and so on. She asserts, "The CLIR experience covered that really well and maybe better than library school." Likewise, another fellow who attended library school after her fellowship agreed that there are things one cannot learn easily in library school, such as understanding relationships among library personnel. One needs to be in the library environment to really understand these dynamics. Yet, she admitted, the fact remains that CLIR Fellows are likely to have trouble finding jobs without the library degree, but in some ways the focus on whether or not CLIR Fellows can qualify as *librarians* misses the point: "I'm not sure that 'librarian' defines what we do—the word seems bound to a physical place and libraries are [moving away from or do more than] that. I prefer 'information professional.' …The tide may turn as digital scholarship becomes the norm and experience may begin to make more difference [on the job market] than whether you have a degree."

A lot seems to hinge on the term *librarian*. When asked the extent to which they came to see themselves as librarians, survey respondents reflected some ambivalence. Of the 22 respondents, two answered "completely," 12 answered "somewhat," and 8 answered "no." This ambivalence or diverse response is a good sign since CLIR's original mission was to produce "a new kind of scholarly information professional."

Interestingly, direct supervisors tended to agree that they themselves would hire CLIR Fellows, in spite of the fact that they may not have received "well-rounded" library training in the course of their fellowships. In at least some situations, the fact that these highly skilled individuals were quick studies, full of ideas and relevant knowledge, carried more weight than credentialing. One supervisor was more cautious, suggesting that CLIR Fellows can be trained as librarians by the time they finish a fellowship but that the fellow needs to decide early on that this is a goal so that the experience can be shaped accordingly. Nevertheless, said another supervisor, the academic library profession still struggles with the question of credentials, background, and training; this program provides a way to have this conversation in a more systematic, formal way because there is "something to point to" when talking about the question of credentials.

The Fellowship Program: Early Challenges and Strategies for Improvement
Growing Pains

As with any new program, there were also aspects of the CLIR Postdoctoral Fellowship Program that did not run as smoothly as they could have. As an enthusiastic proponent of the program, I hesitate to draw attention to these early growing pains but also know that it is crucial to reflect on these early problem points so that program participants can work purposefully to overcome them. Furthermore, many of the problems or challenges experienced by CLIR program participants are not unique to the program and will be instructive for others in the academic library world. A number of the problems that arose relate to a lack of preparation on the part of host institutions, or a disconnect between the position as envisioned beforehand (by CLIR Fellows or by the host institution) and the actual reality as it played out. After describing these problems, I will spend time noting strategies for addressing them going forward.

Some CLIR Fellows were reminded that job advertisements do not always match the reality of the position, which can be problematic or helpful, depending on the situation. On the one hand, there were fellows, like one whose job advertisement sounded "tailor-made," who discovered upon arrival that the project advertised did not actually match its description and had a much different focus, requiring a different set of skills and activities. On the other hand, there is the instance of another fellow who was attracted to the placement she eventually got because of its emphasis on electronic resources and teaching. When she arrived at her host institution she discovered that the assignment was vague; there was no mentor available for her first month; and no office space was set aside for her. As she got going, this vagueness amounted to flexibility, which worked in her favor since she could, as an outgoing self-starter, get involved in a wide range of activities throughout the library.

These disconnects between job advertisements and reality illustrate a common theme expressed in interviews with CLIR Fellows, direct supervisors, and administrators—recognition that a program like this requires even more preparation on the part of a host institution than that required for bringing a new librarian or staff member into an existing position. This needed preparation on the part of the host institution goes beyond figuring out where the CLIR Fellows will sit, although more than one fellow was taken aback to find that their host departments "seemed almost surprised to see me," or had no office space available initially. For one supervisor, the problem of receiving CLIR Fellows was not so much a supervisory one—he had discussions early on with his most recent fellow about expectations for the fellowship— as a bureaucratic one: CLIR Fellows did not fit neatly into the library's human resources framework so it was sometimes difficult to determine the employee category to which CLIR Fellows belonged. In contrast, another supervisor's library had already hired two humanities PhDs without library degrees, so there was already a framework within which to accommodate CLIR Fellows in the library. To be sure, the size and entrenchment of the existing bureaucracy will increase the amount of advanced planning and preparation needed before fellows arrive.

Of course, all new programs have a learning curve involved, and certainly many of us have faced a disconnect between an advertised position and the actual needs and experiences of a job, regardless of field or profession. Nevertheless, new host institutions would do well to learn from peer institutions that have already hosted CLIR Fellows in order to get a sense of what is involved in bringing fellows on board.

Sometimes, the lack of preparation on the part of the host institution had to do with identifying the kinds of activities and projects CLIR Fellows should do. Indeed, one supervisor admitted, "It took me a while to wrap my head around what we were going to do [with the fellows]." As noted earlier, some host institutions benefit from keeping position descriptions in job postings for the fellowship more loosely defined—they can get a pool of applicants with broader ranging areas of expertise and interests, and in this way, make room for highly motivated individuals who bring their own innovative project ideas to the table. However, a number of fellows, particularly those in their host institutions' first cohorts, echoed a current fellow who said, "I think [the host institution] could have thought more carefully about how they were going to use me." For one supervisor, problems figuring out how best to use fellows came about as the result of poor communication—"the administration not laying the groundwork for the program, not being clear about its expectations, not communicating enough to staff and colleagues in the library and in the host department. People receiving the CLIR Fellows didn't have enough information about them and what they themselves could do to participate in the process of incorporating fellows into the library and library projects." Fellows sometimes met with resistance from some of the very colleagues who might have been in the best position to capitalize on collaborations with them. As with other library decisions that may challenge existing staffing expectations—e.g., reorganizing a unit or creating an entirely new position—a crucial factor in the success of such change is to give others in the organization an opportunity to buy into the project by allowing them to identify ways in which this new individual or position or reorganization could improve the work of the library, identifying projects or goals that could be accomplished with this new change in place that could not have been accomplished without it.

Thus, libraries need to think carefully about how to utilize CLIR Fellows in ways that capitalize on their unique sets of expertise and perspectives. One fellow reported feeling like she was given assignments or tasks during her first year that amounted to "paper-pushing." Fortunately, this particular fellow was able to work with her supervisors to shift the focus of her fellowship, but this example should remind host libraries to utilize CLIR Fellows not only as extra pairs of hands during tight staffing times but also as agents of change.

Even with a lot of advanced planning on the part of the host institution, there may still be lingering tension between the host institution's desire for flexibility and CLIR Fellows' need for direction or support. From the perspective of one library administrator, being less specific about what the library wants CLIR Fellows to do "forces them to learn about the organization, to figure out what we do and how, and then to figure out what to do [during their fellowship]. I want the individuals to explore." She admits, though, that the success of this approach does depend upon the individuals involved: "We rely on CLIR Fellows to say what they would like or need…. The challenge for CLIR Fellows at our institution is to have them figure out on their own what to do, to have self-starting approaches." Another administrator also valued keeping the fellowship more loosely structured, at least in terms of providing specific training or instruction to fellows. At his institution, "the thinking behind this loose structure was that learning on the job was better than a lot of formal training."

For one fellow, flexibility of this sort was a benefit, but she noted that it does mean the fellow has no defined identity as a postdoc, which may be unsettling to some participants. As mentioned earlier in this essay, another risk is that, in the case of appointments that favor a jack- or jill-of-all-trades approach rather than a specific project—where fellows take on a variety of tasks and activities that librarians and other staff do not have the time to take on—host libraries may not as readily recognize the significance of fellows' contributions. Libraries, like the corporate world, are trained now to think in terms of deliverables and the significance of "extra time" and "extra pair of hands" can be difficult to quantify. Similarly, another fellow worried that placements with less clearly articulated focus or structure cater to a certain personality type (e.g., the most outgoing) or someone with clear library-oriented career goals. This situation runs the risk of neglecting others who come with equally important sets of strengths or goals but who do not thrive in such a loosely structured environment.

This presents host institutions wishing to preserve flexibility with a delicate balancing act: Ideally, suggested one direct supervisor, CLIR Fellows should have more clearly defined projects in mind without those projects being set in stone before they arrive. The goal of the early months or first year of the fellowship should be to mold these project ideas to suit the needs of the library or campus. So while flexibility is an attractive feature of the CLIR Postdoctoral Fellowship Program, it should go hand in hand with careful consideration of what or who may get lost in the shuffle and what steps can be taken to ensure that the flexibility and structure complement each other rather than work against each other.

Similarly, there should be careful consideration of the working environment that the fellows will be entering, including organizational politics in the library and across campus. As noted earlier, fellows encountered campus and library politics during their appointments—a valuable learning experience but one that occasionally comes at some cost. One fellow's main project was compromised from the start by the campus's fraught relationship to the project's subject matter. The effort needed in order to build the networks and resources to tackle the original project would have exceeded the abilities of any one person or short-term effort. The revised project ended up being much different and ultimately less satisfying for the fellow. Another fellow entered a host organization that was in "a time of intense transition," a situation that magnified the uncertainty of the fellow's expected role. Other fellows encountered turf wars of varying degrees that sometimes made it difficult to get projects off the ground.

Confusion or lack of clarity about the nature of the CLIR program probably lends itself, in at least some cases, to uncertainty about how best to utilize fellows. Said one direct supervisor, "As it stands currently, the CLIR Postdoctoral Fellowship is not so much a postdoctoral fellowship as it is 'work study'; it is not structured like a postdoc in an academic department." Work-study implies doing work *for* rather than work *in*, completing tasks that are already in place rather than rethinking the ways things are done. Another supervisor shared this concern about putting CLIR Fellows to the best use possible. To his way of thinking, it is not a good use of postdoctoral fellows to have them doing a standard library job, but if a library wants to use them in this way, it must be very clear about that so that it attracts suitable fellows. Even still, that "standard" work should lead to something newer or better, such as a closer connection with academic departments. A third supervisor pointed out that for host libraries, the key benefit of participating in the program is that the fellow has the time and perspective to seek out new projects and forge new or strengthen existing relationships on campus. Says this supervisor, if her library hired a CLIR Fellow for a humanities librarian position, "we would not expect this person to do the same things as an MLIS-holding applicant. CLIR Fellows are well suited to the changing environment in academic libraries; libraries ought to be making their jobs fit the changing environment rather than molding new library workers to fit the existing job descriptions."

Regardless how CLIR Fellows get utilized, the biggest issue by far for hosts, and by extension for fellows, is funding. Most, if not all, program participants—fellows and hosts alike—agree that two-year appointments are optimal. Unfortunately, many host libraries cannot commit two years of salary and benefits up front, and due to their budget calendar, may still be making funding decisions in late fall or early winter. Thus, they may offer fellows one year with the possibility of a second year. Anyone who has recently earned a PhD knows that most academic job postings hit in the fall, so fellows who are not assured of a second year may find themselves in the position of having to start job hunting while still in the first months of their fellowship. For the CLIR Fellows who are given one-year contracts with the possibility of a second year, the uncertainty about appointment extensions is extremely unsettling. Furthermore, even without the distraction of job hunting, it is difficult for CLIR Fellows to know what kinds of projects to take on if they do not know whether their appointment will end in one year or two. Happily, CLIR is already taking steps to secure outside funding in order to encourage more campuses to participate and enable more host institutions to commit up front to two-year fellowship contracts.

Most participants agree that the learning curve is steep. Consequently, both libraries and fellows should expect and plan for an introductory learning period—this period can be a source of frustration, especially since fellows can end up feeling like they are "spinning their wheels" for the first months of their fellowship. This is the point at which many participants saw mentoring as critically important. What's more, says a fellow from an early cohort, fellows are encouraged by CLIR to see themselves as potential change agents in academic libraries and the academy, but then shortly into the fellowship, "you have the realization that you really don't know what the hell you're doing." For this reason, she encourages fellows to recognize that this introductory period can be unsettling but is a necessary stage of the fellowship experience. Likewise, a direct supervisor suggested that libraries need a certain length of association with a CLIR Fellow to really get things done and gain a proper understanding of what the fellow can contribute to the organization. This introductory period may be shorter for some and longer for others, but in any case, the host institution and fellow will need to work to get past this period. Unfortunately, though, this means that fellows may not be ready even to identify viable projects until almost halfway through their first year, which in turn means they may not have the time to complete anything of significance unless they are given a second year. Furthermore, because some host libraries make the second year contingent upon demonstrated successes in the first year, fellows may find themselves in an even tougher situation.

If a CLIR Fellow goes on the job market during the first year and is able to secure a tenure-track position right away, a library can still be left feeling like it has received an inadequate return on its investment. Of course, the question remains whether the goal of the fellowship should be to produce results—deliverables—or to transform the fellow herself, that is, to create the potential for a new kind of scholar or new kind of library worker. Is it possible to succeed at the latter without accomplishing the former? Here again, it may be helpful for all CLIR program participants at an institution to reflect together on the goals of the program, especially the goal to create a new kind of scholarly information professional. For instance, participants should ask if there are ways that the host library can continue to benefit from the fellow after she or he has moved on. Can the host library work with the fellow's new hiring institution to establish mechanisms by which to continue collaborations, to launch new projects, or to build scholarly networks between institutions?

Strategies for Moving Forward

To sum up, survey and interview respondents had high praise for the program and high hopes for its future, but also offered suggestions for improvement as the program enters its fifth year. As one fellow pointed out, the CLIR Postdoctoral Fellowship Program is itself a work in progress. When asked what they wanted for the future of the program, some participants enthusiastically called for "more of the same!" while others called for expansion—bringing in a greater number of fellows, increasing the number of host institutions, or including disciplines beyond the humanities. Despite the opportunities that the program currently offers, improvement is needed to ensure that the program plays the most effective role possible in academic libraries and in the academy more broadly.

Host institutions need to recognize the amount of preparation it takes to really capitalize on the opportunity presented them through participation in this program. Many conversations need to happen *throughout* a host library before the fellows arrive and perhaps even before the library posts its position announcement. The library needs to be sure that everyone in the organization knows why CLIR Fellows are there and how to make the most of their presence so that fellows end up doing relevant, innovative things that do not amount to change for the sake of change but do take the library in the direction it wants to go. Having these preparatory conversations throughout the organization can also maximize the extent to which library units and departments can collaborate with fellows to help achieve the library's goals. CLIR can keep leading this process by continuing to offer direction and resources to host institutions as they grapple with questions or issues that arise before, during, and after a fellowship year. For example, some direct supervisors expressed interest in establishing a formal evaluation process at the close of each fellowship year to help them make necessary changes for the upcoming year.

During the application process, the program does need to be better advertised in order to draw a larger pool of applicants. CLIR is already keenly aware of this need—having had to revise and extend its most recent call for applications due to insufficient numbers of responses—and is already taking steps to address it. Academic libraries throughout North America could help by announcing the program to graduate students on their campuses and by bringing the program to the attention of campus career centers, even if these libraries are not themselves hosting fellows.

CLIR is also revamping the process by which applications are distributed to potential host libraries (see note 3). Because applicants are not usually familiar with the libraries to which they are applying, they may not realize that a particular institution and its collections may fit their scholarly interests or expertise like a glove. It is not that applicants do not do their homework; it is that many libraries have hidden collections of which applicants as well as other host institutions would be unaware. In the current application distribution process, institutions listed as top choices on an application may snap up the candidate before other institutions have a chance to point out the opportunity for a closer match of interests.

Involving faculty and other campus units in the process of planning for or vetting potential fellows was another recommendation offered by a number of program participants. This is a suggestion at which at least some host libraries may balk, particularly if they are hoping to retain control over decisions about which CLIR Fellow projects would best serve the library. Here I would reiterate the observation that libraries are evolving past their walls, their staffing lines, and their funding structures. A project that seems outside the library's purview today may become its bread and butter tomorrow. Incoming generations of scholars will need to learn about text encoding and metadata, if not how to do it. Scholars will have to learn about and utilize open-access publishing mechanisms for their own work. Scholars will need to know and participate in data preservation, even if they are humanists. Partnering with faculty and other research units on campus ensures that knowledge gets produced in ways that can be manipulated, disseminated, and preserved to the fullest extent. For their part, libraries can push scholars to think in terms of digital projects that are not just one-offs that benefit a single scholar's research but projects that, as the Mellon Foundation's Donald Waters put it in a recent conversation with CLIR Fellows, *build* a field of study by enabling multiple scholars collectively to further knowledge in their area of research, or perhaps by opening up new paths of inquiry previously unavailable to the field.[23] Furthermore, even if host libraries end up disagreeing with faculty about which potential CLIR Fellow is the best candidate for the incoming cohort, it is in these negotiations that we are forced to articulate our priorities and goals and consider options we may not have thought of on our own. As many CLIR program participants agreed, this diversity of opinion is a good thing.

A final point that bears reiteration is mentoring. Consensus among participants is that mentoring plays a key role in ensuring that fellows are able to make the most of their fellowships. However, it is not enough to provide either someone to show fellows the ropes or to give top-level support; it is important that this mentoring occur at two or three levels, including the supervisory level, the administrative level, and the fellowship level (i.e., CLIR). Moreover, fellows need direction on daily activities, but more important for the academic library and academic faculty professions, fellows also need guidance on the challenge of becoming leaders and innovators.

What fellows themselves need to do is approach this fellowship as an ongoing commitment. "Once a CLIR Fellow, always a CLIR Fellow" should not be merely a quip to entice alumni back to Bryn Mawr College each summer for the program's annual orientation/reunion. It should also be a reminder to stay involved—to build networks of scholarly professionals and library professionals, to be leaders in national initiatives, to continue collaborating with fellows past and present on projects to spur on the creation, dissemination, and use of innovative scholarly information resources.

Conclusion: Doing the Work of the Library

As we can see from the experiences of the first four cohorts of CLIR Fellows, the roles these individuals have played in libraries fall along a broad spectrum. At one end, there are fellows doing what might be considered "traditional" library work—sitting on the reference desk, buying books and monitoring approval plans, and teaching library instruction sessions. These activities would seem to support the status quo, though granted these individuals may not do them in the same ways that a more traditionally trained librarian might do them. At the other end of the spectrum are fellows who are involved in activities that look very little like "traditional" library work, though some librarians are already doing them: they are creating digital manuscript collections, tagging XML documents, doing subject-specific research and teaching, writing grants, advising scholars on copyright issues, and helping scholars to create open-access journals. They are also working in academic departments and other research units outside the library, such as digital humanities centers. In between the two ends of the spectrum are a host of activities that are less easy to categorize as traditional or nontraditional, in part because a lot of librarians may already be doing them or would do them if they had the time or training.

Benefits of the CLIR Model

Roles in academic libraries are becoming less clear, the deeper we go into the digital turn, the 21st century, or however you want to characterize the present paradigm shift. The nice thing about initiatives like the CLIR Postdoctoral Fellowship Program is that they enable libraries to experiment with defining new roles and new ways of accomplishing the work of academic librarianship. After all, thanks to their outsider's perspective, Fellow typically have more fluid assumptions about library structures and services, so they are well suited to such experimentation. This program can, as one administrator suggested, provide structured occasions for libraries to reflect on what they do, to identify their needs, and to determine the kinds of people they need to fill those needs.

As an embodiment of change in academic libraries, the CLIR Post-doctoral Fellowship Program and its fellows thus far have succeeded in spurring on new projects and giving new life to existing ones, as well as generating new ideas and solving problems across institutions. As a model for recruitment and staffing, the CLIR program accomplishes two other very important things: cultivating new leaders and fostering a devotion to academic libraries that exceeds the bounds of the profession itself.

The program produces new leaders by taking highly skilled and articulate individuals; giving them broad exposure to the issues and challenges facing academic libraries; encouraging them to think, study, and write; giving them on-the-ground opportunities to learn; and giving them connections within the profession and beyond. CLIR Fellows are likely to be better networked with existing leaders in the profession and with funding organizations and other resources than most recent library school graduates; networking opportunities are built into the CLIR program, such that fellows meet with the likes of Deanna Marcum (Library of Congress), Clifford Lynch (Coalition of Networked Information), Charles Henry (CLIR), Donald Waters and Susan Perry (the Mellon Foundation), and a variety of top library and library/information studies school administrators.

The program fosters devotion to academic librarianship by making fellows invested in resolving the challenges faced by academic libraries and respectful of the knowledge and expertise of their colleagues. While MLIS degree programs instill devotion within up-and-coming librarians, the CLIR program instills this devotion in individuals who are potential librarians, library staff, faculty members, campus administrators, and other members of the scholarly community.

In addition, the CLIR Postdoctoral Fellowship Program demonstrates that the work of academic libraries is larger than the library organization itself and includes a broader range of people than just traditionally trained librarians and other nonprofessional library staff. Such may always have been the state of affairs, but the culture of the discipline-based academy has worked to reinforce the apparent division of labor among academic departments, other academic units such as research centers, campus administrative units, and the library. This assumed division of labor has pigeonholed librarians and other library staff into a service role in the minds of scholars and perhaps also in the minds of some library professionals and administrators. While service is indeed a *good* thing and is intrinsic to librarianship, it does the academy a disservice to restrict the library's role to one of *serving* scholars. Library professionals can and should be active collaborators in the research and knowledge-production processes. Library professionals can and should be active in changing the academy when such change is called for, as in the need to promote the value and prestige of open-access scholarship in the humanities and social sciences. Similarly, faculty and students can and should be involved in the growth of the library and not merely to the extent that they make purchase requests, participate in focus groups, or respond to LibQUAL+ surveys.

What programs like the CLIR Postdoctoral Fellowship Program do is help to create symbiotic relationships between academic libraries and scholars, that is, relationships that are mutually beneficial and mutually reinforcing. Like a process of cross-pollination, the program carries the work of the library throughout the campus community. At the same time, the program brings the work of scholars into the library profession in concentrated ways; many librarians have come to the profession with advanced degrees, so this is not entirely a new thing, but what the CLIR Postdoctoral Fellowship Program does is to give these scholar-librarians occasions in which to reflect purposefully and engage in dialog about this cross-pollination. These discussions provide opportunities to capitalize on ideas that arise and to create projects designed to be implemented within and across libraries and campus units.

One way that CLIR is seeking to capitalize on these ideas and cross-pollinations is to create a collegium of scholars and librarians in order to facilitate new forms of scholarship and to cultivate new kinds of information professionals and new leaders for 21st-century academic libraries. This collegium program would provide structured occasions in which scholars, librarians, and other members of the campus community can meet to reflect on the work of libraries and the needs of scholars. Out of these meetings could grow project ideas, funding proposals, new initiatives, and inspired collaborations.

A risk of a program like the CLIR Postdoctoral Fellowship, as with other leadership programs, is that it will seem elitist; only a chosen few are given the privilege of stepping back from the daily grind to think through big issues, to take initiative to launch major profession-changing projects, or to network with other movers and shakers. However, the CLIR program can be taken as a model to be applied in a variety of ways throughout the profession, allowing much broader participation in these exciting programs, and enabling us to address other emerging needs in the scholarly information universe.

The CLIR program model consists of a number of key elements: cross-institutional conversations and collaborations; focused seminars in which to reflect, debate, and problem-solve; institutional support to enable projects to be put into motion and to facilitate applications for external funding, if necessary; infrastructure to sustain these new relationships over time and space; a diversity of perspectives among participants. Any alternative application of this model should include each of these elements.

Alternative Applications of the CLIR Model

I can envision a number of alternative applications. For starters, we could create programs for new MLIS graduates that are modeled on the CLIR Postdoctoral Fellowship Program structure and focused on academic libraries, giving these newly minted librarians as much exposure to and involvement in scholarly collaborations as possible. Additionally, CLIR Fellows could partner with LIS faculty to design courses on advanced research in the humanities or other fields in order to benefit current MLIS students. Several past CLIR Fellows are already pursuing ideas for such courses at their current institutions.

Another idea is to create programs for library staff that do more than allow individuals to view a webcast or presentation and then have a discussion before returning to their desks. Rather than be viewed as "professional development"—though undoubtedly all of these programs I am suggesting, including the CLIR Postdoctoral Fellowship Program, qualify as professional development—such programs should be goal-oriented with real opportunities to follow through on projects that emerge. To this end, a program would need to be focused on a key issue or challenge such as space planning, digital preservation, cataloging and metadata issues, open-access scholarship, and so on.

An idea that might address staffing issues and create a more flexible workforce for the profession would be to establish a broad-reaching network of staff exchange programs. Scholars frequently move to other institutions as visiting professors or visiting scholars, thereby reinvigorating their own work and possibly filling a position left vacant by another faculty member's sabbatical or research trip. Occasionally, librarians and library staff may wish to work at another institution, either because personal circumstances require them to be away from home for a time or because they find colleagues or programs at other institutions that are engaged in the kinds of projects they themselves would like to be able to launch at their home libraries. For their part, academic libraries may wish to bring in specific individuals who can provide a particular set of skills or expertise on a short-term basis. With exchange infrastructure in place, libraries could be more nimble about setting up temporary positions that benefit the host institution and provide opportunities for visiting colleagues.

Programs of the kind I am proposing will succeed only if libraries and campuses that host them learn from the experience of the CLIR Postdoctoral Fellowship Program. For instance, host institutions will need to build flexibility into their human resources structures and procedures. They will need to think through the long-term benefits of these programs so that short-term impacts—provision of funding, administrative support, appropriate cyberinfrastructure, and workload coverage for participating staff members—do not become insurmountable hurdles.

With programs like these in place, the profession will create productive dialog as well as occasions for collaboration across academic libraries, such as across ARL (Association of Research Libraries) and non-ARL host institutions, an example offered by one library administrator. We need more discussions within the profession about visions of our collective future, specifically focused on ways in which CLIR Fellows—and other future leaders—can help us get there. Even if we recognize that there is no "there" there and that we will be constantly needing to renew this vision over time, we can collectively shape our own future.

Notes

1.   Council on Library and Information Resources, "CLIR Announces Post-Doctoral Fellowship in Scholarly Information Resources for Humanists," (news release), Dec, 8, 2003, CLIR website, www.clir.org/news/pressrelease/2003postdoc.html.
2.   This history is gleaned from various conversations with early participants in the planning process and from internal documents provided by CLIR.
3.   CLIR, "CLIR Announced Post-Doctoral Fellowship."
4.   The application and hiring process described will change slightly beginning with the sixth application cycle. The program will move to a model akin to the Fulbright scholarship program in order to better accommodate the calendars of the academic job market and the academic library fiscal year.
5.   For examples of positive contributions, see James G. Neal, "Raised by Wolves," *Library Journal* 131, no. 3 (Feb. 15, 2006): 42–44; Daphnée Rentfrow, "Postdoctoral Program Bridges Library, Faculty," *CLIR Issues,* no. 53 (Oct. 2006), www.clir.org/pubs/issues/issues53.html#postdoc; Alice Schreyer, "Education and Training for Careers in Special Collections: A White Paper Prepared for the Association of Research Libraries Special Collections Task Force," Nov. 2004, www.arl.org/bm~doc/sctf_ed.pdf; Elliott Shore, "CLIR Fellows Share Experiences as 'Hybrid' Professional," CLIR , no. 61 (Feb. 2008), www.clir.org/pubs/issues/issues61.html#fell; Christa Williford, comment to Association of College and Research Libraries blog, Oct. 19, 2006, http://acrlog.org/2006/10/16/clirs-program-a-real-or-imagined-shortage-of-academic-librarians.
6.   I was a CLIR Fellow in the third cohort, based in the Charles E. Young Research Library at UCLA. Like some of my colleagues, I learned about the postdoctoral fellowship by accident; I had been working part-time at an academic library while finishing up an interdisciplinary dissertation on U. S. social movement history and literature, and my supervisor's boss put the call for applications on my desk. After one year as a fellow, I became a humanities librarian at Young Research Library, where I do department liaison work, collection management, reference, instruction, digital projects, scholarly communication projects, and some research. Though no longer in a fellowship position, I remain involved in the CLIR Postdoctoral Fellowship Program, collaborating with other fellows on a variety of projects, helping to orient new fellows, and continuing the always invigorating discussions about academic librarianship that I began during my fellowship year.
7.   Rush G. Miller, "The Influx of Ph.D.'s into Librarianship: Intrusion or Transfusion?" *College & Research Libraries* 37, no. 2 (1976): 158–159.
8.   As academic libraries struggle to remain relevant to users, some libraries have opted to try new staffing strategies in order to improve outreach to students. For example, Utah State University created a Library Peer Mentor Program in 2004 in which undergraduates (LPMs) collaborate with librarians to provide reference service and instruction to their peers. Unlike the typical student worker positions within libraries—in access services or interlibrary loan departments, for instance—these paid positions entailed ongoing seminars in addition to training.

See Wendy Holliday and Cynthia Nordgren, "Extending the Reach of Librarians: Library Peer Program at Utah State University," *College & Research Libraries* 66, no. 4 (July 2005): 282–283.

9. Jeffrey S. Bullington and Susanna D. Boylston, "Strengthening the Profession: Assuring Our Future," *College & Research Libraries News* 62, no. 4 (2001): 430–432.

10. Ibid., 432. ACRL now offers the ACRL Dr. E. J. Josey Spectrum Scholar Mentor Program aimed at recruiting and retaining librarians of color: www.ala.org/ala/mgrps/divs/acrl/proftools/mentorprogram.cfm.

11. Rebecca Hankins, Michele Saunders, and Ping Situ, "Diversity Initiatives vs. Residency Programs: Agents of Change?" *College & Research Libraries News* 64, no. 5 (2003): 309.

12. Sean Patrick Knowlton and Becky Imamoto, "Recruiting Non-MLIS Graduate Students to Academic Librarianship," *College & Research Libraries* 67, no. 6 (Nov. 2006): 564.

13. Ibid., 566.

14. Thea Lindquist and Todd Gilman, "Academic/Research Librarians with Subject Doctorates: Data and Trends 1965-2006," *portal: Libraries and the Academy* 8, no. 1 (Jan. 2008): 31–52.

15. Ibid., 40.

16. Ibid., 47.

17. Ibid., 46.

18. For more information about Zoomerang surveys, see www.zoomerang.com.

19. Todd Gilman kindly provided me with a copy of their survey instrument.

20. Marta L. Brunner, 2009). "Ph.D. Holders in the Academic Library: The CLIR Postdoctoral Fellowship Program," UC Los Angeles: UCLA Library, 2009, retrieved from: http://escholarship.org/uc/item/05j228r4.

21. Ibid.

22. An updated list of links to CLIR Fellow projects is available from the CLIR Postdoctoral Fellowship Program website at www.clir.org/fellowships/postdoc/postdoc.html.

23. Conversation with Donald Waters, Bryn Mawr College, July 25, 2008.

CHAPTER 8

THE PUBLISHER IN THE LIBRARY

Michael J. Furlough
Penn State University

Introduction

In the last decade, academic libraries have begun to claim an active role in the arena of scholarly publishing. Their involvement consists of experiments in the electronic distribution of journals, monographs, and conference proceedings, as well as distinct forms of scholarly work that apply researchers' subject expertise and librarians' information management skills to digitized library collections. This remains a highly experimental and fluid field of library programming, one typically cultivated through direct engagement with faculty, and sometimes in collaboration with service partners in campus computing and university presses. Much of the early emphasis on library publishing services drew energy from advocacy efforts that sought to counterbalance the control of research by commercial scholarly publishers. But the success of these services will depend not on advocacy, but on identifying significant needs and promising trends in research and scholarship and creating services to meet them. These programs depend heavily upon IT infrastructure, but also encompass many activities that require capabilities beyond IT management. Developing the appropriate staffing resources and skills to implement and extend such programs will be challenging. This chapter reviews the operations of several library publishing programs to examine their staffing models and the expertise found among the staff, and attempts to describe what publishing demands of librarians and how it may extend their existing and historical roles.

This essay draws extensively upon a series of 13 interviews conducted in May and June 2008 with librarians who direct publishing programs and their operations. I also interviewed university press directors and editors who were involved in collaborative work with a research library. The organizations represented are Cornell University (both the library and the press), Emory University, Indiana University, New York University (both the libraries and the press), Ohio State University, the University of Kansas, the University of California (both California Digital Library and the press). I did not interview anyone at Penn State University, where I am employed, but I drew upon my own knowledge of its publishing services for details included here. (See appendix B for a complete list of interviewees.) Each interview was conducted by telephone and lasted from 30 to 60 minutes. I provide a general script for these interviews in an appendix C of this essay, but each interview was unique and tailored to some degree to the circumstances of the individual. When possible, I reviewed documents supplied by the subjects, such as program proposals, activity summaries, job ads, and job descriptions. The research I have conducted might best be characterized as qualitative, anecdotal, impressionistic, and in some cases speculative. These individuals are my colleagues, and my prior knowledge of some of the subjects and of their programs influenced my choice of questions and general approach. All subjects were asked to name other individuals who might be useful to interview, though I did not pursue all leads. Only one person who was invited to be interviewed declined to respond. All of the subjects agreed to be identified and quoted in this essay, and all were given the opportunity to review quotations for accuracy before final publication.

The chapter first examines the status of library publishing programs in 2008, and then analyzes four sets of activities within them: strategy development and resource management, outreach and recruitment, content production and management, and distribution and marketing. To some extent, each of these areas may build on existing librarian competencies, but also necessitate the integration of additional skills and knowledge that may sometimes conflict with the existing culture. An examination of several programs then in their early stages demonstrates how pilot projects help to assess existing capacities to offer publishing services, frequently drawing upon existing staff who could be widely distributed throughout the organization. Those interviewed for this essay provide further evidence of the hybridization of library staffing, and the programs reviewed in this chapter have capitalized on the diverse professional backgrounds of their staff to create and sustain innovative services. They need a high tolerance for risk, ambiguity, and experimentation, as well as the aptitude for creative problem solving and collaborative work. These programs will also provide opportunities for staff throughout libraries, perhaps especially those in liaison roles, to extend their work to encompass a wider range of services related to scholarly communications. Nevertheless, they may still prove especially challenging because libraries will have to expand their service focus from collections on a local campus to distributing data for a much wider audience in a competitive information environment. Sustaining library publishing will entail unique decision-making processes and financial models, as well as true commitments to collaboration and partnerships. The future growth of such programs will depend upon leadership that can articulate to the campus community the library's role in creating more comprehensive content management strategies for the university or college.

This is a rapidly changing service area for libraries. Nearly two years have passed since I first drafted this chapter in summer 2008 and when it was readied for final publication. Since then a serious economic crisis has had an impact on all institutions represented here, and some of those impacts have been dramatic. In some cases significant organizational changes and realignments have occurred, and some individuals interviewed have assumed expanded duties, new roles, or have since left the organization. I would hazard a guess that many of them of would respond to my questions differently now, and I would probably address some of the topics differently as a result. In no case, however, has a publishing service been eliminated, and all have evolved and even expanded. However, I leave a study of the impact of the recession on library-based publishing services for another day and another author.

Overview of Library Publishing Services

Publishing services have built upon expertise developed in library digitization programs and in institutional repository services (IRs) over the past decade, through which librarians have articulated expanded service roles for fulfilling their mission for collecting, organizing, and preserving information.. Many libraries link new publishing services very closely to preexisting institutional repository services, often based on tools such DSpace and Fedora, and may also use open source publishing software, such as Open Journal Systems and DPubS. These links suggest an organic growth in the library's strategy for supporting scholarly communication needs on the campus. The most comprehensive picture of library publishing services in 2008 can be found in *Research Library Publishing Services: New Options for University Publishing,* a report authored by Karla Hahn and published by the Association of Research Libraries (ARL).[1] Of the 80 member institutions replying to Hahn's survey, 44% (35) reported that their library offered some form of publishing services, and another 21% (16) were planning such services. These libraries publish traditional formats that have well-established print equivalents: journals (88%), conference proceedings (79%), and monographs (71%), and all together reported 265 discrete titles that were either already online or in development. Hahn confirms that each library, in addition to providing hardware and software, directly subsidizes these programs primarily through reallocation of staff time, while a few rely on fee-based services, grants, and other external funding sources. The survey showed that these programs generally do not attempt to replicate full-scale publishing operations, such as those found at university presses. Instead they "are intentionally exploring the boundaries of what several program managers conceptualize as a service core,"[2] built around Web hosting of publications.

The study reports a wealth of information about publishing programs and services, but offers limited specific data about staffing or the roles these staff played in the service. In a later e-mail to the author on July 3, 2008, Hahn explained:

> Although data on staffing were requested, questions about the consistency of the data prevented it from being published in the study report. Comments accompanying the counts suggest that different institutions defined involved staff differently. A second issue is that service managers indicated that startup of a title was much more staff intensive than maintenance suggesting that staffing demands could fluctuate substantially over time. Average FTE was 3, a range from under .25 to over 10, a median of 2 and a mode of 4. The number of individuals averaged 7, with a range from 0–14 (0 representing a vacancy), a median of 5, and a mode of 4.

My interviews with librarians and publishers confirmed Hahn's report of wide variation in levels of staffing. There were also substantial differences in how individuals' time was allocated across projects, and not surprisingly, these variations related to the scale and scope of the program. The report suggests that most library programs are small and have not grown to maturity. But several quite well-developed programs, with well-defined services and staffing, can provide us with illustrations of how the work can be divided and organized.

Three well-established and -staffed programs include Project Euclid and related projects at Cornell University Library, the Scholarly Publishing Office at the University of Michigan Library (SPO), and the eScholarship Publishing Program at the California Digital Library (CDL). Each of these programs has distributed or published a significant number of titles or projects in previous years. (Note: The details in this paragraph and in the one following were compiled from interviews and the public websites of each organization as they appeared in July 2008. See appendix A for the URLs.) Project Euclid began at Cornell in 1999, the Scholarly Publishing Office at the University of Michigan was formed in 2001, and eScholarship Publishing Program at CDL dates from 2000. All have responsibility for a large number of titles or projects and each hosts journals, monographs, and some additional formats. As of July 2008, Project Euclid aggregated and marketed 53 math and statistics journals from 34 different publishers, as well as monographs and conference proceedings. Cornell Library also distributes four other publications that originate from Cornell faculty, using either an open-access model, or a mixed open-access/subscription model. The Michigan Scholarly Publishing Office listed 23 different journals or projects in July 2008, including the hosting of several large for-fee aggregation services, such as the American Council of Learned Societies History E-Book project. CDL's eScholarship hosted 25 "Journals and Peer-Reviewed Series" at the same date. Only CDL provides publishing services exclusively for University of California researchers and programs and distributes exclusively in open-access mode. Both SPO and Project Euclid rely on revenue from external clients and subscription-based titles to underwrite a portion of their operations, and each fund about half of their staff from those revenues. Project Euclid operates as a discipline-oriented, branded business operation, but SPO and eScholarship Services act as distributors for multiple publications across a range of disciplines

At Cornell, Project Euclid staff report through two different lines: Terry Ehling, Executive Director of Euclid and Director of the Center for Innovative Publishing, reports to the associate university librarian for Scholarly Resources and Special Collections, while technical staff, led by director of E-Publishing Technologies David Ruddy, report to the associate university librarian for Digital Library and Information Technologies. Currently at Cornell, three people contribute about 2 FTE support for Project Euclid.[3] Seven FTE in the Scholarly Publishing Office report to Director Maria Bonn, who in turn reports to Michigan's university librarian. Catherine Mitchell, director, eScholarship Publishing Program at the California Digital Library, manages a group of seven FTE and reports to the executive director of CDL. These small groups cannot be very hierarchical, but rely upon specialized work assignments divided among leadership and operational duties. In addition to permanent staff in the publishing group, these programs rely in varying degrees on the IT infrastructure in place throughout the organization and on the financial management operations in the library. Each makes heavy use of external vendors for digitization, markup and metadata creation, or hosting software platforms.

Smaller programs, such as those at Kansas, Indiana, Ohio State, and Penn State, have been operating in start-up mode, having brought projects online only within the year leading up to the date of the interview and not having fully settled on a clear staffing model and plan for publishing. In interviews, their staff described implementations employing teams numbering from two to eight, usually located within a multiple units. These start-up programs tackle many of the same tasks that Euclid, SPO, and eScholarship must, but as start-ups they focus significantly on learning tasks and establishing processes that will be adapted later. Every program discussed in this essay continuously explores various possible new services, but New York University's program was almost entirely investigative at the time of my interview, with a single staff member, the Digital Publishing Program Officer, leading preliminary needs analyses. Finally, Emory University offers publishing services somewhat different from the others discussed in this essay. While the Digital Programs Group unit at Emory Library has provided software to host conference proceedings and journals, the unit focuses on more experimental types of digital scholarly projects and on larger scale digital content preservation and management.

Roles and Staffing for Publishing Services

Several commentators have noted that librarians carry competencies and skills deeply rooted in a service orientation, which can prove valuable in providing publishing services. Kate Wittenberg suggests that librarians have embraced change and that electronic publishing experiments will benefit from the "expertise of librarians in information architecture, design, preservation and retrieval, indexing, and support for users [that] is already available within such library-based publishing organizations."[4] In their 2007 report for Ithaka, *University Publishing in a Digital Age,* Laura Brown, Rebecca Griffiths, and Matthew Rascoff address library skill sets in relation to those of publishers and include an appendix that compares complementary "strengths and weaknesses" of both libraries and university presses.[5] The report identifies the library's most useful strengths as IT infrastructure and staff, expertise in information management and retrieval, as well as librarians' firsthand knowledge of user needs and behaviors gathered through public services, liaison work, and collection development. However, Brown and her colleagues also point out that this service orientation, which is focused on single campuses, has the potential to isolate libraries from forces that commonly affect academic publishing, which tends to address a much broader potential audience. The report notes that strong service-oriented approaches do not always allow for easy prioritization or evaluating demand among competing service needs: library budgets, largely expenditure- and subsidy-based, provide the organization with flexibility to take risks on new services, which for university publishers would be a rare luxury. However, these budgets are not infinitely flexible, and it can also be difficult to continually absorb new services with existing staff. If the library's publishing services do not rely on a revenue-capture business model, like those of a university press, it will likely need to deploy the commercially oriented discipline or expertise to create sustainable new services and programs over longer periods of time. Libraries operate as campus-focused service centers, not market-facing organizations, so they have less incentive to specialize in needs assessments and marketing that will create demand for their content beyond their home campus.[6] Brown refers to one librarian who remarked that "putting these resources online for free is much easier than charging for them, because then they would actually have to consider who the user base would be."[7] Perhaps most significantly, Brown, Griffiths, and Rascoff point out that historically libraries have little direct involvement in the set of processes that go into publishing scholarship.

Raym Crow, in his highly useful SPARC guide, *University-Based Publishing Partnerships: A Guide to Critical Issues,* discusses the cultural, logistical, and business factors that must be negotiated in order for libraries to successfully collaborate with university presses when starting a publishing service.[8] Crow provides a table mapping out the core competencies for university publishing activities that are found in university presses, libraries, academic units, and campus computing. These are: funding, content acquisition, editorial, IP/rights management, pre-press/production, distribution, business management, marketing and sales, archiving and preservation. These competencies cover a broad range of business and technical operations, some of which may demand uncommon or unusual specializations for library staff if a viable collaborative service cannot be established. (This table is reprinted as appendix D.) Crow's listing of library competencies emphasizes those related to content production and management and faculty service and consultation, again pointing to these two areas as the base from which libraries should launch the publishing program.

The following sections examine these specializations in more detail to identify potential gaps, how publishing might expand the skill sets of librarians, and what factors these librarians may find to be most critical to address. I will group my discussion of these competencies more broadly than Crow because the same person or persons may perform multiple functions in these services. Some of the more important competency gaps may be found in *Strategy Development and Resource Management,* suggesting most clearly how the library's mission and culture might frame the operation of publishing services. *Outreach and recruitment* for publishing services overlap in some ways with university press editorial and acquisition activities. But libraries' approaches to recruiting and evaluating projects remain very different from the university press model. Publishing services are one of the many factors changing how libraries may think of their subject specialists' outreach roles. *Production and content management,* comparable to the prepress operations in a publishing house, draw most heavily on existing competencies found in digital library programs. However, orienting the operations towards distributing original scholarly works often forces staff to become more familiar with a range of different standards and to scale operations up for high efficiency. *Distribution and marketing* appear at first to be the simplest of publishing services. But making the content more visible goes beyond putting it online, requiring library staff to focus on the wider audience of scholars and the public that exist beyond the local campus environment.

Defining the Scope: Strategy Development and Resource Management

Maria Bonn explains that when the Scholarly Publishing Office began at Michigan, they defined themselves as an "alternative publisher," but soon had to ask "alternative to what?" A similar question faces each leader of library publishing services, and answering it will be the most complex, and most critical, aspect of beginning a program. Libraries are filled with leaders who engage in strategic thinking when writing collection development plans, disaster recovery protocols, and plans for new services and new facilities. The processes employed in managing and providing access to collections, as well as staffing libraries seven days a week, speak to a strong culture of resource management. At an abstract level, such skills transfer to other domains, but publishing services leadership needs both specific expertise and an ability to adapt an existing culture to include elements of others. Leaders of publishing services must balance oversight of day-to-day operations with longer range planning for program growth and alignment with the larger mission and vision of their library's leadership. These leaders will need specialized knowledge of publishing procedures that move content from raw to readable forms; an understanding of trends in academic publishing, higher education, and information technology; and the legal and policy issues that frame these matters. They must be able to translate these issues to researchers and faculty who may have limited understanding of this framework, while also demonstrating a sensitivity and appreciation of the distinctive research processes and methodologies employed by the researchers in many disciplines. They may be deeply involved in long-range financial planning complicated by multiple funding and revenue streams, and might also manage multiple internal and external relationships with authors, editors, or publishers; subscribers or users; commercial vendors; and possibly units within their own organization that provide them with the support necessary to offer these publishing services. To help incubate these new programs, the leader must have a strong understanding of the goals of the host library, how the service contributes to those goals, and how such service can fit within a continuously changing network of scholarly communications. The program director should be a strong communicator and be capable of feeding strategy up to the administration, especially in linking the program to related issues such as collection development, public services, and digital content services.

Organizational and professional culture may have a special impact on how leaders carry out strategic and tactical planning for their publishing services and operations. Crow and Brown and her colleagues suggest ways that librarians may bring an "outsider" perspective to existing publishing problems, and but also suggests that the culture of libraries (and publishing) can be limiting for new service programs.[9] Their emphasis on "market forces" should not be understood to suggest that library publishing must always be based on revenue generation and fee-based access models. But librarians must acknowledge that publishing by nature exists within a wider set of systems in which information must compete for attention. Sound and exacting attention to questions of sustainability should be applied to any new service in an academic context, and common business-planning processes will still be necessary, even in an open-access model. Given the uncertain future of academic publishing in general, publishing service managers in any operation will likely need to bring an entrepreneurial approach to the work, must be highly tolerant of ambiguity and risk, and must be open to new ideas or collaborations that may in fact radically shift the direction of their program. Terry Ehling explains that start-up library publishing services present "a counterintuitive challenge," noting that the academy's simultaneously decentralized and bureaucratic environment may not offer hospitable environments for incubating start-up services aimed at creating organizational and cultural change. For their publishing services to thrive, librarians will need even "greater flexibility, greater creativity, and [to promote] more risk-taking. . . . Libraries need people who went to business schools and arts schools, not only the traditional I-school."[10]

Monica McCormick, the Digital Scholarly Publishing Program Officer at New York University Library, has previously worked in both academic publishing and other research libraries. She comes into this role with a sympathetic understanding of the financial situations of both institutions, as well as a clear-eyed take on how their organizational cultures may support but also inhibit new publishing services. Academic publishing, a bottom-line-oriented environment even in not-for-profits, relies upon a particular set of rigorous and formalized processes for decision making around book projects: "Publishers, by definition, make choices. Choose one project and you are not going to do another one. There are clear decision-making processes for ruling out" manuscripts for publication. With the exception of collection development, where materials acquisition may well be a zero-sum activity, in libraries decision processes for new services appear more fluid and opaque, with a less urgent sense of binary choice. "My job now is to start a conversation about the criteria for what we will and won't include in a digital publishing service," according to McCormick.[11]

Strategic collaborations with other organizations, such as a campus computing unit, an academic program, or an academic publisher, bring special challenges for management and strategy development. In such cases, cultural differences could prove difficult to overcome, even when well-defined opportunities and needs guide the relationship. As Raym Crow points out, potential partners must see that the benefits and risks of a collaboration are in balance for both sides in order to yield a powerful collaboration that provides a more comprehensive set of services for the researcher.[12] California Digital Library (CDL) and the University of California Press (UCP) present a useful case study. In 2007, the California Digital Library and University of California Press surveyed potential publishing opportunities within the UC system through extensive site visits to and interviews at all system campuses. Together they recommended that the university system create a well-planned, sustainable, and coordinated university publishing program that could allow space for publications derived from novel methodologies and requiring alternative formats.[13] Both organizations had a prior history of working together on the Mark Twain Project Online and other isolated projects. To implement the report, Catherine Mitchell and Laura Cerruti, Director of Digital Content Development at the press, focused on how to move from such opportunistic efforts to the more strategic direction recommended. Working with an outside consultant for several weeks, both acquired what Mitchell diplomatically called "a keen understanding of dramatic differences in cultures" that at times seemed insurmountable. Yet they eventually determined how to structure a working plan and defined a pilot project to initiate it. Their future work will identify shared publishing services, rather than jointly fashioned monograph imprints or journals, according to Mitchell. Cerruti explains that both organizations want to specialize in the processes and systems that they have relied upon, but work together to promote them as "a continuum of publishing services for the university." For an academic department or institute with a book or journal publication series, for example, CDL can provide an infrastructure for manuscript management, peer review, hosting, access, and archiving, while the university press might assist with other services, such as marketing or finding a channel for print-on-demand if appropriate. Strategically, the collaboration reinforces the visibility of both partners with researchers and allows them to begin working towards experiments that would stretch the boundaries of traditional publishing.[14] The California collaboration illustrates one potential path that a strategic partnership might take when partners can align their respective missions and cultures to reinforce the others.

Publishing is about establishing partnerships. No matter who the partners are, the leaders of these programs will probably be most successful if they combine pragmatism with creativity. As managers, they will possibly need to link resources across multiple organizational lines, which will call for strong communication and persuasive negotiation. They must root themselves in their organizational culture and retain the flexibility to question that culture when stepping outside of its traditional library boundaries.

Working with the Researcher: Outreach and Recruitment
How do clients find the publishing service, and who is responsible for ensuring that researchers know who to ask? Who assesses the researcher's needs for publication services, and how? This section explores service outreach and marketing aimed at identifying potential projects and clients to serve. Library subject liaisons and publishing acquisitions editors carry out complementary tasks, and involvement in publishing services provides an opportunity, if not a need, to build on existing roles and relationships with researchers. While outreach might be carried out exclusively by the program manager, it could also be carried out by a designated outreach librarian, subject liaisons, editors in a partnering organization, or even the researchers themselves. Outreach should be based on a thorough understanding of publishing services and broader scholarly communications trends and issues in order to map the researcher's needs onto the services the program can support. More importantly, outreach staff should be able to explore the goals and objectives of researchers and scholarly groups and demonstrate an understanding of the role that scholarly publishing plays in a variety of disciplinary fields. Promoting the service and recruiting projects might include holding workshops, writing marketing materials, meeting with researchers to explore ideas, conducting needs assessments and analyses, and providing advice to solve their clients' publishing needs. This work may also involve others in the publishing services team with more specialized expertise. Because outreach activity entails close working relationships with faculty and a strong understanding of academic practice, it may suggest how library subject specialization may evolve to more actively engage scholarly communication issues.

The California Digital Library, which serves all 10 of the University of California campuses, relies heavily upon a network of liaison librarians at each campus to help CDL staff connect with users at the local level. Catherine Mitchell explains that a new position in the eScholarship Publishing Group, the Outreach and Marketing Coordinator, works closely with these eScholarship liaisons. The Outreach Coordinator works "in the field," moving from campus to campus to advertise the services and to identify new publishing opportunities. For the outreach role, Mitchell sought substantial marketing expertise, with the capability of defining and carrying out a campaign to help promote eScholarship's identity and as a provider of alternative publishing services to the University of California. Yet she also recognizes the potential for marketing to be perceived with suspicion in the academy. "We don't want it to feel like a corporate come-on," says Mitchell, noting that the candidate she recruits must carry the "gravitas" to be taken seriously by the faculty. He or she will "have to understand the cultural differences among disciplines, and campuses" to avoid the "make a compelling case for the relevance and value of eScholarship services."

Mitchell further explains that she saw some affinities between the Marketing and Outreach Coordinator and the role that acquiring editors play in university presses, partly because the individual will be expected to build networks in order to engage partners and identify projects with the potential to grow the service. Similarly, Monica Mc-Cormick at New York University, who was previously an acquiring editor at the University of California Press, explains how critical outreach and networking are to an editor's success. Acquisitions editors, she says, have as a basic requirement "not being shy. . . . To be a good editor, you have to build networks" among potential authors, reviewers, and others who can serve as "feeders" to the editor. Relationship building not only helps an editor to find new manuscripts, but keeps the editor in touch with trends and shifts within her assigned scholarly fields. Editors have the power to reject, but they must also promote, even sell, their press to potential authors in order to land a promising manuscript: "Here's what I can do for you, here's the platform I can offer you, here's the visibility you can get [with me and my publishing house.]" McCormick links her previous role as an acquiring editor and to that of her current colleagues at New York University Libraries who serve as subject area liaisons. A subject liaison must build similar networks to serve her assigned disciplines and departments and to promote the services and collections of the libraries.

But important distinctions remain. A liaison's typical role has historically been tied to collections services, focusing on support for the teaching and research needs of her users through the acquisition of scholarly resources and instruction in their use. Liaison outreach may incorporate marketing elements but it tends to focus not on "selling" and recruitment, but on notification, communication, and adoption of resources. Library liaisons and selectors also do not select materials in the same way that editors do. Editors narrow the field of potential works. Selectors seek to deepen the collections to respond to local research and curricular needs. Peter Potter, editor-in-chief of the Cornell University Press, explains that while collection development clearly involves processes of evaluation, libraries rely upon reputable publishers to make good decisions at an early stage of publication, well before the library acquires the material. "Librarians don't have the same gate-keeping mentality that press editors do," Potter says. "We see a lot of books, and we winnow out the good from the bad. Librarians aren't well versed in that [level of review]." Library publishing programs usually do not take on the same role in vetting original research that a publisher does, where, at least in monograph publishing, the acquisitions editor reviews manuscripts in addition to the peers who provide anonymous assessments. The library publishing service may choose to publish materials that undergo no prior peer review, or might publish materials for which the project sponsors or editors manage the peer review. For a library, the decision to take on a publishing project may rest significantly upon other factors, such as the service's own capacities, skill sets, technologies, schedules, and basic "fit" with the potential client's needs. Publishers may also choose not to publish books based on technical requirements—some presses specialize in heavily illustrated books, others do not and would steer a manuscript requiring many visuals to another publisher. Nevertheless, while librarians have had limited experience cultivating new content, publishing programs and their representatives will have to "sell" the benefits of their service and their distribution platform, just as editors do their press when competing for a manuscript.

In spite of these differences, publishing services within a library are among many scholarly-communications-related activities that may influence the outreach role of liaisons, whose portfolio of responsibilities continues to shift from an exclusive focus on purchased and licensed resources to a broader focus on the processes of scholarship and facilitating them. In some cases, this may still incorporate work that relates to reviewing and selecting scholarly content. Kizer Walker currently serves as an editor for *Signale: Modern German Letters, Cultures, and Thought*, a new print and digital monograph series published by Cornell University Press and in collaboration with the Cornell Library. Walker, who holds both a library degree and a PhD in German, has his primary assignment at Cornell Library in collection development with subject liaison responsibilities that cover the German program. *Signale*'s series editor serves as a senior professor of German and comparative literature, an editorial board includes five Cornell faculty in related fields, and 12 researchers from 11 other universities serve as an external advisory board. Walker's role in *Signale* is defined as "managing editor," and he serves on the editorial board, communicating with authors, editors, and reviewers; calling meetings of the board; and reading manuscripts for discussion. Although Peter Potter, the official acquiring editor for *Signale,* notes significant differences between editorial review and collection development, he observes that Walker's involvement in managing the *Signale* effort can "develop the kind of editorial thinking to apply to projects" that demand peer review. Remarking that acquisitions editors do not necessarily need the deep disciplinary background that some librarians and some editors hold, he suggests that editorial skill relies more upon "personality than subject training. . . . [Walker's] temperament seems similar to university press editors. He has an ability to stand back and apply the right level of judgment."

Walker, however, sees other aspects of his role as a selector for the library relating to "selecting at an earlier stage in the process" of scholarly works, noting that when librarians select and curate materials for collection digitization projects, they create packaged sets of content that shapes a viewer's understanding of the subjects, even though it may not provide the same narrative and analytic arguments found in a scholarly monograph or article. Walker agrees that not all collections librarians would be well suited to working at the level of detail in publishing services that he does. However his deeper involvement in the research and publishing process suggests one way in which the subject specialist's future role might involve more collaborative working relationships in their subject fields, which may in fact demand more specialized knowledge. Programs like *Signale,* he says are "best focused on smaller areas [of scholarship] with greater difficulty in keeping their publications going." In fact, within these specialized niches of scholarship that form small information ecologies, libraries have some of their best opportunities to incubate more active roles in publishing.

Pre- and Postpublication: Content Production and Management

Maria Bonn defines the University of Michigan's Scholarly Publishing Office's primary business activity to be "get[ting] the data into shape so that it can be moved online." These operations involve conversion, processing, and preparation of publishable content for online delivery in aggregations with related publications that bring additional functionality and utility for readers. These technology-dependent operations are frequently cited as a key asset for libraries engaged in publishing. The last decade's expansion of digital library programs and deployments of institutional repository services have created a large base of expertise in the manipulation, markup, and preparation of digital content for electronic distribution. Karla Hahn's report on library publishing reveals that in most cases, publishing services focus primarily on hosting the publications online, a more limited set of services than those found in traditional publishing outlets. In such cases, the library plays a role analogous to that of a printer or a small distributor. As hosting becomes more routine, Hahn writes, libraries often begin to explore more value-added services in pre- and postproduction, such as technical support for workflow and editorial management, metadata production, preservation, ISSN registration, OpenURL support, layout and design, and copyediting/proofreading.[15] Publishers will be more familiar with many of these, especially those that move original material from manuscript to presentable form, such as copyediting, design, and layout. Several of these services lie outside of the established competencies for many existing digital library programs. Peter Potter at Cornell University Press suggested that where complementary and sufficient expertise can be found through a partnership, libraries and publishers should continue to specialize in this way because of the expense of duplicating talent.

A mix of project managers, developers, and technicians carry out the operations in these programs. Project managers and technical leaders frequently work directly with clients and users to define the functional requirements of a publication project. Technologists in these publishing programs carry responsibilities for process automation, system management, access log analysis and reporting, software investigations, and writing of documentation. Technical staff likely will not be the primary contacts with the user community, but it will be critical for them to understand their services from the perspective of users. While these operations managers and technologists must understand the mission and context in which they work and the needs and perspectives of users and clients, their areas of technology specialization are not necessarily specific to publishing. Many of their skills, such as the ability to program in one or more common languages, as well as an understanding of XML/XSLT or webserver administration, are common to other IT operations in libraries. For example, Project Euclid employs a Publishing Systems Developer to maintain the production and hosting platforms, perform service enhancements and upgrades, and provide technical support. The position requires a computer science background, previous work experience, and familiarity with Perl and XML/XSLT, but does not specify an expectation of or preference for experience in a publishing setting.[16] Other staff partially devoted to Euclid perform related duties at a higher systems level, such as architecture design and specifications for elements of DPubS and Euclid. At SPO and the eScholarship Program, junior programmers report to a technical leader or more senior programmer. At Cornell and other libraries, staff already assigned to digitization or production units, or the core IT units, are sometimes assigned duties at less than 100% effort to support the publishing services. Staff within a central technology unit thus can work on multiple digital library, publishing, and integrated library operations, relying upon cross-training or a service team approach. Proper project management and resource management in such contexts will be critical.

Maria Bonn supervises three staff members in these types of roles, including two project managers, one of whom serves as managing editor of the *Journal of Electronic Publishing.* An electronic publications librarian identifies workflow, process, and automation needs; determines appropriate publication formats; and presents clients with design and interface options. Catherine Mitchell at California Digital Library oversees a technical lead, three programmers, and an operations coordinator, in addition to the outreach and marketing coordinator previously discussed.. David Ruddy, director of E- Publishing Technologies at Cornell, now oversees 2 FTE technical staff devoted to Euclid,[17] smaller publishing projects, and maintenance and development of the DPubS publishing platform. David Ruddy says that as Euclid has become larger in scale, distributing more journals and publishers, operational work has concurrently become "simultaneously more intense and more tedious," requiring a detail orientation and an eye for process improvement and efficiency. Project Euclid has kept its costs lower by taking on fewer responsibilities for copyediting, design, and layout, relying on their journal editors to bring them the equivalent of "camera-ready copy." Nevertheless, this material still needs metadata creation and standardization and reference linking via the assignment and use of Digital Object Identifiers (DOIs). Both Bonn and Ruddy discussed when and how they might outsource especially large assignments of digitization or metadata generation to another library unit or to a commercial vendor.

Although the operations staff may not be the primary public face of the program, they may manage its most visible aspect: the Web interface to the publications. Some programs have deployed new software programs, such as Open Journal Systems or DPubS, or used third-party services such as BePress, to distribute the published materials. Such platforms may also provide the editors of publications with Web-based tools to manage the processes of manuscript submission and review. In either situation, responsiveness to the users will become a critical issue. David Ruddy points out that increases in the client base and readership will inevitably entail a greater degree of help desk activity and trouble reports, requiring staff to rapidly triage the problem for referral or resolution. Help desk reports can signal a problem of such severity that it will take precedence over all other work and may take significant time away from other assignments within these small working groups. Furthermore, client needs and subscriber requests for improved service may require customization or further development of the publication software platform. At the time of our interview, the Scholarly Publishing Office at Michigan was initiating planning focused on a significant implementation of OpenURL to comply with a major subscriber's newly announced expectations. Similarly, the eScholarship Publishing Group at CDL has recently begun significant usability testing and redesign, working closely with BePress, the vendor of their Digital Commons platform, to identify and test new functionality to improve the reading experience.

Reaching the Reader: Distribution and Marketing

Because distribution and marketing take place near the end of the production chain, they tend to be less visible to many library staff. Assisting a journal editor in bringing her publication online can be a significant first step in reaching a wider audience. But it is only a first step. Strategic decisions about the publishing business model and targeted audiences direct where the content is marketed and in what forms it will be accessible. In the most basic way, electronic distribution occurs at the moment the publication goes online. But the efforts to improve interface accessibility discussed above will have no effect if staff time cannot also be directed at improving visibility. Doing so would at a minimum entail search engine optimization of the websites and metadata publishing of a variety of forms, ranging from basic OAI publishing/harvesting to the assignment of Digital Object Identifiers to promote citation cross-linking. That may promote visibility, but it stops short of the marketing or promotion of publications that would be necessary to establish awareness of their name or their reputation as a valuable scholarly resource. A key service for a publishing program should be to help publications reach the widest possible reading market, which can entail significantly more promotional effort beyond search engine optimization and OAI publishing. Katharine Skinner, Digital Projects Librarian at Emory University Library, worked briefly in publicity and marketing for nonprofit organizations prior to working at Emory. While she believes the experience gave her "a good understanding of the importance of a broader, wider audience and the ways of reaching it," it also has made her since realize "that's not something that libraries are especially good at doing." Marketing becomes critical if the publishing service's business plan calls for cost recovery through sales or fees. In her survey of library publishing services, Karla Hahn pointed out that most libraries today primarily offer services based on open-access business and access models, but not necessarily because of their advocacy for open access: "Where libraries are supporting only open access publications, there is also a genuine element of pragmatism in the decision—they are avoiding the substantial overhead involved in subscription-based business models and traditional print runs. The costs of restricting access to a small readership may exceed the opportunities to generate revenue that subscriptions create."[18] Long-tail service providers have proliferated, and libraries can use print-on-demand services such as Lulu or outsource to Amazon's CreateSpace or to Ingram's Lightning Source for services more directly connected to broader sales channels. Here, however, library-based publishing begins to move towards more complicated financial arrangements that may necessitate additional expertise. Maria Bonn of Michigan's Scholarly Publishing Office admits that over the years her steepest learning curve has been to learn how publishing works from the perspectives of a producer, marketer, and distributor. "I'm still figuring out the publishing business. [Offering print-on-demand services] has meant understanding the whole world of distribution, trade discounts" and other practices less well understood by librarians.

Where significant marketing needs exist, or when a revenue-based access model is needed or desirable, a formal publishing partner can possibly provide necessary expertise. California Digital Library's partnership with the UC Press provides the eScholarship Program with access to marketing channels and expertise to complement its own hosting services. In early 2008, Cornell established a partnership with Duke University Press that divided responsibilities for Project Euclid operations between the two organizations. Project Euclid's mixed open-access/subscription model involves significant business planning, journal recruitment, and marketing in order to compete with other publishers for sales to libraries and for the rights to distribute journals. Duke, which has a significant e-journal publishing program of its own, now provides marketing, sales, and order-fulfillment services to Euclid publishers and subscribers. Cornell Library continues to provide the technology platform for the Euclid journals, along with metadata, preservation, and consultation services.[19] Euclid's revenue-generating business operations are complicated and unique within Cornell Libraries and would likely be unique in any research library. Duke has extensive experience and capacity in those areas, having developed them as a not-for-profit university press. Ehling describes this mutually advantageous arrangement as another example of how libraries and publishers can partner based on their unique strengths. But not every library has needs like Euclid's, nor can they all work with a university press that has the ability and interest in collaborating in these ways. In such cases, the library may have no choice but to handle these and other capabilities in house or to scope the programs services to a manageable set of responsibilities and provide referrals for what it cannot provide.

Starting Up: Testing the Waters and Building Expertise

The previous discussion of staffing models focused on better developed library publishing programs in order to outline the diversity of processes within them. Assigning staff solely to the publishing operation can allow the program to specialize and create economies of scale. Libraries may hire new staff specifically to begin or manage such programs, and these individuals may come from a variety of nontraditional backgrounds. But libraries just beginning a new publishing service likely cannot dedicate a large number of FTE to a start-up project and will need to link the effort to existing programs or to reallocate existing staff on a permanent or short-term basis. In this section, I will first discuss several pilot publishing projects to identify where needed expertise could be found. Following that discussion, I will look at the education and professional backgrounds of librarians tapped to manage publishing services, and the challenges for their professional development.

Start-Up Programs and Services

Start-up programs might begin in any number of ways: a detailed and concerted needs analysis, requests from one or more faculty, an opportunistic chance to experiment, or some combination of these. Start-ups frequently begin with one or more pilot projects, often defined as technology-dependent tasks and implementations, that create a learning opportunity in which teamwork and problem-solving capacities are critical. Such projects provide the groundwork to define a publishing service strategy, but typically focus first on answering the questions of how the library can publish original materials and later on assessing next steps. Staff assigned to these projects tend to be members of the library who have demonstrated a capacity for operations and process management, as well as a proven willingness to experiment and ability to succeed. The following sections briefly discuss how several publishing projects were initiated at the University of Kansas, Indiana University, Ohio State University, and Penn State University. In three of these libraries, the publishing service has been closely aligned with preexisting institutional repository services, an approach allowing the project to effectively leverage staff expertise even if the IR and publishing platforms are distinct. At Penn State University, no IR service existed at the time the publishing program was initiated. The publishing projects there gave the library an opportunity to begin its program with services that responded to specific needs and strategic collaborations and to build additional repository services from this base of activity.

Though few in number, librarians with prior publishing experience will certainly have an advantage when starting new services. At the University of Kansas, Brian Rosenblum has relied on his previous work at the Scholarly Publishing Office at the University of Michigan to initiate pilot journal and monograph publications. As the Scholarly Digital Initiatives Librarian, Brian manages no one directly, but coordinates work undertaken in the central information technology group and by others in the Scholar Services unit in which he serves. Rosenblum has guided the evaluation and selection of publishing software for the new program, assessed new content with researchers, written specifications, and communicated with vendors for digitization work. He also supports users of the institutional repository, consults with researchers on content preparation, and advises editors on subjects ranging from intellectual property and contracts to how to work with aggregators and indexing services. Rosenblum oversaw the launch of two journals in early 2008 through a service known as Journals@KU before coordinating the preparation of two additional journals and three monographs. However, he also sees limited growth potential without additional resources for technical support or production staff. At the Scholarly Publishing Office at Michigan, he gained proficiency in content production, text markup, and working with faculty. But with no formal training or experience in traditional print publishing, he says that he is well aware of the boundaries of his expertise and where that will limit new services or require external partnerships, especially in the areas of marketing and distribution.

Rosenblum's prior experience allows him to perform as a "jack-of-all-trades" and to provide clear guidance to others in his organization. But where no prior experience exists, pilot publishing projects may rely on a small team with "all hands on deck." Such teams may number as few as two or three people tasked with moving one journal from concept to publication. Frequently these teams cross departmental and divisional lines, even when one department has been identified as the publishing services unit. This allows for a breadth of expertise and a needed division of labor, even though roles may not be distinct at various points in the process. At Indiana, a team of four, made up of a systems analyst, a reference/public services librarian, a graduate assistant, and the associate dean for Collections and Digital Publishing, worked for several months directly with one faculty member to launch a brand-new open-access journal, *Museum Anthropology Review.* Associate Dean Julie Bobay explained that the journal's editor, who also serves as editor of one of field's flagship journals, *Museum Anthropology,* "taught the library as much as about the editorial process as we taught him about online distribution." The project began when the editor, a user of Indiana's IR service, IUScholarWorks , indicated his more pressing need to publish new, original scholarship, rather than archiving postprints. Based on the need for supporting the workflows of editorial review, the library decided not to use its DSpace installation but instead adopt a publishing-specific tool. This small team did "just about everything" to bring the journal online, which involved choosing new software, Open Journal Systems, testing and debugging the installation, customizing the interfaces, and designing the workflows. Because the systems analyst was assigned only half-time to both the publishing effort and institutional repository services, all other members of the team took on as many tasks as possible to enable him to focus on the software services. Bobay explained that with one journal complete, Indiana now has a better understanding of the process and knows that it will need additional staff with more dedicated time to grow the program. Because the publishing project came to the library via the IR service, Bobay believes that the continuum of these services gave the library a stronger grounding for supporting scholarly communications.

Tschera Harkness Connell, head of the Scholarly Resources Integration Department, has responsibility for developing the publishing services at Ohio State University (OSU). The library has recently become the host for *Disability Studies Quarterly* (DSQ), now an open-access journal. Connell also oversees serials and electronic resources cataloging, as well as the Knowledge Bank, OSU's institutional repository. She also serves on the project team, and her unit has been heavily involved in the deployment of OSU:pro, an enterprise system for managing information about the scholarly expertise of the university, that is being phased in as a tool to support the OSU's promotion and tenure-review process. Connell's department carries out a notable range of activities, and in this case, assigning the work to a service unit that had experience in implementing services off the beaten track seems to have been a strategic and effective choice. Overall, the department consists of 10 people, counting Connell, who says that her staff, now specialized, will be asked to cross-train as publishing services become more regularized. When OSU Library initiated the migration of DSQ from a commercial Web hosting firm to OSU, available staff were few in number. At the start, only one individual was heavily involved in the installation, setup, and initiation of DPubS, as well as the content preparation for the journal. Though this allowed for a deeper knowledge of the tool and how it works, Connell expected that these two tasks would be divided for more efficiency. Connell now oversees 1.5 FTE who are responsible for defining workflows, service plans, and assessment methods. Both the Knowledge Bank and the new publishing services have been assigned one FTE in the central IT group. A wider group of staff from her unit and IT services have become involved in evaluating and reviewing needs for further software implementations.

Penn State University Libraries and the Penn State Press formed the Office of Digital Scholarly Publishing in 2005, but it operates largely as a virtual organization. The office is codirected by the author, the Assistant Dean for Scholarly Communications, and the Associate Director of the press, and a distributed project model supports the its programs. Penn State had no previously existing institutional repository services per se, though it had been actively digitizing from its collections for a number of years, and it had been collaborating with Cornell Library to create the DPubS platform. Following the first public release of DPubS in late 2006, the codirectors commissioned an implementation team to publish online large back file sets for two journals, a set of conference proceedings, and three monographs in the newly launched series Penn State Romance Studies. This implementation group consisted of the members of the previously existing Digital Technologies Advisory Group, a cross-departmental team of staff who planned digitization projects from inception to completion, with two more staff added for additional expertise. Membership ultimately comprised staff from the departments of Digitization and Preservation, Metadata and Cataloging Services, I-Tech (a technology applications support and training unit), and Digital Library Technologies (IT networking, hardware, systems), as well as the production editor from Penn State Press and the newly named Scholarly Communications Services librarian. Including production staff from both the Penn State Press and Libraries allowed the two units to better coordinate specifications for design and composition to accommodate both print and electronic products. Relying on a previously existing team with additional expertise ensured that the libraries drew upon known strengths and working relationships, while also testing how well a distributed service and staffing model can work for these programs.

Given the emerging nature of library publishing programs, these experimental pilot projects have served as assessment opportunities. They gave each organization the chance to test assumptions, develop an understanding of process, identify the needed skills and resources to grow such a program, and compare these against the competencies of existing staff. During the interview discussions, several organizational glitches tended to recur. Better established and critical services within the library often placed demands on the staff involved in the pilot so that individuals, especially those assigned from an IT services group, would sometimes have to drop the project's work for a brief period. Sometimes there is no other way to begin, but dividing staff time across multiple efforts can delay or hinder the success of these projects, especially if higher level managers or administrators, who will naturally have competing priorities from other aspects of their jobs, play a critical operational role in the project. During the pilot, it may not be clear to the team how a smaller project would lead to a larger program, giving the effort a feeling of uncertainty that may prove to be unsettling for some of the staff involved. With responsibilities divided across units, internal divisions may surface over communication or protectionist behaviors over turf and influence, even when strong working relationships already exist. Nevertheless, these projects show librarians and staff creating a collaborative, energetic problem-solving environment in which members will do whatever it takes to get the work done. Managers and library leaders must maintain this energy when moving to make those processes more operationally routine.

Finding and Developing Expertise

The ability to adapt and learn quickly on the job is probably the most important skill for anyone working in library publishing services. The programs discussed here have been managed by individuals who have not only experience in libraries and library science, but also advanced degrees in other fields or extensive experience working in the academic publishing or public communications sectors. Because of the small size of the interview pool for this chapter, generalizations about the career history and expertise necessary for a library-based publishing service might be shaky at best. But given the evolving nature of publishing service programs, it is not surprising to find this mix. Some had crossed over to libraries from academic publishing, or other nonprofit sector work, while others held advanced degrees in librarianship, the humanities, or both, and a few combined one or more of these backgrounds. Two of those interviewed would be considered by some to be "career librarians" who held masters or doctorates in library science, had spent many years working in a library, and came up through the ranks of collections, public services, and technical services. Five of those interviewed began working in libraries after obtaining an advanced degree in the humanities, and three of them obtained a library degree afterwards. Among those with a humanities background, all gained additional experience in library digital programs or nonprofit sectors related to publishing, marketing, or Web-content management. Each of this subset told stories of how the humanities background contributed to their success once they began working in libraries. Familiarity with the scholarly research process helps them to "speak the language" of faculty with whom they work, and a PhD often helped to counter what one described as a "degree of snobbishness" that some campus faculty display when working with employees in service units like the library.

Libraries looking to make new hires for these services have cast their net widely and sought unusual blends of education and experiences. Both New York University Libraries and Penn State University Libraries have created new positions to oversee publishing services in their libraries in the recent years, and the postings for these roles indicate a need for flexibility as well as the hope for unique experiences. At both institutions, the university press reports to the Dean of Libraries, and these positions were both structured to develop and manage collaborative programs for the libraries and the press. In their job advertisements, both libraries characterized these roles broadly, sought a blend of publishing and library experience, as well as thorough familiarity with aspects of digital content development and distribution for scholarly purposes. The most significant difference between the two position postings can be found in the scope of the roles. Penn State's position, Assistant Dean for Scholarly Communications and Co-director of the Office of Digital Scholarly Publishing, was defined as a senior administrative role for the libraries. At New York University, the Program Officer for Digital Scholarly Publishing reports to the Dean and to the Director of the University Press and has been defined with a more specific focus on the publishing program. Both positions, however, highlight the ambiguous nature of the planned work, with expectations for facilitating cooperation among a number of nonreporting units.

At Penn State, where the partnership with the press preexisted the search, the assistant dean's portfolio extends beyond publishing services to several related areas that focus on the context for the publishing program within the libraries and the university. The job posting for Assistant Dean for Scholarly Communications, Penn State University Libraries listed these as "planning, organization, policy development, and implementation of the Libraries' scholarly communications program," which would be implemented through "collaborative leadership with computing units, the Penn State Press, and the Libraries departments and collection development groups to coordinate and develop digital publications, collections, electronic repositories and appropriate software and hardware platforms." When the posting was opened, in late 2005, the Libraries' sought a "Masters Degree in Library Science (or an equivalent academic degree), significant experience in a major university with a least five years experience in library collection development, scholarly publishing or communications, and/or digital library programs."[21] I was hired into this position with a master's degree in English and American literature, and nine years' experience in defining and providing digital library services at another research library, with occasional collaborations with a university press. However, because I hold no library science degree, my hire into a senior leadership role was highly unusual for the institution.

At New York University, press Director Steve Maikowski explains that Program Officer position, now held by Monica McCormick, was deliberately structured as a bridge: "We had no program of any kind of collaboration on any publishing projects between press and libraries, nor the time to seriously explore such collaborations or new digital publishing and publishing services we could provide to faculty." According to Steve Maikowski, NYU sought applicants who "understood how libraries operate and could bring the user perspective" to the job, while also demonstrating knowledge of "how a dissertation becomes a book, peer review and how it transforms content, the role of the university press in promotion and tenure, and the financial challenges that might affect what and why they publish." The posting stated that duties would focus on "develop[ing] and manag[ing] a ... program to design and initiate a variety of innovative digital publishing initiatives."[22] Its collaborative responsibilities involved "working with the NYU Press, Digital Library Technology Services, Faculty Technology Services, and the Digital Studio" to "provide a central, advisory, and liaison role in publishing online scholarly content." The posting stated the expectation for "at least five years of related work experience, preferably with a scholarly publishing house or an academic library"[23] and a preference for a master of library science degree. McCormick's position is not defined as tenure-line librarian role, but is instead classified similarly to those of the university press staff. McCormick previously worked at the University of California Press for 16 years, including 10 years as an acquisitions editor responsible for history and ethnic studies. After leaving the press, she earned an MSLS from the University of North Carolina, served as a visiting program officer in special collections at the Association of Research Libraries, and joined North Carolina State University Library as Director of Digital Publishing before moving to NYU.

Others interviewed for this study shared work histories that were similarly diverse, and a few described career arcs that would, at least retrospectively, seem to be on a track towards library publishing. Brian Rosenblum's path from Michigan to Kansas provides one example of a career path within library publishing, but the field is as yet too new and too small to find many such examples. Maria Bonn began work at entry-level humanities text-encoding jobs at the University of Michigan Library in the late 1990s while earning her library degree. She gradually picked up more digital library project management responsibilities in successive roles leading to her assignment as head of the SPO. David Ruddy earned his PhD in English literature at Michigan and began working in digital publishing when he was an editor of the print *Middle English Dictionary* at Michigan around the same time that project began to partner with the library to bring it online. Katharine Skinner, Digital Projects Librarian at Emory's Woodruff Library, started in the library as a graduate assistant on a grant-funded project while finishing her PhD research in American studies. She has continued after completing the dissertation, taking on responsibilities that include oversight of several multi-institution collaborations. Catherine Mitchell at California Digital Library received exposure to the effect of economics on academic publishing while earning her doctorate in English when her colleagues began to write for publication with mixed success. Both Mitchell and Skinner spent time in communications, marketing, or Web-publishing jobs in the nonprofit sector during breaks from the academy. Still others, like McCormick, have crossed over from the publishing industry itself. Terry Ehling joined Cornell Libraries in 1999 after 20 years at MIT Press, where she had served as the Director of the Digital Projects Lab and helped to bring MIT CogNET online. Her previous experience in creating products within academic publishing fit well with Cornell's needs for the newly launched Project Euclid, envisioned as an alternative channel for publishing and aggregating math and statistics journals. Ehling explains that she made the leap because she sensed that libraries were an important and fertile arena for experimentation in scholarly communications and saw the potential for Project Euclid to serve as a "kernel" for the growth of other publishing services and projects within Cornell that are less market-driven and more service-focused. Among all of these stories, each contains some early exposure to and experience with communications using the Web, and a number of them involve work in a publishing environment of some sort.

Although library publishing has generated a great deal of buzz, the opportunities for training, education, and professional development have not grown quickly. Library science programs have offered new specializations in the related areas of digital library management and data curation functions, but publishing issues, if studied at all, are more likely to be treated in relation to collection development. Workshops and training programs on the subjects of scholarly communications and institutional repositories also tend to focus on broader issues, such as open-access advocacy and building awareness, or on specifics such as the selection of IR software and not very much at all on publishing as a set of services and processes for creating, distributing, and promoting content. Unlike librarianship's academic credentialing norms, the publishing profession itself relies heavily on the apprenticeship model, in which staff gain skills through successive assignments and professional networks.[24] Karla Hahn writes that "library publishing programs seem to be developing in something of a vacuum of community discussion."[25] Brian Rosenblum spoke of the difficulty he has had in identifying a network of other librarians "doing publishing." This will remain challenging so long as the field remains small, and so these publishing staff have had to find ways of networking through existing meetings and conferences, even though many of these may not quite fit the full range of topics that staff encounter. Programs specifically about library publishing have appeared at LITA, the Digital Library Federation Forum, the Charleston Conference, and SPARC's 2008 Digital Repositories Meeting. Publishing services may have developed in a vacuum because academic libraries operate primarily within the confines of their own institutions to offer services. But without a professional network, publishing librarians will have limited opportunity to learn from each other, and limited chance to identify areas for collaboration that may benefit the programs.

Conclusion: Staffing for Future Growth

Supporting scholarly communication is the core business of academic research libraries. In the early part of this decade, the phrase *scholarly communications* tended to serve as a signifier primarily for advocacy around the economics of publishing and library collections. It has now become more ambiguous and generally connotes the entire process of creating, distributing, and accessing scholarship and research, not only the economics of the system. Improving how that system works brings increasing needs for more specialization, for more knowledge about more aspects of that life cycle, and for the use of that specialized knowledge to consult and provide advice to faculty and students.

Library publishing programs began in response to economic issues, but should be planned and staffed as part of a more comprehensive service foundation for the entire life cycle of scholarship within the network of research libraries. Linking the programs to institutional repository services can be a promising start, but higher education changes at a notoriously slow pace. The highly complex, competitive, and fast-changing information and technology market beyond the academy will likely have a greater impact on how we use technology to communicate the results of research. Developing library publishing programs requires leadership that is entrepreneurially based, creative, and unrestricted by conventional conceptions of either publishing or librarianship. Today they focus heavily on the processing of scholarly content for online delivery and discovery and sometimes for additional distribution services such as print. Bringing these services into the library can begin to reshape the culture of the organization beyond the technology units. Kizer Walker's work at Cornell suggests how librarians could become more actively engaged with faculty in their role as authors who are shaping the discourse of their field, as opposed to instructors or researchers seeking information. This will not be an overnight change, however, and liaisons will need colleagues in the area of publishing and repository services who can bridge the distance between technology-dependent activities and the specific scholarly needs that the technology should serve.

When speculating about the future, most of those interviewed discussed strategies for building scale, adding new staff, and recruiting new publication partners. Others mentioned the need to collaborate beyond their own organization, and still others mentioned that they needed to create space to explore emerging issues such as large-scale science data, digital preservation, and experimental publication formats. Any library evaluating whether to offer publishing services should assume that these now-experimental efforts will become increasingly important, and that collaborative services and technologies will drive future research and publishing needs. This underscores the need for librarians with deeper subject expertise who can conduct research and development on the same terms as the faculty member.[26] The current emphasis on cyberinfrastructure—those local, national and international initiatives to create more holistic networks of technology services for research and communication of its results in disciplines ranging from "big science" to "digital humanities"—have a direct bearing on how library publishing and related staffing competencies may develop.[27] Publishing and the related services that support scholarly communication form a critical part of that cyberinfrastructure, but the definition of the "publishable unit" and the functionality that accumulates around it will very likely expand. Cliff Lynch has suggested that proliferating data emerging from contemporary scientific research has already begun to change the relationship between scientific articles and this data. According to Lynch, authors and their articles will not simply reference the data, but that data will be incorporated into review processes and into the article in ways that may provide additional tools to allow readers to visualize or analyze the data for themselves.[28] Preliminary efforts are underway at Johns Hopkins to build partnerships between libraries, scientists, and publishers to define new standards and model the practices and relationships necessary for such a system.[29] Data in different formats will drive the humanities too, where digital scholarship has been slower to take root but has begun to do so with the frequent assistance of libraries. As such, librarians have sometimes filled a role that many publishers have been less capable of filling, as Emory University has recently demonstrated in redeveloping the Trans-Atlantic Slave Trade Database as an online service from its original CD-ROM format.[30]

It will be critical to identify staff who can contribute to this emerging cyberinfrastructure, which will draw upon expertise beyond information management.[31] This will be a challenge with existing library staffing patterns and budgets. Both librarians and publishers emphasized the need for more rigorous business planning to sustain these programs and to fully exploit the library's financial capacity for experimentation. Technology supports library publishing, but as a common denominator, it might be an area where libraries could consolidate services and even look to outsource more basic operations. All of the programs discussed in this chapter that needed digitization conversion of any size relied on vended services. Must the content management and delivery platforms, such as OJS, DPubS, or DSpace, remain in house?[32] If libraries had more numerous and viable alternatives that allowed for autonomy over their services to their campuses, how many would choose to manage their own publishing and repository tools? What deeper levels of expertise and service could be offered? Publishing service directors should consider their strategy: whether to build their own publishing infrastructure, rely on other in-house services, or seek outsourcing alternatives outside of the library. On this topic, Laura Cerruti at the University of California Press was clear: "it doesn't make sense now to build capacities for production inside: don't build platforms, build content." CDL's eScholarship Publishing Group, with a large dedicated staff, relies on BePress's Digital Commons to host and distribute its publications and provide workflow infrastructure as well. This frees up its staff to focus on enhancing and extending services rather than building and running basic publishing infrastructure. The content these publishing programs will help to create will live (or die) within a larger scholarly communications ecology with both symbiotic and predatory relationships. Many libraries' publishing programs began in order to provide scholars with viable and economical alternatives to commercially based publishers, thus minimizing the academy's loss of control over its research and its budgets for supporting that research. It might seem ironic to suggest that libraries should outsource more of their technology services, but doing so could leave more room for specialization and for hiring staff who can focus on the activities for which we really must cultivate expertise: services to the experts on our campuses, research and development, and the leadership for both.

Notes

1.   Karla Hahn, *Research Library Publishing Services: New Options for University Publishing* (Washington, DC: Association of Research Libraries, 2008).
2.   Ibid., 5.
3.   In early 2008, Cornell and Duke University Press established a partnership in which Euclid operations are shared between the two organizations. Prior to this, 4 FTE in technical and business operations supported Euclid at Cornell according to Terry Ehling and David Ruddy.
4.   Kate Wittenberg, 2004. "Librarians as Publishers: A New Role in Scholarly Communication," *Searcher* 12, no. 10 (2004). In EBSCO*host*.
5.   Laura Brown, Rebecca Griffiths, and Matthew Rascoff, *University Publishing in a Digital Age* (New York: Ithaka, 2007).
6.   The promotion and marketing of institutional repositories provides some interesting examples here. Foster & Gibbons, and Davis & Connolly have both written about how IRs services, defined as services around the collection of the institution's content, have initially focused too much attention on the needs and benefits to the library and the university in general, often resulting in poor

uptake of the services. Because researchers publish to extend the impact of their research and to make their professional careers, developing and defining services that promote the researcher's "brand" and promote the findability of their work have had more success. This in fact is what publishing seeks to do. (Nancy Fried Foster and Susan Gibbons, "Understanding Faculty to Improve Content Recruitment for Institutional Repositories," *D-Lib Magazine* 11, no. 1 [Jan. 2005]. www.dlib.org/dlib/january05/foster/01foster.html; Phillip M. Davis and Matthew J. L. Connolly, "Institutional Repositories: Evaluating the Reasons for Non-use of Cornell University's Installation of DSpace," *D-Lib Magazine* 13, no. 3/4 [March/April 2007], www.dlib.org/dlib/march07/davis/03davis.html.)

7. Brown, Griffiths, and Rascoff, *University Publishing in a Digital Age,* 16; this librarian is actually speaking about digitized special collections materials, but Brown et al. use the point to refer to publishing skills.

8. Raym Crow, *University-Based Publishing Partnerships: A Guide to Critical Issues* (Washington, DC: The Scholarly Publishing & Academic Resources Coalition, 2009).

9. Ibid.; Brown, Griffiths, and Rascoff, *University Publishing in a Digital Age.*

10. In a 2008 study from Ithaka, Kevin Guthrie, Rebecca Griffiths, and Nancy Maron point out that the academic community has historically not been oriented towards the fiscal sustainability of individual products or projects. They argue that this has now become a significant liability and that core business planning principles need to be put in place in order to ensure the survivability of innovative services (Kevin Guthrie, Rebecca Griffiths, and Nancy Maron, *Sustainability and Revenue Models for Online Academic Resources* [New York: Ithaka, 2008].)

11. McCormick describes the plans for New York University in greater detail in Monica McCormick, "Learning to Say Maybe: Building NYU's Press/Library Collaboration," *Against the Grain* 20, no. 6 (Dec. 2008/Jan. 2009): 28–30.

12. Crow, *University-Based Publishing Partnerships.*

13. Catherine Candee and Lynn Withey, *Report of the SLASIAC Task Force on Publishing Needs and Opportunities at the University of California* (Oakland, CA: University of California Systemwide Library and Scholarly Information Advisory Committee, 2008).

14. This partnership is discussed in greater detail by Mitchell and Cerruti in Catherine A. Mitchell and Laura Cerruti, "Local, Sustainable, and Organic Publishing: A Library-Press Collaboration at the University of California," *Against the Grain* 20, no. 6 (Dec. 2008/Jan. 2009): 22–26.

15. Hahn, *Research Library Publishing Services.*

16. Internal job specification document provided by David Ruddy.

17. According to Terry Ehling and David Ruddy, an additional FTE had previously been assigned prior to the establishment of a new business partnership with Duke University Press in which operations for Euclid are shared between Cornell and Duke.

18. Hahn, *Research Library Publishing Services,* 19.

19. For more detail on this partnership, see Terry Ehling and Erich Staib, "The Coefficient Partnership: Project Euclid, Cornell University Library and Duke University Press," *Against the Grain* 20, no. 6 (Dec. 2008/Jan. 2009): 32–35.

21. Email posting "Position Announcement: The Penn State University Libraries, Assistant Dean for Scholarly Communication" to SPARC-OAForum listserv, January 17, 2006. Archived at arl.org/lists/sparc-oaforum/Message/2694.html.

22. Job advertisement for Digital Publishing Program Officer, New York University. Chronicle of Higher Education, August 17, 2007, p C37.

23. Ibid.

24. Thanks to Chuck Thomas of IMLS and October Ivans of the Society for Scholarly Publishing for the two conversations that led to these points.

25. Hahn, *Research Library Publishing Services,* 28.

26. In its solicitations for funding proposal in the DataNet Program, the National Science Foundation stated that "librarians, archivists, and computer/ computational/information scientists are unlikely to build excellent infrastructure for science and/or engineering without deep engagement with the intended users. In that sense, domain scientists should be full partners in the process." (National Science Foundation, Sustainable Digital Data Preservation and Access Network Frequently Asked Questions December 18, 2007. [Last updated Nov 19, 2008] www.nsf.gov/pubs/2008/nsf08021/nsf08021.jsp .)

27. The ACLS has written that "'Cyberinfrastructure' becomes less mysterious once we reflect that scholarship already has an infrastructure. The foundation of that infrastructure consists of the libraries, archives, and museums that preserve information; the bibliographies, finding aids, citation systems, and concordances that make that information retrievable; the journals and university presses that distribute the information; and the editors, librarians, archivists, and curators who link the operation of this structure to the scholars who use it. All of these structures have both extensions and analogues in the digital realm." (American Council of Learned Societies, "ACLS Commission on Cyberinfrastructure: Summary," www.acls.org/programs/Default.aspx?id=644 [accessed Dec. 15 2008].)

   The National Science Foundation has defined Cyberinfrastructure as the "Computing systems, data, information resources, networking, digitally enabled-sensors, instruments, virtual organizations, and observatories, along with an interoperable suite of software services and tools. This technology is complemented by the interdisciplinary teams of professionals that are responsible for its development, deployment and its use in transformative approaches to scientific and engineering discovery and learning. The vision also includes attention to the educational and workforce initiatives necessary for both the creation and effective use of Cyberinfrastructure." (NSF Cyberinfrastructure Council, *Cyberinfrastructure Vision for 21st Century Discovery,* 1.)

28. Clifford Lynch, "The Shape of the Scientific Article in the Developing Cyberinfrastructure," CTWatch Quarterly 3, no. 3 (Aug. 2007): www.ctwatch.org/quarterly/articles/2007/08/the-shape-of-the-scientific-article-in-the-developing-cyberinfrastructure. The potential for data fraud has also begun to make it more likely that the base data will be reviewed with the research report. See Jeffrey R. Young, "Journals Find Fakery in Many Images Submitted to Support Research," *Chronicle of Higher Education,* May 29, 2008, http://chronicle.com/article/Journals-Find-Fakery-in-Man/846.

29. Sayeed Choudhury, Tim DiLauro, Alex Szalay, Ethan Vishniac, Robert J. Hanisch, Julie Steffen, Robert Milkey, Teresa Ehling, and Ray Plante. "Digital Data Preservation for Scholarly Publications in Astronomy," *International Journal of Digital Curation* 2, no. 2 (2007): 20–30; David Reynolds, Tim DiLauro, and Sayeed Choudury. 2008. "An OAI-ORE Aggregation for the National Virtual Observatory" (presentation, Digital Library Federation Spring 2008 Forum, April 28–30, 2008, Minneapolis, MN).

30. Cambridge University Press originally published the database as a CD-ROM in 1999 (David Eltis, Stephen D. Behrendt, David Richardson, and Herbert S. Klein, The Trans-Atlantic Slave Trade [CD-ROM Database], [New York: Cambridge University Press, 1999],) Cambridge, like many early publishers of CD-based products, later determined that it could not affordably continue to update and release further editions and reverted the rights to Eltis. The Digital Programs Group at Woodruff Library began working with Eltis, Robert W. Woodruff Professor of History, to articulate new goals and parameters for the project. Compared to the original CD version, the Web-based service provides improved functionality for analysis and visualization, new and expanded source data, ancillary content for teachers, and it will readily allow Eltis and an advisory board to update the resource as needed. In projects such as this one, librarians take on roles similar to scholarly collaborators or publishing editors who help shape the project, define its boundaries, and seek the funding needed to create it.

31. For a discussion of the staff development needs arising from "e-science" services in libraries, see Wendy Lougee, Sayeed Choudhury, Anna Gold, Chuck Humphrey, Betsy Humphreys, Rick Luce, Clifford Lynch, James Mullins, Sarah Pritchard, and Peter Young, *Agenda for Developing E-Science in Research Libraries: Final Report and Recommendations to the Scholarly Communication Steering Committee, the Public Policies Affecting Research Libraries Steering Committee, and the Research, Teaching, and Learning Steering Committee* (Washington, DC: Association of Research Libraries, 2007).

32. The outsourcing of information technology services in higher education has become an important topic, but is well beyond the scope of this essay. But with limited resources and increased demand upon our services, we cannot staff to the levels that we would hope or easily grow programs to meet emerging needs. Colin Currie writes that "one of the great ironies for those of us in higher education information technology is that, in the coming years, doing the best-possible job for our institutions will mean finding the optimal ways to replace our functions with outside services. In other words, a critical part of our job will be to outsource ourselves as effectively as possible" (Colin Currie, "Painting the Clouds," *Educause Review* 43, no. 6 (Nov./Dec. 2008), http://connect.educause.edu/Library/EDUCAUSE+Review/PaintingtheClouds/47441.)

Acknowledgments

I wish to thank all of the librarians and publishers who agreed to be interview on the record about their work and their careers. Clearly this chapter could not have been written without their cooperation. Several also provided very helpful comments on early drafts of this chapter as did Patrick Alexander, Sandy Thatcher, Raym Crow, and Karla Hahn. Martha Ney provided some additional research help. Throughout the entire project Ellie Goodman provided much needed advice and support.

APPENDIX A

REFERENCED WEB SITES

Company Name	Company URL
Amazon BookSurge	www.booksurge.com
Berkeley Electronic Press Digital Commons	www.bepress.com/ir
Center for Innovative Publishing, Cornell University Library	http://cip.cornell.edu
Disability Studies Quarterly	www.dsq-sds.org
DPubS	http://dpubs.org
DSpace	www.dspace.org
eScholarship Publishing, University of California Digital Library	www.cdlib.org/programs/escholarship.html
Fedora Commons	www.fedora-commons.org
Journal of Electronic Publishing	www.journalofelectronicpublishing.org
Journals@KU, University of Kansas Library	https://journals.ku.edu
Lightning Source	www.lightningsource.com
Lulu	www.lulu.com
Mark Twain Project Online	www.marktwainproject.org
Museum Anthropology Review	http://scholarworks.iu.edu/journals/index.php/mar
Office of Digital Scholarly Publishing, Penn State University	www.libraries.psu.edu/odsp
Open Journal Systems	http://pkp.sfu.ca/?q=ojs
Penn State Romance Studies	http://romancestudies.psu.edu
Project Euclid	http://projecteuclid.org
Scholarly Publishing Office, University of Michigan Library	www.lib.umich.edu/spo
Signale: Modern German Letters, Cultures, and Thought	http://signale.cornell.edu
The Trans-Atlantic Slave Trade Database Project	www.slavevoyages.org

APPENDIX B

INTERVIEWS CONDUCTED BY THE AUTHOR

NOTE: The individual circumstances of some of those interviewed have changed since this research began. Titles and affiliations listed were current on the date listed for the interview.

Person	Organization	Title	Date of Interview
Julie Bobay	Indiana University Library	Associate Dean for Collections and Digital Publishing	June 25, 2008
Maria Bonn	University of Michigan Library	Director, Scholarly Publishing Office	June 12, 2008
Laura Cerruti	University of California Press	Director of Digital Content Development	June 20, 2008
Tschera Connell	Ohio State University Library	Head, Scholarly Resources Integration Department	May 27, 2008
Terry Ehling	Cornell University Library	Executive Director, Project Euclid, and Director, Center for Innovative Publishing	May 11, 2008
Monica McCormick	New York University Library and Press	Program Officer for Digital Scholarly Publishing	May 27, 2008
Steve Maikowski	New York University Press	Director	June 20, 2008
Catherine Mitchell	California Digital Library	Acting Director, E-Scholarship Publishing Group	June 6, 2008
Peter Potter	Cornell University Press	Editor in Chief	June 13, 2008
Brian Rosenblum	University of Kansas Library	Scholarly Digital Initiatives Librarian	May 12, 2008
David Ruddy	Cornell University Library	Director of E-Publishing Technologies	May 11, 2008
Katherine Skinner	Woodruff Library, Emory University	Digital Projects Librarian	May 27, 2008
Kizer Walker	Cornell University Library	Bibliographer for German Studies and Bibliographer for Classics, Ancient Near East, and Archaeology	June 6, 2008

APPENDIX C

SAMPLE INTERVIEW QUESTIONS

These questions were used only as a starting point for conversations. The author's specific knowledge of the interviewee and his or her organization often led to more detailed lines of questions.

Sample interview questions for individuals holding publishing-oriented jobs in libraries

- What is your title?
- How is your job classified (faculty, classified staff, professional)?
- What is the nature of the program you are working within? What is your role within it? What do you think you are expected to accomplish in this job?
- Can you describe a "typical day," or can you describe what you did in your job yesterday or today?
- With which parts of your library do you work most closely? What requires you to work together?
- Why did you apply for and accept this job? Why do you think you were offered the job?
- What skills are most important in this job? What parts of your work or educational background do you draw upon most?
- How do you think your job will evolve? What other types of jobs might you imagine being necessary to support this program?
- Can you provide me with any documents that may assist me in further analysis of your publishing program and the jobs involved? These might include strategic or project plans, job descriptions, job advertisements, or web sites.
- Who else within your organization, or at another institution, would you recommend that I speak with about these subjects?

Sample interview questions for academic publishers and editors

- Are you familiar with publishing programs in libraries? Do you work in collaboration with a library that has such a program?
- If has a working relationship: What is your working relationship with the individuals in that program? Were you involved in defining or posting the job that XX holds, and were you involved in the hiring process?
- If no working relationship: What role do you believe these individuals fulfill in the program he/she supports?
- Why do you believe the position/the program/programs and jobs like these was/were created? What goal do they serve? What expectations do you have of the program and the job?
- What skills do you believe are necessary to manage and support such programs? What educational and work backgrounds are important?
- Do these programs and individuals have any similarity to traditional publishing/editing jobs? If so, which, and what is the nature of the similarity? What are the key differences?
- How do you expect that publishing-oriented jobs will evolve in libraries? What implications do such programs have for academic publishing?
- Who else within your organization, or at another institution, would you recommend that I speak with about these subjects?

APPENDIX D
UNIVERSITY-BASED PUBLISHING CORE COMPETENCIES

Function	Press	Library	Academic Units	Academic Computing
Funding	• Earned revenue • Retained surplus • Institutional subsidy	• Development/ fundraising capacity • Standing budget resources (aligned w/ institutional needs) • Access to external funding • Institutional political influence	• Access to external development funding • In-kind administrative & casual labor support	• Standing budget resources
Content Acquisition	• Acquisition & editorial selection • Brand & prestige • Relationships w/faculty & external authors • Relationships w/societies • Author marketing	• Mining of library collections • Relationships w/ faculty & researchers within institution via subject specialists • Understanding of curriculum needs	• Content creation	
Editorial	• Vetting & peer review • Substantive editing • Editorial services management	• Digital library creation • Metadata creation • Access to grad student labor	• Vetting & peer review • Access to grad student labor	• Codes of practice governing online publishing • Editorial management systems support
IP/Rights Management	• Publication permissions & rights management • IP management • Author rights	• Author rights education • IP management (retrospective)	• Rights holders/ grantors	

APPENDIX D

UNIVERSITY-BASED PUBLISHING CORE COMPETENCIES

Function	Press	Library	Academic Units	Academic Computing
Pre-press/ Production	• Print production management	• Digital conversion • Digital formatting & tagging		
Distribution	• Print distribution systems & inventory management • Online & print fulfillment management • Online hosting (gated) • Monitoring subscriber usage (e.g., via COUNTER) • Print-on-demand services	• Online hosting (ungated & gated) • Monitoring use metrics • Print-on-demand services • Capacity to develop large-scale digital projects • Online interface design/testing • Acquisition expertise applied to print distribution	• Online hosting (ungated; impermanent)	• Online hosting (ungated & gated) • Online service design & development
(Business) Management	• Financial accounting & control • P&L management • Fulfillment management (subscription & monograph) • E-commerce capacity • Contractual expertise	• Technical project management • Measuring per-capita service provision • Management for publishing cost centers • Contractual expertise		• Technical project management

APPENDIX D

UNIVERSITY-BASED PUBLISHING CORE COMPETENCIES

Function	Press	Library	Academic Units	Academic Computing
Marketing & Sales (Awareness & Visibility)	• Access to markets outside university • Determine market demand • Pricing/value management • Marketing • Sales management (institutional & consumer) • Advertising & sponsorship sales	• Access to markets inside university • Author rights & IP awareness • Publishing issue faculty awareness & outreach programs • Online content visibility & access • Understand information use for research & teaching	• Networking with discipline/field	
Archiving & Preservation	• Post-cancellation access (e.g., via LOCKSS) • Digital preservation (e.g., via Portico)	• Storage & preservation (digital & print)		

Reprinted with permission from Raym Crow, *University-Based Publishing Partnerships: A Guide to Critical Issues.* (Washington, DC: The Scholarly Publishing & Academic Resources Coalition, 2009).

CHAPTER 9

E-SCIENCE, CYBERINFRASTRUCTURE AND THE CHANGING FACE OF SCHOLARSHIP

ORGANIZING FOR NEW MODELS OF RESEARCH SUPPORT AT THE PURDUE UNIVERSITY LIBRARIES

Jake R. Carlson and Jeremy R. Garritano
Purdue University

Introduction

A revolution in scientific research is being driven by the proliferation and wider availability of high-performance computing; the development of visualization, simulation, and other sophisticated analysis tools; and the increasing capacity to store massive amounts of data. As a result, science is beginning to shift away from traditional experiment-based practices and towards computationally driven models of research, in which massive data sets are used to test hypotheses. These developments in scientific practice, collectively known as e-science, are leading to massive changes in how science is conducted. Under e-science, questions that were once relegated to being purely theoretical, such as these:

- What impact does species gene flow have on an ecological community?
- What happens to space-time when two black holes collide?
- What are the key factors driving climate change?

are now within the ability of researchers to explore and answer using cyberinfrastructure.[1]

According to the seminal 2003 report to the National Science Foundation (also known as the "Atkins Report"), cyberinfrastructure consists of the multiple layers of distributed computer, information, and communication technologies upon which e-science models and practices are built. These layers of cyberinfrastructure house the information, data, storage, standards, personnel, policies, tools, services, and social practices that enable e-science to function. As stated in the Atkins Report, "If *infrastructure* is required for an industrial economy, then we could say that *cyberinfrastructure* is required for a knowledge economy."[2]

An example of the potential of cyberinfrastructure to revolutionize how science is practiced is the National Virtual Observatory (NVO). The NVO provides a centralized portal for discovery and access to distributed catalogs of astronomical data gathered from telescopes all over the world. Rather than having to secure access to a high-powered telescope and schedule a limited amount of time to obtain an individual data set, professional and amateur astronomers alike can now easily discover and access high-quality catalogs of data sets at their convenience through the NVO. Although astronomy data collections are gathered and stored at installations across the world, the NVO is able to bring these data sets together in a centralized interface through its use of standard protocols for registering the existence and location of data with NVO and the use of community-based metadata standards to enable the interoperability of the registered data sets. The ready availability of a multitude of interoperable data sets enables astronomers to search for data that match a particular set of criteria and analyze patterns and to better study the complexity of astronomical systems in ways that simply were not previously possible. The NVO also offers a software library and a suite of statistical, visualization, and other tools for the analysis of astronomical data. The NVO promotes community involvement in the development of its services and resources by enabling astronomers to publish their own data or tools through the NVO.[3]

E-science is expanding into a broader paradigm of e-scholarship as other academic disciplines are beginning to create their own cyberinfrastructures for their fields of practice. For example, applying the tools and capabilities of cyberinfrastructure to research in the liberal arts has the potential to change how scholars make sense of the human record.[4] This potential is illustrated in Rome Reborn, a digital 3-D model of the city of Rome as it existed in late antiquity. Produced by the Institute for Advanced Technology in the Humanities (IATH) at the University of

Virginia and its collaborators, Rome Reborn has the primary purpose of communicating the current understanding of the urban topography, infrastructures, and individual structures of ancient Rome. In addition to providing a means to address theories of how the city may have looked, IATH and its partners envision Rome Reborn as a means to explore questions that would otherwise be difficult or impossible to address, such as how the design of the city and its buildings affected ventilation, illumination, or the movement of people.[5]

This chapter will briefly highlight two key components of cyberinfrastructure as identified by the National Science Foundation (NSF)—data curation and preservation, and interdisciplinary research and virtual organizations—and address the challenges and opportunities they pose for academic libraries. A review of new ideas for library organizational structures and staffing models to meet the changing needs of library users in the digital age will follow. Next, this chapter will describe the approaches taken by the Purdue University Libraries to adopt aspects of these ideas and put them into practice to enable librarians to become directly involved in the development of cyberinfrastructure and to provide support for e-science research. The Purdue model includes creating a new organizational structure within the libraries to support librarians' active engagement in working directly with faculty to research and develop solutions to address the problems of data management, organization, dissemination, and preservation, and creating new positions to coordinate the libraries' research efforts and to help leverage the existing skills and relationships of subject librarians. Finally, a case study describing a collaboration between two librarians, the information technology department, and faculty in the chemistry and food sciences departments will be presented to illustrate the Purdue Libraries' model of engagement with faculty.

Data Curation and Preservation

Under the paradigm of e-science, the scientific method shifts from "hypothesize, design and run experiment, analyze results" to "hypothesize, look up answer in a database."[6] In this environment, data are the lifeblood of scientific practice, and access to data becomes as important to the scientist as was the microscope to a traditional laboratory. The problem is that researchers' capability to generate or manipulate data through e-science experiments has far surpassed their ability to manage, organize, or make their data easily accessible. E-science experiments both generate and require massive amounts of data, and the rate of growth in data production is expected to increase as better, faster, and smarter technologies are developed and deployed. The physical and social infrastructures that are needed to manage this "data deluge" have not developed at the same pace as the ability of researchers to produce it.[7] This disparity between the growth of production capability and the lack of tools, infrastructures, workflow systems, and collaboration to address distributed and complex data sets is recognized as a barrier to realizing the full potential of e-science.[8]

In its 2007 cyberinfrastructure report, the NSF articulated a vision of the future "in which science and engineering digital data are routinely deposited in well-documented form, are regularly and easily consulted and analyzed by specialists and non-specialists alike, are openly accessible while suitably protected, and are reliably preserved."[9] Enacting this vision will require much more than just collecting information and putting it on a webserver for access or on a backup hard drive for storage. Data have to be curated and preserved to retain their value and to remain accessible over the long term. Data curation is defined as "the activity of managing and promoting the use of data from its point of creation, to ensure it is fit for contemporary purpose, and available for discovery and re-use."[10] Data that are not curated will become irretrievable or indecipherable and thus lose their value and utility as an information resource.

However, the curation and preservation of data present an array of difficult challenges. For example, research data come in all different types, formats, and sizes, even within individual academic disciplines. The heterogeneity of research data, as well as the diversity of the social and cultural practices of researchers producing the data, means that "one size fits all" solutions will not work.[11] This situation is further exacerbated by the lack of agreement (or even awareness) in many communities on the standards, practices, and technologies to employ for curation and preservation work. The infrastructure supporting data curation and preservation activities must be flexible, scalable, and extensible to accommodate current and future needs. Data sets need to be accompanied by appropriate metadata to provide the context for understanding and using the data. Metadata is required so data sets can be discovered, preserved, administered, and made interoperable with one another. Appropriate and fair intellectual property rights for the owners of research data sets and fair-use exceptions for would-be users will need to be identified, conveyed, and enforced. The preservation of data requires an ongoing commitment of resources, which, in turn, mandates the need for viable economic and technology sustainability plans.[12]

Interdisciplinary Research and Virtual Organizations

The scope of the questions being addressed by e-science goes far beyond what could be addressed in a single academic discipline or even by a single institution. Research performed under the e-science paradigm typically requires the formation of interdisciplinary research teams composed of researchers from multiple disciplines and who are distributed across multiple types of institutions and locations. In addition, the complexities of this new research environment and the amount of support needed to develop and maintain the necessary cyberinfrastructure mandate close collaboration between researchers and computer scientists, software developers, network engineers, data managers, and other IT providers. Other types of professionals possessing an array of diverse skills and abilities will be needed to contribute to an environment in which e-science can flourish. Librarians and archivists, for example, have been identified as having the knowledge necessary to potentially help researchers address data curation and preservation issues.[13] Economists could help craft economic sustainability plans for supporting cyberinfrastructure. Copyright attorneys may be needed to sort out intellectual property issues over the ownership and fair-use dissemination of digital objects.

The high performance networks, advanced data storage capacities, distributed computational tools, and other components that make up cyberinfrastructure enable the formation of virtual organizations to carry out e-science projects. Cyberinfrastructure capabilities have grown to the point where it is now possible for these virtual organizations to carry out all of their work in an online environment. Through shared access to online tools, services, and data, research teams can share information, design experiments, operate scientific instruments remotely, run simulations, and analyze or visualize data in order to conduct their experiments and work together as a cohesive unit. The resources and services used by virtual organizations can be distributed across multiple locations and made centrally accessible in real time, reducing the burden of providing support for any single institution. The creation of viable virtual organizations eliminates the barriers of geography, enabling the creation of cross-institutional teams of researchers in the United States and internationally.[14]

Supporting interdisciplinary research and collaborative cyberinfrastructure is a significant challenge to universities as academic culture and structures are largely geared towards supporting and rewarding the work of individuals. The traditional "cottage industry" approach to research, in which research is driven by individuals, resources are obtained for singular purposes and deployed locally in the department or lab runs counter to the goals of e-science: to make cyberinfrastructure and the data, tools, and other resources available to a wide audience for multiple research and educational purposes. The lack of an overarching approach to cyberinfrastructure makes it difficult for universities to integrate technology resources and open them up to broader access in order to achieve necessary economies of scale and to make the best use of scarce resources.[15] Changing the current environment and realizing the full potential of a sustainable cyberinfrastructure will require innovative thinking, creative approaches, and new synergies within and between academic units and institutions.

Challenges for Libraries

The changes in how research is done under the e-science paradigm will have an effect on how the library carries out its mission of supporting the research and information needs of the university. The nature of scholarly communication, for example, is already undergoing dramatic change in response to technological advances, and the spread of e-science research models will only accelerate the pace of these changes. Research data are already shifting from being a disposable by-product of research into an important outcome, if not the most important outcome, of the experiment.[16] To reflect this shift, some have suggested that scientific publications may transform into databases themselves. The data from these publications would be peer-reviewed and available for researchers to reuse or repurpose in order to create new science.[17] Moreover, researchers participating in e-science will increasingly need more than static sources of information in the form of books and journals to satisfy their information needs. As the effects of "Web 2.0" continue to influence scholarly communication and the sharing of information, libraries will be increasingly called upon to capture, curate, and preserve dynamic streams of raw, loosely structured communication streams.[18]

Beyond simply reacting to the changes in research brought about through e-science, libraries have an opportunity to become actively involved in developing cyberinfrastructure and in addressing the issues and challenges of e-science. Libraries have already realized the need to protect the investments they have made in building digital collections and to ensure their availability for the long term by actively seeking solutions to the many conundrums that surround the preservation of digital materials.[19] Many within the library community are increasingly interested in developing roles for librarians in curating and preserving the digital data generated by research faculty, believing that librarians possess abilities and expertise that will be needed in this area. Librarians bring a long-term perspective to their work and understand the value of maintaining primary documents for the historical record as well as the planning and effort preservation requires. Further, librarians are experienced not only in navigating complex information environments, but in understanding the architecture of these environments and how they connect to the needs of research communities. The function of the librarian has always centered on creating, maintaining, and employing logical systems of organizing and describing information in order to enable its discovery and retrieval for the appropriate audiences. Librarians have long recognized the need for standards to manage heterogeneous sources of information and the benefits of commonly accepted and uniform terminologies, rules, and structures in disseminating information. Finally, librarians have already invested resources to digitize materials and house, preserve, and disseminate digital collections of materials in institutional repositories and developed the expertise needed to manage these repositories.[20]

Recognizing the potential transformative impacts that e-science may have on the role of research libraries, the Association of Research

Libraries (ARL) formed a task force on library support for e-science with a mandate to shape an agenda for developing e-science capacity in libraries. Its 2007 report articulated several focal areas for libraries to explore: data and new forms of scholarly communication, support for virtual organizations, and policy development. The outcomes recommended by this task force included an increased level of interaction with e-science communities and a greater understanding of how libraries can contribute to the continued development and deployment of cyberinfrastructure and e-science. At the organizational and staffing level, the ARL report advocated the development of knowledgeable and skilled library professionals who could undertake new roles to help libraries conceive and implement new services and resources in support of e-science. The ARL report also recommended enabling "research libraries [to be] active participants in the conceptualization and development of research infrastructure, including systems and services to support the process of research and the full life cycle of research assets."[21] To achieve these outcomes, libraries will need to adopt and support new types of organizational and staffing models that encourage innovation and risk taking by librarians and enable librarians to explore possibilities for applying their knowledge and skills outside of the traditional boundaries of the library.

In conjunction with NSF, ARL also held a workshop to examine the role of libraries and other partners in the stewardship of science and engineering research data. The report that followed urged NSF to "facilitate the establishment of a sustainable framework for the long term stewardship of data."[22] This framework would include support for the training and education of a new workforce in data science, support for research and development in understanding what is needed to curate and preserve data for the long term effectively, and support for librarians working on data curation and preservation issues as members of research teams.[23]

Although librarians may be seen as a natural and logical partner in addressing the challenges of e-science, there are many significant roadblocks to overcome if librarians are to play a meaningful role. Some of the larger challenges include these:

- Existing library systems and infrastructures are primarily set up to support a text-based environment and will not translate easily, if at all, to managing and supporting research data.

- A steep learning curve exists to gaining the level of fluency needed to understand e-science issues and practices.
- Librarians generally lack the training and background needed to understand the technical issues involved in data management, curation, and preservation.[24]
- Recent assessments of researchers indicate that libraries are generally not viewed as being connected to the research infrastructure needed to support interdisciplinary research.[25]
- Libraries are institution-centered, whereas most scientific data repositories are subject-based and designed to serve interdisciplinary audiences.[26]
- It is likely that efforts in data curation and stewardship will require libraries to make significant investments in infrastructure and people.

Rethinking the Organizational Structure and Staffing Models of Libraries

Just as the traditional organizational structures and the conservative culture of academia pose barriers to supporting e-science research, the traditional organizational structures and culture of academic libraries pose barriers to the library becoming more actively involved in building cyberinfrastructure and supporting e-science. However, librarians have recognized that the organization and staffing models of libraries need to be rethought and adjusted to become more in sync with developments in research, teaching, and learning in the digital age. Susan Gibbons has written about the need to cultivate an "R&D mind-set" in librarians and to foster an environment in libraries that enables and rewards innovation. Gibbons defines an "R&D mind-set" in libraries as a culture in which all staff are expected to stay connected with developments not only within academic libraries, but in higher education, technology, management, and other fields in order to bring in new ideas from these different perspectives to the library. In this culture, the exploration and development of new ideas is actively encouraged by the library administration, and staff are provided with reasonable amounts of time, resources, and support to experiment without being stigmatized if their ideas do not pan out. Gibbons believes that a library fostering an "R&D mind-set" will be more agile, flexible and able to respond more effectively to change than a library with a more traditional mind-set.[27]

Wendy Pradt Lougee, chair of the ARL e-science task force, has written about the evolution of library roles and foresees libraries and librarians becoming more "diffused" through working directly as collaborators with stakeholders within and beyond their home institutions. Lougee identifies four key shifts in libraries:

- from emphasizing the value of collections to emphasizing the value of librarians' expertise
- from supporting information description and access to taking responsibility for greater information analysis
- from serving as a support agency to serving as a collaborator
- from a facility-based enterprise to a campus-wide enterprise

These shifts mark a path of development that focuses on adopting distributed and open models that enable libraries to take on more varied roles. In the final phase of this evolutionary path, the "diffuse library" has become both more broadly and more deeply ingrained not only in the dissemination of knowledge, but in its creation as well. In addition to its traditional role of collecting research outputs, the professionals housed in, or associated with, the diffuse library work alongside knowledge producers as a part of the research process. Traditional library functions and roles such as collection development and information access are expanded outward to form new paradigms such as the library as a publisher of information, or using metadata to enable new access strategies and techniques for content being used or developed by research communities.[28]

As academic libraries reconsider their organizational systems to better meet the needs of faculty, staff, and students in the digital age, they are also reconceptualizing staffing models for the library and reexamining the skill sets needed by library personnel. James Neal has written about the rise of "feral professionals" in libraries. Neal defines two types of feral professionals. The first type are individuals without a master's degree in library science but who possess skill sets, experience, or other credentials that allow them to effectively assume traditional library positions, such as subject specialist or cataloger. One example might be a PhD chemist who migrated to an information center within industry and then was hired as an academic chemistry librarian. The second type are professionally trained librarians who have positions or responsibilities that lie outside of the traditional library core, such as those related to fund-raising, publishing, or instructional technology. These types of positions are designed to allow libraries to offer additional services, increase the library's capabilities, or to move the library in new directions. These professionals are considered "feral" not only due to the nontraditional nature of their backgrounds or positions, but because they often carry a different set of values, expectations, outlooks, and opinions than a more traditional librarian does.[29] Although "feral professionals" have challenged the status quo of libraries, their nontraditional expertise has helped libraries become more in touch with the core academic mission of the university.[30]

A second new staffing model at academic libraries has been conceptualized by Steven Bell and John Shank. Bell and Shank have observed that the use of information technologies is a disruptive force in the support and delivery of instruction at colleges and universities, changing the way faculty teach and students learn. They note that librarians have not kept pace with developments in information technology and are at risk of being overshadowed or eclipsed as the adoption of information technologies in the classroom and curriculum continues to gain traction and acceptance. Bell and Shank propose the role of "blended librarian" as a remedy. A blended librarian is one who combines the traditional skill set of a librarian with an information technologist's skill set in hardware and software along with an instructional designer's knowledge of pedagogy to understand when and how to apply technology in the teaching and learning process appropriately. The combination of these skill sets places the blended librarian, and the library as a whole, in a better position to offer the kinds of services and resources needed in a new age of technology-enabled teaching and learning.[31]

A third innovative staffing model is centered on librarians working outside of the library setting and more directly with faculty in the classroom or "in the field" to support the faculty's teaching or research. Several university libraries have been experimenting with this type of model. The Community College of Vermont and the University of Rhode Island have embedded librarians into online courses to enable them to connect more directly with students and better address their information needs.[32] Virginia Tech has implemented a college librarian program in which librarians are placed outside of the centralized university library and distributed within the colleges they serve, thus allowing them to be more immersed in all aspects of a researcher's or student's information needs.[33] Building on the Virginia Tech model, the University of Michigan has launched a field librarian program in which the librarian is not only housed with faculty researchers but offers technology skills in addition to subject domain expertise.[34] The underlying goals of these "embedded librarian" programs is for librarians to immerse themselves in the department's environment and to better understand and respond to the individual faculty members needs. Ideally, deeper understanding enables librarians to build trust relationships with faculty and to become more of active partners in faculty research and teaching.

The Purdue University Libraries' Approach to E-science

Dr. James Mullins became the dean of the Purdue University Libraries in 2004, in the midst of major efforts launched by Purdue to actively respond to the changes brought about by e-science and to adapt the university to accommodate the development and expansion of cyberinfrastructure. As at most other research universities, e-science figured prominently in Purdue's strategic for 2001–2006. The characteristics of Purdue's vision and goals under this plan included:

- "Model interdisciplinary and collaborative partnerships in the university community"
- "[An] active role of all disciplines in contributing their disciplinary and interdisciplinary strengths to Purdue's vision"
- "Collaboration with public and private enterprise in Indiana, the United States and abroad as a model for pursuing common objectives"
- "A stimulating and supportive state-of-the-art infrastructure that includes informational, technical, facility and human resources"[35]

Again like many research universities, Purdue has put the e-science–based conceptual goals articulated in its strategic plan into practice. Purdue's notable accomplishments in supporting e-science have been the creation of Discovery Park and the NanoHUB. Discovery Park was created at Purdue in 2001 and serves as a home to Purdue's interdisciplinary research centers through providing space for researchers from different disciplines to work together, and centralized access to resources including cutting-edge scientific instruments and facilities.[36] The NanoHUB is designed to support a virtual community in the interdisciplinary field of nanotechnology. This is accomplished through NanoHUB's online gateway, which provides access to simulation and other computational tools, research materials, resources for teaching and learning, and virtual meeting space and other communication tools. The NanoHUB is designed to be used by a wide audience of researchers, teachers, and students. The complexities of the cyberinfrastructure behind the NanoHUB are hidden from the user, and all of the tools and resources can be accessed using nothing more than a Web browser.[37]

As part of Purdue's research infrastructure, the libraries were given a mandate from the president to define their roles in supporting interdisciplinary research and enabling collaborative partnerships. Early on, Dean Mullins met with almost every department head on campus to better understand the research needs of Purdue faculty. What he heard from these meetings echoed the challenges reported in the literature. Common refrains from faculty were that they are having difficulty managing, organizing, sharing, and archiving their research data and that they lacked the time and the skills to address these problems. Many faculty realized that their data have value beyond their original purpose and expressed a desire to share their data with others, but were not sure how to share their data effectively. In addition, funding agencies were beginning to talk about requiring data management plans to ensure the availability of the data to others outside of the project after a reasonable amount of time and beyond the duration of the project's funding cycle. More than just making data sets available, funding agencies would expect the data to be organized and described well enough so that these data could be mined or repurposed by other researchers. Although faculty were aware that these requirements are coming, they were not sure how to prepare for them.[38]

Dean Mullins saw an opportunity for the Purdue University Libraries to play a direct role in the university's push towards interdisciplinary research by working with faculty to meet the challenges of e-science, focusing on data curation and preservation in particular. He quickly recognized that this endeavor would require transforming the libraries' traditional roles, resources, and services to better suit the information needs of researchers in this new era.

The organizational changes made by the Purdue University Libraries to support librarian involvement in interdisciplinary research have been based upon several assumptions made by the libraries' administration. These assumptions have been articulated in presentations made by Dean Mullins and the libraries' associate dean of research.[39] The first set of assumptions reflect one of the recommendations of the ARL e-science task force: *in order to be effective in addressing data curation and preservation issues librarians will need to reexamine the role they play in the research process and modify their practices accordingly.* Working with faculty and IT professionals to develop effective means for the curation and preservation of data requires that librarians be intimately involved with the project early on in the research process, ideally at its conception.[40] This level of involvement would mean that librarians would need to be fully embedded within the research project, similar to the way that librarians are now becoming embedded within courses and academic departments. The librarian embedded within a research project would generate ideas, solicit partners to work with, participate in the grant application process, conduct the research, and write up and report out the results just as any other researcher would do.

The second set of assumptions is that librarians would be accepted as research partners in developing solutions to address data curation and preservation issues by faculty researchers and information technology professionals. The barriers to data curation and preservation identified in the literature—heterogeneity, lack of standards, the need for metadata, copyright, and so on—pose serious challenges to researchers as they generally do not have expertise in data management, nor do they typically have many resources for effective data management at their disposal. Furthermore, most researchers would rather focus their energies on conducting their research than on managing their data. Information technologists are needed to build the technical systems and infrastructure to support data curation and preservation; however, they are likely to be more interested in the technology aspects of the problem, often overlooking the data management and data description tasks necessary to enable discovery, access, or preservation. Under this set of assumptions, the goals and objectives of the researchers for their data would be difficult to achieve without collaborating with librarians. Thus, librarians would be viewed as problem solvers with applicable and needed skills by faculty researchers and information technology professionals.

A third set of assumptions is that, as no readily apparent solutions to the data deluge exist at this time, resolving these issues will call for a substantial investment in time, effort, and infrastructure, beyond what libraries and other parties could reasonably provide on their own. Enabling these kinds of investments requires resources, specifically the availability of funding through grants or other sources. Government agencies and other funding organizations have already expressed a desire to protect the investments they are making in research by ensuring that research outputs are accessible to others and sustainable for the long term. For example, the 2003 statement on data sharing from the National Institutes of Health affirms its support of sharing research data and puts forth an expectation that researchers requesting more than $500,000 in a single year will design a plan for sharing their data.[41] The National Science Foundation's (NSF) 2005 grant policy manual also states that grantees are expected and encouraged to share their primary data and other supporting materials with other researchers.[42] In late 2007, the Office of Cyberinfrastructure within the NSF released a solicitation to fund the creation of organizations dedicated to developing and sustaining new methods, technologies, and management structures to address the challenges of the data deluge. These organizations, dubbed "DataNet partners" in the solicitation, will be driven by the needs of researchers but will include representatives from the library and archival science communities as well as the cyberinfrastructure, computer science, and information science fields.[43] Therefore, it seems likely that the NSF, NIH, and other agencies will continue to offer support and funding for efforts to address data management, curation, and preservation issues as a component of their solicitations, or as solicitations in and of themselves.

Finally, a fourth set of assumptions is that the Purdue Libraries' involvement in developing solutions in data curation and preservation will affect many, if not all, librarians at Purdue. New library professionals willing to help guide and lead the libraries' efforts in data curation and preservation will be needed. However, the scope of what is required for the libraries to support data curation and preservation effectively will go beyond what is possible for individuals in data curation positions to provide on their own. An effective program in data curation and preservation will require multiple skill sets and the involvement of many different librarians. For example, public service librarians could conduct reference interviews to uncover the data-related needs of the researcher. Librarians with collections expertise could serve as data stewards if the library agrees to take responsibility for data sets. The expertise of technical services or metadata librarians could be brought in to identify appropriate taxonomies or ontologies that could be employed to meet the needs of the researcher. Librarians supporting technology infrastructures or services could be able to design and implement data repositories to provide appropriate discovery, access, and preservation functions.[44] These librarians, while continuing to provide traditional library services, will need to expand their capabilities, knowledge, and skill sets with data curation and preservation to become a different kind of "blended librarian," one with a knowledge and understanding of the production and use of research data instead of instructional design.

The Reorganization of the Purdue Libraries

Working from these assumptions, the Purdue Libraries began reorganizing to create a "diffuse library" with an "R&D mind-set" in which librarians would collaborate with faculty and others through involvement in interdisciplinary research projects and would apply their skills as librarians in new ways to address data curation and other issues in e-science. Realizing that someone would need to take ownership and lead the charge to investigate and assess the libraries' involvement in campus research, Dean Mullins approached D. Scott Brandt, then technology training librarian, to take on this role. In 2004, Brandt became the first interdisciplinary research librarian.

It quickly became apparent that the library needed to realign its organizational structure to more closely resemble that of an academic department so as to gain recognition and acceptance as a legitimate research organization. Most colleges at Purdue have an associate dean of research who fosters and facilitates research initiatives and serves as liaison to the Office of the Vice-President for Research (OVPR). Many important decisions are made at the OVPR's Strategic Research Initiatives group meetings, and so it was important for the libraries to have representation on this group. Attendance at group meetings is limited to associate deans and the heads of research centers, however, and so Dean Mullins proposed the creation of a formal research department within the libraries which would be headed by an associate dean of research. The associate dean position would coordinate the libraries' research initiatives and give the libraries access to people and resources, such as membership on the Strategic Research Initiatives group, that would otherwise be difficult to obtain. The libraries' proposal for the creation of a research department was approved by the provost in November 2005, and Brandt was appointed as the first associate dean of research.

The mission of the libraries' Research Department is to support the libraries' research initiative in applying the knowledge and expertise of librarians to provide organization, enrichment, and dissemination of e-science.[45] This mission is currently accomplished in several different ways. First, research department faculty and staff help librarians in more traditional library roles to identify and resolve access, organization, dissemination, and other issues in data curation and e-science. Second, the research department sponsors activities that support and promote research, such as hosting informational and brainstorming sessions on research or funding opportunities for librarians. Third, the research department oversees the investigation of the Purdue Libraries' Distributed Institutional Repository (DIR) system. The DIR system will consist of multiple repositories that will enable the dissemination of research at Purdue as well as its curation, storage, and preservation as appropriate for the nature of the content, available infrastructure, and the needs of the users. A hallmark of the DIR will be the federation and interoperability of metadata between these repositories to enable cross-disciplinary discovery and research. The DIR consists of three interconnected repositories: one for publications, one for archives and special collections, and one for research data (in development). Finally, the research department seeks out grants and other opportunities for the libraries to obtain the funding necessary to pursue their research objectives and assists librarians in navigating the process of applying for these grants. Research is also supported by the Libraries Research Council, which is charged with addressing issues and policies related to the libraries' research activities.

In 2006, the libraries created the Distributed Data Curation Center (D2C2) at Purdue as another means to further the diffusion of the libraries into the research culture and infrastructure of Purdue. The goals of the D2C2 are to enable the libraries to align itself with the university's strategic mission and to make connections with researchers in ways that they and funding agencies would understand and accept.[46] Faculty and administrators are not used to working with the libraries as research partners, but are used to collaborating with research centers, so creating a research center has given the library greater access to resources and key individuals throughout the Purdue community and elsewhere. The board of directors for the D2C2 is comprised of several deans, a director of a research center at Purdue, Purdue's chief information officer, and others. These board members enable the D2C2, and by extension the Purdue Libraries, to stay abreast of important developments within the university.[47]

The D2C2 seeks to address the challenges presented by the increasingly data-intensive and highly networked nature of academic research. Its mission is "to investigate and resolve curation issues of facilitating access to, preservation of, and archiving for data and data sets in complex and distributed environments" through the application of the practice and principles of library science.[48] This mission is primarily accomplished through working directly with researchers and embedding librarians within their research projects to add value to their data sets. The D2C2 defines data sets broadly to include a wide range of digital collections or objects. Adding value to data sets may include such tasks as helping to identify and apply appropriate metadata standards and ontologies to data sets, designing models and workflows to better enable the access, curation, and preservation of data, and ensuring that data are available for the long term by capturing provenance information or stewarding data in the libraries' e-data repository. The D2C2 also pursues its own teaching and research agenda, which includes addressing the higher scope of data curation through the development of best practices, teaching others about data curation theory and application, and building community-based curation profiles and policies to define appropriate access to and use of data.

New Staffing Models at the Purdue Libraries

The reorganizations at Purdue, the new strategic plan, and the "diffusion" of the library across campus through the creation of the libraries' research department and the D2C2,\ have all been undertaken with an overarching purpose in mind: to enable librarians, not only to adopt an "R&D mind-set," but to think of themselves as academic researchers in their own right. Purdue's approach has been to assert that librarians have what Dean Mullins refers to as "a natural research domain" in the management, organization, dissemination, and preservation of information. However, as is often the case, many librarians at Purdue are focused on the operations of a library and have only limited experience in applying their skills on projects or research outside of a library setting. Working to design and build solutions to address problems in data curation and preservation and partnering with faculty in their research projects directly are not only a major paradigm shift to the organizational models of libraries but a significant change in how librarians view themselves and their place in the university. Therefore, enabling librarians to become involved in interdisciplinary research requires more than reorganizing the structure of the libraries; it requires librarians, along with faculty and others outside of the profession, to reconceptualize the role of a librarian.

The Purdue University Libraries approach to staffing its research initiative is two-fold. First is to adopt the "feral professional" approach by bringing new personnel into the library to focus directly on building the libraries' capacity and expertise in researching data curation and related areas to support the new paradigm of e-science–based research. Second is to adopt the "blended librarian" approach through the reapplication of the specialized skill sets of traditional librarians at Purdue towards providing the new services and resources that are needed to meet the information needs of researchers practicing e-science. This approach entails not only a role for librarians in assisting in the libraries' research efforts, but operational roles as well. One of the desired outcomes of this approach is to develop the data management and curation skills of librarians to the point where they become a natural part of the core skill set of librarians at Purdue. Ultimately, it is envisioned that librarians will build and maintain collections of digital research data sets as they would build and maintain a collection of electronic books or journals.

The Data Research Scientist Position

The data research scientist is a new position created by the Purdue Libraries to help drive its efforts in developing the libraries' capabilities and services in data curation and preservation. The idea for this position came out of a report by the National Science Board (NSB): *Long-Lived Digital Data Collections: Enabling Research and Education in the 21st Century.* This report describes the roles and responsibilities of individuals in curating research data including a position it labels "data scientist." The role of the data scientist differs from the role of the data manager, as the data manager would be directly responsible for the operation and maintenance of databases. The role of the data manager roughly corresponds to the role envisioned for Purdue's librarians as stewards of collections of data sets. In contrast, the role of the data scientist centers on enabling others to conduct research and educational activities using collections of digital data through consultation, collaboration, and coordination. The NSB notes that individuals who are serving as data scientists hail from a variety of backgrounds, including the technology and programming fields, disciplinary science fields, and library/archival fields. No matter the background, the feature uniting data scientists is their ability to enable others to get more out of their data than they could have otherwise on their own. This is accomplished by the data scientist developing a deep understanding of the project's data and workflows, obtaining an intimate knowledge of the needs of the researchers who are using the data, and having the creative capacity to create the resources, tools, and services that will connect researchers with the data in ways that would not have otherwise been possible.[49]

The idea of a data librarian is not a new one. There are academic librarians who provide data services and resources, particularly in the social sciences. However, although some position descriptions do include data management and archival responsibilities, data librarian positions are often more centered on incorporating data into traditional library services: reference, instruction, collection development, and so on.[50]

What makes the data research scientist position different is the lack of public service and other traditional librarian responsibilities and the primary focus on building interdisciplinary research initiatives in data management, curation, and preservation and related areas. At a high level, the data research scientist is charged with developing an awareness and knowledge of available data management, access and preservation tools, and services and standards, as well as understanding how they could be employed effectively to address specific needs and enrich research outcomes. The data research scientist applies this knowledge in order to add value to digital data collections being generated or used for research at Purdue through consultation, collaboration, and coordination with researchers. On the ground level, the data research scientist is responsible for helping the libraries move research strategically forward through increasing awareness and visibility of Purdue Libraries' research on campus and elsewhere, fostering interactions between librarians and research faculty on campus, leveraging interdisciplinary research collaborations and co-investigations (particularly on grant funding) and increasing the libraries' capabilities and opportunities to work in data-related research and applied activities.

New Roles for Existing Positions: The Subject Specialist

In addition to building expertise in data curation and preservation, the data research scientist serves as a resource for subject specialists needing to develop the skills and abilities necessary to become "blended librarians" and include data curation in their own work. Perhaps the largest responsibility of the data research scientist is to act as a catalyst in initiating and building connections between researchers with data management, curation, dissemination, and preservation or other related needs and librarians who possess the knowledge and expertise to develop solutions to address these needs. These connections are built through the libraries' having an understanding of the research being conducted at Purdue and reaching out to faculty who are generating or using data as a component of their research activities.

Collaborations between the data research scientists and subject librarians to identify faculty researchers with data needs are critical. Subject librarians have already invested time and effort in building connections with faculty, learning about their particular area of research, and understanding their information needs. These existing connections can also help the data research scientist identify which faculty may be receptive to working with the library to address their issues and needs with regards to their research data. The relationship between a subject librarian and a faculty member can open the door to a discussion about the researcher's data needs and how the library may be able to address these needs.

However, the role of the subject librarians in the libraries' data curation initiatives goes far beyond simply making introductions for the data research scientist. As specialists in the information environment of a particular discipline, subject librarians are a vital part of any data curation project undertaken by the libraries and need to be actively involved in every step of the process as collaborators with the data research scientist if the project is to succeed. Their understanding of a subject includes such things as knowledge of the information sources that exist for the discipline and how they are constructed and used, along with an awareness of the metadata standards, thesauri, and taxonomies or ontologies that are used to organize and manage information in their field. Many of the subject librarians at Purdue have advanced degrees in their field, and even if they do not, they have gained an understanding of the cultural practice of research and the research process in their respective disciplines. Subject librarians can use their knowledge of a discipline to identify what data sets might be of use to others in the field and can articulate what description, documentation, or other information will be needed to enable the data to be used beyond a particular faculty's research project. Finally, subject librarians have connections to professional societies within their discipline and have an understanding of the trends and the direction the discipline is likely to go in the future.

Once a researcher or research group with possible data management, dissemination, preservation, or other related needs has been identified, the data research scientist, with the help of the subject librarian, may contact the researcher to arrange a face-to-face meeting. The purpose of the meeting is typically to conduct a needs assessment to learn more about the specific data needs of the researcher or research team, and then to convey how the library may be able to address these needs.

The needs assessment is often done through a data interview with the faculty researchers and others who are connected to the data and is conducted by the data research scientist and/or subject librarian. The questions asked will vary according to the nature of the research being conducted and the data being collected; however, there are some fairly standardized broad categories of inquiry. Beyond learning about the nature of the data (its format, size, type, and other attributes), the interviewer seeks to uncover the unmet needs of the researcher or group generating or using the data and to obtain specific details about these needs. For example, if researchers state that they would like to make the data accessible to others beyond their own research group, then the interviewer asks about what data should be available to whom, at what point in the research cycle (immediately after the data has been processed, in conjunction with the publication of the results, six months after publication, etc.), and how the data should be made available. A sample of the types of questions that are typically asked during the data interview is provided in figure 9.1.[51]

FIGURE 9.1
Sample Data Interview Schedule

- What's the story of the data?
  - Asked to obtain background information, context, and insight into the value of the data.
- What's the expected lifespan of the data?
  - Asked to obtain information about provenance and preservation needs.
- Who are the potential audiences for the data?
  - Asked to determine how the data might be used by others as well as if any restrictions on accessing need to be created.
- Who owns the data?
  - Asked to identify and clarify intellectual property issues.
- Does the data include any sensitive information?
  - Asked to identify any confidentiality issues that may have to be addressed.

As the needs of the researcher are articulated, the data research scientist and subject librarian consider and communicate ways in which the library could potentially address these needs as appropriate. In these instances, the work of the library is driven by the needs of the researcher, and so the exact nature of the libraries' proposals will vary accordingly. For example, if the researchers need a data management plan to satisfy a requirement of a funding agency, we may assist in creating such a plan. If the researcher needs to develop a means of sharing data with others, we may propose developing metadata based on the community accepted standards to enable the data to be shared with the intended audiences. If the researcher wants to preserve his or her data for the long term, we may discuss what decisions, documentation, and resources would be required to do this effectively and then develop a preservation model for the data. As a part of this communications stage, the data research scientist may ask for a sample of the researcher's data. Having a sample of the data allows the data research scientist to become more familiar with the nature of the data under consideration. The sample can also serve as a test bed for the efficacy of the ideas being generated.

After the possible roles of the libraries in addressing the needs of the researchers are discussed and solidified, the data research scientist will often write up a summary of the articulated needs of the researcher and the initial work the libraries propose to do in response. This document spells out the resources that are needed and the responsibilities of everyone involved in the project, provides an estimate for the amount of time allotted to the project, and describes the expected results. This written summary ensures that both sides have a shared understanding of the expectations and the work involved in achieving these expectations.

These initial collaborations are often smaller "pilot" projects conducted to test out the ideas, demonstrate the benefits of what the library has to offer, and get a sense of the time, effort, and resources that would be required in a larger scale project. Frequently, however, the stated expectation is that the smaller pilot project will lead to a significant collaboration with the researcher to build and implement a full-scale project. These larger projects usually require more resources than the library is able to provide on its own, and so grant funding is sought. The pilot projects also serve to demonstrate to funding agencies the feasibility of the work being proposed in the grant application.

Faculty will typically seek grant funding in order to obtain the resources necessary to conduct their research projects. E-science projects are typically conducted in teams, with each team member bringing a different set of skills and expertise to the project. In pursuit of grant funding, the principal investigator of the project will seek out partners who can address the requirements of the funding agency, contribute to the project in meaningful ways, and increase the likelihood of success. Ideally, the work done by the data research scientist and the subject librarian and their relationship with the principal investigator would lead to an invitation for them to participate in the grant proposal as co-principal investigators or senior personnel. As a co-PI or senior personnel, the data research scientist and subject librarian collaborate with the other faculty and staff in the grant-building, negotiating, and writing process. They work as a part of the research team in all of the tasks that go into creating a grant proposal, including: defining the specifics of the project and proposal, contacting the program officers of the grant, writing up the proposal following the terms and guidelines specified in the grant, negotiating a budget for the project, soliciting letters of support, and creating or gathering other needed documentation.

Collaboration in Practice: The CASPiE Project

One example of how the Purdue University Libraries Research Department is working to support e-science is the collaboration between the libraries and the faculty and staff of the Center for Authentic Science Practice in Education (CASPiE). This collaboration enabled the data research scientist and chemical information specialist to embed themselves within the CASPiE project and to work closely with CASPiE administration.

CASPiE is a multi-institutional NSF-funded undergraduate research center headquartered at Purdue University.[52] It provides authentic research experiences to first- and second-year students in order to increase student interest and retention in the sciences. Rather than simply answering textbook questions or conducting experiments in which the results are already known, students enrolled in CASPiE courses investigate a real-world research problem to support the work of a faculty member. The nature of the research problem is explained through a course module developed by a faculty member (subsequently referred to as the module author). After students complete a series of introductory lab sessions, they then develop their own hypotheses and design their own experiments. The module author then receives the results of the experiments to investigate whether anything of interest has been discovered by the students.

The students in CASPiE courses have access to a system of networked high-quality scientific instruments to gather research-quality data for their experiments if required by the module. These highly advanced instruments—including a Raman spectrometer, a liquid chromatograph with array detector, and a gas chromatograph—are not typically available for use by undergraduate students. CASPiE investigators collaborating with Information Technology at Purdue (ITaP) developed a means to network these instruments and make them available for students through the Internet while monitoring how these instruments are accessed and used. This network allows many students at different geographic locations to access the instrument network hosted by Purdue and to run their samples remotely.[53]

The libraries' involvement with CASPiE began in April 2007 when the data research scientist and the chemical information specialist attended a seminar given by the director of instrumentation networking for CASPiE. Although the seminar focused more on the technical aspects of CASPiE's instrumentation network, it was apparent to the librarians by the end of the seminar that data management was a growing problem for the project. CASPiE and ITaP had built a very powerful and secure high-throughput system of remote instrumentation, but they lacked the means to manage these data as effectively as desired. It was clear that as more instruments came onto the network, as more institutions participated in the CASPiE project, and as more CASPiE courses were created, the data being generated would quickly become unmanageable.

The data research scientist made contact with the director of instrumentation networking to introduce the libraries' interest in supporting data curation and to request a meeting to learn more about the CASPiE project and its needs in managing and archiving data. Over the course of several meetings, these librarians met with CASPiE staff involved with the management and operation of the instrumentation network. CASPiE did not have a data management plan that reflected what they wanted to accomplish with their data or the infrastructure in place to support the effective use, access, or preservation of the data they were generating. Furthermore, there was a lack of metadata describing the data, which made the data difficult to use. From these meetings, the librarians began to understand the workflow outside the instrumentation network, including how students generated additional data through in-class experiments, how students recorded additional information during and after lab in their notebooks, and how the final data and conclusions were forwarded to the module author for review and future exploration.

After these meetings, the data research scientist and chemical information specialist met to design a pilot project that would address the issues articulated by CASPiE's administration. In consultation with the libraries' associate dean for research, the data research scientist and chemical information specialist worked out what the library could offer CASPiE at this stage, defined the boundaries of the pilot, obtained the necessary resources, and worked out release time for the chemical information specialist to work on the pilot. The libraries' initial offer was to provide 200 hours of staff time for a pilot project to design a prototype model for managing and archiving the data from one of CASPiE's modules based on its existing workflows.

For the libraries, the expectation was that building this prototype would serve two purposes. First, the prototype might serve as an example solution that could potentially be extended to a full data management and archiving model for the entire CASPiE program and eventually be applied to other similar research projects or situations. The second expectation was that the prototype could be used to leverage additional grant funding for the libraries and CASPiE that would provide the necessary resources to undertake the development of the full-scale system. CASPiE administration understood these expectations and identified a suitable module to serve as the basis for the pilot project. The librarians worked step-wise through the module, identifying where students and instruments were generating and recording data.

In order to be successful in our efforts with this pilot project, the data research scientist and chemical information specialist had to become more familiar with

- the interests of the module's author (the faculty researcher) with the data, with the particular lab module itself, and with the purpose of each of the analytical methods used

- the workflow of the students and CASPiE staff as they implemented the module and generated data
- the size, format, type, and other attributes of the data
- the desired services and outcomes for the data for all parties involved
- the metadata and other documentation that would be required to enable these services and outcomes

A data management plan for the selected CASPiE module was developed over the course of several months. As the data research scientist and the chemical information specialist gathered the information necessary to create the plan from CASPiE's staff and from reviewing the data generated by the students, three distinct stages emerged. First, in the "educational" stage, the data are generated by the students enrolled in the course and reviewed by the instructors for evaluation. The instructor teaching the course (who may or may not be the module author) needs to have access to the data and sufficient documentation to complete the educational aspects of the CASPiE project. Second, in the "research" stage, the module author needed access to the data in order to analyze them further and to apply the results towards answering the research question he or she had set forth. This would require sufficient metadata for the module author to understand enough of how and why the data had been generated to be able to trust in its quality and to reproduce the data if necessary. Access to the data at this point would be determined by the module author. Finally, in the "archive" stage, once the module author had exhausted the value of the data for his or her own purposes and published the results, the data could be ingested into the libraries' e-data repository to be preserved for the long term. The data would be freely available, and the metadata would be in openly accessible formats and structured according to community standards that would enable the reuse of the data by others.[54]

The final report for the libraries' pilot project was presented to CASPiE administration in early February 2008. The report contained a description of the proposed data management model, a discussion of the types of metadata that would be needed to enable desired functionality, details of what the challenges might be in implementing this model, and a list of recommendations for actions and future directions to overcome these challenges.

Knowing that implementing this model would require additional funding, the librarians, CASPiE, and ITaP began pursuing sponsored funding in late fall of 2007. Once a suitable call for proposals was identified, the first step was to define and articulate the role the libraries could and should play in the overall solicitation. The approach was to take what had already been learned about the data management needs of CASPiE from the work that had been done and to adapt that knowledge to meet the requirements of the grant proposal. Collaborating with the other co-PIs on the grant also required the libraries' Research Department to negotiate for the resources it would need to accomplish its part of the proposal, while still remaining within the overall budget of the grant. The data research scientist was made one of the co-PIs and designated to coordinate the libraries' efforts in the process of data capture, curation, and preservation for the project. The chemical information specialist was named as senior personnel in the grant to identify and translate research and instrument methodologies into data curation and archive functions. If this grant is awarded, the libraries will be an integral part of the research team driving the CASPiE project. If this grant is not awarded, the administration of CASPiE is still committed to partnering with the libraries in seeking out the sources of funding needed to build data management, curation, and preservation tools for the CASPiE project.

The partnership between the data research scientist and the chemical information specialist was essential in designing and developing the prototype model to address CASPiE's data needs and in applying for grant funding to continue this work. The data research scientist had little previous experience in chemistry and needed assistance in understanding the nature of the instrumentation and the processes used to generate the data. This project was the chemical information specialist's first direct involvement with data management and curation issues, and he needed guidance in navigating the many aspects involved in addressing data issues effectively. The data research scientist served as the project manager and conducted the interviews to identify the specific needs of the CASPiE administration and the module author with regards to their data. He reviewed CASPiE's processes and scientific workflows to determine how data management, curation, and preservation functions could best be incorporated into their existing systems and investigated the metadata that might be needed to enable discovery and preservation. The data research scientist also helped to guide the chemical information specialist through the process of applying for grant funding. The chemical information specialist researched what descriptive, administrative, and structural metadata standards might be applicable to address CASPiE's needs for their data. He tutored the data research scientist in the research techniques that were used in the CASPiE module and provided insight as to how the data might be used by the researcher or repurposed by others. The work on the CASPiE project was a team effort and would not have succeeded without the collaboration between the data research scientist and the chemical Information specialist.

Skills Needed for Support E-Science Research

The collaboration between research faculty and staff of CASPiE, ITaP, and the Purdue University Libraries is only one illustration of how librarians at Purdue are defining roles for themselves in the era of e-science. The Purdue Libraries' model of building the capacity and capabilities of librarians to participate in interdisciplinary research as equal partners with academic faculty and IT professionals has pushed librarians at Purdue to adapt their skill sets to this new role. Different types of librarians at Purdue are continuing to build up or rework their specific abilities as appropriate to their particular specialties in the library; however, from our experiences we have already begun to see that all librarians who will play an active role in interdisciplinary research will need to develop a set of shared skills as well. The need for librarians to develop strong technical skills should not be underestimated, but technical skills alone are insufficient for success. Soft skills such as communication, creativity and flexibility, and risk taking are equally important. These skill sets are interrelated, but require some explanation individually.

First, a strong set of communication skills is a key component in enabling librarians to participate in interdisciplinary research and collaborate with faculty and IT professionals. This skill set includes the ability to actively listen, understand, and empathize with the information needs of the researcher within the context of the particular research project. The librarian must also be able to articulate what the library has to offer and translate library science concepts so that all parties can understand them and see how they would add value to the project. The hard work of meeting on common ground helps build strong relationships, which is critical as the researchers must get to know the librarian personally and be able to trust that the librarian will be able to deliver if the librarian is to become part of the research team. Negotiation skills are also important as librarians will need to ensure that enough resources are allocated to support their role in the research project.

Second, success in interdisciplinary research rests on creativity and flexibility. Librarians need to be willing and able to conceptualize how their skills could be applied in new ways outside of the traditional domains of the library. This requires the creativity to be able to see possibilities for the application of library science and the involvement of librarians in a new and relatively undefined frontier. In order to lay their claim to this new ground, librarians must expand their knowledge base beyond the library science field and become familiar with the discussions that are taking place in other fields as Gibbons noted in her description of the "R&D mind-set." Obtaining this familiarity is essential in bridging the "language barrier" that may exist (*curation,* for example, means different things to different people) and in conceiving possibilities for librarians to become more directly involved. Finally, events and circumstances in data projects often change or evolve over time as things progress or as more information becomes known. In this type of environment, librarians will need the flexibility to react accordingly and reframe their role in the project to reflect any changes that occur.

Third, entering this new frontier involves a willingness to take risks. As has been illustrated in the previous skill descriptions, embedding oneself in an interdisciplinary research project entails leaving the comfort zone of the well-established practices and procedures of library science and venturing into unknown territories. Even beyond leaving one's comfort zone, investing time and effort in interdisciplinary research, such as data curation and preservation projects, is a risky endeavor for librarians. The amount of effort required just to design a project and get it off the ground demands a high degree of commitment and investment from all team members, especially when it comes time to locate, write, and submit a grant proposal. Unfortunately, even with this investment, the logistical challenges of putting a project together and the nature of grant funding are such that a lot of effort may not lead to any tangible results. Despite the prospect of failure, however, the Purdue Libraries have found it worthwhile to take the risk. Enough of the projects that we have been involved in have received support and funding, thereby justifying the investment of librarians' time and effort. Furthermore, even in situations where the project did not take off as planned, the experience of having been a part of a research team as a full partner is a valuable learning experience for librarians, because it better prepares us for future opportunities and helps us forge deep relationships with faculty and IT professionals that otherwise would not have developed.

Conclusion

The Purdue University Libraries initiatives in supporting e-science through the active involvement of librarians in collaborations in inter-disciplinary research projects have been quite successful thus far. Since the initiative began in 2005, more than 22 librarians have participated in more than 47 multidisciplinary grant proposals, including proposals from the National Institutes of Health, the National Science Foundation, the National Endowment for the Humanities, and the United States Department of Agriculture, as well as regional and local grants. Fourteen of these grants have been awarded.

The creation of a libraries research department and related positions such as associate dean of research and data research scientist have enabled individual librarians as well as the Purdue Libraries as a whole to expand their participation in research support in the age of e-science and cyberinfrastructure. This new organizational structure can coordinate the libraries' efforts in contacting potential collaborators, seeking sponsored funding, and educating and assisting subject librarians in becoming more comfortable with enacting data services for faculty and research groups. The Purdue Libraries are now in the process of disseminating and sharing our experiences in this area through such events as participating in the University of Illinois at Urbana-Champaign's summer data curation institute and hosting a Committee on Institutional Cooperation (CIC) conference on libraries and e-science.[55]

To be sure, the Purdue University Libraries have only just begun to explore new roles for librarians, and there are still many challenges yet to face in defining what the role of librarians could or should be in curating or preserving data or in supporting e-science in general. However, as e-science continues to provide new capabilities—and even requirements—for exploration and research, librarians and the services they provide must also evolve to meet the information needs of their patrons in emerging data-driven research environment of the 21st century. Furthermore, data curation and preservation activities give librarians an opportunity to reclaim our status as the central provider and steward of research information, no matter in what form it is captured. By so doing, the profession will add value to e-science as it evolves, equipping its discoveries to persist and to remain accessible into the years ahead.

Notes

1. Cyberinfrastructure Council, "Cyberinfrastructure Vision for 21st Century Discovery" (Arlington, VA: National Science Foundation, 2007), available online from www.nsf.gov/pubs/2007/nsf0728/nsf0728.pdf (accessed July 18, 2008).
2. Blue-Ribbon Advisory Panel on Cyberinfrastructure, "Revolutionizing Science and Engineering through Cyberinfrastructure," (Arlington, VA: National Science Foundation, 2003), available online from www.nsf.gov/od/oci/reports/atkins.pdf (accessed June 18, 2008).
3. G. Sayeed Choudhury, "The Virtual Observatory Meets the Library," *Journal of Electronic Publishing* 11, no.1 (Winter 2008), available online from http://hdl.handle.net/2027/spo.3336451.0011.111 (accessed Sept. 22, 2008); Sayeed Choudhury, Tim DiLauro, Alex Szalay, Ethan Vishniac, Robert Hanisch, Julie Steffen, Robert Milkey, Teresa Ehling, and Ray Plante, "Digital Data Preservation for Scholarly Publications in Astronomy," *International Journal of Digital Curation* 2, no.2 (2007): 20–30, available online from http://jhir.library.jhu.edu/handle/1774.2/32796 (accessed Sept. 22, 2008); U. S. National Virtual Observatory, www.us-vo.org/index.cfm (accessed Sept. 22, 2008).
4. Commission on Cyberinfrastructure for the Humanities and Social Sciences, "Our Cultural Commonwealth." (New York: American Council of Learned Societies, 2006), available online from www.acls.org/cyberinfrastructure/OurCulturalCommonwealth.pdf (accessed July 18, 2008).
5. Institute for Advanced Technology in the Humanities at the University of Virginia, "Rome Reborn 1.0," 2007, available online from www.romereborn.virginia.edu (accessed July 18, 2008).
6. Stephen Emmott, ed., *Towards 2020 Science* (Cambridge, UK: Microsoft Research Ltd., 2006), 15.
7. Tony Hey and Anne Trefethen, "The Data Deluge: An E-Science Perspective," in *Grid Computing: Making the Global Infrastructure a Reality,* ed. Fran Berman, Geoffrey Fox, and Anthony J. G. Hey, 809–824 (Chichester, UK: Wiley, 2003).
8. Ewa Deelman and Yolanda Gil, "Workshop on the Challenges of Scientific

Workflows: Executive Summary," (Arlington, VA: National Science Foundation, 2006), available online from http://vtcpc.isi.edu/wiki/images/7/71/NSF-Work-fow-Summary.pdf (accessed June 18, 2008).

9. Cyberinfrastructure Council, "Cyberinfrastructure Vision," 24.

10. Philip Lord, Alison Macdonald, Liz Lyon, and David Giaretta, "From Data Deluge to Data Curation," (UK e-Science All Hands Meeting, Nottingham, UK, Aug. 31–Sept. 3, 2004), available online from www.ukoln.ac.uk/ukoln/staff/e.j.lyon/150.pdf (accessed June 18, 2008).

11. ARL Workshop on New Collaborative Relationships, *To Stand the Test of Time: Long-Term Stewardship of Digital Data Sets in Science and Engineering,* (Washington, DC, Association of Research Libraries, 2006), available online from www.arl.org/bm-doc/digdatarpt.pdf (accessed June 18, 2008).

12. Michael Witt, "Institutional Repositories and Research Data Curation in a Distributed Environment." *Library Trends* 57, no. 2 (Fall 2008): 191–201.

13. Christopher L. Greer, "A Vision for the Digital Data Universe," 2007, available online from www.nanohub.org/resources/2291 (accessed July 19, 2008).

14. Cyberinfrastructure Council, "Cyberinfrastructure Vision," 31.

15. Mark C. Sheehan, *Higher Education IT and Cyberinfrastructure: Integrating Technologies for Scholarship,* ECAR Research Study 3 (Boulder, CO: EDUCAUSE Center for Applied Research, 2008), available online from www.educause.edu/ir/library/pdf/ers0803/rs/ERS0803w.pdf (accessed July 18, 2008).

16. Nicholas Joint, "Data Preservation, the New Science and the Practitioner Librarian." *Library Review* 56, no. 6 (2007): 450–455.

17. Emmott, *Towards 2020 Science,* 19.

18. Richard E. Luce, "A New Value Equation Challenge: The Emergence of Eresearch and Roles for Research Libraries," in *No Brief Candle: Reconceiving Research Libraries for the 21st Century* (Council on Library and Information Resources, 2008), available online from www.clir.org/pubs/reports/pub142/luce.html (accessed July 23, 2008).

19. Andy Guess, "At Libraries, Taking the (Really) Long View." Inside Higher Ed, July 23, 2008, available online from www.insidehighered.com/news/2008/07/23/preservation (accessed Aug. 31, 2008).

20. Joint Task Force on Library Support for E-Science, "Agenda for Developing E-Science in Research Libraries," Association of Research Libraries, Nov. 2007, available online from www.arl.org/bm-doc/ARL_EScience_final.pdf (accessed June 18, 2008).

21. Joint Task Force. "Agenda for Developing E-Science," 17.

22. ARL Workshop. *To Stand the Test of Time,* 12.

23. Ibid , 12–13.

24. Anna Gold, "Cyberinfrastructure, Data and Libraries, Part 1: A Cyberinfrastructure Primer for Librarians," *D-Lib Magazine* 13, no. 9/10 (Sept./Oct. 2007), available online from www.dlib.org/dlib/september07/gold/09gold-pt1.html accessed June 11, 2008).

25. Research Information Network and Consortium of Research Libraries, *Researchers' Use of Academic Libraries and Their Services,* (London: Research Information Network, 2007), available online from www.rin.ac.uk/files/libraries-report-2007.pdf (accessed July 29, 2008); University of Minnesota Libraries, "Sciences Assessment," 2005, available online from University of Minnesota Libraries, "Understanding Research Behaviors, Information Resources, and Service Needs of

Scientists and Graduate Students," 2007, available online from conservancy.umn. edu/handle/5546.

26. David G. Messerschmitt, "Opportunities for Research Libraries in the NSF Cyberinfrastructure Program," ARL Bimonthly Report no. 229, Association of Research Libraries, Aug. 2003, available online from www.arl.org/resources/ pubs/br/br229/br229cyber.shtml (accessed Feb. 9, 2008).

27. Susan Gibbons, *The Academic Library and the Net Gen Student: Making the Connections* (Chicago: American Library Association, 2007).

28. Wendy Pradt Lougee, "Diffuse Libraries: Emergent Roles for the Research Library in the Digital Age," Council on Library and Information Resources, Aug. 2002, available online from www.clir.org/pubs/reports/pub108/pub108.pdf (accessed July 23, 2008).

29. James G. Neal, "Raised by Wolves: Integrating the New Generation of Feral Professionals into the Academic Library," *Library Journal* 131, no. 3 (Feb. 15, 2006): 42–44.

30. Stanley Wilder, "The New Library Professional," *Chronicle of Higher Education*, Feb. 20, 2007, available online from http://chronicle.com/jobs/ news/2007/02/2007022001c.htm (accessed July 18, 2008).

31. Stephen J. Bell and John D. Shank, "The Blended Librarian: A Blueprint for Redefining the Teaching and Learning Role of Academic Librarians." *College & Research Libraries News* 65, no. 7 (July 2004): 372–375.

32. Victoria Matthew and Ann Schroeder, "The Embedded Librarian Program: Faculty and Librarians Partner to Embed Personalized Library Assistance into Online Courses," *EDUCAUSE Quarterly* 29, no. 4 (2006): 61–65; Karen M. Ramsay and Jim Kinnie, "The Embedded Librarian: Getting Out There via Technology to Help Students Where They Learn," *Library Journal* 131, no. 6 (April 2006): 34–35.

33. Nancy H. Seamans and Paul Metz, "Virginia Tech's Innovative College Librarian Program." *College & Research Libraries* 63, no. 4 (July 2002): 324–332; Jane E. Schillie, Virginia E. Young, Susan A. Ariew, Ellen M. Krupar, and Margaret C. Merrill, "Outreach through the College Librarian Program at Virginia Tech." *Reference Librarian* 34. no. 71 (2001): 71–78.

34. Brenda L. Johnson and Laurie A. Alexander, "In the Field: An Innovative Role Puts Academic Librarians Right in the Departments They Serve," *Library Journal* 132, no. 2 (Feb. 1, 2007), Available online from www.libraryjournal.com/article/ CA6407750.html (accessed Sept. 1, 2008); Lougee. "Diffuse Libraries," 19.

35. "The Next Level: Preeminence: Strategic Plan 2001–2006." Purdue University, Nov. 2001, available online from www.purdue.edu/strategic_plan/2001-2006 (see Vision and Goals links; accessed June 18, 2008).

36. Discovery Park, Purdue University website, available online from www.purdue. edu/dp/index.php (accessed July 23, 2008).

37. nanoHUB, Network for Computational Nanotechnology, Purdue University, available online from www.nanohub.org (accessed July 19, 2008).

38. James L. Mullins, interview by Jake R. Carlson, June 9, 2008.

39. D. Scott Brandt and James L. Mullins, "Building an Interdisciplinary Research Program in an Academic Library," Coalition for Networked Information (April 4, 2006), available online from www.cni.org/tfms/2006a.spring/abstracts/hand-outs/CNI_Building_Mullins.ppt (accessed June 23, 2008); James L. Mullins, "Enabling International Access to Scientific Data Sets: Creation of the Distribut-

ed Data Curation Center (D2C2)." (presentation, 28th IATUL Conference, June 11–14, 2007, Stockholm, Sweden), available online from http://docs.lib.purdue.edu/lib_research/85 (accessed June 18, 2008).

40. Joint Task Force, "Agenda for Developing E-Science."

41. "Final NIH Statement on Sharing Research Data." National Institutes of Health, Feb. 26, 2003, available online from http://grants.nih.gov/grants/guide/notice-files/NOT-OD-03-032.html (accessed June 18, 2008).

42. "Chapter VII: Other Grant Requirements," section 734: Dissemination and Sharing of Research Results, Grant Policy Manual, National Science Foundation. July 2005, available online from www.nsf.gov/pubs/manuals/gpm05_131/gpm7.jsp (accessed June 18, 2008).

43. Office of Cyberinfrastructure, "Sustainable Digital Data Preservation and Access Network Partners (DataNet)." National Science Foundation, available online from www.nsf.gov/funding/pgm_summ.jsp?pims_id=503141 (accessed June 18, 2008).

44. Brandt and Mullins, "Building an Interdisciplinary Research Program"; Mullins, "Enabling International Access to Scientific Data Sets."

45. D. Scott Brandt, "Librarians as Partners in E-Research: Purdue University Libraries Promote Collaboration." *College & Research Libraries News* 68, no. 6 (June 2007): 365–367, 396.

46. For a more complete account of how the D2C2 was created see Mullins, "Enabling International Access to Scientific Data Sets."

47. Mullins interview.

48. D. Scott Brandt, "Vision," Distributed Data Curation Center website, available online from http://d2c2.lib.purdue.edu/vision.php (accessed June 18, 2008).

49. National Science Board, *Long-Lived Data Collections: Enabling Research and Education in the 21st Century*, (Arlington, VA: National Science Foundation, 2005), available online from www.nsf.gov/pubs/2005/nsb0540/start.htm (accessed June 18, 2008).

50. Michael N. Cook, John J. Hernandez, and Shawn Nicholson, *Numeric Data Products and Services: SPEC Kit 263* (Washington, DC: Association of Research Libraries, 2001).

51. Michael Witt and Jake R. Carlson, "Conducting a Data Interview " Purdue University, Dec. 2007, available online from http://docs.lib.purdue.edu/lib_research/81 (accessed June 24, 2008).

52. "The Center for Authentic Science Practice in Education." CASPiE (2004). Available online from http://www.purdue.edu/dp/caspie/ (Accessed June 24, 2008).

53. Fred E. Lytle, Gabriela C. Weaver, Phillip Wyss, Debora Steffen, and John Campbell, "Making Instrumentation a Secure Part of the Cyberinfrastructure," (working paper, 2008).

54. Jake R. Carlson and Jeremy R. Garritano, "Preserving Undergraduate Research Data," Purdue University, Nov. 2007, available online from http://docs.lib.purdue.edu/lib_research/82 (accessed June 18, 2008).

55. CIC Library Conference: Librarians and E-Science: Focusing toward 20/20, May 12–13, 2008, West Lafayette, IN, available online from www.cic.uiuc.edu/programs/centerforlibraryinitiatives/Archive/ConferencePresentation/Conference2008/home.shtml (accessed Aug. 24, 2008).

CHAPTER 10

CREATIVE DISORDER
THE WORK OF METADATA LIBRARIANS
IN THE 21ST CENTURY

Kevin Clair
Pennsylvania State University

Introduction

The increasing prevalence of information in digital formats is radically changing the way libraries describe their resources and make them available. In addition to the ongoing digitization of "hidden collections" and unique holdings, academic and research libraries are increasingly tasked, in their role as archives and records managers for their institutions, with managing born-digital materials. Concurrently, the communication channels for this information are continually evolving. Emerging data and metadata formats, both within the library community and outside of it, will ultimately allow for the development of a new generation of information-discovery tools. Web resources such as Delicious and Flickr[1] have demonstrated the possibilities of user-driven resource description, providing end users of digital resources with new ways of organizing information on the Internet and sharing that information with others. These changes are indicative of a richer and more sophisticated information landscape, affecting very deeply how digital library resources are accessed and used.

Metadata librarians are at the forefront of these changes. While the skills inherent in traditional cataloging remain relevant to the work performed by metadata librarians on a daily basis, new skills and competencies derived from information science and technology play an important role in the work they do as the types of resources they are charged with describing become more diverse. Frequently crossing departmental boundaries within their institutions, from technical services to digital production units to public services and back again, metadata librarians must be aware of the new channels through which users are accessing digital library resources, keep up with emerging technologies, and be able to separate which of those technologies will truly allow for enhanced access and use of digital library content in their institution. Some of these tasks may be completed in new and unexpected ways.

This chapter will detail the new tasks that metadata librarians are now charged to complete, the work areas in which they now function, and the core competencies required for them. These skills are profoundly affected by the changes in information discovery wrought by the Internet. Libraries are currently in the process of adapting to life in a networked environment, and metadata librarians play a key role in ensuring that library resources will continue to be discovered and used in a world where library metadata needs to be findable in as many environments as possible. In light of this, the life of the 21st-century metadata librarian may be characterized as an "all-creative trip"[2] in which the orderly world of traditional cataloging practice and existing metadata standards will need to be balanced with the disorderly world of user-generated metadata and distributed, reusable Web content. This chapter will offer suggestions as to how such a balance might come about and the skills required of metadata librarians to make it happen.

Environmental Scan

One of the first writers to touch on the effects of the networked environment was Lorcan Dempsey, who described one of its primary effects as "providing the material base for new ways of working and interacting."[3] The networked environment and the unprecedented flow of data it allowed gave libraries the opportunity to work with each other and with other institutions in a "shared space" in which content providers and content users would be able to work together on more similar terms. Many of the active areas of engagement in the profession today—for all librarians, not strictly those working primarily with metadata—derive from Dempsey's observations about active end users, effective rights management, and other phenomena accompanying the move to the network.

Metadata librarianship could well be defined as the practice of cataloging in the networked environment, whether through new description of digital resources or through the repurposing of existing catalog records for network use. To this end, investigating the effects of librarianship's transition to the networked environment is instructive in determining the role of the metadata librarian in the future. Because this transition has occurred so rapidly and because many of the questions brought about by it remain open, it is difficult to determine any one single answer regarding the current state of metadata librarianship. There are, however, select areas in which these changes are taking place that may be identified. They are all areas in which the work of metadata librarians is critical; therefore, metadata librarians will play a key role in determining how these trends affect the future role of the academic library in the networked environment.

The Future of Cataloging

Within the network, the catalog is only one hub, usually a minor one, in the much broader information landscape; often users will not consult it as a first-choice Internet resource when they have information needs. In direct response to this problem, the Library of Congress convened the Working Group on the Future of Bibliographic Control to prepare a report on how the network and network-level applications and user behaviors were changing the way people discovered information and what libraries could do about it. The final report recommended extending library metadata by participating in more cooperative cataloging projects, both within the profession and outside of it.[4] To expand the practice, the report suggested shared catalogs and repositories, such as those already in place in statewide and regional library consortia, as well as shared digital repository projects such as the HathiTrust.[5]

While the broad recommendation to "enhance access to rare, unique, and... hidden materials" was explicitly mentioned as an option in the area of leadership by the report,[6] the Working Group stopped short of taking steps in the world of bibliographic control beyond the bailiwick of traditional librarianship. In particular, though the report emphasized the importance of engaging with "Web standards" while developing the next generation of library descriptive standards, it did not mention areas of development in which the library community (and particularly the metadata community) can play a strong role, such as developing standards for describing large data sets and integrating library catalog information with the Semantic Web.

Scholarly Communication and Cyberinfrastructure

The networked environment has brought about new channels for scholarly communication, with accompanying new challenges for resource description. The best known of these is the institutional repository, defined by Clifford Lynch as "a set of services that a university offers to the members of its community for the management and dissemination of digital materials created by the institution and its community members."[7] The original promise of the institutional repository was to respond to the needs of university faculty and researchers to communicate their work, in whatever format, by utilizing the skills of academic and research librarians in description and preservation. In execution, the role of the institutional repository still shows some variance across (and sometimes within) institutions.[8] As they begin to take root, the need to develop interoperable metadata schemes meeting local description needs while also having the capacity to connect with other repositories sharing a disciplinary or format-centric focus will come to the fore.

Parallel to the emergence of institutional repositories in research libraries is the development of *cyberinfrastructure,* defined by a National Science Foundation study as "infrastructure based on distributed computer, information, and communication technology."[9] For academic libraries, cyberinfrastructure reinforces the trend toward developing institutional repositories, as well as the importance of developing metadata standards to ensure that the information—in this context, primarily large data sets—is preserved and made discoverable. Efforts being made in this area include the Data Documentation Initiative (DDI), the next iteration of which will document not only the data itself, but also the entire life cycle of data collection and presentation.[10]

Institutional repositories play an important role in the development and maintenance of cyberinfrastructure. Because of their focus on "grey literature" and materials not generally subjected to peer review, particularly raw data in the sciences, institutional repositories represent important nodes in the exchange of information that cyberinfrastructure hopes to facilitate; to this end, metadata will play a crucial role in determining the success of cyberinfrastructure initiatives. Furthermore, because the ultimate goals of institutional repository projects are complementary with those of the emerging cyberinfrastructure, metadata initiatives for institutional repositories, such as DDI, will also play an important role in making cyberinfrastructure work in the future.

Digital Libraries and Emerging Technologies

The primary task of metadata librarians is to integrate new and existing descriptive information generated by catalogers into the digital environment and make it as universally accessible and usable as possible. Digital asset management systems and the establishment of interoperable data and metadata standards help to make that information accessible; new Web applications developed inside of libraries, and more frequently by independent third parties, can make that metadata usable in a wider variety of contexts—providing the metadata is made open and accessible. As these operating conditions evolve, metadata librarians will need to find new ways to create and present the metadata generated by their own institutions.

Libraries are increasingly interested in reformatting new and existing metadata so that it is more compatible with Web data standards. Some are looking toward the Semantic Web as a primary location of innovation in this area. Conceived as a place where machine-readable information will allow Web applications (or "agents") to more intelligently process information based on the relationships between entities,[11] it has recently entered into the awareness of librarians and people working closely with library data as an avenue through which library data may be used in more meaningful ways. Within the world of cataloging, the work being done by researchers at Talis to represent MARC21 catalog records in RDF format[12] and at the Library of Congress in doing the same with MODS, controlled vocabularies, and authority files[13] shows the great potential inherent in placing library data on the Semantic Web and the benefits in doing so for both academic and research libraries and for the value of the Semantic Web itself.

The Web standards development arena is not the only venue in which library metadata may have an influence. Over the past several years, Web applications such as Flickr and Delicious have emerged. One of the most noteworthy characteristics of these applications is the fact that they allow for user-generated description of the resources contained within them, whether they are images, videos, or links to other resources on the Internet. These user descriptions, or "tags," add significant value to digital resources by permitting user development of tag vocabularies from the ground up. Libraries have recently begun to take advantage of these applications in a significant way. For example, the Library of Congress and the National Library of Australia are both Flickr users as a means of more widely distributing their digital resources.[14]

Integrating user contributions into metadata records for digital resources is not the only way in which new Web applications challenge traditional conceptions of cataloging. Applications such as Google's Maps and Earth initiatives derive a great deal of their value from the ability to seamlessly integrate outside content and to have their own content embedded elsewhere on the Internet through the use of application programming interfaces (APIs). This allows content created in one location to be repurposed and made available in one or more entirely different locations, through entirely different interfaces, than where the content originated. As mobile devices such as the iPhone evolve and become more common, digital library content may no longer even be exclusively accessed through personal computers; particularly in the case of geographically oriented data and metadata, it may indeed be more convenient to have those resources available through mobile, handheld devices. Generally, metadata can no longer be expected to stay in one place on the Web, at least not for very much longer; not only should libraries expect that to be the case, but they should also expect the value of their resources and metadata to be enhanced by allowing for that possibility.

The Roles of Metadata Librarians

The challenges of making digital library resources as accessible and usable as possible in the networked environment compel a rethinking of how cataloging will be practiced in the future, whether by metadata librarians or those working in traditional cataloging environments. For metadata librarians, the traditional skills of cataloging will still be of use, especially for those working in cataloging and technical services environments. Much of the work ahead consists of repurposing existing catalog records within a digital library framework; this work will require at least a passing familiarity with MARC records and with cataloging rules, and consultations with cataloging departments will be essential.

Into the skills of "creative order" associated with this work will need to be integrated new cataloging skills required for the integration of digital library content into the network. New forms of scholarly communication demand metadata practices different enough from the practice of applying metadata to special collections materials as to require distinct metadata librarian positions able to handle the demands of both. Additionally, new data formats and emerging metadata schemas from communities of practice outside of librarianship require constant vigilance on the part of metadata librarians in order to ensure that library metadata is able to interoperate with them and to be reused creatively by application developers when appropriate. In exploring the ramifications of these new developments for library services, metadata librarians may find themselves in need of information technology competencies such as systems analysis, assessment, and potentially programming and interface design. The job of metadata librarians will require a great deal of creativity in order to ensure that future library metadata is able to satisfy the needs of researchers while also contributing to the development of open metadata that may be used by application developers to enhance its value to everyone.

As Traditional Catalogers
Many metadata librarian positions, regardless of their current administrative location, have their origin in technical services departments; their primary responsibilities will likely always include cataloging within the digital production environment. To this end, it is worth investigating their roles within this model in detail. In a 2007 article in *Library Resources and Technical Services,* John Chapman detailed the specific roles played by metadata librarians within the technical service model.[15] He noted four such roles—collaboration, research, education, and development. As a developer and researcher, the metadata librarian is responsible for being aware of emerging standards as well as revisions to existing ones, and for successfully implementing and integrating these standards into local cataloging practices. As a collaborator and educator, the metadata librarian is responsible for developing best practices to ensure the greatest possible findability for library resources, as well as for training library cataloging staff in the execution of these best practices to ensure a level of widespread specialization and redundancy

of skills throughout their departments.

The focus in Chapman's work was on the role metadata librarians play at large research institutions, but within smaller research libraries the roles share some similarities. Recent job postings at institutions such as Georgetown University[16] and the University of California, San Francisco[17] indicate that metadata librarians in smaller academic and research libraries still tend to couple work in non-MARC metadata standards with traditional MARC cataloging in emerging formats such as electronic theses and dissertations (ETDs). Such distinguishes the continuing evolution of metadata librarian positions in academic and research libraries. Often new responsibilities will be added to a metadata librarian's job description as new digital initiatives take root or as the quantity of digital library production work increases to the point of displacing other electronic resource cataloging tasks. Small or mid-sized academic and research libraries lacking the labor and capital resources of a larger institution may continue to couple MARC cataloging work for electronic resources with work in non-MARC formats in their metadata librarian positions. The roles described above, and the means by which metadata librarians execute them, will likely differ from institution to institution, and different skills may be needed depending on the circumstances.

That said, certain tasks are required of all metadata librarians at any research institution in order to create the necessary preconditions for library metadata to be useful, not only as a guide for researchers, but as a tool to allow users to draw connections between digital resources and add value to them. Primarily this will have to do with making sense of the multitude of metadata standards available to catalogers today, as well as those that have not yet been developed or implemented widely, and developing broadly applicable best practices and use cases for them. Most metadata librarian positions place emphasis on candidates being familiar with several flavors of non-MARC metadata, particularly Dublin Core, MODS, METS, and EAD. Standards from the library community serving more specialized purposes, such as PREMIS for preservation or MIX for image-oriented technical metadata, may also be important for metadata librarians to be aware of, depending on the digital initiatives in place at a given institution. Furthermore, as the Internet has opened up unprecedented opportunities for collaboration among libraries, archives, and museums, a knowledge of the different cataloging and metadata practices in use in the archival and museum sectors may be of use to metadata librarians; indeed, metadata librarians may increasingly find homes working in archives and museums as their own digital initiatives begin to take root and grow.

The different types of digital initiatives being adopted by academic and research libraries and their collaborations with other cultural institutions and university departments outside the library will necessitate conversations about merging the different cataloging and metadata models in place outside of the library environment. Metadata librarian position announcements and discussions at conferences regarding the implementation of non-MARC metadata within libraries have largely focused on metadata standards. As the use of non-MARC metadata for digital initiatives becomes a standard practice, the next step will be to integrate digital resources and the metadata describing them into the broader network. Interoperability across sectors operating on the network will be essential to this process. Many institutions are adopting application profiles[18] as a way to combine elements from many different metadata schemas in order to satisfy a particular application instance within their institution, such as profiles for cartographic materials or audiovisual resources. Using application profiles has the benefit of making library digital collections more compatible with those created outside of the library sector, using metadata standards often quite different from those used in libraries. Metadata models such as the Dublin Core Abstract Model (DCAM) and the Singapore Framework for designing application profiles play an important role in framing this work, and ultimately it will be as important for metadata librarians to be familiar with conceptualizing metadata applications using these models as it is to actually apply the various metadata schemas that exist in the field.

Many of these tasks are still in early stages. Developing and sharing documentation for them will be quite valuable in establishing best practices and guidelines for implementing metadata standards and application profiles, not only in libraries, but across the spectrum of cultural institutions. There are many forms this type of development and communication can take. Central metadata registries, where collaborators working on similar metadata applications can share and comment on application profiles, will play an important role in standardizing metadata practice going forward. The NSDL Metadata Registry is one example of such a resource, where users may upload controlled vocabularies in use at their institutions.[19] The Dublin Core Metadata Initiative has been active for many years in establishing central registries; these would facilitate reuse and exchange of data in a given schema as well as allowing for the distribution of the schemas themselves.[20] Metadata librarians may lead or participate in such efforts in the coming years, especially as they move out of the research and development phase (many are still in various beta stages) and into production.

The documentation and communication process for metadata librarians extends itself to education as well. Being able to present research findings, applications of metadata practices at one's home institution, and so forth are as important for metadata librarians as they are for any other member of the profession. Within one's institution, education of cataloging staff who may not have worked with non-MARC metadata before is equally important. As digital library production work increases and more library cataloging paraprofessionals begin to have non-MARC metadata responsibilities added to their job descriptions, it will be up to metadata librarians (possibly in conjunction with IT training staff) to develop training programs for instructing them, not only in the various standards and cataloging rules applicable to the digital environment, but in any application profiles or metadata applications unique to the institution. Knowledge of the digital asset management systems and other repositories in place at the institution will also be an important part of this training process, as these may have different interfaces or processing procedures from the ILS in use at the library. These experiences too may be shared with colleagues at other institutions in order to develop best practices for training library staff in the procedures developed globally by metadata librarians.

Finally, it will be important for metadata librarians to participate in library-wide assessment and maintenance activities vis-à-vis their digital library projects. As digital production activities are relatively new at most libraries, such analysis may not have been done at a systematic level; however, because of the ever-changing nature of digitization work and the Internet generally, assessment and occasional maintenance of digital library content in order to bring it up to newly emergent standards is useful. Metadata is no exception, as many standards iterate in order to encompass new and perceived user needs not addressed by previous versions of the standard. Additionally, as more information about the specific uses of digital collections becomes available to librarians, adjustments to local metadata practice may need to be made in response to concerns from faculty, researchers, or the general public about the utility of metadata records within local repositories. It should also be noted that this type of assessment of metadata is not strictly limited to simply changing local application practices to account for changing standards or cataloging rules. With the trend toward network-level uses of local digital library content, assessment may also include investigating the possibility of making metadata available through external channels such as Flickr. This type of assessment will require metadata librarians to be able to work collaboratively, not only with other librarians active within or having an interest in the digital production environment, but with a wide variety of digital library users, whether they are faculty making research or teaching use of the collections, students, or interested members of the general public.

Many of these roles and responsibilities are relatively canonical skills for catalogers. The skills of traditional cataloging will always be useful for metadata librarians as they process digital resources and make them available. As this chapter has begun to demonstrate, though, these skills are being applied in new and sometimes unexpected ways in response to the demands, promise, and challenges associated with the networked environment. Some of the tasks that have arisen before metadata librarians as a result of this process are indeed brand new and require skills that set metadata librarians apart from their colleagues in library technical services units; it is to these roles and responsibilities that we now turn.

As Untraditional Catalogers

The key element defining the networked environment and providing its character is the increased capacity—indeed, the necessity—for working productively across institutional and professional boundaries. One of the main challenges facing libraries as they adapt to the network, as identified by Dempsey, is simply coming to terms with what it means for them as institutions: developing resources focused on user needs rather than on content, realizing that the library is one information resource among many, and so on.[21] This does not have to be a limiting factor for providing access to library resources. Knowing how to position those resources at several access points within the network will ultimately draw new visitors to those services and allow for the possibility of new uses of them. High-quality, reusable metadata is what allows this process to happen. In the network, it is no longer sufficient simply to create metadata records describing the digital resources; those resources, and by extension the metadata belonging to them, should be able to be located within other contexts by their end users, whether through a digital asset management system or externally in a third-party Web application. That metadata will need to be reusable in other applications without losing its connection to the resource it describes. Metadata librarians should be leaders and innovators in laying the groundwork for this.

Some of the ways in which this may be accomplished are addressed using skills already inherent to the traditional cataloging model. The ability to reuse metadata outside of a given repository or digital asset management system and to utilize digital resources in external third-party applications may be identified as a legitimate feature of future library systems by metadata librarians and other interested parties, and as such enter into the previously addressed realm of systems analysis. Additionally, protocols allowing for this possibility already exist, in the form of data standards such as OAI-PMH and microformats; research and development in the Semantic Web or in other areas will assuredly lead to more advances in this area. A fluency in these standards will be useful to metadata librarians as they begin to create network-accessible metadata.

The novelty comes in the totally unforeseen characteristics of the network. The Web allows for two unique additions to the way metadata has traditionally been created by libraries. First, there are new types of metadata to be put to use to describe digital resources. Lorcan Dempsey identifies three: "contributed metadata" from users of library resources, "programmatically promoted metadata" generated by aggregating metadata from separate collections into one central resource (as the Open Archives Initiative does), and "intentional metadata,"[22] also called "attention metadata,"[23] which tracks the sites users are looking at on the Web in order to gain information about their interests and browsing habits. In addition to these new forms of metadata, there are new uses, distributed across the network, to which all of this metadata may be put. The changing nature of catalog records themselves is most acutely felt by metadata librarians; integrating all of the network-inspired changes into cataloging and metadata workflows will be the primary challenge faced by them in enabling creative disorder as well as creative order.

"Contributed metadata," annotations to library resources provided by their users, is probably the best known manifestation of these new types of metadata. Most commonly associated with recent Web applications such as Flickr and Delicious, annotations can also include reviews and user descriptions of content, similar to what one might find on the Amazon page for a book. Libraries have recently begun utilizing such features in their own interfaces. Projects such as PennTags[24] have done much to introduce the idea of personal tag libraries as supplements to traditional library cataloging into the professional consciousness of librarians. Applications of these ideas will become more common in the years ahead as more users grow accustomed to using them in their own work; within specific repository frameworks, metadata librarians will need to determine how annotations and community-generated resource descriptions can be effectively integrated into the cataloging work done professionally by librarians.

The use of attention metadata can potentially enhance the ways users interact with digital resources. Probably the most common use of this metadata is through e-commerce sites such as Amazon, where users viewing a particular book will see the other books viewed or purchased by other users who also purchased that book. Using similar principles, digital libraries can practice a sort of researcher's advisory for their users by allowing them to discover other digital resources similar to the material on which they initially landed, based on the behavior of previous visitors. Such metadata would draw heavily on access logs and other regularly collected statistics, allowing it to play a key role in digital library assessment activities and future collection development. Metadata librarians, working with library IT departments, will play a role in ensuring that these new sources of metadata are successfully integrated into library digital collections.

The evolution of metadata on the Web includes not only the emergence of new forms of metadata, but also the changing ways in which people are putting it to use. Because the Web makes it much easier to extract data from their original repository and reposition them in new contexts, developers are creating new Web applications drawing upon data from several points of origin to create new resources. Many of these uses were unanticipated by the developers of the original resources; however, thanks to embeddable content and APIs, these developers can prepare for unanticipated uses from third parties. The most successful Web applications encourage this type of use. Libraries already use Google Maps to provide access to digital collection resources[25] as well as the entire library catalog generally.[26] Such instances will undoubtedly increase in the future. Closer to home, the Open Library project[27] is building an open database of every book, using contributions of catalog records from publishers, libraries, and Internet users. Once populated, this database will be open in kind, allowing any user who wishes to have access to and build applications around its data to do so.

These ideas are a challenge to the way in which the catalog has traditionally been conceived. Where before metadata functioned primarily as descriptive content related only to the resource it described in a catalog, on the Web metadata can exist in a number of different formats capable of being used outside of its original context. Metadata librarians face the challenge of balancing necessary controls over the application and use of library metadata with the lack of such controls that has allowed for the freedom of use of data on the Internet and traditionally made it such a successful medium. Clay Shirky makes the point that Google's overwhelming success with respect to Yahoo on the search market stems from its decision to bypass traditional methods of information retrieval—essentially, extensive categorization—by allowing the links between documents themselves to describe the relationships between units of content on the Web.[28]

This is not to say that such classification cannot work within particular contexts; Shirky himself notes that in situations where domains are well defined and users are expert, classification systems such as LCSH work very well. The larger challenge is twofold. First, digital libraries need to make their resources visible elsewhere on the network.

This is made difficult because the standards used by librarians to describe content are not used outside of the library community, and digital asset management systems generally leave this content constrained within a single institution. The second challenge is to create digital repositories that are themselves destinations, drawing a regular base of users who, while not necessarily making it their first stop for information, perhaps visit the repository independently of a Google referral. Metadata librarians can play a key role in meeting both of these challenges, through creating metadata that is reusable in a number of different protocols and personalized to suit the needs of individual users.

In order to meet these challenges, developing metadata standards and best practices valuable beyond the local environment will become essential work. Metadata librarians will need to appraise their work in developing local metadata standards and practices to ensure that they are not *too* local; that is, that they do not entrap metadata in inaccessible silos. In addition to collaboration across institutions, collaboration across operating units *within* institutions will be important, in order to ensure that no two (or more) parties within a single research institution are reinventing the wheel when it comes to developing local metadata practices. Additionally, integrating nontraditional methods of cataloging into metadata workflows can allow metadata librarians to fulfill their role as developers. In the process of ingesting new resources and descriptive metadata into the various digital repositories employed by libraries, metadata librarians should be able to evaluate library systems in order to ensure that they allow this information to be discovered through alternative channels beyond the repository itself, such as the Library of Congress Flickr initiative. Metadata librarians could also be leaders in preparing library content to be repurposed in new ways, such as preparing digital map collections to be integrated with geospatial services such as Google Earth or OpenStreetMap. They may also tap into the expertise of the community in order to harvest user-generated metadata to enhance that already provided by trained catalogers, such as the National Archive of Australia's *Mapping Our Anzacs* project.[29] Projects and initiatives such as these do not demand that metadata librarians live double lives as programmers, but they should have an awareness of what different library systems can do and how they can be made to allow for innovative distribution and enhancement of library resources and metadata.

How to Get There: The All-Creative Trip

The extent to which the nontraditional cataloging work described above will truly enter into the canonical metadata librarian job description is still uncertain. Much of this is due to the fact that digital library operational standards are still very much in development; as more libraries begin to appraise the processes by which they have put digital projects into production and develop documented workflows based on the lessons learned from those processes, digital library frameworks will begin to take shape. Additionally, there is some degree of convergence between the work of metadata librarians and librarians working in public service environments that can be seen in this nontraditional work. Because metadata is such a necessary component for linking digital library resources to the external applications that can get the most use out of them, metadata librarians will need to collaborate with subject specialists and reference librarians in order to determine what user needs, if any, are not being met by the metadata and metadata standards provided and calibrate their practices accordingly.

Elements of traditional cataloging, though deemphasized, will always remain part of the work plan for metadata librarians. The four roles of metadata librarians delineated by Chapman are present in both traditional and nontraditional cataloging work. There are differences in character, however. In the traditional cataloging work described above, metadata librarianship is in the process of adapting changes in metadata practice to traditional cataloging workflows: for example, implementing crosswalks from MARC to MODS or developing application profiles for use in audiovisual resource collections. Where nontraditional cataloging work is concerned, metadata librarians are in the process of defining the boundaries of the work. To what extent will (or should) metadata librarians be responsible for controlling social tagging applications in repositories or OPACs? How much input should metadata librarians have in developing digital research tools around the collections that libraries have already digitized? As digital library production processes become more standardized within academic and research libraries, questions of what to do to enhance the services they provide will inevitably arise; metadata librarians will play a key role in answering them.

There are, to be sure, clear distinctions to be noted between the work of metadata librarians and the work of traditional catalogers. The information technology competencies, awareness of trends and standards on the Web, and so on, are tools not traditionally held in cataloging departments, and metadata librarians will necessarily need to be ahead of the curve in this respect. This is not to say that traditional cataloging skills should be devalued as integral parts of the metadata librarian's tool set. Attention to detail, an awareness of cataloging rules and procedures, and an ability to work across formats and domains are just as useful for metadata specialists now as they have always been for catalogers. The challenge, from the standpoint of description and access, is that the amount of material requiring description—and the possible points of access to it—have grown exponentially in recent years and by all accounts will continue to do so.

Ensuring that metadata skills are present in new cataloging librarians requires a look at the current cataloging curriculum and what might be done to teach metadata skills. Surveying LIS schools in the early years of the decade, Ingrid Hsieh-Yee identified a number of trends in cataloging courses affecting the way metadata is integrated into them. Noting that cataloging courses themselves are being deemphasized in the library science curriculum—itself a discouraging trend from the standpoint of training metadata professionals—Hsieh-Yee found that while there was a canonical list of skills needed for traditional cataloging work shared by most cataloging courses, only 71% of those cataloging courses gave an overview of metadata, with a lower percentage delving deeper into issues such as the relationships between metadata and traditional cataloging.[30] A handful of programs reported having metadata courses separate from those on traditional cataloging; these reported similar problems, with even less focus on the relationships between traditional cataloging and metadata than in cataloging courses. At the time, metadata was still a fairly new concept within the library world, and the survey did find that educators were interested in ensuring that students did know more about metadata and its role in cataloging and classification in libraries. With more metadata specialists on the permanent and adjunct faculty of library and information science programs and emerging curricula in digital library management,[31] there will undoubtedly be increasing convergence between cataloging and metadata courses at the graduate level.

What might such a converged curriculum look like? While training in cataloging rules will still remain important, required coursework for catalogers will expand to include material from the information science curriculum. For metadata, this will include not only an introduction to METS, MODS, PREMIS, and the like (and the ways in which they interoperate), but also to metadata models such as FRBR and the Dublin Core Abstract Model. Such adjustments to the cataloging curriculum in library schools may encompass not only metadata standards, but also principles of knowledge organization, of systems analysis, and of Web architecture.

No graduate program in library and information science, no matter how conscientious about cataloging and information organization instruction it is, can fully prepare librarians for the changes happening constantly in this area. To that end, continuing education is vital to enhancing the skills of current metadata specialists, training MARC catalogers in other metadata standards, and introducing metadata skills to paraprofessional staff in technical services and digital production departments. Hider surveyed cataloging professionals to discover their needs and concerns with respect to continuing professional development opportunities.[32] He found an interest in organized "short courses," particularly in emerging metadata formats such as Dublin Core and in cataloging for nonprint formats—something of increasing interest to metadata librarians, with technology advanced to the point where libraries are beginning to digitize more of their audiovisual holdings.

The role of metadata librarians as educators will of course put them in a good position for communicating these skills to others, particularly to catalogers who do not currently work with metadata but who might like to add that skill set to their repertoire. It is tempting to structure metadata education in a way similar to how cataloging curricula in library schools have been constructed and simply teach the proper mapping from MARC records to MODS; however, the abstract models and principles such as application profiles upon which current metadata practice is based are just as important as the rules and standards themselves and should be an integral part of this training. Additionally, the sheer volume of digital information being created by libraries, as well as the various sources from which it is generated, will necessitate that the roles of metadata librarians be distributed across more than one position within technical or digital collection services. Such a strategy will allow for subject expertise to inform metadata creation decisions, and potentially allow for richer metadata records.

As libraries are charged with the management of increasing numbers of digital resources, and as those resources begin to encompass more and more distinct formats and resource types, it makes sense to distribute the work among multiple positions charged with describing particular types of information. The most obvious such division is that between metadata applications for special collections and those related to ETDs and other materials destined for institutional or shared repositories. The skills of metadata librarianship, particularly the new and nontraditional skills, may also find their way into the job descriptions of traditional catalogers working in special formats as those formats begin the conversion process from analog to digital. The traditional cataloging skills possessed by current special formats catalogers, combined with the knowledge of information search and retrieval in the networked environment possessed by metadata librarians, will be essential in ensuring that newly digitized library resources are as useful for end users as possible. Continuing education and cross-pollination of ideas between metadata librarians and traditional catalogers, no matter where the former find themselves aligned administratively, will be of the utmost importance as this process continues.

Conclusions: The Road Ahead

This chapter has been an attempt at sketching out the bailiwick for metadata librarians in the years ahead. Many of these ideas have been based on the volume of work facing metadata librarians right now. As the amount of newly created digital information increases in the future, both born-digital and reformatted, the division of labor for metadata specialists will likely change as old forms of metadata become routine and new forms need to be researched and applied locally and globally. The changes currently being wrought by new technology and the evolution in library user behavior caused by those changes will force metadata librarians to be especially agile in their fulfillment of institutional roles and acquisition of new skills. Though relative metadata stability is certainly a goal of most developers in this area, it has not yet arrived, as more standards are developed and merged with each other.

Metadata librarian positions have changed rapidly over the course of the last several years, as the ramifications of the networked environment for librarians became known and the roles of catalogers in making digital library resources available in it clarified themselves. As existing digital initiatives become systematized and new types of digital initiatives begin to be developed within academic and research libraries, the role of the metadata librarian may become more standardized across institutions, and more cataloging positions will deal in non-MARC metadata as the volume of digital resource creation increases to keep up. The challenges of the "all-creative trip" of positioning academic and research libraries within the network are formidable, but there are many rewards for meeting them, and metadata librarians in the 21st century will play a key role in ensuring that they do so successfully.

Notes

1. Delicious, http://delicious.com; Flickr, www.flickr.com.
2. Kerry Thornley, *Principia Discordia* (Port Townsend, WA: Loompanics Unlimited, 1990), 63.
3. Lorcan Dempsey, "The Network and the Library: Working in a New Shared Space: Infrastructure and Institutions," *Electronic Library* 17, no. 4 (1999): 207–211.
4. Library of Congress, "On the Record: Report of the Library of Congress Working Group on the Future of Bibliographic Control," Jan. 9, 2008, www.loc.gov/bibliographic-future/news/lcwg-ontherecord-jan08-final.pdf (accessed Oct. 27, 2008).
5. Hathitrust, http://hathitrust.org.
6. Library of Congress, "On the Record," 21.
7. Clifford Lynch, "Institutional Repositories: Essential Infrastructure for Scholarship in the Digital Age," *portal: Libraries and the Academy* 3, no. 2 (April 2003): 328.
8. Soo Young Rieh, Karen Markey, Beth St. Jean, Elizabeth Yakel, and Jihyun Kim, "Census of Institutional Repositories in the United States: A Comparison across Institutions at Different Stages of IR Development," *D-Lib Magazine* 13, no. 11/12 (Nov./Dec. 2007), www.dlib.org/dlib/november07/rieh/11rieh.html (accessed Oct. 27, 2008).
9. National Science Foundation, "Report of the National Science Foundation Blue-Ribbon Advisory Panel on Cyberinfrastructure," Jan. 2003, 5, www.nsf.gov/od/oci/reports/atkins.pdf (accessed Feb. 25, 2008).National Science Foundation study.
10. Data Documentation Initiative (DDI) 3.1, www.ddialliance.org/specification/ddi3.1.
11. Tim Berners-Lee, James Hendler, and Ora Lassila, 2001. "The Semantic Web," *Scientific American,* May 17, 2001, www.sciam.com/article.cfm?id=00048144-10D2-1C70-84A9809EC588EF21&print=true (accessed Oct. 27, 2008).

12. Rob Styles, Danny Ayers, and Nadeem Shabir, "Semantic MARC, MARC21 and the Semantic Web," 2008, Preprint, www.talis.com/applications/assets/Semantic_Marcup.pdf (accessed Oct. 27, 2008).
13. Corey A. Harper and Barbara Tillett, "Library of Congress Controlled Vocabularies and Their Application to the Semantic Web," *Cataloging and Classification Quarterly* 43, no. 3/4 (2007): 47–68.
14.   Flickr: The Library of Congress' Photostream, http://flickr.com/photos/library_of_congress; Flickr: National Library of Australia's Photostream, http://flickr.com/photos/national_library_of_australia.
15. John Chapman, "The Roles of the Metadata Librarian in a Research Library," *Library Resources and Technical Services* 51, no. 4 (Oct. 2006): 279–285.
16. Georgetown University Library, "Metadata Librarian," 2008, www.library.georgetown.edu/employment/positions/MetadataLib.pdf (accessed May 5, 2008; page now discontinued).
17. University of California, San Francisco Library, "Metadata and Cataloging Librarian," 2008, www.library.ucsf.edu/jobs/metacat.html (accessed May 5, 2008; page now discontinued).
18. Rachel Heery and Manjula Patel, "Application Profiles: Mixing and Matching Metadata Schemas," *Ariadne* 25 (Sept. 2000): www.ariadne.ac.uk/issue25/app-profiles (accessed Oct. 27, 2008).
19. NSDL Registry, http://metadataregistry.org; incidentally, the NSDL Metadata Registry is also a validated implementation of the Simple Knowledge Organization System (SKOS), a key data standard in the Semantic Web—one concrete example of the ways in which digital library metadata applications can contribute to Web standards.
20. Rachel Heery and Harry Wagner, "A Metadata Registry for the Semantic Web," *D-Lib Magazine* 8, no. 5 (May 2002): www.dlib.org/dlib/may02/wagner/05wagner.html (accessed Oct. 27, 2008).
21. Dempsey, "The Network and the Library," 211.
22. Lorcan Dempsey, "Four Sources of Metadata about Things," Lorcan Dempsey's Weblog, May 20, 2007, http://orweblog.oclc.org/archives/001351.html (accessed May 16, 2008).
23. Jehad Najjar, Martin Wolpers, and Erik Duval, 2006. Attention Metadata: Collection and Management. (presentation, WWW2006 Workshop on Logging Traces of Web Activity, Edinburgh, Scotland, 2006), www.kbs.uni-hannover.de/Arbeiten/Publikationen/2006/www/www2006-LoggingTracesWS_wolpers.pdf (accessed Oct. 27, 2008).
24. PennTags, http://tags.library.upenn.edu.
25.   Chris Fleet, "Life Beyond the Paper Graphic Index: Evaluating New Geographical Retrieval Technologies for the Future Map Library," *LIBER Quarterly* 18, no. 2 (September 2008), http://liber.library.uu.nl/publish/articles/000253/article.pdf (accessed Apr. 9, 2010).
26.   Michael Vandenburg, "Using Google Maps as an Interface for the Library Catalogue," *Library Hi Tech* 26, no. 1 (2008): 33-40.
27. Open Library, http://openlibrary.org.
28. Clay Shirky, "Ontology Is Overrated," 2005, Clay Shirky's Writings about the Internet, www.shirky.com/writings/ontology_overrated.html (accessed October 27, 2008).
29. Mapping Our Anzacs: http://mappingouranzacs.naa.gov.au (accessed April 9, 2010).

30. Ingrid Hsieh-Yee, 2004. "Cataloging and Metadata Education in North American LIS Programs," *Library Resources and Technical Services* 48, no. 1 (Jan. 2004): 62–63.

31. Jeffrey Pomerantz, Sanghee Oh, Seungwon Yang, Edward A. Fox, and Barbara Wildemuth, "The Core: Digital Library Education in Library and Information Science Programs," *D-Lib Magazine* 12, no. 11 (Nov. 2006), www.dlib.org/dlib/november06/pomerantz/11pomerantz.html (accessed Oct. 27, 2008).

32. Philip Hider, 2006. "A Survey of Continuing Professional Development Activities and Attitudes amongst Catalogers," *Cataloging and Classification Quarterly* 42, no. 2 (2006): 35–58.

CHAPTER 11

LISTEN UP, LIBRARIANS
IT'S ALL ABOUT THE MESSAGE

Eric Bartheld
University of Maryland

We all know the library is the heart of the university, because we all like to say it is. Referring to an academic library in this way points to its centrality to the educational experience and confers a life-sustaining importance that validates our hard work. Plus, it fits nicely on bookmarks.

At Indiana University, a similarly pithy sentiment is chiseled above the entrance to one of the oldest library spaces on campus. Cross the threshold of Franklin Hall, look toward heaven, and you'll see John Milton's inspirational quote cherished by librarians since the building was constructed in 1906: "A good book is the precious lifeblood of a master spirit."[1] For decades IU students and faculty have found encouragement and security in the phrase penned by Milton in 1644 and made a permanent part of IU's famous limestone architecture. It's a feel-good quote that we have dutifully printed on bookplates, note cards, and webpages.

The problem here is that Franklin Hall hasn't served as the university library for nearly 40 years—and in a strange twist of fate, it is now home to the university's vice president for information technology. At a time when the very concept of a book is not such a straightforward notion anymore, what with Google digitization, networked discovery tools, and download-and-go files, one might argue that the library is clearly not the heart of a university. I'm here to tell you it is. But listen up, librarians: Nothing lasts forever, even if it's chiseled in stone.

Why It Matters

Now more than ever, academic libraries must prove their relevance to campus constituents. Librarians cannot assume that the role of the library will not be challenged by the administrators, donors, or faculty and students who have traditionally defended or supported it.

In much the way that development and fund-raising functions have matured over the past decade in academic libraries, communications and marketing functions are emerging as an ever more strategic role. Just as library administrators learned that libraries must solicit donations to supplement eroding budgets, so too must academic libraries communicate their value—not only to the faculty and students whose needs libraries traditionally serve, but also to administrators and influencers who set budgets and determine institutional priorities.

As we think about the skills required in the 21st-century library, we will be well served to create a marketing orientation within the library culture—and in so doing, coordinate disparate activities, identify and prioritize messages, and leverage support among librarians not necessarily accustomed to promoting collections and services in an aggressive and cohesive way. Key to the success of academic libraries at Indiana University and elsewhere in the coming years will be not only to determine which services constituents and faculty need (a fast-moving target indeed), but also to communicate effectively in a highly complex marketplace. Branding, targeted messaging, and media savvy will all contribute to this success. Increasingly this work falls beyond the scope of traditional librarianship and requires skills librarians often do not embrace or develop.

We must also redefine expectations. Librarians, though long involved in outreach, are being asked to be more strategic and collaborative than ever before. It's not enough for a librarian with add-on public relations responsibilities to create an occasional newsletter or to host an event because "it's good PR." A marketing committee of engaged librarians or a Lone Ranger communications director cannot accomplish desired goals without broad-based commitment. Librarians and staff at all levels must contribute to a marketing effort and embrace the need for heightened communications.

Communications professionals can help lead this team effort in a meaningful way, and in so doing raise the profile of the library among key constituents, deliver messages that can advance library capital or funding priorities, and advance overall goals. "But wait," some library directors will say. "Don't we already communicate with students and faculty? Why coordinate these efforts under a single person or department and spend precious resources to refine an effort that's already underway?" Answer: to leverage current resources to the greatest effect and ensure the whole is greater than the sum of the parts. Librarians have proved again and again to be creative and resourceful, and they frequently promote their areas with great skill and enthusiasm, but a central communications officer can ensure that librarians' individual efforts "hang together" and complement institutional priorities. When someone coordinates the overall effort, libraries can avoid common pitfalls: the lack of coherent or overarching communications strategies, cannibalization of messages by conflicting needs, and lost momentum because marketing efforts are not sustained for the long term.

Specifically, communications professionals can help ensure librarians advance their messages with a common voice; coordinate "big-picture" institutional messages; offer a neutral bridge between library departments or committees that might otherwise work in isolation or with competing priorities; contribute new perspectives in ways that resonate with nonlibrarian constituents; serve as liaisons with sophisticated campus or university marketing operations; and offer specialized writing, design, or marketing expertise. By aligning with development officers, communications officers can assist in cultivating and stewarding donors in ways that affect the bottom line. Because library budgets are under greater scrutiny than ever, it seems that now is the time for library directors to get serious about communicating with decision makers. Good or bad, perceptions among administrators, donors, faculty, and students already exist. The challenge becomes aligning those perceptions with the needs, plans, and goals of a library that may well be struggling to find its way in the digital future.

Facing Facts and Understanding Contradictions

Academic libraries have a long and glorious history of being perceived as benign and helpful institutions. Those of us who work in libraries do so because we believe in the mission and in the value we add as information providers: we exist to serve every student and faculty member, we're impartial, and we advance knowledge. Who can disagree with that?

Turns out, lots of people. A quick review of OCLC's pivotal 2005 marketing study reminds us that too many of today's students have grown up bypassing libraries completely. In searching for information, students don't necessarily think of the library as the place to start. The Joint Information Systems Committee points to the study in defining the "Google generation." Eighty-nine percent of college students use search engines to begin an information search (while only two percent start from a university website). More students express satisfaction searching in this way than having a librarian assist them. And, though college students still use the library, they are using it less (and reading less) since they started using Internet research tools.[2]

Those of us in academic libraries once prided ourselves on having a near-monopoly as the source for quality information. But we've lost our stronghold. In the olden days—just a few years ago—patrons knew that if they couldn't get information at the library, it probably wasn't available. In a good-humored but face-slapping reality check, one of our librarians put it to me this way: "We don't have it all anymore," she said. "We never will. And we have to get used to it."

Increasingly, our goal in this environment is to push library resources and services outward: to meet students where they work, to become fully integrated in course management systems, for example, or to maximize the utility of RSS feeds or pack nontraditional resources such as Wikipedia with links to our materials. Our goal is to become seamless in our delivery of information. We operate with the assumption that students don't necessarily want to know the source of information, they just want information. This transparency in the delivery of our resources, then, becomes key to making libraries and library resources more accessible and relevant. But it also introduces an unsettling contradiction. How do we heighten awareness of our value while we are simultaneously working to make ourselves invisible?

One solution is to do a better job conveying who we are, what we do, and the benefit this activity imparts to our core audiences. In other words, to heighten our marketing communications. Doing so in a crowded marketplace, however, means that we must necessarily filter, target, and simplify our messages to ensure they resonate. These can be difficult objectives for librarians who pride themselves on providing unbiased information, and more rather than less. Within the context of describing how librarians collaborate with information technology groups, Peter Brantley, executive director of the Digital Library Federation, noted that librarians stereotypically focus "more on the long haul, more on thoroughness, more on well-described and studied approaches."[3] This mind-set is also often at odds with basic communications goals—the most common, perhaps, to increase awareness simply by repeating key messages. Don't tell me how the clock works, helpful librarian, just tell me the time.

We cannot moan that libraries and librarians are taken for granted—not only by students, but also by funders, administrators, and campus marketers whose job it is to advance the university—if we don't get better at communicating with our core audiences and selling ourselves aggressively. For too long we have assumed that faculty love us, serious students will find us if they need us, and administrators will support us. In a blistering indictment, Stephen Abram, vice president of innovation at SirsiDynix, puts marketing at the top of his list of activities that libraries do poorly. "We are poor at marketing and promoting the library and librarians," he writes in an article suggesting how libraries can compete with Google. "We lack confidence; we don't seek and sustain attention. I can't think of another institution that has consistently done such a poor job for so long."[4]

On the Rise

As sobering as Abram's observations may be, I do believe there's hope. And I do believe we're making progress. Though outreach and marketing are not new to academic libraries, it seems from my perspective—as the director of communications for the Indiana University Bloomington Libraries—that the field is gaining momentum and importance, and the level of investment in formal communications programs is maturing in much the way that fundraising efforts matured over the past decade or two. (After trending upward, the number of libraries with formal development programs peaked in the years between 1995 and 1999.[5]) Increased competition is demanding that libraries work harder. Promoting library services and collections requires a strategic approach, and one I argue requires greater commitment and accountability than many current models. Distributing promotional duties to a committee or adding part-time responsibilities to a bibliographer's job description may be good first steps, but they are not enough in today's environment. Thanks to forward-thinking library directors, communications efforts are beginning to be perceived within library cultures as a determinant, not an afterthought.

In addition to rethinking how we market libraries (a truly broad and complex topic, including everything from purchasing resources and understanding student learning patterns to leveraging technology and tackling parking issues), we can do a better job communicating what we are doing. The drumbeat has already started. The toolkit for Academic and Research Libraries published by the American Library Association and the Association of College and Research Libraries makes the case for straightforward communication: "For an awareness campaign to be successful," the report emphasizes, "there must be a clear and consistent message." Messages included in the toolkit were designed to focus on the unique contributions of academic and research libraries; they were developed based on research conducted by a public relations and communication management firm in consultation with ACRL members. Among the messages and talking points: college and research libraries are an essential part of the learning community; they connect faculty and students with a world of knowledge; and they are investing in the future while preserving the past.[6]

Our marketing communications plan at the Indiana University Bloomington Libraries, developed by an ad hoc marketing group of librarians, includes goals and objectives, to which we linked key messages and even key words. The plan identifies what we want to say about ourselves and how we wish to be perceived by our various audiences. We created the plan understanding that it's for internal use only. Messages are not intended to be produced verbatim; instead we operate with the expectation that their deliberate and consistent application will influence perceptions.

Here's one example: Within the overall goal to convince audiences of our value as an information provider, we seek to improve understanding that the IUB Libraries select and pay for information. We work toward educating core audiences of the relative values of different types of information and to position librarians as information experts. A corollary message: The IUB Libraries provide the resources, services, and environments that the academic community needs to succeed. We can help students and faculty take full advantage of the vast resources we select, purchase, and manage for them. (Please see appendix for all key messages.)

My favorite of our four marketing communications goals looks inward by directing us to develop a marketing orientation within the library. One of its underlying objectives is to strengthen the understanding of the need for consistent messaging; another is to engage key internal groups in marketing activities and promote broad ownership.

Our messages are printed on red cardstock folded to a size that can be easily slipped into a pocket. It's gimmicky, I know, but producing them in this way signals that they should be referenced, not filed. I'm surprised—though I shouldn't be—how often I reach for my own copy when I'm pounding out donor thank-you letters, writing an article for the parents' association newsletter, responding to student reporters, or contributing text to the admissions viewbook. My greatest hope is that every employee remembers our marketing communications messages and gently casts them outward—whether teaching a workshop, authoring a blog, or meeting with a campus colleague. During orientation sessions for new library employees, I make a point of distributing these undersized brochures and speaking to their importance. It's not that I'm asking anyone to drink the Kool-Aid, but I do suggest that if we work together, we'll all have greater success in demonstrating our collective value. It pleases me to no end when I see brochures tacked up in employee workspaces, serving as implicit reminders to speak with a common voice. Even our dean has a copy. It stands upright on the corner of her desk like a bird on a post.

Another way of creating a marketing orientation within the library is by ensuring library employees recognize, adopt, and promote a visual brand or identity. At campuses large and small, libraries are often perceived as utilities, serving many constituents but lacking an overarching look that can integrate and bring value to many disparate units or services. Liene Karels, director of communications at the University of Michigan Library, believes such organizations are at a disadvantage. "Without a coherent visual identity, an organization is like grass, or a pervasive mist," she says. "It's everywhere, but nobody notices it."

Her solution was to create and cultivate a graphic identity that not only worked within university branding guidelines, but also tied together a system of 11 different libraries and countless services. "Get a face," she says, "then you can make it talk."

The University of Michigan Library (MLibrary) developed visual identity standards that included rationale and examples of the new look and tied it to core messages. A key part of the Michigan strategy was to ensure that library employees embraced the identity. Karels put the logo on items staff members used every day, like pens and notepads, so they'd be constantly reminded of the power of an integrated look. She also distributed gold pins bearing the logo, which staff soon began to wear with pride. "A brand begins inside," Karels says, "then grows organically. If we identify with it internally, we can carry that message outward. Everyone becomes part of the marketing effort; it's the face that everyone wears."[7]

Thinking in this way may be somewhat new for librarians, but will become increasingly important. No longer is it enough to rely on inconsistent or uncoordinated messaging and branding, or to think we can operate as productively unless each of us has an understanding of institutional priorities.

Messaging In Action

To maximize their impact, key messages should bubble up in as many contexts as possible, and many of them should reveal themselves in simple and straightforward ways. Certainly they should also influence broad-based strategic thinking. At IUB, three larger examples illustrate the ways in which we have advanced the value of the IUB Libraries among undergraduate students and faculty.

Our executive associate dean, who for years instructed business students about library resources, nurtured a relationship with a professor who taught a popular course on organizational management. As a result of that partnership, in the fall of 2006 more than 700 students evaluated the branch library that serves the Kelley School of Business and the School for Public and Environmental Affairs. The assignment required the students, who worked in teams of five or fewer, to assess library offerings and make recommendations for improvement. Students were instructed to address the core issues of space, services, and marketing and to work within a budget of $500,000. Innovative thinking and use of research materials were key measures of successful proposals. Students competed for top honors, and the highest-ranking teams presented their plans to a panel comprised of library administrators. The dean had the final vote.

The assignment forced students to rethink traditional library services and to examine the role a library can play in meeting their academic needs. For us at the IUB Libraries, the assignment offered unparalleled insight into student expectations: it was a large and responsive focus group. We found the presentations to be thoughtful and well considered. Priorities emerged. Among them: community space that reflects the culture and stature of the schools; quiet and group space; technology; comfortable furnishings and café services; presentation rooms; and heightened branding.

Student recommendations were generally consistent with findings of our own previous studies, including a task force comprised of faculty representatives and librarians. Recommendations also reflected national trends. Students want choices. As one business student wrote: "When I go into a library, I want to be able to find an area suitable to my needs. Sometimes I need a computer, sometimes group space, and sometimes a quiet area. And parking space."[8] Some suggestions were particularly imaginative. And although creativity counted, it didn't necessarily make for a winning proposal. Ideas that didn't fly: nap pods (to reenergize); aquariums (to help relieve stress); a computer dedicated to ordering food (to refuel); and scented air fresheners (as presented, to provide a psychological boost , but perhaps to mask the smelly food that would inevitably result from the streamlined ordering system). I can't say these were all bad ideas, but they perhaps fell beyond our ability to pay for or maintain them.

A primary motivator for the students—beyond earning a good grade—was the opportunity to leave a positive imprint on their university and to help create a successful library. "The assignment allowed me to realize that I did have input," said a member of the winning team. "Students do have a voice."[9] The project was a superb exercise for the IUB Libraries on two counts. First, it offered a chance to increase awareness and promote current services. (Remember one of our key messages: Libraries provide the resources, services, and environments students need to succeed.) Stories in the student newspaper[10] and our donor newsletter advanced awareness among core audiences, and a forum, which included the class professor, engaged library staff in a discussion about the changing expectations of students. Second, the project provided first-rate user research that is guiding renovation planning and changes in services now under way as we work to make their recommendations a reality.

Last year we launched an awareness campaign targeted to freshmen and anchored by a survival handbook. Our *IU Survival Guide: Libraries Edition* provided the tactical framework for a multimedia campaign that included a companion website.[11] In developing our creative strategy, we knew tone would be important. We decided at the outset to avoid repackaging standard promotional blather and to be brutally honest. Our spot-on instructional services librarian identified the tone this way: *We know what you think of us: libraries aren't cool. But we know the truth about you, too. Some days you just want to get by in your everyday life as a college student. Some days you just want to survive.* Yes, we were saying, we can help you get by if that's what you want. But be careful, because in the process we can help you succeed. (Again, a key message.)

We surveyed marketing pieces produced by other campus units and academic libraries. We considered the deluge of slick admissions brochures freshmen receive for a full year before enrolling. We learned from focus groups that fliers we had previously photocopied on goldenrod-colored paper didn't cut it. We teamed up with a highly creative designer. We started writing. The result: a 56-page perfect-bound handbook (durability and longevity were also important to us). The content was cheeky and reassuring. But more than humorous, it was strategic and targeted. Among the chapters: Glitches, Crashes, and Natural Disasters; Necessary Evils; and Oh, Crap! Crisis Management.

Entries included:

- what to do if you flunked your first test
- what to do if you find an article in Google and need to pay for it
- how to survive your first all-nighter
- what to do if you get stuck in the library elevator
- what to do if your paper's due tomorrow and you don't know how to start
- how to impress weekend visitors

Library-based solutions were woven into many, but not all, of the answers. "We can save you time, money and resources," the introduction stated. "What's not to love?" An integrated campaign reinforced messages in a variety of media and outlets, thereby increasing their impact. We promoted the survival tips on bus ads, podcasts, posters, and cafeteria tray liners—bypassing expensive ads in the student news-paper in favor of these less costly but targeted vehicles. The campaign was well received, memorable, and can be easily revised and extended. Wrote one reviewer in an unsolicited response: "So flippin' awesome."

Like many other academic research libraries, we at Indiana have worked hard recently to build awareness of and support for our in-stitutional repository as part of our broad-based strategy to support open-access publishing. (Communications objective: Grow support for scholarly communications initiatives.) Key to this effort has been leveraging the longstanding relationships that librarians have nurtured with faculty. Our approach was personal. The director of scholarly communications, joined by committed subject librarians and collec-tion managers, met with more than 50 faculty members in various departments or centers to introduce the service and build awareness of scholarly communications issues. We hoped to position the libraries at the forefront, so when faculty were ready to act, they'd know they could rely on the IUB Libraries for support.

Brochures, postcards, websites, and electronic news announce-ments supplemented those meetings and reinforced a key message. "We at the IUB Libraries are working on your behalf to realize the full benefits of this digital era," the brochure read. "As your partner, we can create new publishing models to advance your discipline. We can offer parallel channels to disseminate your research within your community of scholars. And, most importantly, we can help you advance your academic goals at IU." (Sound at all like a key message you've already heard? The IUB Libraries provide the resources and services faculty need to succeed.)

In one notable success story, an anthropology professor created an open-access supplement to a journal he edits and now makes it avail-able via our repository, IUScholarWorks. It's our first faculty-generated electronic journal. We congratulated him in a postcard sent to faculty, which had the added benefit of increasing awareness of the service to other potential users. He kindly acknowledged our support, thanking, in an editorial (later quoted in *Library Journal* Academic Newswire),[12] the "remarkable, visionary librarians" with whom he partnered. Nice stuff.

We knew at the outset that integrating the institutional repository into the daily lives of faculty would be a long process. And frankly, asking librarians to promote the service aggressively was new territory for us. The campaign—I resist calling it a crusade—did far more than promote a service. It fostered two-way communication about what faculty need and how librarians can help. The conversations have led to heightened awareness, informative exchanges, and, often, meaningful partnerships. I believe librarians will be asked to take on similarly proactive roles as academic libraries reposition themselves in the coming years.

News Judgment and Audiences

Conveying messages to audiences beyond the academic community, particularly via the news media, takes a concerted effort that I suggest requires skills not necessarily taught or learned in library school. And yet, librarians on the front lines are often the ones who make the news, have the best understanding of key issues, and consequently are best positioned to demonstrate our value. Remember that positioning librarians as experts is part of our communications plan. It's helpful, then, when they respond to news inquiries, and it's doubly helpful if they advance our key messages when doing so.

General news media, of course, reach not only external audiences, but also our core groups of administrators, faculty, and influencers. Working with the university media relations staff, who are masters at generating publicity, can be extremely helpful in placing stories in more general outlets. This group of professional editors has a far broader mandate than promoting library activities. Foremost they advance mission-critical priorities, tuition-based degree programs, and messages directed specifically to their own target markets, which at a state-supported institution such as IU are often legislators or taxpayers.

If awareness among external audiences is our goal, we in libraries need to understand how to work with the university news staff to make our stories more broadly appealing (just as fund-raisers work with colleagues at the university foundation or fund-raising arm). This means making it as easy as possible for university editors to assist us in advancing our own messages. Provide clear, well-written releases. Master the inverted pyramid. Don't bury the lead. Follow Associated Press, not Chicago, style. As ProQuest reminds in its Library Marketing Toolkit,[13] avoid jargon and library-speak. Think about the audience. Know you've lost all perspective when you call a book a monograph.

Brent Lang, who served as communications and external relations specialist at Brown University Library, understands the value in thinking a bit outside the box, or at least outside the librarian box. Not a librarian himself, Lang served Brown after working as a researcher at *Forbes* magazine and as a communications officer for a U.S. senator. Experience in the political realm taught him the need to cultivate reporters to get the message out. So, although he worked with the university's media relations department, he also recognized the importance of following up on news releases they'd distribute on his behalf. He identified reporters, learned their interests, and sent notes describing why the release might lead to a fruitful story. One such interaction landed a high-profile article and photographs in the *Chronicle of Higher Education* about the library's digitization of a Garibaldi panorama, an impressive 273-foot-long, double-sided watercolor from the 19th century.[14]

Lang also sent stories about library donors to their local newspapers and featured stories about library donors in library and campus alumni publications. "My thought process was," Lang says," you never really know who's going to be interested, so it's good to pepper many outlets." He set up Google alerts to notify him of far-flung media hits.

Lang sees advantages in not having a library degree. "Like any field, people can drift into techno-speak," he says. "Outsiders think in terms of clarity." But he also values the role librarians play in advancing story ideas and publicity. "The germ of the idea has to come from the librarian," Lang says, "because they know the collections and resources."[15]

In my role at Indiana as media liaison (and not a librarian), I am a filter and a promoter. I get my best leads from the librarians with whom I work. They purchase interesting items, interact with students and faculty, and introduce new services. We support each other. And we will have greater opportunities for success as librarians increasingly recognize and value the need to promote themselves aggressively in a way not necessarily required of them in the past. This means talking to the media, identifying news stories that support institutional communications goals, and, yes, occasionally beating their chests.

The curator of books at Indiana University's renowned Lilly Library for rare books and manuscripts has a good sense for news.

He told me one day last fall about a recent acquisition I might be interested in promoting: a first-edition book that relates the origins of Oktoberfest. Published in 1811, it describes the Bavarian harvest festival that celebrated the wedding of the Crown Prince Ludwig. The 46-page book includes two engravings, one of which folds open to reveal music composed for the occasion. Gold-stamped and leather-bound, the book is apparently one of only a few copies known to exist worldwide.

I pounced. The story had all three elements that would make it appealing to editors of the student newspaper: it was timely (it being October), newsworthy (consider the book's rarity), and beer-related (the clincher). Somehow I knew the editors would respond. If there's anything that piques the interest of a campus newspaper reporter, it's the opportunity to explore a known topic.

Sure enough, the curator and I both fielded phone calls from an enthusiastic student reporter, and we were delighted to read later that week a bit of publicity about the book. The article[16] reinforced the perception of the Lilly Library as a local trove for IU students and scholars who can visit the library any time. (Communications objective: Increase visibility of IUB Libraries within the campus community.) A professor from the department of Germanic Studies commented on the advantage of having the original text available for researchers.

Perhaps to contextualize the story, the reporter somewhat expect-edly shifted the focus from a story about the book acquisition to one about the revelry associated with Oktoberfest. Noting that the tradi-tion is still celebrated in Munich, Germany, he reported that every fall people from around the world meet for the celebration "known for its excessive amounts of beer and partying." Said one party animal quoted in the story: "It was awesome."

The news release I wrote about the acquisition was appealing enough for the university communications team, which distributed it broadly via their Listservs. Radio stations, print media, and a rare-book website frequented by bibliophiles all picked up the story. It was a good lesson that topicality and timeliness matter. The curator, however, remains a bit befuddled. Given all the treasures in the magnificent Lilly Library, he was somewhat dismayed that a relatively minor purchase about Oktoberfest could garner such attention. The lesson I take from this: Speak to your audience, reinforce your key messages, and never underestimate the power of a good brew.

Consistent application of messages can help achieve communications goals. Sometimes a bit of creativity helps, too. The Friday morning I stumbled to the curb to retrieve my empty garbage cans and the local newspaper, I was more than a little surprised to read the front-page headline: "That sinking feeling: Library story won't die."[17] What's more, I was quoted top-of-the-fold, in a 16-point callout: "It's entertaining and somewhat believable," I had told the reporter, "but entirely untrue." Apparently, not only was it garbage day, it was also a painfully slow news day. I'd need more coffee.

As shocking as the placement was, I was extraordinarily pleased by the outcome. I'd actually pitched the story the day before about the "sinking library" legend as a possible news feature. The myth—by no means unique to IU—suggests that the library is slowly sinking because architects didn't account for the weight of the books. Parents of incoming freshmen, who were participating in summer orientation held at the library, had noticed construction crews at the library entrance. "Was the rumor true?" they asked, only half joking. "Is the library really sinking?" (Workers were repairing worn concrete in the entry plaza.) Our folklore librarian would warn against perpetuating an urban legend even by denying it, but because one of our communications objectives that year was to promote the value of an offsite shelving facility, it helped to advance stories about the library being overcrowded with materials. I told the reporter about the myth and the momentum it seemed to be gaining. It worked to our advantage. The prominent story created buzz about the library and the millions of materials contained within. "We're not sinking," an on-message librarian was quoted in the story, " but we're bursting."

An aside: At the Bloomington campus of Indiana University, known for its beautiful limestone buildings, the library sits on a 330-million-year-old, 94-foot-thick layer of limestone.[18] The building is definitely not sinking. The myth gains credibility among some Hoosiers, however, in a homespun version that suggests the incompetent architects hailed from rival Purdue.

Another aside: Years ago a colleague suggested hanging on the front of the library a giant banner that reads: "This building is not sinking"—and then lowering the banner a foot or so every week. I haven't yet pulled this prank, but I think about it every April Fools' Day. (Fast forward to 2006, when on a blustery December day some of our catalogers noticed slabs of limestone dangling from the side of the building. The year long project to reattach them and safeguard passersby cost the university millions of dollars. Clearly no joke.)

Social media and Web 2.0 are blurring the lines of communication. As important as they are, traditional media outlets are not the only means to advance messages, and they are clearly not the only vehicles that shape the perceptions of those whose opinions we value. In this age when it seems that everyone blogs and we're all potential publishers, we risk losing control of the institutional messages we have worked so hard to develop. But we also have an extraordinary opportunity to reach audiences in a highly focused manner and to leverage the credibility that's gained when messages are embraced by many within the institution. Casting messages in this way can be especially effective if we are thoughtful about our approach.

Perspective matters. We all have perspective, but essential judgment in relating messages to key audiences is often cultivated precisely from not thinking like a librarian. Too often we in academic libraries look inward rather than outward. What is important to us—perhaps because it's the focus or culmination of endless meetings, resources, and deliberations—isn't necessarily meaningful to others. If our goal is to communicate with external audiences, we must think beyond the walls of the library or the edge of campus. This essay is written in the first person in part to underscore the impact a different perspective can make.

Try as I might, I cannot forget an encounter with a coworker who years ago came into my office, closed the door, and with eye-popping, red-faced disbelief asked why we had not announced which vendor we had selected to provide our integrated library management system. Huh? I confess I'm still not sure I know what an integrated library management system is, but at least I now know enough to pretend I do. And if such a system is a mystery to me as a seasoned full-timer, does a student or faculty member really care, let alone a donor or community member? Who is the audience? How do they benefit? Furthermore, as an employee of a state-funded university, should I really be in the business of promoting for-profit companies whom we pay for services? (We happily cooperated with the vendor's own publicity machine, and as good citizens provided a delicious endorsement of their product they could use for their own purposes, which of course benefited us as well.) I now know about OCLC, metadata, and APIs. But guess what? Our core audiences—including many in our innermost circle—have never heard of them. They're interested in benefits, not process.

Lone Ranger

Library communications specialists are typically writers, or designers, or some combination of both. They work with or hire the services of photographers, Web administrators, technologists, and commercial printers, all of whom contribute to producing the vehicles that carry institutional messages. Managing these relationships, understanding their value, and appreciating how these complementary roles interact is critical to success in pushing messages outward. In the best world, a library communications office would include a dynamic mix of these professionals. By working together in house, a communications team would gain firsthand insight to the issues important to librarians and offer their complementary skills as graphic designers, wordsmiths, programmers, or business-tested marketers. They would ideally collaborate creatively and fuel each other's strengths. They would manage communications, ensure consistency of delivery and presentation, and serve as a resource for librarians who will increasingly be called on to develop many of these skills themselves.

Today, however, a common challenge for directors of communications in academic libraries—and one frequently shared by development officers—is that they act as lone rangers. There is often no Office of Communications per se, no formal reporting structure that links communications activities to the overall effort of public services or IT or other functions essential to the marketing effort. At Indiana, I sit on committees and am at the table, but essentially operate independently. Like development officers who also operate in peripheral orbits, communications officers must work to build relationships and embed themselves in the library culture as much as possible. In establishing a marketing communications program, or even hiring a Lone Ranger, library directors may benefit from understanding that the program or individual should:

- *Concentrate on institutional priorities.* Everyone in your library may potentially want a piece of the communications effort: a new brochure for an individual unit, heightened publicity for a pet project, giveaways for an event. (It's all PR, right? It's all communications, right?) Be selective. Which activities advance the goals and priorities of the library? Which advance the communications plan? If you try to do everything, you will do nothing well.

- *Set a budget.* If a budget does not follow priority planning, it will force the planning on its own. Broad buy-in and enthusiastic support for a communications program would certainly be simpler to accomplish if budgets were flush, but libraries typically don't work this way. If, however, plans are created jointly with staff, participants will then also understand the logic behind them and be more understanding of priorities. Pointing to a budget makes it easier to decline requests of entrepreneurial librarians whose good ideas fall beyond the scope of a communications office working to establish itself.

- *Manage expectations.* Say no at the outset to projects for which there is not adequate time or money. Centralize selectively. Stay on track, and make sure everyone understands the reasoning. At the same time, encourage staff to be a part of the marketing effort. Don't insist that every calendar listing, flyer, or blog be channeled through the communications office. It's more important that staff are on board with the message and are working to promote their own activities.

- *Promote ownership and share successes.* Solicit advice, input, and ideas. Make it easy for staff to carry the message, use the brand, adhere to guidelines, and adopt the principles. Marketing communications requires a team approach. A director can coordinate the effort by helping prioritize and by advancing key initiatives , but an overall communications program will ultimately be successful only if everyone within an organization owns it.

- *Remain flexible.* Don't say no to every project or idea that falls outside the communications plan or budget. Plans and priorities change. Just keep the goals in sight.
- *Grow a program.* Like their fund-raising counterparts (called development for a reason), communications programs also take time to mature. Your library can identify a look, advance key messages, and create a cohesive family of communications materials in print and digital formats, but doing so may take longer than you'd like. Stage the implementation by concentrating on high profile or essential efforts first. You'll be encouraged by the cohesion or momentum that develops, and its success will help all contributors sustain the effort.
- *Show the results.* The effectiveness of library communications plans can be difficult to measure, and in this way are unlike development operations. Fund-raising offers a demonstrable if indirect link: annual giving rises or falls, contributions and donor lists grow. Communications activities can certainly influence attendance at events, items checked out, or hits to webpages, which may be barometers of communications efforts, but are often hard to assign a one-to-one correlation. And furthermore, how does one reliably measure credibility, prestige, or influence?

The LibQUAL+ survey produced by the Association of Research Libraries and attitudinal measures of our own creation can help us understand snapshot impressions, and over time we may glean the impact of communications efforts. For example, local trends in response to the LibQUAL+ question about a library helping distinguish between trustworthy and untrustworthy information may help us determine how effectively our communications messages resonate. Focus groups can help measure success of awareness campaigns. Analysis of hits to websites tied to a specific campaign or promotion can help measure reach. Including communications messages in our culture of assessment and measuring their impact, when possible, should be a priority. Doing so reminds us that the best communication is two-way, and with quantifiable evidence we have a positive influence not only on individuals but also on the university. Librarians will have more leverage in the coming years if they can show in very real terms that the strength of the library contributes to the overall strength of the institution. Numbers will help.

Conclusion

When I first started at IU, deans of academic libraries were seeking grant funding to help combat the graying of the profession and the lack of area studies specialists. Faced with too few librarians in certain area studies programs, they faced a dilemma: was it better to hire a subject specialist—a PhD in a certain area—and train him or her to be a librarian, or vice versa. I ask a similar question today: When hiring someone to advance a communications strategy, is it better to hire a librarian with marketing skills or a marketer who understands libraries?

In the best world, the boundaries would be so blurred the distinction would be hard to make. The solution will be, I believe, that librarians will have to think more and more about marketing their services and communicating their value. This will come eventually, no doubt led by those who have the skills and duty to push communications to the forefront, but everyone will one day contribute.

At a recent gathering of our librarians and staff, a guest speaker surveyed the audience to help him focus his remarks. "Who works in Technical Services?" he asked. "Raise your hand if you're in Public Services. Are there any IT folks here?" My short-lived fantasy was that he'd ask who markets the library—and we'd all raise our hands.

As we work toward advancing the academic library in the coming years, our goal, collectively, should be to capitalize on the goodwill that many still feel for libraries and librarians. To reach out in a coordinated and forceful way to those who have yet to discover how wonderful academic research libraries truly are. To rethink how we define external relations and to work beyond simple promotion to include broader strategies. To communicate our value by working toward shared and well understood goals. To embrace a plan with direct and simple messages. To implement the plan and delight in its success.

And that, librarians of the 21st century, you can chisel in stone.

Notes

1. John Milton, "Areopagitica," trans. Judith Boss and Risa Stephanie Bear (Eugene, OR: University of Oregon, 1997), 4, http://hdl.handle.net/1794/739.
2. Joint Information Systems Committee, "Information Behaviour of the Research-

er of the Future," Jan. 11, 2008, www.jisc.ac.uk/media/documents/programmes/reppres/gg_final_keynote_11012008.pdf (accessed June 6, 2008).

3. Peter Brantley, "Architectures for Collaboration: Roles and Expectations for Digital Libraries," *Educause Review* 43, no. 2, (March/April 2008), 36.

4. Stephen Abram, *Out Front with Stephen Abram: A Guide for Information Leaders.* Judith A. Siess and Jonathan Lori, comp., (Chicago: American Library Association, 2007), 96.

5. Karlene Noel Jennings and Jos Wanschers, *Library Development: SPEC Kit 297* (Washington, DC: Association of Research Libraries, 2006), 18.

6. Linda Wallace, ed., *The @ your library™ Toolkit for Academic and Research Libraries,* (Chicago: American Library Association and Association of College and Research Libraries, 2003), 5.

7. Karels, Liene. Telephone interview. August 29, 2008.

8. Attendance assignment from a business student, Nov. 11, 2006.

9. Indiana University Bloomington Libraries, Sources, "Flip This Library," www.indiana.edu/~library/sources/spring2007/story1.html, 2006 (accessed May 13, 2008).

10. Jessica Anderson, "Students Propose Renovations to Business/SPEA Library," *Indiana Daily Student,* March, 27, 2007.

11. Indiana University Bloomington Libraries, "Survival Tips," www.libraries.iub.edu/survival (accessed June 25, 2008).

12. Reed Business Information, Library Journal Academic Newswire, "Indiana University Library Publishes First Faculty E-Journal," Feb. 21, 2008, www.libraryjournal.com/info/CA6534369.html?nid=2673#news2 (accessed June 25, 2008).

13. "ProQuest Introduces Marketing Toolkit for Academic Libraries," *Information Today,* Jan 2008: 36.

14. Lawrence Biemiller, "Art on an Epic Scale," *Chronicle of Higher Education,* Oct. 5, 2007, http://chronicle.com/article/Art-on-an-Epic-Scale/21399 (accessed Sept. 8, 2008).

15. Lang, Brent. Telephone interview. September 5, 2008.

16. Ben Phelps, "Lilly Library Now Home to Valuable Oktoberfest Book," *Indiana Daily Student,* Oct. 26, 2007.

17. Steve Hinnefeld, "That Sinking Feeling: Library Story Won't Die," *Bloomington (IN) Herald-Times,* June 27, 2003, sec. A.

18. Response to letter to the editor, *IU Alumni* magazine, Nov./Dec. 1997, 7.

WHAT WE WANT TO SAY
WORDS AND MESSAGES

These messages describe how we wish to be perceived by our various audiences. They are not intended to be reproduced verbatim, but will guide our communications and ensure we speak with a consistent voice.

Key Messages		
The IUB Libraries provide the resources, services, and environments that you need to succeed.	**We are information experts.**	**The IUB Libraries share the teaching, learning, and research goals of the university.**
Corollary messages		
We can help you take full advantage of the vast resources we select, purchase, and manage for you.	The IUB Libraries have a long and respected history of providing trustworthy, reliable, and diverse information.	We support all academic disciplines on campus and are essential to the academic mission.

CHAPTER 12

TEACHING THE TEACHERS

DEVELOPING A TEACHING IMPROVEMENT PROGRAM FOR ACADEMIC LIBRARIANS

Beth S. Woodard and Lisa Janicke Hinchliffe
University of Illinois at Urbana-Champaign

Introduction

Job ads for academic librarians consistently mention, for those in public service, roles in instruction of users, and often, for those in technical services positions, mention roles in training for library staff.[1] The "Draft College and University Professional Association Position Descriptions for Academic Libraries"[2] list teaching, instruction, and training with surprising regularity. Librarians, new and veteran, are expected to have skills in teaching and training and to understand how people learn and what motivates learning.

Many library schools have developed stand-alone instruction-related courses.[3] Despite these offerings, many newly graduated librarians did not take these courses, perhaps not realizing that instruction would be a component of their future jobs, and those already in the field often did not have the opportunity to do so. The Immersion Program offered by the Association of College and Research Libraries through its Institute for Information Literacy has filled the gap for some through its Teacher Track, but many libraries cannot afford its steep registration fees.[4] In addition, instructional improvement programs have long been offered in specific institutions, and several attempts have been made to summarize and describe them. Alice Clark, over 20 years ago, reported on a survey of programs in ARL libraries,[5] and Scott Walter and Lisa Janicke Hinchliffe updated this information several years ago.[6] Priscilla Atkins and Catherine E. Freirichs describe a process used to develop in-house programming, very much like those at other institutions.[7] Programs like the Instructor College at University of Michigan, instruction in-services at The Ohio State University Libraries, "Tips and Techniques for Library Instruction" at the University of Texas Libraries, the very theoretically grounded staff development initiative at Queensland University of Technology, and "teacher meetings" at the University of Washington-Bothell all recognize that training and continual development of instructional skills are important to the development of instructional programs in academic libraries.[8]

Professional development is an important responsibility not only for individual librarians but also for academic libraries.[9] The term *instructional improvement* is used by Paulsen and Feldman to describe the practice of offering professional development activities for college instructors that help them improve their performance in the classroom.[10] Academic librarians have these classroom and instructional professional development needs as well.

This case study will examine the programs and workshops of the University Library of the University of Illinois at Urbana-Champaign as it attempts to orient approximately 100 librarians to their instructional roles and to meet the continuing education needs of the University Library's instructional staff, which includes librarians as well as support staff and a contingent of approximately 60 graduate assistants enrolled in the Graduate School of Library and Information Science working in preprofessional public services positions.

Institutional Environment

The University of Illinois at Urbana-Champaign is a land grant public institution in a nonurban environment. The institution is considered a research-extensive institution according to the Carnegie Classification.[11] As such, there is an important emphasis on scholarship for faculty. Although teaching and service are important criteria in promotion and tenure, the overriding factor is the level of research and publication. Librarians have faculty status and professorial rank at Illinois and face the same expectations as other faculty for tenure and promotion decisions. Consequently, in addition to high levels of involvement in national service through association committee service and presentations at conferences, excellence in research and scholarship in the form of published papers, articles, chapters in books, and monographs is expected in both annual review and tenure and promotion processes. In addition to its emphasis on research, the university has been pursuing initiatives related to quality undergraduate education for a number of years. The institution sees its role as a leader in research, teaching, and public engagement in pursuit of its vision to "become the preeminent public research institution."[12]

In order to serve the needs of its faculty and research students, the library developed into a multilibrary system, with over 40 departmental libraries distributed in more than 25 buildings across the campus. There is a legend, which exemplifies the value of decentralized library services, in which the chemistry library became the first departmental library because by the time a chemistry faculty member ran across campus to check some data in a reference book, the experiment in his lab had failed. Consequently the current system of collections based on subject disciplines being housed separately, and often within the building with offices of the faculty being served, was established. Though evolving through the University Library's New Service Model Programs initiative,[14] changes being made are guided by a commitment to "retaining the greatest strengths of the departmental library service model."[15]

Because fewer than half of the departmental libraries were housed within the main building, and because of the characteristics of librarian faculty status at Illinois, an environment that recognized individual autonomy and authority developed, and individual librarians developed unique strategies and approaches to providing services to their clientele.

Organization of User Education at Illinois

With a history of great emphasis on collection development and support of faculty research needs, as well as the concomitant unique and varied approaches to collection development and reference services, it is no surprise that a systematic approach to user education within the library system has been slow to develop. The Undergraduate Library focuses on students in the first and second years of college, primarily working with writing-intensive and speech communication courses that fulfill the basic composition requirement. Subject librarians serve the courses in their colleges or departments and have had mixed successes with integrating information literacy into research-intensive courses.

In the mid-1980s, a loosely knit group of librarians from across the campus met for lunch once a month to discuss bibliographic issues. No formal committee existed until 1986, when the OPAC User Education Committee was created. This committee focused specifically on user instruction workshops and handouts for the new online catalog. Gradually, responsibilities for CD-ROM databases, end-user searching, and Web-based indexes were assigned to this group, with the committee taking on an increasingly comprehensive charge and developing basic instructional materials for the library's webpages in 1995. Though much was accomplished through the committee, eventually renamed the User Education Committee, the revolving nature of committee membership and competing demands on committee members' time hampered the development of instructional leadership for the library as a whole.

A Coordinator for Information Literacy Services and Instruction, reporting to the Associate University Librarian for Services, was hired in 2002 and charged to lead efforts to develop a more systematized approach to offering instruction. Initial steps in the development of the information literacy program included taking stock of existing instructional efforts, identifying unserved and underserved groups, providing support for librarians teaching instruction sessions or developing instructional materials, and selecting strategic directions for short- and long-term efforts. Developing instructional facilities was another important aspect that needed to be addressed to improve instructional efforts by librarians, as librarians repeatedly stated they were hampered in developing instruction programs by not having spaces in which to teach. In addition, the coordinator was charged to "nurture the professional development of librarians as educators and serve as a resource person for library faculty and staff in this area... the Coordinator will ensure that library staff have the necessary knowledge and skills to provide information literacy instruction and other services at the highest level possible."[16] A year after the Coordinator for Information Literacy was hired, the University Library also appointed a Coordinator for Staff Development and Training, a key position in helping with the developing instructional improvement program.

To create a foundation for the information literacy program and a common understanding throughout the University Library of instructional goals, the coordinator worked with the User Education Committee to develop guiding documents for the program—specifically a vision statement and a statement on learning goals. User education services are guided by a vision that states:

> The Information Literacy Services and Instruction programs offered by the University Library teach library users to identify, retrieve, evaluate, judge, use and value information and information tools while attending to the legal and ethical considerations involved in doing so. The services and programs are developed in a strategic and systematic manner but are expected to vary in approach and composition of strategies utilized based on curriculum needs, user skills and experiences, and library resources. Methods in use include formal group instruction, including course-integrated sessions, credit courses, and open workshops; individual one-to-one instruction; and independent learning opportunities including both print and web-based point-of-use instructional materials. Librarians collaborate with campus faculty and staff to develop instruction that is responsive to teaching and learning needs and furthers the development of student information literacy. The programs are characterized by assessment of student learning outcomes and systematic program evaluation and particular attention is paid to identifying unserved and underserved groups.[17]

The University Library's "Statement on Learning Goals" incorporates both the "Model Statement of Objectives for Academic Bibliographic Instruction" and the "Information Literacy Competency Standards for Higher Education" in order to provide frameworks for developing learning goals.[18]

Objectives for the Instructional Improvement Program

The unique environment of the Illinois Library—decentralized libraries, a highly autonomous library faculty, and many staff and graduate assistants also teaching but without any central instruction unit beyond the Coordinator for Information Literacy Services and Instruction and one graduate assistant—led to the approach adopted by the University Library in providing support for librarians developing themselves as teachers. The focus is on creating opportunities for development rather than a set curriculum or a mandate for attendance at specific functions. As such, the instructional improvement program is one that focuses on "continual growth that anticipates and complements the evolving information needs of our institutions and of society"[19] and is at the same time sensitive to and reflective of the University Library organization structure and culture.

The library hopes to improve librarians' teaching and to establish a community of teachers who can provide mutual support and feedback by always considering instructional improvement from the perspective of library faculty members who are choosing to better their skills and abilities. Training and development related to teaching is not part of a remedial or annual evaluation system. This program for teaching improvement shares the goals of the University of Michigan's Instructor College:

- fostering interest and enthusiasm
- encouraging reflection and creativity in teaching
- improving confidence in teaching abilities
- improving knowledge and skills in teaching
- understanding the impact of teaching on student learning
- changing work practices
- creating a community and developing, maintaining, and strengthening social networks among those involved
- formalizing library instruction as the ultimate goal[20]

The Illinois Library's "Vision for Information Literacy Services and Instruction" specifically states that "library faculty and staff have opportunities to participate in professional development opportunities that improve their instructional skills and understanding of student learning,"[21] and this is an integral component of achieving the vision for the library. Librarians and other instructional staff are encouraged to participate in offerings through the library itself, the Teaching Alliance (a joint program of the University Library and the Graduate School of Library and Information Science), the university, and consortia and professional organizations.

Library Offerings

Opportunities for developing baseline skills and knowledge are the foundation for the instructional improvement program within the

University Library. Without such knowledge and skills, instructors will not be able to further their own abilities and will struggle with logistical basics, impeding their own effectiveness.

The "Checklist for New Librarians and Others with Teaching Responsibilities: Information Literacy" is the foundational document for orienting those responsible for provision of instruction. It recognizes that the decentralized nature of the institution and the autonomous culture would not ensure that new librarians received the information they needed to be successful instructors. The Coordinator for Information Literacy Services and Instruction worked with the User Education Committee to develop this checklist, which the coordinator reviews with new librarians to orient them to roles of individuals, continuing education opportunities, existing programs, and resources. See the appendix for this checklist.

In contrast, graduate assistants are trained to provide instruction within their own library units by the librarians in the unit. As a complement to this, an overview presentation, "Teaching and Learning in Academic Libraries," is given once a year to provide background information for those who do not have instructional components for the assistantships or who wish additional training. The Undergraduate Library and the Reference Library have held initial discussions regarding how they might cooperate to develop a more robust approach to training graduate assistants since graduate assistants have specific and rather extensive assigned instructional responsibilities in each unit.

Library/GSLIS Teaching Alliance

In addition to offerings within the library, librarians and instructional staff can also attend programs offered by the Teaching Alliance, a joint program of the university's Graduate School of Library and Information Science (GSLIS) and the University Library, which provides professional development programs related to teaching to both librarians and library and information science professors, as well as doctoral and master's degree students in library and information science. Events offered through the Teaching Alliance have formed the bulk of the instruction improvement workshops sponsored by the University Library.

The Teaching Alliance sponsored two to three events per semester from its inception in 2001 until 2005, when regularly allocated campus funding was changed to a grant program and programming slowed to one to two events per semester. With the appointment of new leadership for the Teaching Alliance in fall 2008, including a liaison from the campus Center for Teaching Excellence, and a reconsidered funding model, programming is projected to grow and return to former levels.

An initial retreat, inspired by Anna Litten's work,[22] provided the foundation for the collaborative programming. During a lunchtime discussion facilitated by the Library and Information Science Librarian, retreat participants brainstormed topics for future sessions, which gave participants the opportunity to share their interests and needs regarding professional development topics. The choice of events centered around improving confidence in teaching abilities, improving knowledge and skills in teaching, and understanding the impact of teaching on student learning. Many of the topics highlighted in the "Seven Principles for Good Practice in Undergraduate Education"[23] were topics of discussion, including encouraging contact between students and faculty, encouraging active learning, giving prompt feedback, communicating high expectations, and respecting diverse talents and ways of learning. This framework provides a useful approach to organizing a summary of the events as it is more reflective of themes pursued since 2001 than a chronological approach would be.

Encourage Contact between Students and Faculty

According to educational research, frequent student-faculty contact in and out of classes is the most important factor in student motivation and involvement,[24] but librarians were not comfortable using technology to make that contact. Christine Jenkins and Jill Gengler, both of the library school, addressed teaching with technology in a session entitled "Teaching in an Electronic Classroom." They shared information and teaching strategies that related to teaching with various modes of technology. A large part of the presentation focused on the technology used for real-time distance education classes within GSLIS. A handout summarized technology available in GSLIS to support distance teaching and learning and described the advantages of each type of technology. The session reviewed different forms of synchronous and asynchronous technologies that support classroom work.

A second event on the same topic provided a more hands-on view of specific techniques for teaching in an electronic classroom that would be applicable for both library and GSLIS faculty. In a computer classroom, Lisa Janicke Hinchliffe, at that time working at Illinois State University, presented a session on general considerations for teaching in a computer lab. The content covered sight lines, layout of the room, and principles for effective presentation in a computer lab setting rather than specific software or technology usage.

Encourage Active Learning

Active learning refers to a wide range of teaching and learning activities that require or encourage students to do more than sit passively and listen. Chickering and Gamson suggest that beyond listening, students must read, write, discuss, or be engaged in solving problems.[25] "Most important, to be actively involved, students must engage in such higher-order thinking tasks as analysis, synthesis, and evaluation."[26]

A two-part series, led by Dean Papajohn of the campus Office of Instructional Resources, was offered on effective lecturing. The first session was devoted to presentation and discussion of the principles and strategies of effective lecturing, while the second session gave participants an opportunity to teach a minilesson for eight minutes and receive peer feedback. Most participants attended both sessions and participated in the microteaching. In the first session, the basics of lecturing were reviewed as well as hints for preparing and delivering lectures that actively involve learners. The goal for the session was to review the features and strategies of lectures, including defining lecture objectives, profiling audiences, distinguishing between weak and strong openings, creating relevant examples, determining appropriate organizational structures, and practicing delivery skills. In pairs, the participants discussed how lecturers and learners can be active or inactive. The group suggested that active lecturers ask questions, are flexible and change course based on students' questions, supplement talking with visuals and hands-on experiences, show enthusiasm, cultivate interest in the topic, guide students in preparing before class so there is knowledge upon which to build, consider the sequence of what is to be learned, provide feedback to gauge comprehension, think through assignments and prepare compelling questions before class, demonstrate current knowledge of the topic, and prepare current and relevant examples.

Active students are seen as those who make eye contact, ask questions, contribute ideas and experiences, make connections, take notes, and participate in group discussions and student presentations.

Distinguished Teacher/Scholar Jim Gentry from the College of Commerce and GSLIS faculty member Pat Lawton presented an interactive session to outline some of the qualities of an exemplary teacher. With Jim Gentry as facilitator and participants divided into a group of "students" and a group of observers, Pat Lawton taught a minilesson, which Jim then analyzed for aspects of exemplary teaching. A very popular and effective teacher at GSLIS, Pat used a variety of teaching techniques to engage the "students" in the learning process as she demonstrated a host of exemplary teaching strategies. During the debriefing session facilitated by Jim, observers commented on the level of engagement of the "students" and the effectiveness of using concrete models in representing the abstract ideas of classification, which was the theme of the minilesson. Following the debriefing session, participants broke into small groups for further discussion over lunch. Facilitators from the campus Office of Instructional Resources were present so that each roundtable had a discussant to lead a dialogue on the principles and practices of effective teaching.

Developed in response to the requests of a number of participants, a workshop was designed to provide small-group instruction on the basics of HTML coding with the aim of being able to post teaching materials on the Web. With such a small-group approach, individualized instruction was possible. Jeni Weidenbenner, the Teaching Alliance graduate assistant, began with a brief overview of considerations for basic Web design and then facilitated a workshop where participants could work on their own HTML projects. The basic presentation was posted on a website, and the URL was disseminated to interested people who were unable to attend the workshop. During the session, one participant chose to work on a basic website for her library, while another participant worked on a personal homepage. The diversity of goals for Web design was well suited to the atmosphere of individualized instruction.

Give Prompt Feedback

Feedback is the teacher's way of communicating with students, and it is key to helping the student learn. According to Wlodkowski and Ginsberg, teachers should provide feedback that is informational rather than controlling, based on agreed-upon standards, specific and constructive, quantitative, prompt, frequent, positive, and personal and differential.[27]

Sandra Finley, Education Specialist at the campus Center for Teaching Excellence (formerly named the Office of Instructional Resources), led a workshop entitled "Keeping Your Ship on Course: How to Use Classroom Assessment Techniques (CATs)." Several exercises were administered during the discussion, and handouts outlining some of the major CATs were distributed.

A follow-up session, "Create a Classroom Assessment Technique," was facilitated by Teaching Alliance coordinators Linda Smith (GSLIS) and Lisa Hinchliffe (library). Participants were asked ahead of time to think of ways in which they would like to implement CATs in their instructional program. The session then attempted as far as possible to present some practical considerations and highlight three techniques that would best suit the needs expressed: Background Knowledge Probe, One-Minute Paper, and Classroom Opinion Poll.[28]

Communicate High Expectations

Research has shown that expecting students to perform well becomes a self-fulfilling prophecy, having direct impact upon student learning,[29] and that how these expectations are communicated is important.[30] Communicating these expectations was the focus of other sessions. For the Teaching Alliance's first online, synchronous event, a small group facilitated by Linda Smith discussed issues of academic integrity and brainstormed approaches to preventing cheating and confronting cheaters. Initial discussion considered the university's academic code, for which all students are responsible, as well as the range of infractions of the code (e.g., cheating, fabrication, facilitating infractions, and plagiarism).

Participants decided that the chat conversation would focus on plagiarism, the inherent pitfalls of dealing with such infractions, and options for instructing students about how to avoid plagiarism, for which it was noted that instructors can exercise authority and discretion in handling infractions. Much of the discussion focused on the inability of students to distinguish fair use from plagiarism in many cases. The group considered options for educating students about academic writing, in particular the utility of creating a tutorial for new students (including master's level students). The discussion focused on the creation of assignments that minimize a student's ability to plagiarize. As a whole, the group agreed that creative writing assignments like autobiographies were most useful in avoiding instances of plagiarism but noted that traditional research projects could also be framed in a way that would minimize opportunities for plagiarism (e.g., requiring drafts during the writing process). Furthermore, resources exist to aid instructors in uncovering instances of plagiarism.

In concluding the session, participants reiterated the need for effective awareness and prevention programs on campus, including ways to make students more aware of the code. Additionally, several participants mentioned that citation requirements differ by discipline (e.g., journalism vs. history) and the need to change campus culture without making librarians appear as if they are the citation police. Participants also raised the possibility of organizing a formal campus initiative to support plagiarism detection (with librarians aiding instructors in uncovering instances of student plagiarism) and the need for "just in time" instruction. Collectively, the group agreed that the focus should be on prevention rather than detection.

Respect Diverse Talents and Ways of Learning

While there has been much recent debate on the validity of learning styles, which suggest that people have preferred ways of learning and that teachers should adapt their teaching to address these preferences, both supporters and detractors agree that classes are composed of a variety of people and that understanding who these people are and how they learn can help improve teaching.[31]

Early on, the Teaching Alliance sponsored a workshop led by Beth Woodard that focused on learning styles. Participants in the workshop took the *Kolb Learning Style Inventory*,[32] followed by a debriefing of the inventory and its implications for teaching. Participants then created sample instructional sessions that addressed a variety of learning styles.

A panel presentation with discussion, "Who Are Our Students?" started with Dean of Students William Riley presenting a timeline of demographics, attitudes, behavior, and interests of incoming students of recent years, up to about 10 years ago. Panelists, including Riley; Jordan Seymour, a former Illinois undergraduate and then GSLIS master's degree student; and Dana Wright, Assistant Undergraduate Librarian for Diversity Services, explored issues surrounding the needs of those students. Questions were invited after the presentations, and a lively discussion ensued, addressing issues specific to the interests of the participants. Three handouts were provided: "University of Illinois Student Profile Quiz," "Profile of John Doe, The University of Illinois at Urbana-Champaign 'Model' Student," and a PowerPoint presentation entitled "Illinois Student Profile."

A third event focusing on diverse talents and ways of learning was led by Arlette Ingrim Willis, Associate Head of the Department of Curriculum and Instruction. She showed a video and then led a discussion on "Teaching a Diverse Population."

Caroline Haythornthwaite, co-editor of the then recently published "Internet in Everyday Life," led a discussion that centered around "The Internet Goes to College: How Students Are Living in the Future with Today's Technology."[33] Internet links to the report and suggested questions were provided before the event, and hard copies of the report were also on hand during the event.

Chip Bruce of the GSLIS faculty presented an event entitled "What Do We Know about Undergraduate Learning?" which addressed the developmental theory of learning as it relates to undergraduates. This was followed with a discussion session on how experts differ from novices, facilitated by GSLIS-Library Teaching Alliance coordinators Linda Smith and Lisa Janicke Hinchliffe. Discussed was "How Experts Differ from Novices," a chapter from the book *How People Learn.*[34] The Internet link to the online book was provided before the event, and hard copies of the chapter were on hand as participants entered the room.

Reflective Practice

Donald Schon's articulation of reflective practice, whereby one considers one's own knowledge and experience at the same time as being coached or mentored by an experienced professional, has had a profound influence on teacher education and improvement programs.[35] The work of Stephen Brookfield further explored the importance of critical reflection to improve teaching and learning.[36] Peer coaching, creating teaching portfolios, and the use of action research are all techniques that help improve reflective practice.

Peer coaching uses the same process as evaluation, using preconference, observation, and postconference, but peer coaches do not evaluate; they use the observation opportunity to gather data and start a professional dialogue to help improve teaching.[37] Some libraries have also instituted this process as an evaluative method for documenting the quality of teaching for promotion purposes.[38]

Kirby Barrick, from the College of Agriculture, Consumer and Environmental Sciences, led a session on "Peer Observation of Teaching." Kirby presented strategies for making these peer observations positive by providing constructive feedback for change. His focus was on a voluntary process that would not be used for evaluative purposes. Unfortunately, the next logical step of creating peer groups was stymied by being unable to create appropriate groups. This remains a project the group would like to revisit in the future.

The creation of teaching portfolios encourages the articulation of a teaching philosophy and asks teachers to provide evidence of the effectiveness of their teaching. Judith Arnold and K. B. Pearson wrote one of the first descriptions of how this process can be applied by librarians.[39] Jane Tuttle further explored the use of teaching portfolios, highlighting how the process can illuminate areas about which library instructors may not have awareness.[40]

A presentation and discussion on "The Ins and Outs of Teaching Portfolios" was led by Beth S. Woodard, then Central Information Services Librarian. Based upon a workshop presented at an ACRL conference, this workshop featured discussion about the purposes for which portfolios can be used; reflective writing on teaching philosophy; brainstorming evidence of teaching performance, philosophy, and practice; and highlights of assessment techniques. A follow-up session for feedback on teaching philosophy statements was offered at a later date.

"What Kind of Teacher Are You? Models from the Movies" was presented by Jane Alsberg and Laura Hahn from the campus Center for Teaching Excellence and provided a light-hearted but deeply engaging approach to discussing difficult teaching issues and student learning challenges. Clips from *Mona Lisa Smile, Dead Poets Society, Finding*

Forrester, and other films were used to highlight teacher effectiveness and identify particular characteristics and approaches that can be incorporated into teaching in libraries.

The use of action research is another technique that helps improve instruction through the facilitation of reflective practice. The presentation and discussion of "Action Research as a Methodology for Inquiry" was facilitated by Ann Bishop, associate professor, GSLIS, who described a project entitled "Community Inquiry and LIS." The presentation outlined definitions and examples of participatory action research, participatory evaluation, appreciative inquiry, and service learning. These approaches to inquiry involve learners to a greater degree than more experimental methods and can be easier for librarians to implement in their teaching environments.

"The Scholarship of Teaching and Learning (SoTL) Unmasked" was facilitated by guest Kathleen McKinney, Cross Chair in the Scholarship of Teaching and Learning and professor of sociology at Illinois State University. Prior to the event, an article entitled "The Scholarship of Teaching and Learning: Past Lessons, Current Challenges, and Future Visions"[41] was distributed in order to provide a common point of entry among participants. Discussion topics for small groups included these:

- What Is the Scholarship of Teaching and Learning (SoTL) in Higher Education?
- Research Methods for Doing the Scholarship of Teaching and Learning
- Ethical Issues in the Scholarship of Teaching and Learning

Copies of all handouts were sent to interested persons who were unable to attend. Kathleen McKinney also donated several books to the Teaching Alliance to be used as SoTL resources.

Campus Opportunities

Librarians and instructional staff are also able to take advantage of the campus Center for Teaching Excellence, which provides resources, training, and consulting services related to teaching and learning.[42] In addition to the workshops mentioned above that have been offered through the Teaching Alliance and the new liaison to the Teaching Alliance, the center offers additional workshops open to all campus instructors on a variety of topics including metaphors, concept mapping, storytelling, grading, creating tests, connecting learning theories to classroom activities, writing teaching philosophy statements, and syllabus development.

The center also sponsors an annual Faculty Retreat on Active Learning, a one-day event to which all Illinois faculty are invited to learn more about teaching from a nationally known keynote speaker and concurrent and poster sessions featuring local faculty. These events have been held since 1995, and librarian attendance has been steadily increasing. Librarians have also presented sessions about their own teaching projects and recently have also had a resource table showing how the library supports campus faculty in their teaching.

Beginning in fall 2004, as a follow-up to the 2003 Faculty Retreat, which featured Lee Schulman speaking on the scholarship of teaching and learning, the Center for Teaching Excellence has been holding discussions during the academic year on the Scholarship of Teaching and Learning as a systematic investigation into issues of student learning, bridging the acts of teaching and research. Librarians have been active participants since its inception and the Coordinator for Information Literacy Services and Instruction serves on the advisory board for the SoTL group.

Librarians also participate in and present at the campus's Faculty Summer Institute, a four-day conference sponsored by the campus Educational Technologies group and the Illinois Online Network.[44] This conference offers more than 50 presentations, including hands-on workshops, forums, poster sessions, keynotes, and roundtable discussions, for those interested in the application of Web-based technologies to the teaching and learning process and in the planning, administration, and management of online education programs.

The codirectors of the Teaching Alliance also serve as members of the campus Teaching Academy Leadership Network (TALN), a grassroots group of the leaders of the teaching academies in the colleges across campus. Through TALN, the codirectors share information with other instructional improvement leaders on campus and gain ideas for implementation in the Teaching Alliance. In 2008–2009, TALN sponsored a Diversity in the Classroom workshop..

Instructional Development Opportunities in the Profession

The main consortium impacting instructional librarians at Illinois is CARLI (Consortium of Academic and Research Libraries in Illinois), a consortium of all the academic libraries within the state. In its previous iterations, this group typically held forums twice a year focusing on public services aspects of using the statewide online catalog. Instructional applications beyond the catalog were generally not discussed. After the reorganization of the consortium, CARLI has been taking a more proactive role and sponsored an ACRL Institute for Information Literacy Regional Immersion Program in summer 2007 with 46 attendees, three of whom were from the University of Illinois at Urbana-Champaign. In fall 2006, CARLI also began holding forums that focus on information literacy and instruction and now has a very active instruction team.[45]

The Coordinator for Information Literacy Services and Instruction has also obtained a commitment from the library administration for regular funding for attendance at the Institute for Information Literacy Immersion Program each year. At present, Illinois has had five attendees in program track, five in teacher track, and one each in intentional teacher and the assessment programs. These four tracks focus on different areas:

- teacher track on teaching techniques for those librarians new to teaching
- program track on coordinating and leading instruction programs
- intentional teacher on development opportunities for experienced teachers
- assessment on improving knowledge and practice of both classroom and program assessment

Four librarian hires have attended immersion prior to being hired, and two University Library faculty are faculty in the immersion program.

Library funding has also been set aside for attendance at other instruction conferences, for example, LOEX (Library Orientation Exchange), LOEX-of-the-West, and WILU (Workshop on Instruction in Library Use), as well as other higher education conferences that focus on student learning and instructional improvement, such as those put on by the American Association of Colleges and Universities and the Educause Learning Initiative. Librarians are also eligible to apply for additional campus funds to supplement internal travel money for attendance at instructional conferences.

Conclusions

Over the past two or three decades, instruction has evolved at Illinois from a concern of a small committee and the Undergraduate Library to a core service responsibility for all public service and subject liaison librarians in a transition similar to that of public services positions throughout the country. With the creation of the position of Coordinator for Information Literacy Services and Instruction came the opportunity and expectation for the development of an instructional improvement program supporting the librarians and other instructional staff. As the professional development offerings for instructional improvement expanded, the User Education Committee also created a subcommittee, the Professional Development Working Group, to help guide and further the growth of the instructional improvement offerings. The working group is also fortunate to have the guidance of the relatively newly disseminated ACRL "Standards for Proficiencies for Instruction Librarians and Coordinators"[46] in identifying areas of need.

By indicators of participation numbers and positive evaluations, the instructional improvement program of the University Library has enjoyed great success. Program evaluations indicate that participants appreciate the variety of topics addressed, the variety of presenters who have led sessions, careful attention to logistics (e.g., starting and ending on time, provision of snacks and beverages, and Web-based registration for events), and how responsive the selection of topics has been to instructional needs. These strategies are reflective of the overall philosophy of the program—to create opportunities for development, not a mandated one-size-fits-all prescription.

While successful, however, the University Library still has many ways to further develop its instructional improvement programs. Little assessment of the program has investigated the impact of the offerings—for example, do librarians change their teaching approaches, do they incorporate new techniques, are they more reflective in their practice, or have they adopted a focus on student learning outcomes? In addition, some librarians attend most of the sessions and many attend none, so there is a need to engage a broader group of participants as well as identify experts in particular instructional improvement areas beyond the Coordinator for Information Literacy who might be called upon more one-on-one for consultations and assistance. Building a local instructional community that encompasses all who have instructional responsibilities is the guarantee that everyone is able to engage their instructional responsibilities successfully and in personally fulfilling ways.

Notes

1. Beverly P. Lynch and Kimberley Robles Smith, "The Changing Nature of Work in Academic Libraries," *College & Research Libraries* 62, no. 5 (Sept. 2001): 407–420.

2. College and University Professional Association, "The Draft CUPA Position Descriptions for Academic Libraries," May 2007. www.ala.org/ala/mgrps/divs/acrl/issues/personnel/cupataskforce.pdf (accessed April 6, 2010).

3. ACRL Instruction Section Professional Education Committee, "Library Instruction Courses Offered by Accredited Master's Programs in Library and Information Studies," March 21, 2007, www.ala.org/ala/mgrps/divs/acrl/about/sections/is/projpubs/ceprogram/libraryschools.cfm   wikis.ala.org/acrl/index.php/IS/Library_Instruction_Courses (accessed April 6, 2010)

4. ACRL, Immersion Program website, http://www.ala.org/ala/mgrps/divs/acrl/issues/infolit/professactivity/iil/immersion/programs.cfm (accessed Feb. 20, 2008).

5. Alice S. Clark, "In-House Training: The Situation in ARL Libraries," in *Teaching Librarians to Teach: On-the-Job Training for Bibliographic Instruction Librarians,* ed. by Alice S. Clark and Kay F. Jones, 32–44 (Metuchen, NJ: Scarecrow Press, 1986).

6. Scott Walter and Lisa Janicke Hinchliffe, *Instructional Improvement Programs. SPEC Kit No. 287* (Washington, DC: Office of Leadership & Management Services, Association of Research Libraries, 2005).

7. Priscilla Atkins and Catherine E. Freirichs, "Planning and Implementing a Teaching Workshop for Librarians." *College & Undergraduate Libraries* 9, no. 2 (2002): 5–20.

8. "Instructor College," University of Michigan website, www.lib.umich.edu/instructor-college (accessed June 13, 2007); "Instruction In-Services" Ohio State University Libraries website, /library.osu.edu/sites/staff/ioc/insvc.php (accessed April 6, 2010); "Tips and Techniques for Library Instruction," University of Texas Libraries website, www.lib.utexas.edu/services/instruction/tips/index.html (accessed June 13, 2007); Judith Peacock, "Teaching Skills for Teaching Librarians: Postcards from the Edge of the Educational Paradigm," *Australian Academic and Research Libraries* 32, no. 1 (May 2001), http://alia.org.au/publishing/aarl/32.1/jpeacock.html (accessed Dec. 12, 2007); Sarah Leadley, "Teaching Meetings: Providing a Forum for Learning How to Teach," *Reference Services*

Review 26, no. 3/4 (Dec. 1998): 103–108.

9. Association of College and Research Libraries, "ACRL Statement on Professional Development," July 8, 2000, www.ala.org/ala/mgrps/divs/acrl/publications/whitepapers/acrlstatement.cfm (accessed June 18, 2007).

10. Michael B. Paulsen and Kenneth A. Feldman, *Taking Teaching Seriously: Meeting the Challenge of Instructional Improvement,* ASHE-ERIC Higher Education Report No. 2. (Washington, DC: The George Washington University, Graduate School of Education and Human Development, 1995).

11. Carnegie Foundation for Higher Education, "Carnegie Classifications," 2000, www.educause.edu/CarnegieClassifications/1051 (accessed June 6, 2007).

12. University of Illinois at Urbana-Champaign, ":Campus Strategic Plan," March 2007, 4, www.strategicplan.uiuc.edu/documents/Illinois_StrategicPlan.pdf (accessed June 17, 2007).

14. University of Illinois Library at Urbana-Champaign, "New Service Model Programs," www.library.illinois.edu/nsm (accessed Oct. 12, 2008).

15. University of Illinois Library at Urbana-Champaign, "Challenge, Change, and the Service Imperative," April 21, 2008, www.library.illinois.edu/nsm/background/service_imperatives.html (accessed Oct. 12, 2008).

16. University of Illinois Library at Urbana-Champaign, "Coordinator for Information Literacy Services and Instruction Job Announcement," 2002.

17. University Library, University of Illinois at Urbana-Champaign, "Vision for Information Literacy Services and Instruction," Fall 2002.

18. University Library, University of Illinois at Urbana-Champaign, "Statement on Learning Goals," 2003; Association of College and Research Libraries Bibliographic Instruction Section, *Read This First: An Owner's Guide to the New Model Statement of Objectives for Academic Bibliographic Instruction* (Chicago: American Library Association, 1991); Association of College and Research Libraries, "Information Literacy Competency Standards for Higher Education," 2000, www.ala.org/ala/mgrps/divs/acrl/standards/informationliteracycompetency.cfm (accessed June 6, 2007).

19. ACRL. "Statement on Professional Development."

20. Emily Mazure, Nicole Scholtz, and Maura Seale, "An Outcome-Based Evaluation of the Instructor College," Winter 2007. www.lib.umich.edu/files/SI623report_summary.doc (accessed June 13, 2007).

21. University Library, "Vision for Information Literacy Services."

22. Anna Litten, "We're All in This Together: Planning and Leading a Retreat for Teaching Librarians," *Journal of Library Administration* 36, no. 1/2 (2002): 57–69.

23. Arthur W. Chickering and Zelda F. Gamson, "Seven Principles for Good Practice in Undergraduate Education," *AAHE Bulletin* 39 (March 1987): 3–7, ED 282 491.

24. Ibid.

25. Ibid.

26. Charles C. Bonwell and James A. Eison, "Active Learning: Creating Excitement in the Classroom," ERIC Digest ED 340 272 (Washington, DC" ERIC Clearinghouse on Higher Education, Sept. 1991). www.ntlf.com/html/lib/bib/91-9dig.htm (accessed June 6, 2007).

27. Raymond J. Wlodkowski and Margery B. Ginsberg, "Feedback," in *Diversity and Motivation: Culturally Responsive Teaching.* 242–246 (San Francisco: Jossey-Bass,

1995).

28. Thomas A. Angelo and K Patricia Cross, *Classroom Assessment Techniques: A Handbook for College Teachers*, 2nd ed. (San Francisco: Jossey-Bass, 1993), 121-125, 148-153-258-262

29. Kathleen Cotton, "Expectations and Student Outcomes," School Improvement Research Series Close-up 7 (Nov. 1989), http://educationnorthwest.org/webfm_send/562 (accessed June 13, 2007).

30. U.S. Department of Education, "Hard Work and High Expectations: Motivating Students to Learn," June 1992, www.kidsource.com/kidsource/content3/work.expectations.k12.4.html (accessed June 13, 2007).

31. Frank Coffield, David Moseley, Elaine Hall, and Kathryn Ecclestone, *Should We Be Using Learning Styles? What Research Has to Say to Practice* (London: Learning and Skills Development Agency: 2004), www.lsnlearning.org.uk/search/Resource-32186.aspx (accessed Dec. 12, 2007); Marcia L. Conner, "Introduction to Learning Styles." Ageless Learner website, http://agelesslearner.com/intros/lstyleintro.html (accessed June 13, 2007); David Hargreaves, chair, *About Learning: Report of the Learning Working Group* (London: Demos, 2005), ww.demos.co.uk/files/About_learning.pdf?1240939425 (accessed April 3, 2010)

32. David A. Kolb, *Kolb Learning Styles Inventory* (Boston,: Hay Group Transforming Learning, 2007).

33. Mary Madden and Steve Jones, "The Internet Goes to College: How Students Are Living in the Future with Today's Technology," Sept. 15, 2002, report, PEW Internet & American Life Project, www.pewinternet.org/Reports/2002/The-Internet-Goes-to-College.aspx (accessed June 13, 2007).

34. "How Experts Differ from Novices," chapter 2 in *How People Learn: Brain, Mind, Experience, and School,* ed. John D. Bransford, Ann L. Brown, and Rodney R. Cocking. (Washington, DC: National Academy Press, 1999), 17–38, www.nap.edu/html/howpeople1 (accessed Dec. 12, 2007).

35. Donald A Schon, *Educating the Reflective Practitioner: Toward a New Design for Teaching and Learning in the Professions* (San Francisco: Jossey-Bass, 1996); Joan M. Ferraro, "Reflective Practice and Professional Development," ERIC Digest ED 449 120 (Washington DC: ERIC Clearinghouse on Teaching and Teacher Education, 2000).

36. Stephen D. Brookfield, *Becoming a Critically Reflective Teacher* (San Francisco: Jossey-Bass, 1995).

37. Lee-Allison Levene and Polly Frank, "Peer Coaching: Professional Growth and Development for Instruction Librarians," *Reference Services Review* 21, no. 3 (Fall 1993): 35–42; Cheryl Middleton, "Evolution of Peer Evaluation of Library Instruction at Oregon State University Libraries," *portal: Libraries and the Academy* 2, no. 1 (Jan. 2002): 69–78.

38. Patrick Ragains, "Evaluation of Academic Librarians' Instructional Performance: Report of a National Survey," *Research Strategies* 15, no. 3 (1997): 159–175.

39. Judith M. Arnold and K. B. Pearson, "Using the Teaching Portfolio to Define and Improve the Instructional Role of the Academic Librarian," in Linda Shirato and R. Fowler (eds.), *Change in Reference and BI: How Much Help and How? Papers and Session Materials Presented at the Twenty-Second National LOEX Library Instruction Conference Held in Ypsilanti, Michigan 13 to 14 May 1994*, 29–42 (Ann Arbor, MI: Pierian Press, 1996).

40. Jane P. Tuttle, "Bringing the 'Invisible' into Focus: Teaching Portfolios for the

Instruction Librarian," in J. K. Nims, and A. Andrew (eds.), *Library User Education in the New Millennium: Blending Tradition, Trends, and Innovation: Papers and Session Materials Presented at the Twenty-Seventh National LOEX Library Instruction Conference Held in Houston, Texas 12 to 13 March 1999,* 141–149 (Ann Arbor, MI: Pierian Press, 2001).

41. Kathleen McKinney, "The Scholarship of Teaching and Learning: Past Lessons, Current Challenges, and Future Visions," *To Improve the Academy* 22 (2004): 3–19. www.sotl.ilstu.edu/downloads/pdf/definesotl.pdf (accessed June 13, 2007).

42. Center for Teaching Excellence website, http://cte.illinois.edu (accessed June 13, 2007).

44. Faculty Summer Institute, www.ion.uillinois.edu/institutes/fsi/2006 (accessed June 13, 2007).

45. Consortium of Academic and Research Libraries in Illinois, "I-Share Instruction Team," www.carli.illinois.edu/comms/iug/iug-instr.html (accessed Oct. 12, 2008).

46. Association of College and Research Libraries, "Standards for Proficiencies for Instruction Librarians and Coordinators,"2007, www.ala.org/ala/mgrps/divs/acrl/standards/profstandards.cfm (accessed Oct. 12, 2008).

APPENDIX

CHECKLIST FOR NEW LIBRARIANS AND OTHERS WITH TEACHING RESPONSIBILITIES:

INFORMATION LITERACY

- ☐ Role of Coordinator for Information Literacy Services and Instruction, Office of Services, and the Relationship between Coordinator and Library Units
- ☐ User Education Committee (http://www.library.uiuc.edu/committee/usered)
- ☐ Library Instruction Reporting and Unit Annual Reports
- ☐ Professional Development Opportunities
  - GSLIS-Library Teaching Alliance and Campus Teaching Academies
  - Active Learning Retreat
  - PITA Grants
  - ILI-L Listserv
  - ACRL Instruction Section
  - LOEX Resources
- ☐ General Programs
  - New Student Week Tours
  - Library Fall Festival
  - Virtual Tours
  - Undergraduate Library Programs
- ☐ Instructional Materials and Resources
  - Statement on Learning Goals
  - Information Literacy Vision Statement
  - GEN Handouts
  - Library Brochure
  - Information Literacy Website
- ☐ Equipment and Facilities
  - Classrooms
  - Portable Instruction Unit

Approved April 18, 2005—User Education Committee, University Library, University of Illinois at Urbana-Champaign

CHAPTER 13

CREATING SMOOTH SAILING

THE BENEFITS OF ORGANIZATION DEVELOPMENT FOR THE EXPERT LIBRARY

Elaine Z. Jennerich
University of Washington

M. Sue Baughman
University of Maryland

Introduction

The practice of organization development (OD) can be messy, unsettling, time-consuming and sometimes costly. Why would any organization want to sail on OD waters? Because, to paraphrase Kenneth Grahame (from his classic, *The Wind in the Willows*), "There is nothing absolutely nothing half so much worth doing as simply messing about in organizations." Incorporating organization development practices into the expert library of the 21st century enables a library to position itself effectively to meet ongoing challenges and to remain an agile organization. OD provides ways to eliminate obstacles, to prepare staff and the organization to change, and to improve implementation endeavors. Using a sea chest full of techniques, OD focuses on a number of means to move the organization forward. OD "messing about" in libraries has many worthwhile, gratifying, and valuable benefits for the organization and its people. Moving toward the goal of becoming the expert library, OD can help the organizational boat maintain course while navigating the sea of change that the future brings.

What Is Organization Development?

Organization development (OD) as a field emerged from the areas of group dynamics and planned change and has existed since the late

1950s and early 1960s. With its foundation in the behavioral sciences such as psychology, sociology, organizational behavior, and management, OD focuses on the human side of organizations. With the beginning of OD centered in human relations, the theory and practice of OD has evolved over time. Leaders in this field include Kurt Lewin, Chris Argyris, Abraham Maslow, Douglas MacGregor, Edgar Schein, Richard Beckhard, and Rensis Likert, to name a few who linked theory and practice. They promoted the need to understand how organizations operated in order to identify ways to help them improve. Several of the earlier activities that led to the evolution of OD included:

- *Sensitivity Training, T-Groups, or Laboratory Training*—"small group discussions in which the primary, almost exclusive, source of information for learning is the behavior of the group members themselves.[1]
- *Sociotechnical Systems*—based on the "premise that an organization is simultaneously a social and a technical system."[2] Both the social system (the people who perform the work) and the technical system (what is produced, whether something tangible or a service) are subsystems of the total organization. Both must be considered to bring about any change in the organization.
- *Survey Feedback*—influenced by industrial psychology. Surveys have been used to assess employee morale and attitudes in organizations dating back to the late 1940s.

As these early activities evolved, leaders in the field continued to espouse many ways to describe and define OD as a way of expressing not only the value of it as a change agent, but also its diversity in approaches. A review of the current literature still finds this to be true. Paying attention to the evolution of OD by building on past knowledge and incorporating new ideas embraces the basic tenet of continuous learning. Organizations over time have faced the need to change for a myriad of reasons ranging from economical to social to technological.

There are a number of people who are given credit for coining the term *organization development*. In fact, in the literature the terms *organization development* and *organizational development* are often used interchangeably. One explanation of where the term comes from is that individual development speaks to human growth and change, so therefore the growth and change of the organization should be called organization not organizational development.[3] For this discussion, the authors will use Richard Beckhard's definition of OD: "Organization development is an effort (1) *planned,* (2) *organization-wide,* and (3) *managed* from the top, to (4) increase *organization effectiveness* and *health* through (5) *planned interventions* in the organization's "process," using *behavioral-science* knowledge."[4]

Beckhard explains each of these elements, which are helpful as organizations define what their OD program will entail. As planned change, OD should involve a systematic diagnosis of the organization, including a plan for improvement and the resources to carry it out. Whether the change effort is large and thus affecting the entire organization or done on a smaller scale with subsystems, the overall results impact the total organization. The top management must be invested in the program and the outcomes. This requires the knowledge of what is going on and a commitment to the change goals. To know when you get there, it is important to have a picture in mind of the ideal effective, healthy organization. The framework of behavioral-science knowledge ensures that alternate ways of working, relating, or rewarding are used. This could include processes such as motivation, communication, problem solving, goal setting, and interpersonal relationships.

While there are various definitions of the ideal state of an effective, healthy organization, there are several characteristics that are held in common. These characteristics are (a) all work is done in conjunction with the organization's goals; (b) communication (in all directions) is clear and transparent; (c) decisions are made at the source closest to the information; (d) conflicts are treated as situations for which problem-solving methods are used to solve them; (e) feedback mechanisms are used for continuous learning; (f) recruitment and development of talent is a priority; (g) there is an organizational identity that people feel attracted to; (h) there is high morale among the employees; and (i) the organization is able to cope with its changing environment because it is agile and adaptable.[5] Striving towards a healthy organization presents a strong case for creating a successful OD program. The expert library should seriously consider embracing the techniques and methods of OD because, by its nature, OD forces us to consider the big picture, the interrelatedness of components, patterns, and culture, as well the positive contributions of each individual in the organization. From the crow's nest at the top of the mast, the views out to the horizon and looking down and observing activity are much different than the narrower vantage points on or below decks!

Implementation and Management of OD

A successful OD program requires three basic components: diagnosis, action, and program management, which can involve a variety of interventions depending on the situation or need. The diagnosis component seeks to understand the strengths, opportunities, and problem areas. Identifying what information is already at hand or gathering new data ensures a clear picture of the current situation. The action component follows with activities or interventions intended to improve the organization's functioning, whether on an individual, team, or organizational level. The program management component addresses all of the other issues that come into play: creating a vision for the organization development strategy; identifying who is involved in the process and what this involvement looks like; communicating the goals, process, and evaluation mechanisms; motivating staff to become engaged; and sustaining momentum.[6]

Interventions that address any given situation are many. The intention of any intervention as a structured activity is that it results in a desired change or goal based on the diagnosis of the situation. Understanding the capability of a particular intervention will ensure that its implementation is most effective. There are several points to consider when choosing to use an intervention activity. The first is to make sure the activity has relevance to the participants affected by the situation. When the participants have a stake in the problem or opportunity, the activity has a better chance of being successful. Second, structure the activity so that it includes both experiential and conceptual learning. Learning through experience and incorporating this with conceptual models allows the participants to more effectively internalize the new knowledge and skills. Third, integrate both the task, what the participants are working on, with the process, how the participants are working together. All three are important as they support continuous learning—learning from an experience can lead to increased enlightenment by applying the new knowledge and skills to other situations.

The range and scope of OD interventions are quite extensive and are generally organized by categories. These broad categories can aid in the determination of the appropriate intervention needed for a particular situation. Table 13.1 illustrates the various categories with examples of activities or interventions that we believe would most likely be used successfully in academic libraries.[7]

TABLE 13.1 OD Interventions by Category	
Categories	Interventions
Diagnostic	Activities are designed to ascertain the state of a system and can include interviews, questionnaires, surveys, etc.
Team Building	Activities focus on enhancing the operation of teams and can include role and task clarity, ground rules, interpersonal dynamics, etc.
Intergroup	These activities are designed to improve the effectiveness between groups that must work together to accomplish a goal and can include activities that help them understand how to do this.
Education & Training	The activities improve an individual's skills, abilities and knowledge. They can be geared toward task or interpersonal competencies and include such things as decision-making, problem solving, goal setting, etc.
Process Consultation	This is an approach that is used to help the "client" gain insight into what is happening within the organization and develop the skills to diagnose and manage what is occurring. The focus is on processes such as leadership, authority, communication, problem solving and decision-making.
Planning & Goal Setting	Activities focus on the theory and practice of setting goals and using problem solving models.
Strategic Management	Activities that direct attention to the organization's mission and goals as well as environmental factors such as strengths, weaknesses, threats and opportunities are effective for planning short or long term efforts.
Organizational Transformation	Activities that involve large-scale change paying attention to systems such as rewards, values, culture, structure, management philosophy, etc. can lead to lasting transformation.

OD allows for flexibility in developing strategies to adapt to change. Because change can be planned or unplanned, continuous or incremental, utilizing the appropriate OD technique to address the issue is important. OD can be messy, unsettling, and time-consuming, but a well-designed program provides a clear implementation plan for managing change. Beckhard identifies a number of characteristics of a successful OD program. In addition to being managed from the top, other characteristics include the following:

- The program is well thought out and involves the whole organization.
- It focuses on improving the organization's ability to achieve its mission.
- It can include short-term goals, but overall it is a long-term effort.
- The activities are action-oriented with the intention that change will take place after the activity. These activities are designed to enable participants to build "connections and follow-up activities that are aimed toward action programs." They focus on changing attitudes and /or behaviors and include some form of experiential learning.
- Activities focus primarily on working with groups.[8]
- Above all, there is a strategic goal or need that the above characteristics will address.

Libraries and OD

Libraries have been engaged in OD practices since the 1970s beginning with the efforts conducted by the Association of Research Libraries' (ARL) Office of Management Studies. Maureen Sullivan notes that the "Management Review and Analysis Program (MRAP) was the first and most comprehensive program of its kind. It led the way for the development of the series of OD programs offered by ARL throughout the 1980s and 1990s."[9] Many libraries have been engaging in a variety of practices such as strategic planning, process improvement or total quality management, visioning, and training for quite some time without naming these practices as OD. The naming of these activities is not as critical an issue as understanding the need for implementing an activity based on some identified goal or change. In some cases, libraries have intentionally embarked on systemic or systematic change processes, while in other cases the change process has been focused on one area of the library.

There are a number of reasons that libraries have used OD to manage change. Karen Holloway describes technology as one of the key drivers for organizational change, notably that "information technology in the 1990s is advancing more rapidly than our profession is prepared to assimilate the changes."[10] She further notes that dealing with technological changes required consideration of nontraditional organizational structures. Other drivers have moved libraries to change, including an ever-changing financial climate, customer needs, new or changing skills for staff, accountability, and assessment.

Libraries face continuous change, and it is imperative to prepare the organization and its staff to deal with change, no matter how small or large. Not all change is within the control of libraries. While organizations respond to change drivers, the resulting adjustments can occur on three levels: individual, team or work unit, and the organization. Learning, or growth on an individual level, often occurs as a result of team or organizational changes but may not be enough in itself to affect change within the team or work unit or across the organization. By developing an organization on these three levels so that it is capable of learning about the key drivers of change and creating ways to address them, the more successful the library will be in the future. The more flexible the library is in adjusting to change, the better staff will be positioned to adapt. Libraries have learned that there is no one solution that works for every library or in every situation.

Selection of OD Tools

The authors have selected eight OD tools to describe in more detail and to demonstrate their application in practical terms to a major change effort. The tools selected are action research, appreciative inquiry, organizational assessment, facilitation, coaching, change management, organizational learning, and systems thinking. The key is to use a tool, an approach, or a process that works to solve a problem or to create an opportunity.

Action Research

Action research is considered both a tool and a process and is characterized as a "cornerstone of organization development."[11] In simple terms, action research means taking action based on what was learned from the data collected to understand a problem situation. The goal is to create a process for change that leads to practical results. Kurt Lewin, an applied social scientist, is credited with creating "action research" in the 1940s. Lewin presented this research model as a cyclical process beginning with "analysis, fact finding and re-conceptualization, planning, execution of actions, observing and collecting more facts, and lastly to reflecting and acting again."[12] It is important to note that these steps might overlap, and in some cases, more emphasis could be placed on one step than another. The cyclical process is described in three fundamental steps: unfreezing, moving, and refreezing. Unfreezing takes place when there is an awareness of the need to change—acknowledging that there is a problem. Diagnosis of the problem, collection of data, and a plan of action take place first. Sometimes this first step is the hardest as it takes time for people to think differently. Transformation begins when actions are taken in the "moving" step. This involves some kind of learning, often through workshops, with change integrated into one's job. The last step, "refreezing," begins when results of change are evident. There is a new sense of order. Gathering more data to test if the behaviors are working assesses the application of new behaviors, whether individually, in a team, or in the organization.

The use of action research as a tool has evolved over time, and a number of OD activities are used to implement the basic steps. However, an important element of action research is the engagement of the people who are involved in the problem. The more people are engaged in the process of collecting and analyzing data and taking action to manage or improve the problem, the more likely that the implementation of any change process will have a lasting impact. Action research can be used in a variety of ways, from improving staff meetings, to improving a workflow process, to more effectively meeting customer needs.

In an academic library, one can employ action research to change something, but also along the way to help staff people understand the change thus creating wider and deeper participation and learning. For example, a library may want to improve its information literacy program for a segment of the student population. As data are gathered and effects are studied, self and organizational reflections are part of the process. Consequently, librarians plan improvements for the program overall, while at the same time adopting new or different teaching methodologies within their own personal performance. They look at not only improving the program, but improving *themselves.*

Appreciative Inquiry

Appreciative inquiry (AI) is a tool that helps an organization learn through discovery and analysis of what works in the organization instead of what is wrong with it. The process encourages people, whether from the individual, team/work unit, or organizational level, to explore how they can function at their best. It embodies a philosophy and practice for positive change. By creating settings where people can talk about the positive elements of an experience or an event, people can create transformative change. AI is attributed to David Cooperrider, who, as a graduate student at Case Western Reserve University along, with his faculty mentor, Suresh Srivastva, developed an action research approach that focused on factors that contributed to the success of the Cleveland Clinic rather than what was not working well. The process encouraged people in this consultation to talk about success stories— discussion about the factors contributing to the organization's effectiveness. This activity was widely successful for the Cleveland Clinic. As Cooperrider and colleagues continued to experiment with this process and began sharing this research, appreciative inquiry was quickly developing into a practice for organizational change.[13] The popularity of AI is far-reaching, as evidenced by the number of books that have now been written on the subject.

As an action research tool, appreciative inquiry is suited for a variety of organization development interventions such as strategic planning, customer satisfaction, leadership development, recruitment and retention, performance appraisal, meeting management, and new employee orientation. The possibilities are endless and positive because you are always asking "What's going well?"

The "appreciation" in appreciative inquiry focuses on recognizing and valuing the best in people, affirming "past and present strengths, successes, assets, and potentials."[14] Inquiry occurs when people have the opportunity to explore, study or discover what they know. There are eight principles of AI, five of which stem from the writings of Cooperrider and Srivastva. Three additional principles have been added through the work of Diana Whitney and Amanda Trosten-Bloom. Each of the principles is briefly described below:

1. *Constructionist Principle*—Stories and words create people's reality and when they are brought together to discover, dream, design the organization they most desire, positive change occurs.

2. *Simultaneity Principle*—As soon as people begin to ask questions, change begins. Questions can stimulate creativity and innovation.

3. *Poetic Principle*—Organizations are endless sources of learning, with each individual adding a piece to the puzzle. What an organization chooses to learn about, whether positive or negative, will become the "world as we know it."

4. *Anticipatory Principle*—People create images of their future through their conversations with others. These collective conversations can create positive images of the future.

5. *Positive Principle*—Asking positive questions brings out the best in people. Bringing out the best in people can bring out the best in an organization.

6. *Wholeness Principle*—Gathering all of the stakeholders together to hear each other's stories or perspectives fosters creativity and builds the collective capacity of the group.

7. *Enactment Principle*—Modeling the behaviors that we want to see in practice.

8. *Free Choice Principle*—When people choose how and what they will contribute, they will perform better and be more committed to the organization.[15]

These principles are the underpinnings for all AI activities and should always be kept in mind when using this tool.

The AI process is a 4-D Cycle that begins with a topic to be studied, something that is of strategic importance. *Discovery* uses an interview process where people are led through a series of questions to talk about what they see as positive or exemplary. People affirm what they believe to be good about a situation or the organization. *Dream* explores "what might be" and gives people an opportunity to explore hopes and dreams. This is a time to explore the potential and create a vision for the future. *Design* begins the discussion of "what should be" and allows people to create a picture of how things will be when the end is reached. *Destiny* focuses on individual or organizational commitments to move forward.[16] By exploring these four areas of the cycle, people can begin to grow and change towards what they want to become, individually and as part of the whole system.

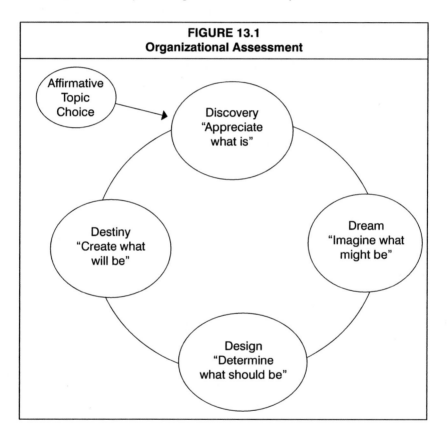

FIGURE 13.1
Organizational Assessment

D. D. Warrick posits the commonsense notion that it is important to understand organizations "before trying to change and improve them so that the strategies fit the unique characteristics, needs and circumstances of each organization."[17] Understanding the organization means more than measuring library user satisfaction or the cost-effectiveness of outsourcing a particular process. It also means understanding the culture and climate of the organization. *Climate* and *culture* are often used interchangeably, but there are subtle differences. *Climate* generally describes employee feelings, attitudes, and shared perceptions. It can also include general behavior patterns (e.g., that's how we do it around here). *Culture* is deeper, encompassing the organization's values and principles (e.g., commitment to service). The culture of an academic library is intrinsically tied to the college or university of which it is a part. The values, principles, and other attributes of the culture are frequently featured in mission, values/vision statements, and strategic plans. Climate is more difficult to gauge, but both can be assessed in a variety of ways.

Organizational assessment may be used in an academic library to elicit from staff members more specific information about the organization rather than relying on hearsay, rumors, and gut feelings. For example, employees may make statements such as, "Communication is not good here," "There is no decision-making transparency," or "Morale is poor." By using a combination of survey, structured interviews, and focus groups, the organization can get definitions and deeper understanding of the current situation. Only then can an organization begin to recognize and change critical facets.

Organizational climate or culture assessment should never be taken lightly. Asking library staff members to talk about their feelings and attitudes, what, in their perception, is working or not working, is important work that raises hopes for improvement and empowerment. Assessing climate and culture must have the strong support of management. More damage than good is done if (a) there is no intention to release the results of the findings or to release only the positives; (b) there is no effort to follow up or to strive for improvement; or (c) there is no effort to involve staff in action planning for change.

Surveys generally come to mind first when organizational assessment is mentioned, but there are other ways to assess an organization. An examination of existing data, such as documents, vision statements, Web sites, strategic plans, committee meeting notes, customer satisfaction surveys, and other published information, can be very useful in noting themes, values, the major players, or the pace and path of decision making. Although time-consuming, structured and nonstructured interviews as well as focus groups are rich sources of data. Observation and anecdotal data are also of use.

Recently, an organizational assessment tool, ClimateQUAL—Organizational Climate and Diversity Assessment, was developed as a joint project with the University of Maryland Libraries, the University of Maryland Industrial/ Organizational Psychology Program, and the Association of Research Libraries.[18] Other academic libraries have developed their own assessments using internal expertise or in conjunction with faculty or university staff experts. Still others have used standard surveys that have been developed over the years for business, nonprofits, and other organizations.

Every one of the OD techniques mentioned in this chapter comes into play when climate and culture assessment is undertaken. For instance, assessment is a classic example of systems thinking as an organization tries to understand how pieces of the whole relate to each other. The "pieces" can be processes, programs, or employees. Once data are collected and gaps and problems are identified, action research methods can help to define issues, diagnose problems, and plan action for change. Change management models can be used to engage staff in visualizing and understanding those changes. The expert library is one that learns how to assess its climate and culture in order to understand the ethos of employees and the organization as a whole. It uses that knowledge in appropriate ways to enable smooth sailing through change.

Facilitation

Facilitation and coaching are two approaches that enable groups, individuals, and organizations to make progress, modify behaviors, and cope positively with change. Facilitation is used most effectively in groups, while coaching techniques are more applicable to individuals. "Facilitation may not be as glitzy or fancy as some OD work," but it is extremely useful to an organization.[19] Meant to improve dialogue in the workplace, facilitation is one way to increase understanding among individuals in a group and for the group as a whole. Facilitators use a variety of skills, knowledge, techniques, and methodologies. Asking questions, steering decision-making processes, assisting in problem solving, guiding planning, and enhancing collaboration are just a few of the ways a good facilitator can be of use. Such facilitation does not have to be used only at high levels of the organization, but is feasible at all levels. Facilitators do not need intimate knowledge of a topic or process to be successful because they are focusing mainly on process and progress.[20] In fact, objectivity is increased by having a facilitator who is not extremely knowledgeable about the subject and can remain neutral. Basic facilitation skills such as asking questions to fuel the conversation in groups or teams can be learned by anyone in the organization. An effective OD program will focus some energy on teaching key players facilitation techniques or developing a group of employees from around the organization who can serve as facilitators.

An approach called "facilitative leadership" takes the technique one step further by providing facilitators with core values, ground rules, and exercises. Facilitative leadership may be practiced by anyone in the organization. A description of the major facilitative leadership approaches is described by Thomas Moore in a 2004 *Library Trends* article.[21] In Roger Schwarz's approach, for example, facilitators are led by the core values of valid information, free and informed choice, and internal commitment. "One first seeks and shares valid information, uses that valid information to make an informed decision, and is internally committed to the decision and to continuing to seek valid information."[22] This *reinforcing circle* means that, although a decision has been made, a facilitative leader continues to seek valid information to verify that the path determined by the decision continues to be viable. Chris Argyris's work identifies two theories of action, *model one* and *model two*. Argyris says that 98 percent of managers operate using model one which is a unilateral win-lose theory.[23] He advocates model two, mutual learning and win-win, which is facilitative leadership at its best.

An organization development consultant can be invaluable as a facilitator. Even more importantly, the OD professional can teach and coach others in the organization to use facilitation methods to improve meeting management, group decision making, and problem solving. No matter what the approach, improving results through conversations that move work forward is what facilitation is all about.[24]

Coaching

From the book *Practicing Organization Development* comes this lovely and intriguing sentence: "There are two basic paths to personal development coaching, corresponding to the two Medieval spiritual development methods: the via negative (the negative road) and the via positive (the positive road)."[25] Gap analysis and identifying the restraining forces in a situation are traditional ways that coaching has taken place in the via negative realm. The via positive strategy is closely aligned with appreciative inquiry, that is, identifying what is working and building upon it. Both roads can lead coach and client on a successful voyage. Coaching can be a planned event or series of events, but coaching also often occurs ad hoc. OD practitioners learn to seize such spontaneous opportunities and can teach others, such as managers, to seize those moments.

Coaching is often thought of as high-level or "executive" support where a consultant is hired to improve the performance and/or relationships of an executive. It can happen in academic libraries for directors, deans, and the like. General benefits of such coaching are alluded to in the literature, but specifics are difficult to find. In an illuminating piece by Barbara Pate Glacel, she iterates what lessons a client specifically learns from coaching: (a) perception is reality; (b) trust and credibility are the basis for all good relationships; (c) common ground overcomes interpersonal difficulties; and (d) blind spots matter.[26] Such lessons are important results from any coaching no matter what the level!

The single most important purpose of coaching is to focus on the goals, hopes, and questions of the person being coached. "A great coach talks little, listens a lot, and facilitates the thinking of the client."[27] Performance coaching is an excellent mechanism for changing the dreaded performance evaluation into a focused conversation that is a positive experience for both managers and employees. Effective OD practice trains and encourages managers to start coaching before problems start. A positive climate of coaching rather than disciplining should be an important goal for any organization. To paraphrase Bruce Tulgan in *It's Okay to Be the Boss*, it's better to coach employees when they are doing great or just okay so that they develop good habits before they have a chance to develop bad ones.[28]

Change Management

The expert library needs change agents, now and in the future, to guide, lead, and monitor change. The term *change agent* is sometimes used as the definition of an OD professional who is frequently working to improve some aspect of the organization or even the whole culture.

"For the purpose of managing change, the important thing to note is that the *pull* of the future *must* be stronger than the combined *pull* of the past and the distractions of the present."[29] Creating a vision of the future that compels people to change behavior; to begin new programs or to let go of habits or activities is no easy task. People make changes. In order to do that, they must understand why the change is needed, be encouraged to ask questions and seek information, gather and make suggestions, agree on action plans, and evaluate progress. In addition, employees must be rewarded and recognized for their willingness and ability to change. In his groundbreaking work *Managing Transitions,* William Bridges emphasized that it is not the speed or type or degree of change that is the problem for human beings.[30] It's the voyage. Going from the home port to another destination creates problems because people must deal with emotions (their own and others') and uncertainty along the way.

Whenever a change, small or extensive, is anticipated in an academic library, thought should be given to *managing* the change. Simply deciding to impose a change with no thought to progression, effects on personnel, or consequences seldom results in successful outcomes. Closing a service desk, outsourcing a process, instituting mandatory training of some type are just some examples. Each change must be managed thoughtfully, and that's when change management tools are very helpful.

Individual OD intervention techniques are especially useful during transitions. Appreciative inquiry is a powerful tool in this context. Thinking about what works rather than what doesn't work is potent. It enables visioning, positive thinking, and the ability to transfer successful skills and attributes to the new situation. Facilitation is an objective method for moving groups ahead and keeping discussions and disagreements focused ultimately on the goal—the change. Because coaching is about the person being coached, it is an effective way to move individuals through the continuum of change.

Models of change can be used by OD professionals to illustrate and help staff to understand what individuals and organizations are experiencing and to plan. One well-known model is Stephen Haines's "rollercoaster of change."[31] Individuals going through change psychologically travel from their current stage at the beginning of change through shock/denial, anger, hope, and eventually to rebuilding. Each person goes through those stages in varying degrees and at varying times, which can create problems in communication and acceptance of change.

Richard Chang posits that change can be managed by using a six-step model:

1. Clarify the need, which includes explaining why the change is necessary and gauging emotional reactions of staff.
2. Define results, ensuring that it is determined who will be affected.
3. Produce a draft plan, get input from staff, and develop action plans.
4. Implement the plan and monitor activity.
5. Stabilize the outcome, including recognition of those who supported the change.
6. Assess the process.[32]

The model may seem simple, but organizations often skip some of the steps in the haste to make changes happen. Avoiding some of the steps can result in increased resistance and decreased acceptance. Successful organizations are those that actually manage change rather than impose it or let it happen serendipitously. Change management is a key factor in helping to ensure that most crew members are on board and looking forward to the journey.

Organizational Learning

The concept of the learning organization was first introduced by Chris Argyris and Don Schon as a way to improve organizations in the 1970s. They believed the combination of behavioral and cognitive learning increases the capacity to change. Learning can also help build the capacity to challenge the routine.[33] This concept reached its highest popularity as a model with the 1994 publication of *The Fifth Discipline,* in which Peter Senge describes the learning organization as one "where people continually expand their capacity to create the results they truly desire, where new and expansive patterns of thinking are nurtured, where collective aspiration is set free, and where people are continually learning how to learn together."[34] There are five dimensions of learning that must work in tandem to have true learning, no matter at what level in an organization. They are systems thinking, personal mastery, mental models, building a shared vision, and team learning. A brief explanation of each follows.

- *Systems Thinking*—understanding how parts of a whole, whether a process, an activity, or a system, relate to other pieces of the whole.
- *Personal Mastery*—developing a personal vision and then focusing one's energies on that vision. It means identifying what is really important to us personally.
- *Mental Models*—understanding the assumptions we have and bringing them under scrutiny.
- *Building a Shared Vision*—creating a genuine vision that is shared with others to which people are voluntarily committed.
- *Team Learning*—recognizing how teams of people can work effectively together by analyzing what gets in the way of this learning. Creating space for true dialogue where the free flowing of ideas is possible.

Organizations can create an environment that encourages learning, whether on the individual, team, or organization level. When employees become engaged in learning, they increase their ability to create and test ideas. Their ability to understand the big picture leads to their understanding of how the various parts of the organization fit together to meet the goals that it sets forth. Learning must take place at all levels of the organization. It is important to tap the capacity of individuals and groups. Without learning, the organization may not grow effectively from its mistakes. There is no sense of urgency to learn if the organization does not place value on its importance. Creating a sense of curiosity to know more, to know why something happens the way it does, to understand how one process affects some other part of an organization or group, to take risks to try new things—all of these manifest learning. Organizations that value learning and build a culture of learning create organizations that are adaptable to change.

Organization development plays a key role in creating an environment for continuous learning. The systems in place that support learning can include training programs, communication processes, or tools such as flow charts, fishbone diagrams, and storyboards to develop skills for learning. Learning is a critical contributor to a healthy organization.

Systems Thinking

First developed in the 1950s at Massachusetts Institute of Technology by professor Jay Forrester, systems thinking has further evolved through the work of a number of social scientists and theorists including Eric Trist, Gregory Bateson, Ludwig von Bertalanffy, and others who broadened its applications. It encompasses a relatively large body of methods, tools, and principles. Links and loops, unintended consequences, strategic thinking, environmental scan, whole systems, vision statements, and paradigm shift are just some of the words, phrases, and concepts that have emanated from this discipline.

What systems are we talking about? Every academic library has systems that are internally created or externally imposed. There are hiring and compensation systems, performance evaluation systems, and systems for dealing with emergencies. Others include communication systems, technology systems, and budgeting systems. Specific or temporary systems are sometimes created to deal with unique events, programs, planning, or projects. These could be strategic planning or moving materials to remote storage or marketing a new service to users.

Any time the expert library is confronted with a situation or need that requires the interplay, collaboration, and cooperation of various elements of the organization, systems thinking and planning should be employed. It is extremely valuable for situations such as (a) getting many people to see the big picture and not just their small part; (b) problems that worsened due to past fixes; (c) problems stemming from ineffective coordination among those involved; and (d) problems that do not have obvious solutions.[35] Most organizational change comes from traditional analytical thinking where problems are broken down into smaller components and each component is fixed separately. The work of OD involves helping the organization and individuals to become strategic or systems thinkers because change, even though perceived as quite small, can and does affect the entire organization. OD practitioners guide the organization and individuals through stages and phases that include asking the following:

- Where do we (the organization, team, department) want to be? (goals, objectives, vision)
- Will we know when we get there? How? (assessment)
- What's the environment like now? (issues, problems, scan)
- How do we close the gap to our goal, vision? (action plans)
- How will/might things change as a result in the future?[36] (visioning, scenario building)

All the characteristics of an effective, healthy organization mentioned earlier in this chapter are enhanced by the systems thinking approach, and the quality and transparency of the decision-making process can certainly be improved.

OD in Action

When an organization, or one part of an organization, is involved in change, the responsibility for process and outcomes is often murky and unclear. Using OD to successfully address change efforts requires bringing several elements together. The first element to consider is who is going to lead the efforts. The second is the implementation of tools and processes that support the efforts. Someone educated in organization development embodies the leadership elements along with the tools and processes.

Is having a staff member on board whose focus is primarily organization development crucial to the success of an organization? A variety of opinions abound, ranging from saying that an OD professional is an important human resource to OD can be incorporated into the functions of Human Resources (HR), Staff Training, Planning, or some other administrative area. Often what is missing is the consideration of how an OD professional can bring added value by observing the whole organization and how each of the pieces, such as HR or training, fit and contribute to the whole. A successful OD program pays attention to the development of individuals, teams, *and* the organization. What is important is that the organization clearly defines and works toward its goals whether its change efforts are small, large, or all-encompassing. That's one of the primary objectives of OD... keeping everyone focused on the goals.

The OD professional can add value to what is already happening in libraries. Much attention is given to the overarching goals of the organization and bringing the systems together to address the critical issues. Here are some examples of how the OD professional adds value:

- Bringing the processes of facilitation, training, planning, and change strategies to *Teams, Committees, and Other Groups.* An OD professional, for example, might build a program that trains a cadre of staff members in the organization in facilitation techniques. Those staff members can be invaluable in facilitating cross-functional teams.
- Assisting the *Administration of the Library* in planning, assessing systems, and communicating on a number of levels—campus, with external customers, and with staff. We need more "open communication" and "decision-making transparency" is often heard from employees, particularly in large organizations. The OD professional can assist administration in defining those terms and creating ways to assess and improve the communication satisfaction factor.
- Focusing on enhancing models for change, developing performance review processes, and workforce planning within *Human Resources.* As a partner with HR, an OD practitioner can jump in with training, coaching, or assessment to support and foster HR programs.
- Providing coaching and training for *Managers and Supervisors* in the areas of communication, change management, and leadership development. Coaching of managers and supervisors is a key element in OD work. This one-to-one work, done successfully, can improve and enhance the performance of managers who affect the daily working lives of many employees.

With an OD professional on board, successful change efforts show an investment from top management and the commitment to give staff an added resource to deal with change. The OD professional can serve in a variety of ways that free up the administration to focus on strategic issues.

There are many beneficial OD tools and processes to choose from, and their application to situations provide boundless opportunities to affect change based on a library's goals. The tools and processes presented in this chapter have been exceptionally useful in academic libraries and have helped to create solid OD programs. The tools were also selected as a means of demonstrating how they might be applied to a real situation. The scenario presented in the appendix illustrates how OD tools and techniques may be used in the *early, critical* stages of a change that will affect a whole organization.

OD work most often deals with reaction to planned changes, so it can be extremely effective in helping staff members plan, cope with, and embrace change. Remember that organization development "is planned change that focuses on all levels of the organization—individual, group, intergroup, total system, and interorganizational—rather than limiting the practice to one or two levels."[37] Because OD deals with people and their reactions, it does feel like it's messing about in the organization. The tools and methods we described in this chapter sound systematic and clear-cut, but they don't always appear that way, and they take time. It is impossible to change processes and organizational climate or culture overnight.

Think of the sailing vessel working its way toward its destination. For sailors, the journey is as important as the destination. Along the way, although the captain is always in command, crew members learn teamwork and observe the talents and abilities of individuals. Surprises, unexpected and serendipitous, happen on every voyage. Dealing with the nuances and changes in the climate and the intricacies of the systems (sails, rigging, lines, instruments, etc.) attunes the crew to a heightened awareness of the need to be flexible and optimistic and to rely on each other. Like a well-crewed sailing vessel, the Expert Library of the 21st Century will take full advantage of the possibilities of organization development to create smooth sailing.

Notes

1. W. Warner Burke, "Where Did OD Come From?" in *Organization Development: A Jossey-Bass Reader,* ed. Joan V. Gallos (San Francisco: Jossey-Bass, 2006): 14–15.
2. Ibid, 17.
3. Joan V. Gallos, "The OD Field: Setting the Context, Understanding the Legacy" in *Organization Development: A Jossey-Bass Reader,* ed. Joan V. Gallos (San Francisco: Jossey-Bass, 2006): 2.
4. Richard Beckhard, "What Is Organization Development?" in *Organization Development: A Jossey-Bass Reader,* ed. Joan V. Gallos (San Francisco: Jossey-Bass, 2006): 3.
5. Ibid, 3–7.
6. Wendell L. French and Cecil H. Bell, Jr., *Organization Development: Behavioral*

Science Interventions for Organization Improvement, 6th ed. (New Jersey: Prentice Hall, 1999): Chapter 7.

7. Ibid, 151–152.
8. Beckhard, "What Is Organization Development?" 8–10.
9. Maureen Sullivan, "Organization Development in Libraries," *Library Administration & Management* 18, no. 4 (2004): 179.
10. Karen Holloway, "The Significance of Organizational Development in Academic Research Libraries," *Library Trends* 53, no. 1 (2004): 8. See also Charles A. Schwartz (ed.), *Restructuring Academic Libraries: Organizational Development in the Wake of Technological Change* (Chicago: American Library Association, 1997): vii.
11. French and Bell, *Organization Development,* 130.
12. Linda Dickens and Karen Watkins, "Action Research: Rethinking Lewin" in *Organization Development: A Jossey-Bass Reader,* ed. Joan V. Gallos (San Francisco: Jossey-Bass, 2006): 194.
13. Diana Whitney and Amanda Trosten-Bloom, *The Power of Appreciative Inquiry: A Practical Guide to Positive Change* (San Francisco: Berrett-Koehler, 2003): 82–83.
14. Ibid, 2.
15. Ibid, 53–79.
16. Ibid, 6–10.
17. D. D. Warrick, "Launch: Assessment and Action Planning" in *Practicing Organizational Development* , ed. William J. Rothwell and Roland Sullivan (San Francisco: Pfeiffer, 2005).
18. University of Maryland Libraries, "ClimateQUAL—Organizational Climate and Diversity Assessment," www.lib.umd.edu/OCDA (accessed July 10, 2008).
19. Lisa Haneberg, *Organization Development Basics* (Alexandria, VA: ASTD Press, 2005): 86.
20. Lois B. Hart, *Faultless Facilitation* (Amherst, MA: HRD Press, 1996): 17.
21. Thomas L. Moore, "Facilitative Leadership" *Library Trends* 53, no. 1 (2004): 231
22. Ibid, 232.
23. Ibid, 234.
24. Haneberg, *Organization Development Basics,* 95.
25. Udai Pareek, John J. Scherer, and Lynn Brinkerhoff, "Person-Centered OD Interventions" in *Practicing Organization Development,* ed. William J. Rothwell and Roland Sullivan (San Francisco: Pfeiffer, 2005): 390.
26. Barbara Pate Glacel, "Why Executive Coaching? Significant Lessons Learned" in *2006 Pfeiffer Annual Consulting,* ed. Elaine Biech (San Francisco: Pfeiffer, 2006): 174–176.
27. Haneberg, *Organization Development Basics,* 99.
28. Bruce Tulgan, *It's Okay to Be the Boss* (New York: HarperCollins, 2007): 51.
29. Bob Shaver, "Rubber Bands: Envisioning the Future," in *2003 Pfeiffer Annual Consulting,* ed. Elaine Biech (San Francisco: Pfeiffer, 2003): 82.
30. William Bridges, *Managing Transitions: Making the Most of Change* (Reading, MA: Addison-Wesley, 1991).
31. Stephen G. Haines, *The Systems Thinking Approach to Strategic Planning and Management* (Boca Raton, FL: CRC Press, 2000): 260.
32. Richard Y. Chang, *Mastering Change Management* (Irvine, CA: Richard Chang Associates, 1994): 14.

33. John R. Austin and Jean M. Bartunek, "Theories and Practices of Organizational Development" in *Organization Development: A Jossey-Bass Reader,* ed. Joan V. Gallos (San Francisco: Jossey-Bass, 2006): 107–108.

34. Peter Senge et al., *The Fifth Discipline Fieldbook,* (New York: Doubleday, 1994): 3.

35. Daniel Aronson, "Overview of Systems Thinking" Thinking Page website, www. thinking.net (accessed July 10, 2008).

36. Stephen G. Haines, "Becoming a Strategic Thinker on a Daily Basis" in *2007 Pfeiffer Annual Consulting,* ed. Elaine Biech (San Francisco: Pfeiffer, 2007): 271.

37. W. Warner Burke and David L. Bradford, "The Crisis in OD" in *Reinventing Organization Development: New Approaches to Change in Organizations* (San Francisco: Pfeiffer, 2005): 10.

APPENDIX

CREATING A SUPERVISORS TRAINING PROGRAM
A SCENARIO USING OD TOOLS

*Note: All words or phrases in **bold** are OD tools or processes.*

The scenario takes place at the libraries of Nautical University. The libraries have recently gone through a strategic planning process. One of the goals of the strategic plan is to create a training program for supervisors within the next two years. There are currently 60 staff members, both staff and librarians, who serve in supervisory roles. Some supervisors have been in their positions for a number of years, while others are relatively new. The team or work units range in size from 3 to 15. The need for a supervisory training program is based on a recent **internal organization survey,** with the results indicating that the skill levels of supervisors vary tremendously. The survey results show that both supervisors and those they supervise see the need for improving skills. The improvements range from problem solving and decision making, to conflict management and performance management. There is no formal staff development program, but the need for one has been discussed for several years. Any training available to staff is through the campus training office. The topics for campus offerings are wide-ranging but not available on a regular basis.

During the **strategic planning** process, there was much interest in a supervisory training program. A number of staff, including supervisors and nonsupervisors, volunteered to help develop a program. The libraries' administration appointed a task force of six staff members from across the organization, with the head of the science library serving as chair. Membership included all types of positions and classifications of staff.

The task force agreed at its first meeting to review programs at other academic libraries and to conduct a literature search on skills needed by supervisors. Considering that other stakeholders should be involved in the project, the task force met with the libraries' and university's human resources officers. The HR conversations revealed that **performance review processes** were integrally connected to the role of the supervisor. It was also suggested by HR that providing individual **coaching** after the training might be advisable for supervisors who requested it or in targeted situations. After a few meetings, the task force identified a number of topics for workshops and developed a draft list of competencies for supervisors. It was agreed that all supervisors should attend every workshop.

The task force decided to invite all staff to a meeting to hear about the plans. The meeting started off on a positive note until the point about mandatory attendance was mentioned. A heated discussion focused solely on why attendance was required ensued. The task force members became frustrated and discouraged and were not sure what to do next.

So what happened? Let's consider how OD tools and processes could have helped to create better initial outcomes. The task force's work to date seemed on target. Developing a supervisors training program on the surface appeared to be a simple task—identify training needs, provide the training, and watch the skills improve. Seems simple, yes? Not really.

Very early in the process, **a model for change** could have been used to ensure that systematic steps were taken to assure a successful result. The steps would be to clarify need; define results; produce the plan; implement the plan; stabilize the outcome; and assess the process. Using the change model, the task force began working on the first two steps, that is, clarifying the need for the improvements and defining the results, but they jumped to developing a plan too quickly. As part of the clarification of need, the task force should have tried to *gauge the emotional reactions* of supervisors and staff members. Setting aside time to talk with staff, especially those in supervisory positions, was important. Starting off with a few ideas about goals based on what was known from the survey results could be the basis for the conversations. **Appreciative inquiry** (AI) would be an excellent process to use during these conversations. Framing questions to encourage staff to talk about what they believed were the qualities of a good supervisor and to imagine the aspects of a supervisory program that has positive results could set the stage for looking to the future. The task force would help the organization create a picture of a new program and establish buy-in for the program by affirming the positives.

But clarification and defining were not yet finished! Task force members needed to get together with library administrators to talk about their goals for the program. At that point, the task force members should discuss what they perceived as some of the critical components of a program and what reactions they were seeing and hearing from staff and supervisors. Early in the process, the task force should be soliciting buy-in and feedback from the administration, determining what resources were available, and what administrators' expectations were. Only then has the task force clarified need and defined results with all the major players... administrators, supervisors, and staff members.

An OD facilitator or internal or external consultant for the task force would be extremely helpful. Keeping the group on track in terms of the change model and assisting with tools, such as AI, that move the group from point A to point B are activities that are useful. **Facilitating** the task force's discussion enables all members of the group to participate fully. Perhaps the task force might want to use **focus groups** of supervisors and nonsupervisors, which would be valuable in eliciting additional information and hearing reactions. A facilitator, using OD principles, might help the group to understand the purpose of focus groups, perhaps lead the focus groups, or train members of the task force to do so.

Another option might be an **assessment tool,** such as a supervisor's skills inventory, that could help supervisors identify their strengths and areas for improvement and would be an effective way to analyze what training was needed. Here again, an OD facilitator or consultant could make sure the pros and cons of using a skills inventory were understood and recommend possible tools.

Once the task force clarified the need and defined the results, the goals could be developed in a number of ways, but what is most important is a shared organizational understanding of results and outcomes. Specific outcomes that staff would support were critical for ensuring a successful program, and staff had to be engaged (through focus groups, conversations, surveys, etc.) in the process. The supervisory program has the potential to impact everyone in the organization, and behaviors are expected to change as a result. Consequently, the task force had to spend a significant amount of time on the clarification and defining steps. The reaction at a staff meeting describing the new supervisory training could have been "How soon can I attend the training?" rather than "Why do I have to attend?

A goal is beginning to take shape and is now stated as: *The Nautical University Libraries will insure that supervisors have the necessary skills to do their jobs effectively so that staff members are able to meet the needs of faculty, students, and staff of the university.* The goal is broad enough to allow for multiple outcomes and results. With a goal, written outcomes determined, and the steps of clarification and defining complete, the group can begin the activities of creating an action plan, implementing it, stabilizing the outcomes, and assessing the program. As with the initial steps, these steps in **change management** should not be rushed or skipped.

As the plan is created, **systems thinking** can be used to determine who and what will be impacted by the supervisory program. Deciding on necessary resources such as time, money, people, or expertise will be important. Figuring out who does what and when, is critical.

During the implementation phase of the program, the task force might want to create a **communication plan** to let the staff know how things are progressing. Logistics and event planning will come into play. All along the way, the above activities should be **monitored** for consistency and unintended outcomes.

Taking time to stabilize the outcome is a step frequently skipped in organizations. Recognition, rewards, and celebrations are valuable for staff members who support the change and work hard to make it happen. A program such as supervisory training is obviously not a one-time event, so sustainability must be built in. How does the organization keep this program going?

Finally, **assessment** is essential. What went well and what could be improved in the process of managing the change? Were the goals of the program met? Did supervisory skills improve?

The Nautical University libraries, like many academic libraries, are using larger OD organizational strategies such as strategic planning and internal organization surveys to determine what changes are desirable in the organization. It is at the next level, that is, introducing new ideas, implementing programs, and managing specific changes that organizations often fail to use OD tools on a regular basis.

ABOUT THE AUTHORS

Eric Bartheld is director of communications for the University of Maryland Libraries. Before coming to Maryland, he served as director of communications at the Indiana University Bloomington Libraries, where he had also served as associate director of development. Before joining the IUB Libraries, Bartheld wrote fundraising proposals and development publications for the Indiana University Foundation. He has a background in not-for-profit fundraising, grant writing, and marketing, having worked for organizations ranging from an opera company and public aquarium to a jewelry trade association. His annual reports for the IUB Libraries have been recognized by the Council for Advancement and Support of Education, winning silver and bronze honors in the Circle of Excellence Awards competition. He holds a bachelor's degree in journalism from the University of Missouri and says he found it unimaginably difficult to abandon Associated Press style for this article.

M. Sue Baughman is the Associate Deputy Executive Director of the Association of Research Libraries (ARL). Prior to joining ARL, she served as Assistant Dean for Organizational Development at the University of Maryland Libraries. She received her MLS from the University of Maryland. Previous positions held include the Manager of Public Services in the McKeldin Library, University of Maryland Libraries, Executive Director of the Essex-Hudson Regional Library Cooperative (NJ), Branch Chief of the Public Services and State Networking Branch at the Maryland State Department of Education, and Branch Manager for the Anne Arundel (MD) County Public Library.

Baughman has authored or co-authored and presented on the topics of teams, staff development and organizational learning. She is co-author of the book chapter "University of Maryland Libraries: Case Study for Program Review" in *Teams in Library Technical Services* (The Scarecrow Press, Inc., 2006), co-author of "Research: Theory and Applications: Impact of Organizational Learning," *portal: Libraries and the Academy*, 2002, and author of the book chapter "Development of a Customer Service Attitude," in *Staff Development: A Practical Guide* (3rd ed. American Library Association, 2001).

Marta L. Brunner was a CLIR Postdoctoral Fellow at UCLA's Charles E. Young Research Library (Fall 2006 – Summer 2007), having earned her Ph.D. from the History of Consciousness Department at the University of California, Santa Cruz in 2005. She is the author of "The Most Hopeless of Deaths… Is the Death of Faith": Messianic Faith in the Racial Politics of W. E. B. Du Bois," published in *Re-cognizing Du Bois in the Twenty-first Century*, edited by Mary Keller and Charles Fontenot (Mercer University Press, 2007). She has taught courses in early American history, U.S. labor history, and rhetoric and composition, and has assisted on courses in American studies, myth and religion, art history, and cultural studies. Prior to becoming a CLIR Fellow, she worked for two years as Lead Bookstacks Assistant in the University of Chicago's Joseph Regenstein Library.

Brunner is currently Librarian for English and American Literature, Comparative Literature, Folklore, and Translation Studies at Young Research Library. In addition to her collection development and maintenance, reference, and instructional responsibilities as a literature librarian, she is active in a number of digital projects. Extending a project she began as a CLIR Fellow, she is directing a pilot project to digitize oral histories related to Los Angeles social movement history, in collaboration with the UCLA Center for Oral History Research and the UCLA Digital Library Program. She is also co-managing a discipline-specific research portal project sponsored jointly by the UCLA Library and the California Digital Library.

Jake R. Carlson is a Data Research Scientist with the Distributed Data Curation Center (D2C2) and the Research Department at the Purdue University Libraries. His work centers on the investigation of community-driven data curation needs for archiving e-research at Purdue University. He received a BA from Clark University, an MA from Washington University in St. Louis, and an MLIS from the University of Pittsburgh. Before coming to Purdue he served as the Coordinator of Electronic Resources and as the Librarian for the Social Sciences and Government Documents at Bucknell University. His research interests focus on the continually evolving practices of science and the role of the libraries in supporting these practices, with a particular concern towards the capture, maintenance, and preservation of disparate data sets for sharing, reuse and repurpose.

Kevin Clair is Metadata Librarian at the Pennsylvania State University Libraries. He holds a Bachelor of Arts degree in history from Carleton College and received his MSLS from the University of North Carolina at Chapel Hill in May 2006, where his academic focus was on digital library development and digital preservation. His current research interests are in bridging the gap between library metadata standards and those of the Semantic Web, promoting metadata interoperability for the purposes of application development, and the ways in which digital libraries might contribute to the construction of identity and the development of social capital online.

Stephanie H. Crowe is the assistant archivist at the University of Minnesota's Charles Babbage Institute. She first came to the University of Minnesota in 2007 as a fellow in the Association of Research Libraries' ARL Academy program, through which she organized and began implementing the KSA project documented in this chapter. She completed her MLS in 2007 at the University of North Carolina-Chapel Hill and also holds a master's degree in public history from North Carolina State University.

Jamie Wright Coniglio holds a Master of Library Science degree from Indiana University Bloomington and a Bachelor's degree in History from Saint Mary College (Kansas). Her professional experience is extensively in public services in a variety of libraries. She has served on the library faculties of Bradley University, Iowa State University and George Mason University, and has also worked as a special librarian at the Council on Foundations (Washington, DC). Her areas of specialization and professional interest include reference and research, academic liaison work, communications, marketing, public relations, and creative approaches to library services and spaces.

Michael J. Furlough joined Penn State University Libraries in 2006 as the Assistant Dean for Scholarly Communications and the Co-Director of the Office of Digital Scholarly Publishing, a collaborative venture with the Penn State Press. He has extensive experience in consulting with scholars on the application of a wide range of technologies to their teaching and research. Furlough is the former director of Digital Research and Instructional Services at the University of Virginia Library, where he developed programs in support of digital scholarship based on collaborations among researchers, librarians, and technologists.

Jeremy R. Garritano is Chemical Information Specialist and Assistant Professor of Library Science at the M.G. Mellon Library of Chemistry at the Purdue University Libraries. His work is focused on instruction and outreach to all Purdue constituencies that require chemical information for their research and coursework, emphasizing the use of technology based tools to enhance discovery through visualization and manipulation of data and text. He received a BS ChE from Purdue University and an MLS from Indiana University. Before arriving at Purdue he was Visiting Science Librarian at the Wildman Science Library at Earlham College and previously Science Reference/Liaison Librarian at George Mason University. His research interests focus upon re-envisioning the traditional role of the librarian towards delivering new types of information sources, such as research data sets, to patrons and in training those who will become the 21st Century workforce in chemistry in making effective use of these sources.

Heather Gendron is Head of the Sloane Art Library at the University of North Carolina at Chapel Hill, and previously managed the Art and Architecture Library at Virginia Tech. Her other library experience includes working as a library assistant for the research libraries of the American Craft Council and Metropolitan Museum of Art. As Chair of the Professional Development Committee in the Art Libraries Society of North America (ARLIS/NA) and the Core Competencies sub-committee (also ARLIS/NA), Ms. Gendron lead a research and publishing project to identify and communicate what are the core competencies for art information professionals working today ("Core Competencies and Core Curricula for the Art Library and Visual Resources Professions" ARLIS/NA, 2006).

Craig Gibson has been Associate University Librarian for Research, Instructional, and Outreach Services at George Mason University in Fairfax, Virginia, since 1996. In addition to these responsibilities he previously held a one-quarter time appointment as consultant in the University's Department of Instructional and Technology Support Services, whose purpose is in part to assist faculty and students integrate information technology resources into the curriculum. He has collaborated with the University's Center for Teaching Excellence on pedagogical workshops for faculty and on continuing education for Librarians, and with the Office of Institutional Assessment to benchmark assessments of technology skills. He was a member of the ACRL Task Force on Information Literacy Competencies that wrote the *Information Literacy Competency Standards for Higher Education*, and helped to develop the initial set of online workshops co-sponsored by ACRL and the TLT Group. From 1997 to 2006, he was recorder for the National Form on Information Literacy, an umbrella group of library, educational, governmental, policy, and nonprofit organizations concerned with information literacy and lifelong learning both in the U.S. and in other countries. Since 1999, he has been a member of the faculty of the ACRL Immersion Program, an annual summer institute for reference and instruction librarians focused on information literacy—pedagogy, learning theory, assessment, program planning, and leadership. He edited *Student Engagement and Information Literacy* (ACRL, 2006), and is the incoming editor for the *ACRL Publications in Librarianship*, a series of monographs focused on research and scholarly thinking in academic librarianship. He previously held positions as Head of Library User Education at Washington State University (1988-1996), where he was the first-ever coordinator of the Libraries' instruction program; as Reference/Instruction Librarian at Lewis-Clark State College (1986-1988); and as Government Documents Librarian at the University of Texas at Arlington (1985-86). He holds a BA in English Education from West Texas State University (1976), an MA in English from the University of Mississippi (1980), and an MA in Librarianship from the University of Denver (1984).

Lisa Janicke Hinchliffe, MLS, EdM, is the Coordinator for Information Literacy Services and Instruction at the University of Illinois at Urbana-Champaign. Lisa previously served as the Head of the Undergraduate Library at Illinois and as Library Instruction Coordinator at Illinois State University. She is on the faculty of the Institute for Information Literacy, and is currently serving as the President of the Association of College & Research Libraries (2010-11).

Janice M. Jaguszewski is Director of Academic Programs for the Physical Sciences and Engineering at the University of Minnesota Libraries. Prior positions at the University of Minnesota include Collections Coordinator for the Physical Sciences and Engineering, and Geology and Mathematics Librarian. She enjoys working with librarians and staff to help them build their skills and expertise as they prepare for the future. In addition to her work with Stephanie Horowitz on the KSA project described in this chapter, she recently led an initiative to assess the computer competencies of all library staff at her institution. She describes this initiative and the assessment tool that was used in an article that she co-authored with Linda Eells entitled, "Propel Your Staff to New Heights: Computer Competencies for All" (/*Technical Services Quarterly*/, vol. 25, no. 4 (2007)). Janice received her MLS in 1990 from the University of Illinois, Urbana-Champaign.

Elaine Z. Jennerich is the Director, Organization Development and Training, at the University of Washington Libraries in Seattle, WA. She received her doctorate in Library Science from the University of Pittsburgh and held a variety of academic positions including Head of Reference at Baylor University in Waco, TX, Director of the Library at Emory & Henry College in Emory, VA and Coordinator of Staff Development and Training at the University of Washington.

Jennerich is the co-author of *The Reference Interview as a Creative Art* (2ⁿᵈ ed. Libraries Unlimited, 1997) as well as the author of a number of articles such as "The Long Term View of Staff Development", *College and Research Libraries News,* Nov. 2006.

R. David Lankes is Director of the Information Institute of Syracuse, and an associate professor in Syracuse University's School of Information Studies. Lankes has always been interested in combining theory and practice to create active research projects that make a difference. Past projects include the ERIC Clearinghouse on Information and Technology, the Gateway to Education Materials, AskERIC and the Virtual Reference Desk. Lankes' more recent work involves how participatory concepts can reshape libraries and credibility. This work expands his ongoing work to understand the integration of human expertise in information systems.

Lankes is a passionate advocate for libraries and their essential role in today's society. He also seeks to understand how information approaches and technologies can be used to transform industries. In this capacity he has served on advisory boards and study teams in the fields of libraries, telecommunications, education, and transportation, including at the National Academies. He has been appointed as a visiting fellow at the National Library of Canada and the Harvard Graduate School of Education, and as a senior researcher at ALA's Office for Information Technology Policy.

John Lehner is the Assistant Dean for Library Systems, Personnel, and Planning at the University of Houston Libraries. He received his MLS from the University at Albany (SUNY). He has a long standing interest in human resources management issues in academic libraries and oversees all librarian recruiting for the UH Libraries. He holds an MBA with a concentration in human resources management (Tulane), a Master of Industrial and Labor Relations (Cornell), and a JD (Washington University).

David W. Lewis has a BA in History form Carleton College (1973), an MLS from Columbia University (1975), two certificates of advanced study in librarianship, one from the University of Chicago (1983) and one from Columbia University (1991).

He began library life as a reference librarian and became an administrator. He has worked at SUNY Farmingdale (1975-76), Hamilton College (1976-78), Franklin and Marshall College (1978-83), Columbia University (1983-88), and the University of Connecticut (1988-93). He came to Indiana University Purdue University Indianapolis (IUPUI) in 1993 as the Head of Public Services and has been the Dean of the University Library since 2000.

He has written on reference services, management of libraries, and scholarly communication. (Many of his works can be found at <http://idea.iupui.edu/dspace/handle/1805/>). He is professionally active on the state and national levels and is a masters swimmer who enjoys cooking, scuba diving, and traveling to parts of the world where red wine is made.

James G. Neal is currently the Vice President for Information Services and University Librarian at Columbia University, providing leadership for university academic computing and a system of twenty-five libraries. His responsibilities include the Columbia Center for New Media Teaching and Learning (CCNMTL), the Center for Digital Research and Scholarship, the Copyright Advisory Office, and the Center for Human Rights Documentation and Research. He participates on key academic, technology, budget and policy groups at the University. Previously, he served as the Dean of University Libraries at Indiana University and Johns Hopkins University, and held administrative positions in the libraries at Penn State, Notre Dame, and the City University of New York. At Columbia, he has focused on the development of the digital library, special collections, global resources, instructional technology, library facility construction and renovation, electronic scholarship, and fundraising programs.

Neal has served on the Council and Executive Board of the American Library Association, on the Board and as President of the Association of Research Libraries, on the Board and as Chair of the Research Libraries Group (RLG), and as Chair of OCLC's Research Library Advisory Council and Chair of the RLG Program Committee of the OCLC Board. He is on the Board and incoming Chair of the National Information Standards Organization (NISO), and on the Board of the Freedom to Read Foundation. He has also served on numerous international, national, and state professional committees, and is an active member of the International Federation of Library Associations (IFLA).

Neal is a frequent speaker at national and international conferences, consultant and published author, with a focus in the areas of scholarly communication, intellectual property, digital library programs, organizational change and human resource development.

Scott Walter is Associate University Librarian for Services and Associate Dean of Libraries at the University of Illinois at Urbana-Champaign. He holds faculty appointments at Illinois as Professor of Library Administration and Professor of Library & Information Science, and is an Affiliate member of the faculty of the Department of Educational Organization and Leadership. Since 2003, Scott has also served as a Lecturer in the San Jose State University School of Library & Information Science.

Scott received his MA in Russian Area Studies from Georgetown University, his MA in Education from American University, his MLS and MS in History & Philosophy of Education from Indiana University, and his Ph.D. in Higher Education Administration at Washington State University.

Scott has published a number of articles in journals such as *College & Research Libraries, Information Technology & Libraries, Reference Services Review,* and *Reference & User Services Quarterly.* His work has also been included in edited collections published by Neal-Schuman, Indiana University Press, and the Association of College & Research Libraries. He is the co-editor (with Dawn Shinew) of *Information Literacy Instruction for Educators: Professional Knowledge for an Information Age* (2003), co-author (with Lisa Janicke Hinchliffe) of *Instructional Improvement Programs* (ARL SPEC Kit No. 287) (2005), editor of *The Teaching Library: Approaches to Assessing Information Literacy Instruction* (2007), and co-author (with Lori Goetsch) of *Public Engagement* (ARL SPEC Kit No. 312) (2009).

Karen Williams is Associate University Librarian for Academic Programs at the University of Minnesota.

Beth S. Woodard, MLS, is the Staff Development and Training Coordinator and Head of the Reference Library at the University of Illinois at Urbana-Champaign. Since 2000, Beth has been on the faculty of the Association of College and Research Libraries' Institute for Information Literacy, and has taught in the Immersion program as well as the Intentional Teacher program.